Better Homes and Gardens®

COMPLETE STEP~BY~STEP COOK BOOK

© 1978 by Meredith Corporation, Des Moines, Iowa.
All Rights Reserved. Printed in the United States of America.
First Edition. Eleventh Printing, 1981.
Library of Congress Catalog Card Number: 77-74601
ISBN: 0-696-00125-X

On the cover: Slices of luscious Cherry-Pecan Bread enhance any breakfast, brunch, or coffee break. The icing adds just the right touch of sweetness. (See recipe on page 222.)

BETTER HOMES AND GARDENS® BOOKS

Editor: Gerald Knox
Art Director: Ernest Shelton
Associate Art Director: Randall Yontz
Production and Copy Editors: David Kirchner,
Paul S. Kitzke
Food Editor: Doris Eby
Complete Step-By-Step Cook Book Editors:
Sharyl Heiken, Senior Associate Food Editor
Diane Nelson, Associate Food Editor
Flora Szatkowski, Associate Food Editor
Senior Food Editors: Sandra Granseth,
Elizabeth Woolever
Associate Food Editor: Patricia Teberg
Senior Graphic Designer: Harijs Priekulis
Graphic Designers: Faith Berven,
Linda Ford, Richard Lewis,
Sheryl Veenschoten, Neoma Alt West
Test Kitchen Director: Marion Viall
Photography Specialist: Sharon Golbert
Test Kitchen Home Economists: Kay Cargill,
Marilyn Cornelius, Maryellyn Krantz,
Marge Steenson
Photographers: Mike Dieter, George de Gennaro,
Vincent Maselli

"How do you make stirred custard?" "I wouldn't know how to cook a lobster." "But my cream of tomato soup always curdles." These and similar pleas for help are frequently expressed by beginning and experienced cooks alike. They don't know how to learn unfamiliar cooking techniques, and so they continue to make "the same old things."

That's where this book can help. It's designed to teach 122 basic cooking techniques. Each one is presented in the form of a representative recipe accompanied by a series of photographs detailing the steps involved in its preparation. Whether your questions concern cooking meats or just making good coffee, you'll find the answers in this book.

Once you've mastered the basic technique, turn to the accompanying recipe pages. Here you'll find selections to round out the section and broaden your creative cooking experience. And, these recipes are cross-referenced to technique steps whenever applicable.

CONTENTS

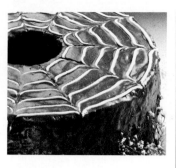

5

Clockwise from left: Fried Chicken (see recipe, page 36); Devilish Beef Stew (see recipe, page 19); Apricot Glazed Ham (see recipe, page 17); and Shrimp Cocktail (see recipe, page 67).

MEAT

On the following pages, we'll discuss the roasting, braising, baking, broiling, grilling, browning, and frying of meats.

Throughout, special tips will give you information on shaping ground meats, plus stuffing, marinating, and microwave-thawing other meats.

Cherry-Almond Glazed Pork

Techniques: Dry heat roasting and glazing meat

1 **3-pound boneless pork loin roast**
   Salt and pepper
1 **10-ounce jar cherry preserves**
¼ **cup red wine vinegar**
2 **tablespoons light corn syrup**
¼ **teaspoon salt**
¼ **teaspoon ground cinnamon**
¼ **teaspoon ground nutmeg**
¼ **teaspoon ground cloves**
¼ **cup toasted slivered almonds**

1 Trim excess fat from roast. **2** Rub roast with a little salt and pepper. **3** Place on rack in shallow roasting pan. **4** Insert roast meat thermometer. **5** Roast, uncovered, in 325° oven for about 2½ hours.
6 In saucepan combine preserves, vinegar, corn syrup, salt, cinnamon, nutmeg, and cloves. **7** Cook and stir to boiling. Reduce heat; simmer 2 minutes. **8** Add almonds; keep warm. **9** Spoon some of mixture over roast to glaze. Continue cooking about 30 minutes more or till meat thermometer registers 170°. Baste several times with glaze mixture.

10 Remove roast to carving board. Let stand 15 minutes; slice. Pass remaining glaze. Serves 8.

1 Trim any excess fat from the roast. Place roast on cutting board. Use a sharp knife to cut away the excess fat. Leave a very thin layer of fat over the meat to protect the lean portion from drying out.

2 Rub roast with a little salt and pepper. Sprinkle the seasoning on all sides of the roast, pressing and rubbing it in with your hands.

6 To prepare the glaze, in a saucepan combine the cherry preserves, red wine vinegar, corn syrup, salt, cinnamon, nutmeg, and cloves.

7 Cook and stir the glaze mixture until it boils, as shown. Reduce the heat and simmer the mixture 2 minutes, stirring occasionally.

3 Place roast, fat side up, on a rack in a shallow roasting pan. Use an adjustable rack, as shown; or use a flat rack which is large enough to hold the entire roast off the bottom of the pan.

When rib bones are left on the roast, as for a standing rib, no rack is needed.

4 Insert a roast meat thermometer into roast. For the most accurate reading, position the thermometer so that the bulb rests in the center of the thickest portion of meat and does not rest in fat. (In cuts with a bone, the thermometer should not touch bone.)

Using a meat thermometer is the most accurate way of determining doneness.

5 Roast, uncovered, in a 325° oven for about 2½ hours. This is known as dry heat roasting since no water or other liquid is added and the roast is not covered. This method can be satisfactorily used only with cuts of meat that are already naturally tender, such as those from the loin area.

9

TIP Glaze a bone-in pork loin roast with this same cherry-almond glaze. *When you buy the roast, have the meatman loosen the backbone from the ribs without cutting into the meaty portion.*

After roasting, remove the backbone, as shown, leaving as much meat on the roast as possible. Turn roast so that rib bones face you. Insert fork in top of roast. Carve by cutting between rib bones so that each slice includes a bone.

8 Add the toasted slivered almonds to the simmering mixture. (Notice that at simmering, the glaze mixture is still bubbling, but not as much as in the previous step.) Stir in the almonds. Keep the mixture warm.

To toast almonds, spread in a shallow baking pan. Place in 325° oven with roast for 10 to 15 minutes, stirring often.

9 Carefully spoon some of the warm mixture over the roast to glaze. Continue cooking roast about 30 minutes more or till meat thermometer registers 170°. Occasionally spoon more of the glaze mixture over the roast.

10 Remove roast to carving board, using two metal spatulas. Do not use forks since they will cause some of the juices to be lost. To allow these juices to set, let the roast stand about 15 minutes before carving. Pass the remaining glaze with the sliced meat.

Two boneless top loin roasts tied flat sides together also may be used. Leave the roast tied during cooking, but cut the strings before carving.

Meat

Beef Pot Roast

Technique: Pot roasting meat

1 **3- to 4-pound beef pot roast**
All-purpose flour
Salt
Pepper
½ **cup water**
Potatoes, peeled and cut up
Small whole onions
Carrots, cut in 1-inch pieces

1 Trim excess fat from roast; reserve trimmings. **2** Coat all sides of roast with flour. **3** Heat trimmings in Dutch oven till about 2 tablespoons hot fat accumulate; discard the trimmings.

    4 Add roast; brown slowly on all sides. **5** Sprinkle roast with salt and pepper; add water. **6** Cover and roast in 325° oven 1 to 1½ hours. **7** Add vegetables to meat. **8** Cover and continue cooking about 45 minutes or till meat and vegetables are tender. If desired, use pan juices to make Pan Gravy (see recipe and tip on pages 100–101). Makes 6 to 8 servings.

Tomato-Juiced Pot Roast: Prepare as above *except* add ½ cup *tomato juice* instead of water before cooking. If making gravy, use *tomato juice* instead of water in cooking and for gravy. Season gravy with ½ teaspoon *worcestershire sauce* and salt and pepper to taste.

Spiced Pot Roast: Prepare as above *except* slice 2 small *onions* over the meat after browning. Substitute ¼ cup *vinegar* and ¼ cup *water* for the ½ cup water; add 5 whole *cloves* and 2 *bay leaves*. Omit the small whole onions, if desired.

10

1 Trim excess fat from roast; reserve trimmings. Any of the roasts considered less tender are suitable for pot roasting (braising). These include those cut from the chuck (arm and blade) and round (rump).

5 Sprinkle roast with a little salt and pepper. Add the ½ cup water, pouring it directly onto the meat, as shown.

    If desired, for a change of flavor, use apple juice, pineapple juice, beef broth, wine, or beer instead of the water.

    Additional seasonings also may be used, if desired. Try adding 1 bay leaf; ½ teaspoon dried basil, crushed; or ½ teaspoon dried thyme, crushed.

2 Coat all sides of roast with all-purpose flour, using about 1 tablespoon in all. Coating with flour gives the meat, and later the gravy, a richer brown color.

However, you may brown the meat without flour, if desired.

3 Heat the reserved trimmings in Dutch oven till about 2 tablespoons of fat accumulate. Discard the trimmings.

If desired, you may use 2 tablespoons cooking oil or shortening instead.

4 Add roast to the hot fat. Slowly brown the roast on both sides. Use a metal spatula and tongs to turn the roast easily.

If the roast is more box-shaped (as rump roasts often are), brown it on all sides.

TIP Pot roasts also may be prepared atop the range. *Simply trim and brown meat as directed at left. Add seasonings and liquid. Cover and simmer for the suggested time. Add additional water as needed to prevent sticking.*

To make pot roast in an electric slow crockery cooker, *first cut roast to fit in cooker, if necessary. Trim and brown as directed. If adding vegetables, slice them and place in bottom of cooker; place meat atop. Add seasonings and liquid; cover and cook on low-heat setting for 8 to 10 hours.*

11

6 Cover and roast in 325° oven 1 to 1½ hours. The cooking time depends as much on the shape of the roast as on the weight. A flat or thin roast will cook more quickly than a box-shaped roast.

Pot roasting refers to cooking at a low temperature in a covered pan with added liquid. This method—sometimes called braising—helps to tenderize the meat by breaking down its tough connective fibers.

7 Add potatoes, onions, and carrots to roast. Since these need less cooking time, they are added toward the end of cooking.

If desired, substitute or add any of these vegetables: sweet potatoes, rutabagas, turnips, parsnips, or celery.

If you want to cook the roast without added vegetables, simply continue cooking the roast.

8 Cover pan and continue cooking about 45 minutes or till vegetables and meat are tender. Use a fork to check doneness, as shown.

Meat

Deviled Swiss Steak

Techniques: Pounding, browning, and braising meat

1 **3-pound beef round steak, cut 1 inch thick**
2 **teaspoons dry mustard**
1½ **teaspoons salt**
¼ **teaspoon pepper**
2 **tablespoons cooking oil**
1 **4-ounce can mushroom stems and pieces**
1 **tablespoon worcestershire sauce**

1 Trim excess fat from meat; remove bone. Cut meat in half for easier handling. **2** Mix dry mustard, salt, and pepper; sprinkle over surface of meat. **3** Pound seasonings into both sides of meat. **4** In heavy 12-inch skillet quickly brown meat on both sides in hot oil. **5** Remove pan from heat; spoon off excess fat.

6 Drain mushrooms, reserving liquid. Add water to liquid, if necessary, to make ½ cup; add worcestershire sauce. Pour liquid mixture over meat. **7-8** Cover; simmer 1¼ to 1½ hours or till meat is tender. Add mushrooms; heat through. Transfer meat to platter; cut each half into 4 pieces. **9** Spoon the excess fat from pan juices; pour juices and mushrooms over meat. Makes 8 servings.

1 Using a sharp knife, trim the excess fat from the meat. Remove the round leg bone. Cut the steak in half for easier handling.

2 In a custard cup or small bowl combine the dry mustard, salt, and pepper. Sprinkle about one-fourth of the seasoning mixture over top surface of each piece of meat.

6 Drain mushrooms, reserving the liquid. Set mushrooms aside. Add water to the reserved liquid, if necessary, to make ½ cup; add worcestershire sauce. Pour liquid mixture over meat.

7 Cover; simmer 1¼ to 1½ hours. This method of cooking meat is often called braising. It refers to the covered pan, low heat, and added liquid which help tenderize the meat by breaking down its tough connective fibers.

12

3 Pound seasonings into meat. Use a metal or wooden meat mallet to pound from center out to edges of meat. Pounding with the coarse-toothed edge of a mallet also breaks some of the meat fibers and helps make the meat more tender.

Turn meat over and pound in remaining seasonings.

4 In heavy 12-inch skillet, heat oil. Add meat and brown quickly on both sides.

If desired, you may brown the meat in hot fat rendered from the trimmings (refer to step 3 on page 11).

5 Remove pan from heat. On an electric range, move the pan off the burner; on a gas range, simply turn off the flame.

To skim the fat, carefully tip the skillet so that drippings run to one side, and spoon off the oily liquid that rises to the surface

TIP To make Deviled Swiss Steak in the oven, *simply trim, pound, and brown the meat as directed at left. Skim fat, add liquid, cover, and roast in 325° oven for the suggested time.*

To make Deviled Swiss Steak in an electric slow crockery cooker, first cut meat to fit in cooker. Trim fat, pound, and brown meat in skillet as directed at left. Place meat in cooker; pour liquid (and mushrooms) over. Cover and cook on low-heat setting for 8 to 10 hours. Remove meat to platter. Skim fat from cooking liquid; serve with meat.

Thicken the cooking liquid, if desired. Measure liquid; add water, if necessary, to make 1½ cups. Return to cooker; cover and turn to high-heat setting. Bring to boiling. (Or, place in saucepan; bring to boiling.) Blend ⅓ cup cold water with 3 tablespoons all-purpose flour; add to hot liquid. Cook and stir till thickened and bubbly.

13

8 To test meat for doneness, poke with a fork to check for tenderness. Spoon mushrooms atop meat; heat through.

Transfer meat to serving platter; cut each half into 4 pieces.

9 Using a large metal spoon, skim the excess fat from pan juices by tilting the pan and lifting off the clear, oily-looking liquid, as shown.

Spoon remaining pan juices and mushrooms over the meat.

Meat

Cider Stew

Technique: Making stew

1	2½-pound beef chuck pot roast (about 2 inches thick)
3	tablespoons all-purpose flour
2	teaspoons salt
¼	teaspoon pepper
¼	teaspoon dried thyme, crushed
3	tablespoons cooking oil
2	cups apple cider *or* apple juice
½	cup water
2	tablespoons vinegar
4	carrots, quartered
3	potatoes, peeled and quartered
2	onions, sliced
1	stalk celery, sliced
1	apple, cored and chopped

1 Trim roast; cut into 1-inch cubes. **2** In plastic bag combine the flour, salt, pepper, and thyme. Add meat cubes, a few at a time, shaking to coat. Place coated cubes on waxed paper. **3** In Dutch oven heat oil; add about ⅓ of the meat cubes, turning to brown evenly on all sides. Repeat with remaining meat cubes. **4** Return all meat to Dutch oven. Add apple cider or juice, water, and vinegar. **5** Cook and stir till mixture comes to boiling. **6** Cover; reduce heat and simmer 1½ to 2 hours or till meat is nearly tender.

7-8 Add carrots, potatoes, onions, celery, and apple. Cover and continue cooking about 30 minutes more or till vegetables and meat are tender. Makes 6 to 8 servings.

14

1 To cut roast into 1-inch cubes, first trim excess fat from roast. Cut roast into 1-inch slices, as shown. Cut each slice in half lengthwise, then cut into 1-inch pieces.

Remember to place roast on a cutting board and to use a sharp knife.

If desired, you may use 2 pounds pre-cut stew meat.

5 Heat the meat-cider mixture over medium to high heat till the mixture boils. Stir occasionally to keep meat from sticking.

2 In a plastic bag combine the flour, salt, pepper, and thyme. Add meat cubes, a few at a time, shaking to coat. Place on waxed paper and continue till all meat is coated.

Coating the meat with flour helps give it a richer brown color. Adding seasonings to the flour ensures that all the meat will be seasoned.

3 In Dutch oven heat oil; add about ⅓ of the meat cubes, turning to brown evenly on all sides. Transfer browned meat to bowl; repeat with remaining meat.

If desired, you may brown the meat in hot fat rendered from trimmings (refer to step 3 on page 11).

4 Return all of the meat to the Dutch oven. Pour the apple cider or apple juice, the water, and vinegar over the meat cubes.

TIP To prepare stew in an electric slow crockery cooker, *cut, coat, and brown meat as directed at left. Chop all the vegetables; place in cooker. Add the apple and browned meat. Add the apple cider or apple juice, omit the water, and add only 1 tablespoon vinegar.*

Cover and cook on low-heat setting for 10 to 12 hours. Turn cooker to high-heat setting. Blend ½ cup cold water with ¼ cup all-purpose flour; stir into stew. Cover and cook about 15 minutes or till thickened. Season to taste with salt and pepper.

15

6 Cover the meat-cider mixture. Reduce the heat so mixture simmers. Simmer for 1½ to 2 hours or till the meat is nearly tender.

7 Add the carrots, potatoes, onions, celery, and apple to stew mixture. Cover and continue simmering about 30 minutes.

8 To check stew for doneness, remove a piece of meat and one or two vegetable pieces. Meat should be easy to cut and vegetables should be fork-tender.

Meat

Boeuf En Croûte

1 4-pound beef eye of the round
   roast
¾ cup burgundy
¾ cup dry sherry
2 bay leaves
1 onion, quartered
8 ounces fresh mushrooms,
   chopped (3 cups)
1 large leek, chopped
2 tablespoons butter
½ cup liver pâté *or* 1 4¾-ounce can
   liver spread
¼ cup fine dry bread crumbs
2 cups all-purpose flour
½ teaspoon salt
⅔ cup shortening
⅓ to ½ cup cold water
1 slightly beaten egg
3 tablespoons all-purpose flour
(continued next column)

16

TIP Wrapping meat in pastry *takes extra time, but is not hard to do. Center the meat atop the rolled-out pastry. Carefully lift up long edge, as shown above, pressing against meat. Repeat with the remaining long side, overlapping pastry atop meat. Brush edges with a little beaten egg; seal.*

Trim excess pastry from ends; fold up. Brush with a little beaten egg; seal. Place, seam down, on greased baking sheet. Brush egg over all. Reroll pastry trimmings. Cut into strips; crisscross on roast. Brush with remaining egg.

Place roast in clear plastic bag; set in deep bowl. For marinade, mix the burgundy, sherry, bay leaves, and onion; pour over meat in bag, referring to the tip on page 19. Close bag. Chill overnight; turn bag occasionally to distribute the marinade.

Next day, remove meat from bag; reserve marinade for use in filling and gravy. Referring to steps 3 and 4 on page 9, place meat on rack in shallow roasting pan. Insert meat thermometer. Roast, uncovered, in 425° oven about 55 minutes or till thermometer registers 130°. Remove meat from pan; cool 20 minutes. Reserve drippings for gravy. Trim any fat from meat.

Meanwhile, prepare the filling. Cook mushrooms and leek in butter about 6 minutes; remove from heat. Stir in the liver pâté or liver spread, bread crumbs, and *3 tablespoons* of the reserved marinade. Cover; chill at least 1 hour.

Prepare pastry, referring to page 276. Stir together the 2 cups flour and salt. Cut in shortening till size of small peas. Gradually add water, 1 tablespoon at a time, tossing with fork till all is moistened; form into a ball.

On lightly floured surface, roll out pastry to a 14×12-inch rectangle. Spread with filling to within 1 inch of edges. Center the partially cooked roast atop. Wrap pastry around meat, referring to tip at left and using beaten egg to seal the edges. Transfer to greased baking sheet; bake in 425° oven for 30 to 35 minutes or till pastry is golden (meat will be rare).

To make gravy, heat the reserved drippings with ¾ cup *water* till solids dissolve. Blend the 3 tablespoons flour with ½ cup cold *water*; stir into drippings. Add ¼ *cup* of the reserved marinade. Cook and stir till bubbly; season with salt and pepper to taste. Serve with roast. Serves 12.

Sensational Veal Stew

2 to 2½ pounds boneless veal, cut
   in 1-inch cubes
6 tablespoons butter *or* margarine
1 pound small whole onions (16)
12 ounces fresh mushrooms, sliced
   (4½ cups)
1 clove garlic, minced
1 teaspoon salt
⅛ teaspoon freshly ground pepper
⅓ cup all-purpose flour
1 10½-ounce can condensed
   chicken broth
¾ cup dry white wine
1 carrot, halved
1 leek, sliced
1 stalk celery, halved
2 sprigs parsley
¼ teaspoon dried thyme, crushed
1 bay leaf
3 tablespoons lemon juice
2 egg yolks
¾ cup whipping cream
   Grated nutmeg
   Lemon wedges

In a Dutch oven or large saucepan simmer veal in butter or margarine over low heat, uncovered, for about 10 minutes (do not brown). Add onions, mushrooms, garlic, salt, and pepper; cook, uncovered, 10 minutes more. Sprinkle flour over meat; stir till blended. Add chicken broth, wine, carrot, leek, and celery.

Tie parsley, thyme, and bay leaf in cheesecloth bag; add to mixture. Cover and simmer, stirring occasionally, for 30 minutes or till meat is tender, referring to step 8 on page 15. Remove and discard cheesecloth bag, carrot, and celery. Stir in lemon juice.

Beat together egg yolks and cream. Stir about *1 cup* of the hot mixture into the egg yolk mixture; return all to hot mixture, stirring constantly. Heat till mixture is bubbly and slightly thickened. Transfer to serving bowl; sprinkle with nutmeg. Serve with lemon wedges. Makes 6 to 8 servings.

Boeuf En Croûte

Beef-and-Kraut Skillet

1 2-pound beef round steak, cut ½
  inch thick
6 fully cooked smoked sausage
  links
2 tablespoons shortening
1 16-ounce can tomatoes, cut up
½ cup chopped onion
1 teaspoon caraway seed
1 16-ounce can sauerkraut, drained
¼ cup cold water
2 tablespoons all-purpose flour

Cut steak into 6 pieces. Pound each to a 5-inch square, referring to step 3 on page 13. Season with a little salt and pepper. Place a sausage link on each piece of steak. Roll up; secure with wooden picks. In skillet brown steak rolls on all sides in hot shortening; drain. Add *undrained* tomatoes, onion, and caraway. Cover; simmer 1 hour. Add sauerkraut; cook 15 minutes more. Remove steak rolls; keep warm. Blend water into flour; add to kraut mixture. Cook and stir till bubbly. Serve meat atop kraut. Serves 6.

Apricot-Glazed Ham

(pictured on page 6)

1 5- to 7-pound fully cooked
  boneless smoked ham
  Whole cloves
½ cup apricot preserves
1½ teaspoons cornstarch
1 teaspoon finely shredded
  orange peel
3 tablespoons orange juice
⅛ teaspoon ground cinnamon

Refer to: Dry heat roasting and glazing meat, page 8. Score ham using a sharp knife to make shallow cuts diagonally across ham in a diamond pattern. Stud with cloves. Place ham on rack in shallow roasting pan. Insert meat thermometer. Bake, uncovered, in 325° oven for 1¾ to 2¼ hours or till thermometer registers 140°. In saucepan blend preserves with cornstarch. Stir in orange peel, juice, and cinnamon. Cook and stir till thickened and bubbly. Spoon some over ham 2 or 3 times during last 30 minutes of baking. Serves 12 to 16.

Round Steak Italiano

1 2-pound beef round steak, cut ¾
  inch thick
1 tablespoon cooking oil
½ pound bulk Italian sausage
1 8-ounce can tomato sauce
¾ cup apple juice
½ cup chopped onion
½ teaspoon garlic salt
¼ teaspoon dried oregano, crushed
⅛ teaspoon pepper
  Hot buttered noodles
  Grated parmesan cheese

Refer to: Pounding, browning, and braising meat, page 12. Cut steak into 8 pieces; pound to ½-inch thickness. In skillet brown steaks in hot oil. Remove steaks.

In same skillet brown the sausage, breaking into small pieces; drain. Add tomato sauce, apple juice, onion, garlic salt, oregano, and pepper. Return steaks to skillet. Reduce heat; cover and simmer about 50 minutes. Skim fat. Remove steaks to platter; pour sauce over. Serve with noodles; pass parmesan. Makes 8 servings.

Meta

Rump Roast Supreme

- 1 4- to 6-pound boneless beef round rump roast
- 2 tablespoons shortening
- 1 cup dry red wine
- 1 cup beef broth
- ½ cup chopped onion
- 1 teaspoon salt
- ¼ teaspoon dried thyme, crushed
- ¼ teaspoon pepper
- 1 bay leaf
- 1 clove garlic, minced
- ¼ cup all-purpose flour

Refer to: Pot roasting meat, page 10. In Dutch oven brown meat in hot shortening. Add ½ *cup* of the wine, broth, onion, salt, thyme, pepper, bay leaf, and garlic. Cover; roast in 325° oven 2½ to 3 hours or till meat is tender.

Remove strings; discard. Transfer roast to platter; keep warm. Discard bay leaf. Skim excess fat from pan juices; add water to juices to make 2 cups. Return juices to pan. Blend remaining ½ cup wine into flour; stir into juices. Cook and stir till bubbly. Pass with meat. Serves 8 to 10.

Corned Beef Dinner

- 1 3- to 4-pound corned beef brisket
- ½ cup chopped onion
- 2 cloves garlic
- 2 bay leaves
- 6 medium potatoes, peeled
- 6 small carrots
- 6 cabbage wedges
- 1 teaspoon prepared mustard
- 3 tablespoons brown sugar
  Dash ground cloves

Place meat in Dutch oven; add water to cover (about 7 cups). Add onion, garlic, and bay leaves. Cover; simmer 3 to 4 hours or till tender. Remove meat. Add potatoes and carrots to cooking liquid. Cover and bring to boiling; cook 5 minutes. Add cabbage; cook 25 minutes more or till vegetables are tender. Meanwhile, place meat, fat side up, in shallow pan. Spread with mustard; sprinkle with mixture of sugar and cloves. Bake in 350° oven 15 minutes. Serve meat with vegetables; pass cooking liquid to spoon atop, if desired. Makes 6 to 8 servings.

Fruited Beef Stew

- 1½ pounds boneless beef chuck, cut in 1-inch cubes
- 2 tablespoons cooking oil
- 3 medium sweet potatoes, peeled and quartered (3 cups)
- 1 16-ounce can tomatoes, cut up
- 1 cup chopped onion
- ½ cup chopped green pepper
- ½ cup water
- 2 inches stick cinnamon *or* ¼ teaspoon ground cinnamon
- 1 clove garlic, minced
- 1 teaspoon salt
- ⅛ teaspoon pepper
- 2 ears corn, cut crosswise in 2-inch pieces
- 2 medium zucchini, sliced
- 1 16-ounce can peach slices, drained

Refer to: Making stew, page 14. In a Dutch oven brown meat, ⅓ at a time, in hot oil; drain. Return all meat to pan. Add sweet potatoes, *undrained* tomatoes, onion, green pepper, water, cinnamon, garlic, salt, and pepper. (If desired, transfer mixture to 3-quart casserole.) Bake, covered, in 350° oven for 1¼ hours. Stir in corn and zucchini; bake 45 minutes longer. Add drained peach slices to stew; season to taste with salt and pepper. Serves 6 to 8.

Country Pork Dinner

- 1 1½-pound smoked pork shoulder roll
- 1 16-ounce can sauerkraut, drained
- 2 cups apple juice
- 1 large bay leaf
- 6 medium potatoes, peeled
- 6 small onions
- 6 small carrots, quartered

Place the pork shoulder roll in a 5-quart Dutch oven; add drained sauerkraut, apple juice, and bay leaf. Referring to steps 6–8 and the tip on page 11, cover and simmer about 1¼ hours. Add the potatoes, onions, and carrots. Simmer, covered, about 45 minutes more or till tender. Remove meat and vegetables to warm platter. Makes 6 servings.

18

Fruited Beef Stew

Devilish Beef Stew

(pictured on page 6)

1½ pounds beef stew meat, cut in
     1-inch cubes
⅓ cup all-purpose flour
2 tablespoons cooking oil
2 cups water
1 tablespoon dry mustard
1½ teaspoons salt
1 clove garlic, minced
1 teaspoon chili powder
1 teaspoon worcestershire sauce
¼ teaspoon pepper
1½ cups water
4 medium potatoes, peeled and
     quartered
6 small onions, quartered
4 carrots, quartered
2 stalks celery, cut in 1-inch pieces
¼ cup cold water

Refer to: Making stew, page 14. In plastic bag toss beef cubes with flour to coat, reserving remaining flour. In a large saucepan or Dutch oven brown the beef, ⅓ at a time, in hot oil. Return all meat to pan; remove from heat. Add the 2 cups water, mustard, salt, garlic, chili powder, worcestershire sauce, and pepper. Simmer, covered, 1 to 1½ hours or till meat is almost tender.

Add the 1½ cups water, potatoes, onions, carrots, and celery. Simmer, covered, about 30 minutes or till vegetables are tender.

For gravy, remove meat and vegetables; skim fat from liquid, if necessary. Blend the ¼ cup cold water into the reserved flour till smooth. Slowly stir into hot liquid. Cook and stir till thickened and bubbly. Season to taste with salt and pepper. Return meat and vegetables to gravy mixture. Heat through. Makes 8 servings.

Curry-Horseradish Pork

1 teaspoon curry powder
½ teaspoon salt
½ teaspoon pepper
1 4- to 5-pound boneless pork loin
     roast
  Milk
½ cup chopped onion
2 to 3 teaspoons curry powder
2 tablespoons butter *or* margarine
2 tablespoons all-purpose flour
¼ teaspoon salt
½ cup dairy sour cream
1 tablespoon prepared horseradish

Refer to: Dry heat roasting meat, page 8. Combine the 1 teaspoon curry powder, the ½ teaspoon salt, and the pepper; rub over meat. Place meat on rack in shallow roasting pan. Insert meat thermometer.

Roast, uncovered, in 325° oven for 2½ to 3 hours or till meat thermometer registers 170°. Remove meat to hot platter; keep warm.

To make gravy, refer to Making pan gravy, page 100. Skim fat from pan juices; measure pan juices. Add enough milk to make 1¼ cups liquid; set aside. In medium saucepan cook the onion and 2 to 3 teaspoons curry powder in butter or margarine till onion is tender but not brown. Stir in flour and the ¼ teaspoon salt; add milk mixture all at once. Cook and stir till bubbly. Stir in the sour cream and horseradish; heat through (do not boil).

Spoon some of the gravy over roast; pass remaining. Garnish meat with fresh mint and poached apple slices, if desired. Makes 10 to 12 servings.

Seasoned Leg of Lamb

1 6- to 7-pound leg of lamb
  Olive oil
½ cup fine dry bread crumbs
3 tablespoons snipped parsley
2 tablespoons butter *or* margarine
2 teaspoons finely shredded lemon
     peel
1 clove garlic, minced
1 teaspoon salt
1 teaspoon dried oregano, crushed
1 teaspoon dried basil, crushed
1 teaspoon dried rosemary, crushed
⅛ teaspoon pepper

Refer to: Dry heat roasting meat, page 8. Have meatman bone leg of lamb, leaving shank bone intact. Remove fell (thin fat covering). Rub roast with oil. Combine bread crumbs, parsley, butter, lemon peel, garlic, salt, oregano, basil, rosemary, and pepper; mix well. Spread over entire inside cut-surface of roast. Skewer roast shut. If necessary, tie with string.

Place roast on rack in shallow roasting pan. Insert meat thermometer. Roast, uncovered, in 325° oven for 2 to 2½ hours or till thermometer registers 150°. Makes 12 servings.

19

TIP Marinating meat *is easier if you use a plastic bag. Place the roast, steaks, or meat cubes into the bag, then set in a deep bowl. Pour the marinade mixture over the meat in the bag. Close the bag; turn to distribute the marinade evenly over the meat. Turn occasionally during the marinating period.*

Meat

1 To make a pocket in the chop, first cut a 1½- to 2-inch-long slit in fatty side of chop. A sharp paring knife works well for this step.

2 Insert knife into slit, as shown, drawing from side to side to form a larger pocket inside the chop. Try not to make the initial slit much larger (so it will be easier to close). Repeat with remaining chops. Season the chops and pockets with salt and pepper.

Corn-Stuffed Pork Chops

Technique: Cutting pocket in chops

6	pork loin chops, cut 1¼ inches thick
½	cup chopped celery
⅓	cup chopped onion
2	tablespoons butter *or* margarine
1½	cups soft bread crumbs (2 slices)
1	8¾-ounce can whole kernel corn, drained
½	teaspoon salt
¼	teaspoon ground sage
	Dash pepper
	Paprika

1-2 Make a pocket in each chop by cutting from fat side almost to bone. Season the chops and pockets with salt and pepper. **3** Cook celery and onion in butter or margarine till tender but not brown. **4** In large bowl combine the bread crumbs, drained corn, salt, sage, and pepper. Add the celery and onion; mix well.

5 Spoon about ⅓ *cup* of the stuffing mixture into pocket of each chop. **6** If desired, securely close pocket opening with wooden picks. **7** Place stuffed chops in a 15×10×1-inch baking pan (use a rack, if desired). **8** Cover pan with foil. Bake in 350° oven for 45 minutes. **9** Remove foil; continue baking 30 to 35 minutes more or till meat is tender. **10** Spoon pan juices over meat; sprinkle with paprika. Remove picks. Makes 6 servings.

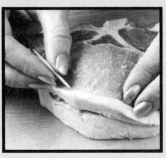

6 If desired, securely close the pocket opening with 1 or 2 wooden picks inserted diagonally. This is done to help ensure that the stuffing stays inside the pocket during baking.

7 As each chop is stuffed, place it in a 15×10×1-inch baking pan. If desired, you may use a rack to keep meat from resting in pan juices during cooking.

3 In saucepan cook the celery and onion in butter or margarine over medium heat for about 5 minutes. Stir the vegetables occasionally, cooking them till they are tender but not brown.

4 In a large bowl combine the bread crumbs, drained corn, salt, sage, and pepper. Add the cooked celery and onion.

Be sure to use a bowl that is large enough to allow for lightly tossing the mixture till it is well combined.

5 Using a tablespoon, carefully spoon about ⅓ *cup* of the stuffing mixture into the pocket of each pork chop.

8 Carefully cover the pan of chops with foil, crimping edges to sides of pan. This helps retain moisture in the meat so that the chops don't dry out during the long baking period. Bake in 350° oven for 45 minutes.

9 Carefully lift off and remove foil from pan. Take care to avoid the hot steam that will escape when you lift off the foil.

Continue baking, uncovered, for 30 to 35 minutes more or till meat is tender (test with a fork).

10 Before serving, spoon some of the pan juices over the pork chops and sprinkle with some paprika. Remove the wooden picks.

Meat

1 Place steak on cutting board. Without cutting into meat, carefully slash the fat edge at 1-inch intervals. This helps prevent the meat from curling during broiling.

Broiled Steaks

Technique: Broiling steaks

Beef porterhouse, T-bone, top loin, sirloin, or tenderloin steak, cut 1 to 2 inches thick
Salt
Pepper

1 Place steak on cutting board. Without cutting into the meat, slash the fat edge at 1-inch intervals. **2** Place steak on unheated rack in broiler pan. **3** Place steaks that are up to 1½ inches thick so surface of meat is 3 inches from heat. Place 1¾- to 2-inch steaks 4 to 5 inches from heat.

4 Broil on one side for about half of the total cooking time indicated in the chart below for the desired doneness. Season with salt and pepper, if desired. **5** Turn steak with tongs. Broil for remaining time. Season again, if desired.

6 Test for doneness by slitting the center. If inside color is still red, the steak is rare; if pink, it is medium; if gray, it is well-done.

To serve, remove bone, if present, then slice across the full width of the steak. For thick steaks, such as this, diagonal slicing rather than crosswise slicing is recommended.

Thickness of Steak	Rare	Medium	Well-Done
	(approximate total cooking time in minutes)		
1-inch	8 to 10	12 to 14	18 to 20
1½-inch	14 to 16	18 to 20	25 to 30
2-inch	20 to 25	30 to 35	40 to 45

4 Broil steak on one side for about half of the total cooking time indicated in chart at left for desired doneness. Season browned side with salt and pepper, if desired.

Reduce the cooking time if steak is less than 1-inch thick.

22

2 Place steak on the un-heated rack in broiler pan. Using a preheated rack would cause the meat to brown too much before the inside cooked to the desired doneness.

If you don't have a broiler pan, you may use a wire rack set in a shallow baking pan.

3 Place steaks that are up to 1½ inches thick so top surface of meat is 3 inches from heat. Place 1¾- to 2-inch steaks 4 to 5 inches from heat.

Check oven manufacturer's directions for adjusting the broiler and also for whether to completely close the door. Most electric ranges require the door to be ajar, while gas range doors should be closed.

TIP To broil hamburgers, *shape into patties, referring to steps 1 and 2 on page 24.* *Place on unheated rack in broiler pan so top surface of patties is 3 inches from heat (check range manufacturer's instructions). Broil to desired doneness, turning once. For medium doneness, allow 10 to 12 minutes total for ½-inch-thick burgers, and 12 to 15 minutes for ¾-inch thick burgers.*

To broil pork loin chops, slash fat edge at 1-inch intervals. Place on unheated rack in broiler pan so top surface of chops is 3 inches from heat (check range manufacturer's instructions). Broil till chops are well-done, turning once. Allow 22 to 25 minutes total for 1-inch chops, and 30 to 35 minutes for 1½-inch chops.

To broil lamb chops, use rib, loin, loin double, or leg sirloin chops. Slash the fat edge at 1-inch intervals to keep chops flat. Place on unheated rack in broiler pan so top surface of chops is 3 inches from heat (check range manufacturer's instructions). Broil to desired doneness, turning once. For medium doneness, allow 10 to 12 minutes total for ¾-inch chops; 11 to 13 minutes for 1-inch chops; and 15 to 18 minutes for 1½-inch chops.

23

5 Carefully turn steak with tongs (do not use a fork, as this pricks the meat and causes loss of juices).

Broil for remaining time. Season again, if desired.

6 Test steak for doneness by making a small slit in the center. If the inside color is still red, the steak is rare. If the inside is pink, the steak is medium. And if the inside is gray, the steak is well-done.

To serve, remove bone, if present, then slice across full width of steak. For thick steaks, such as this, diagonal slicing rather than crosswise slicing is recommended.

Meat

Grilled Burgers

Technique: Shaping and grilling burgers

1½   **pounds ground beef**
¾   **teaspoon salt**
     Dash pepper

1 Combine the ground beef, salt, and pepper. **2** Shape into six 4-inch patties. **3** Mound the briquettes in a pyramid in the center of the firebox. Drizzle with liquid lighter or jelly fire-starter; wait 1 minute, then ignite with match. **4** Let the coals burn for 20 to 30 minutes or till they look ash-gray. Then spread them out in a single layer. **5** Position grill 4 inches above *medium-hot* coals; add burgers. **6** Grill burgers for 5 to 6 minutes; turn and grill for 4 to 5 minutes more. Makes 6 burgers.

Variations: Prepare burgers as above *except* add any of the following to the meat mixture: 2 tablespoons chopped *green onion*, 2 tablespoons drained *sweet pickle relish*, 2 tablespoons chopped *pimiento-stuffed olives*, 1 tablespoon prepared *horseradish, or* ¼ teaspoon *minced dried garlic.*

Preparing the firebox: *If you're using a brazier grill, protect the firebox by lining it with heavy-duty foil. Top with a 1-inch layer of pea gravel. This bedding foundation allows some air to circulate under the briquettes so the coals will burn better. It also protects the firebox from the intense heat of the coals, distributes the heat more evenly, and reduces flare-ups by absorbing dripping fats and meat juices.*

24

1 Combine the ground beef, salt, and pepper. Using your hands, blend mixture thoroughly but carefully. Too much handling will give the burgers a compact texture.

4 Let coals burn for 20 to 30 minutes or till they appear ash-gray by day, or glow red after dark. Spread in a single layer.

Test the temperature by holding hand, palm-side down, about 4 inches above the coals. Begin counting "one thousand one, one thousand two, . . ." If you need to withdraw your hand after 2 seconds, the coals are *hot;* 3 seconds, *medium-hot;* 4 seconds, *medium;* and 5 or 6 seconds, *slow.*

2 Shape meat into six 4-inch patties. Use ⅓ to ½ cup meat mixture for each. Or, form meat into a roll 4 inches in diameter and cut into 6 slices.

Making all of the burgers a uniform size helps ensure that they will cook more evenly.

3 Mound briquettes in a pyramid in center of firebox (or to one side, as shown, if brazier has a larger surface area than is needed). Don't waste briquettes; six burgers require fewer than a large, thick cut of meat.

Drizzle liquid lighter or jelly fire-starter over briquettes. Wait 1 minute, then ignite with a match. Never use gasoline or kerosene.

TIP Using a wire grill basket *makes it much easier to turn burgers. Choose a hinged basket that allows adjustment to the thickness of the burgers. Open the basket and place the burgers on one side, as shown. Hook the other side atop. To turn the burgers, simply invert the grill basket—you don't need to turn them one by one.*

5 Position grill 4 inches above *medium-hot* coals. Carefully place burgers atop grill using a long-handled metal spatula. Burgers should be directly over coals. Leave a little space between them.

6 Grill burgers for 5 to 6 minutes; turn and grill for 4 to 5 minutes more or to desired doneness.

If the burgers cook too quickly because the coals are too hot, raise the grill, close the vents, or remove some of the hot briquettes.

If the burgers cook too slowly because the coals aren't hot enough, lower the grill, open the vents, move the coals closer together, or tap the ashes off burning coals with tongs.

Meat

Everyday Meat Loaf

Technique: Combining and shaping ground meat mixtures

        2   **beaten eggs**
       ¾   **cup milk**
       ½   **cup fine dry bread crumbs**
       ¼   **cup finely chopped onion**
        2   **tablespoons snipped parsley**
        1   **teaspoon salt**
       ½   **teaspoon ground sage**
       ⅛   **teaspoon pepper**
      1½   **pounds ground beef**
       ¼   **cup catsup**
        2   **tablespoons brown sugar**
        1   **teaspoon dry mustard**

1 In bowl combine the eggs and milk; stir in bread crumbs, onion, parsley, salt, sage, and pepper. Add ground beef. **2** Thoroughly mix meat and seasonings. **3** Spoon meat mixture into a 5½-cup ring mold. **4** Firmly pat meat into mold. **5** Unmold meat mixture in shallow baking pan. Bake in 350° oven for 50 minutes. **6** Spoon off the meat drippings and fat.

7 To glaze meat loaf, combine the catsup, brown sugar, and dry mustard; carefully spread over top of meat loaf. Bake 10 minutes longer. Makes 6 servings.

1 In bowl combine the eggs and milk; stir in the bread crumbs, onion, parsley, salt, sage, and pepper. Add the ground beef, breaking it into chunks, as shown.

5 Unmold meat mixture in shallow baking pan with sides; do not use a baking sheet. Bake in 350° oven for 50 minutes.

Unmolding the meat mixture lets the fat and juices that form during baking drain away from the meat, allowing it to brown.

2 Thoroughly mix together meat and seasonings till blended. Mix lightly; too much handling will produce a meat loaf with a compact texture. As shown, mixing with your hands is often easier than with a spoon.

3 Evenly spoon the ground meat mixture into a 5½-cup ring mold; do not grease the mold. To check the size of your mold, fill it with a measured amount of water.

Shaping the meat mixture into a ring is an easy way to dress up the loaf for company dinners. Ring-shaped loaves also cook faster than traditional shapes.

4 Firmly pat the meat mixture into the mold so that it will hold its shape when it is unmolded. Use your hands or the back of a spoon.

27

TIP To shape meat into a loaf, *prepare meat mixture as directed at left. Turn meat into an 8×4×2-inch loaf pan. Slightly press meat down around edges, pulling it away from sides of pan, as shown. Smooth the top.*

Or, shape meat into an 8×4-inch loaf and place it in a larger pan with sides, such as a 13×9×2-inch baking pan. Smooth the top.

Bake the loaf-shaped meat mixture in a 350° oven for 1¼ hours. Either metal loaf pans or glass loaf dishes may be used.

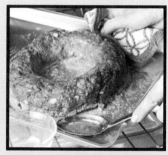

6 Using a large spoon, carefully spoon off the meat drippings and fat, as shown; a bulb baster also may be used.

It may be easier to leave the pan in the oven for this step. If you do remove it, be careful not to spill the drippings over the shallow pan edges.

7 To glaze meat loaf, stir together the catsup, brown sugar, and dry mustard. Carefully spread mixture over top of meat. Bake 10 minutes longer.

If desired, instead of glazing the meat, bake for 1 hour then serve the meat ring with creamed vegetables filling the center. Or, spoon on a cheese sauce (see tip on page 99).

Meat

Sausage Pizza

Technique: Making pizza crust and browning ground meat

1 package active dry yeast
¾ cup warm water (110°)
2½ cups packaged biscuit mix
   Cooking oil *or* olive oil
1 pound Italian sausage
1 16-ounce can tomatoes
6 ounces mozzarella cheese, thinly sliced and
     torn in pieces
1 6-ounce can tomato paste
2 cloves garlic, minced
1 tablespoon dried oregano, crushed
1 tablespoon dried basil, crushed
½ cup grated parmesan *or* romano cheese

1 Soften yeast in warm water; add biscuit mix. **2** Beat vigorously for 2 minutes. **3** Turn out onto a lightly floured surface; knead 25 strokes.

4 Halve dough. On floured surface, roll each piece of dough into a 12-inch circle. **5** Place each on a greased pizza pan; crimp edges. **6** Brush with oil.

7 Remove sausage casing, if present. In skillet break sausage into bits. Cook over low heat about 10 minutes; stir occasionally. Drain. **8** Drain tomatoes, reserving ½ cup juice. Cut up tomatoes and spoon evenly over the two pizza crusts. Sprinkle with salt and pepper. **9** Top tomatoes with mozzarella. Spoon on the sausage, dividing evenly between the two crusts.

10 Combine the tomato paste, reserved tomato juice, garlic, oregano, and basil; mix well and spread over the two pizzas. Sprinkle generously with salt and pepper. Scatter about *¼ cup* of the parmesan or romano cheese over each pizza. Bake in 425° oven for 15 minutes or till crusts are golden. To serve, cut in wedges. Makes two 12-inch pizzas.

28

1 In mixing bowl soften the yeast in warm water (110°). Add the packaged biscuit mix, stirring in with a wooden spoon.
   Measure biscuit mix by lightly spooning it into a dry measure. Do not pack or tap it; just level with a spatula as shown on page 367.

2 Vigorously beat the dough mixture with a wooden spoon for 2 minutes. The texture of the beaten dough should be similar to that shown above.

6 Using a pastry brush, brush each dough circle with a little cooking oil or olive oil. If you do not have a pastry brush, use a folded piece of paper toweling.

7 Remove sausage casing, if present. In skillet break sausage into bits with a wooden spoon. Cook over low heat about 10 minutes or till meat is lightly browned, stirring occasionally to brown meat evenly. Drain off excess fat.

3 Turn out dough onto a lightly floured surface (a pastry cloth works well). Sprinkle surface of dough with a little additional biscuit mix or all-purpose flour.

Knead 25 strokes (refer to steps 6 and 7 on page 182). Dough should have a smooth consistency, as shown.

4 Divide the dough into two equal portions. On a lightly floured surface, roll each half into a 12-inch circle. Again, a floured pastry cloth works especially well.

5 Place each of the dough circles on a greased pizza pan or baking sheet. Crimp the edges by pinching dough between fingers, as shown.

29

8 Drain the tomatoes, reserving ½ cup of the juice for use in the sauce. If desired, use a colander or sieve to drain the tomatoes.

Cut up tomatoes and spoon evenly over the two pizza crusts. Sprinkle with some salt and pepper.

9 Top tomatoes with the mozzarella, dividing between the two pizzas. Spoon half of the browned sausage over each pizza, distributing it as evenly as possible.

10 To make pizza sauce, combine the tomato paste, reserved tomato juice, garlic, oregano, and basil; mix well. Spread evenly over the two pizzas. Sprinkle generously with salt and pepper. Scatter about ¼ *cup* of the parmesan or romano cheese over each pizza.

Bake in a 425° oven for about 15 minutes or till crusts are golden.

To serve, cut into wedges using a pizza wheel, sharp knife, or kitchen shears.

Meat

Walnut-Glazed Lamb Chops

  4 lamb loin chops, cut ¾ inch thick
  ¼ cup honey
  1 tablespoon lemon juice
  ¼ cup finely chopped walnuts
  2 tablespoons snipped parsley

Referring to the tip on page 23, slash fat and place lamb chops on unheated rack in broiler pan. Broil about 3 inches from heat for 5 minutes. Sprinkle with some salt and pepper. Turn; broil 5 to 6 minutes more.

Meanwhile, in small bowl blend honey and lemon juice; stir in walnuts and parsley. Spoon walnut-honey mixture over chops; broil 1 minute longer. Makes 4 servings.

Herbed Lamb Kabobs

  1½ pounds boneless lamb, cut in
       1-inch pieces
  ¾ cup Russian salad dressing
  3 tablespoons lime juice
  ½ teaspoon dried oregano, crushed
  ¼ teaspoon dried tarragon, crushed
     Boiling water
  2 cups small fresh mushrooms
  2 medium green peppers, cut in
     1½- to 2-inch squares

Place lamb pieces in a plastic bag; set in a deep bowl. To make marinade, combine salad dressing, lime juice, oregano, and tarragon; pour over lamb. Close bag; turn to evenly distribute marinade over the meat. Cover and let stand 2 hours at room temperature or overnight in refrigerator; turn occasionally. Drain; reserve marinade.

Pour some boiling water over mushrooms to moisten; drain. Alternately, thread lamb, mushrooms, and green peppers on 6 long skewers. Place on unheated rack in broiler pan.

Referring to step 3 on page 23, broil 3 inches from heat for 10 to 12 minutes; turn and baste occasionally with marinade. Makes 6 servings.

Broiled Short Ribs

  4 pounds beef short ribs
  ⅔ cup catsup
  ¼ cup light molasses
  ¼ cup lemon juice
  1 tablespoon dry mustard
  ½ teaspoon chili powder
     Dash garlic powder

Trim excess fat from ribs; season with salt and pepper. Place ribs in Dutch oven; add water to cover. Simmer, covered, about 2 hours or till tender. Drain; place ribs on unheated rack in broiler pan, referring to steps 2 and 3 on page 23.

Combine catsup and remaining ingredients; brush over ribs. Broil 4 to 5 inches from heat for 10 to 15 minutes, turning often and basting with sauce. Makes 4 servings.

Country Barbecued Ribs

  4 pounds pork country-style ribs
  1 cup chopped onion
  1 clove garlic, minced
  ¼ cup cooking oil
  1 8-ounce can tomato sauce
  ½ cup water
  ¼ cup packed brown sugar
  ¼ cup lemon juice
  2 tablespoons worcestershire sauce
  2 tablespoons prepared mustard
  1 teaspoon salt
  1 teaspoon celery seed
  ¼ teaspoon pepper

In large saucepan or Dutch oven, cook ribs, covered, in enough boiling salted water to cover for 45 to 60 minutes or till ribs are tender; drain well.

Meanwhile, in saucepan cook onion and garlic in hot oil till tender but not brown. Stir in tomato sauce, water, brown sugar, lemon juice, worcestershire sauce, mustard, salt, celery seed, and pepper. Simmer, uncovered, for 15 minutes; stir once or twice.

Grill ribs, referring to steps 3 and 4 on page 24. Place ribs on rack over *slow* coals for about 45 minutes or till done; turn every 15 minutes. Brush with sauce till ribs are well-coated. Serves 6.

Beer Burgers

  1 egg
  ½ cup beer
  ½ cup crushed saltine crackers
  ¼ cup finely chopped onion
  6 tablespoons creamy French salad
     dressing
  2 tablespoons grated parmesan
     cheese
  ¼ teaspoon salt
  1½ pounds ground beef
  6 hamburger buns, split

Refer to: Shaping and grilling burgers, page 24. Combine egg, *¼ cup* of the beer, cracker crumbs, onion, *2 tablespoons* of the dressing, the cheese, and salt. Add meat; mix well and form into 6 patties, ¾ inch thick. For sauce, mix remaining ¼ cup beer and remaining 4 tablespoons dressing. Grill meat over *medium* coals about 10 minutes or to desired doneness. Turn once; baste occasionally with sauce. Serve on buns; pass remaining sauce. Makes 6.

Pork Chops in Sour Cream

  6 pork loin chops, cut ½ inch thick
     (about 2½ pounds)
  ¾ teaspoon dried sage, crushed
  2 tablespoons shortening (optional)
  2 medium onions, sliced (1 cup)
  1 teaspoon instant beef bouillon
     granules
  ½ cup hot water
  ½ cup dairy sour cream
  1 tablespoon all-purpose flour
  2 tablespoons snipped parsley

Trim excess fat from chops; set aside. Rub chops with sage; sprinkle with salt and pepper. Heat shortening or trimmings, referring to step 3 on page 11. Brown chops; drain. Add onions. Dissolve bouillon granules in water; pour over chops. Cover; simmer 35 to 40 minutes or till meat is tender. Transfer meat to platter; keep warm. Skim excess fat from drippings; measure ½ cup drippings and set aside.

Combine sour cream and flour; slowly stir in reserved drippings. Return all to skillet. Cook and stir till bubbly. Pour over meat; garnish with parsley. Makes 6 servings.

Fennel-Stuffed Pork Chops

- 6 pork chops, cut 1 inch thick
- 2 cups small dry bread cubes (3 slices bread)
- 1 cup finely chopped apple
- ¼ cup finely chopped onion
- 2 tablespoons butter *or* margarine, melted
- ½ teaspoon fennel seed, crushed
- ¼ teaspoon salt
- 2 tablespoons water
- 2 tablespoons cooking oil

Cut pockets in chops, referring to steps 1 and 2 on page 20. Sprinkle with a little salt and pepper. Mix bread cubes, apple, onion, butter, fennel, and salt. Sprinkle with water; toss lightly. Stuff into pockets of chops, referring to steps 5 and 6 on page 20.

In large oven-going skillet, slowly brown chops on both sides in hot oil for 10 to 15 minutes. Drain off excess fat. Bake, uncovered, in 350° oven for 45 minutes or till meat is tender. Serves 6.

Texas Beef Skillet

- 1 pound ground beef
- ¾ cup chopped onion
- 1 16-ounce can tomatoes, cut up
- 1 15½-ounce can red kidney beans
- ½ cup quick-cooking rice
- ½ cup water
- 3 tablespoons chopped green pepper
- 1½ teaspoons chili powder
- ½ teaspoon salt
- ½ teaspoon garlic salt
- ¾ cup shredded sharp American cheese (3 ounces)
- Corn chips, crushed

In a skillet cook ground beef and onion till meat is browned and onion is tender. Drain off fat. Stir in the *undrained* tomatoes, *undrained* beans, rice, water, green pepper, chili powder, salt, and garlic salt. Reduce heat; simmer, covered, for 20 minutes, stirring occasionally. Top with cheese. Cover and heat about 3 minutes or till cheese melts. Sprinkle corn chips around edge. Serves 6.

Beef Stroganoff

- 1 pound beef tenderloin
- 3 tablespoons cooking oil
- 1½ cups sliced mushrooms (4 ounces)
- ½ cup dry sherry
- ¼ cup beef broth
- 1 cup dairy sour cream
- Hot cooked fine noodles

Cut beef tenderloin across grain in ¼-inch-thick strips. In skillet heat cooking oil. Quickly brown the meat in oil, 2 to 4 minutes. Remove meat from skillet. Add sliced mushrooms and cook 2 to 3 minutes; remove mushrooms. Add sherry and beef broth to skillet; bring to boiling. Cook, uncovered, till liquid is reduced to ⅓ cup. Stir in dairy sour cream and ½ teaspoon *salt*; stir in meat and mushrooms. Cook slowly till heated through; *do not boil*. Serve over hot cooked noodles. Serves 4.

31

Pork Chop Supper for Two

- 2 pork chops, cut ¾ inch thick
- ⅓ cup long grain rice
- 2 tablespoons chopped onion
- 1 cup water
- 1 teaspoon instant chicken bouillon granules
- ½ cup chopped apple
- 1 tablespoon butter, melted
- 1 tablespoon brown sugar
- ¼ teaspoon ground cinnamon
- ½ cup sliced apples

Trim fat from chops. Cook trimmings in skillet till 2 tablespoons fat accumulate, referring to step 3 on page 11; discard trimmings. Slowly brown chops in hot fat; remove chops. In same skillet cook rice and onion till rice is golden, stirring constantly. Stir in water and bouillon granules. Bring to boiling; stir in chopped apple. Turn mixture into a 6½×6½×2-inch baking dish; arrange chops atop.

Bake, covered, in 350° oven for 30 minutes. Combine butter, sugar, and cinnamon. Brush sliced apples with mixture; arrange around chops. Bake, uncovered, about 20 minutes or till apples and pork are tender. Makes 2 servings.

Pork Chop Supper for Two

Meat

Salad Burgers

¼ cup cider vinegar
¼ cup water
2 tablespoons sugar
1 teaspoon salt
⅛ teaspoon pepper
1 cup chopped onion
1 tomato, diced (1 cup)
½ unpeeled cucumber, sliced paper-thin (1 cup)
2 pounds ground beef
1½ teaspoons salt
⅛ teaspoon pepper
¼ cup chopped sweet pickle
8 hamburger buns, split and toasted

Combine the vinegar, water, sugar, the 1 teaspoon salt, and ⅛ teaspoon pepper. Add the onion, tomato, and cucumber. Cover and refrigerate for 1 to 2 hours; drain well.

Prepare meat patties, referring to Shaping and grilling burgers on page 24. Combine ground beef, the 1½ teaspoons salt, and ⅛ teaspoon pepper; mix lightly. Shape into sixteen 4-inch patties. Grill burgers over *medium* coals 8 to 10 minutes, turning once.

Drain the tomato-cucumber mixture. Stir in the chopped pickle. For each burger, top a bun half with a meat patty. Spoon on some of the tomato mixture. Add second beef patty and more of tomato mixture. Cover with bun top. Makes 8 sandwiches.

Sausage-Kraut Skillet

1 pound bulk pork sausage
1 8¼-ounce can crushed pineapple
1 16-ounce can sauerkraut
2 medium apples, cored and sliced
1 tablespoon cornstarch

In skillet brown the pork sausage, referring to step 7 on page 28; drain. Drain 2 tablespoons of syrup from pineapple; set aside. Stir pineapple with remaining syrup and undrained sauerkraut into meat. Cover; cook over low heat for 20 minutes. Add sliced apples; cook 10 minutes.

Blend the 2 tablespoons reserved syrup into cornstarch; stir into sausage mixture. Cook and stir till thickened. Makes 4 to 6 servings.

Salad Burgers

Best-Ever Chili

2 pounds ground beef
1 cup chopped onion
1 cup chopped green pepper
1 cup sliced celery
2 15½-ounce cans red kidney beans
2 16-ounce cans tomatoes, cut up
1 6-ounce can tomato paste
2 cloves garlic, minced
1 to 1½ tablespoons chili powder
2 teaspoons salt

In Dutch oven cook beef, onion, green pepper, and celery till meat is browned and vegetables are tender. Stir to break up chunks of meat. Drain kidney beans, reserving liquid. Add beans and remaining ingredients. Cover; simmer 1 to 1½ hours. If desired, stir in some reserved bean liquid to make desired consistency. Makes 10 servings.

Porcupine Meatballs

1 beaten egg
1 10¾-ounce can condensed tomato soup
¼ cup long grain rice
2 tablespoons finely chopped onion
1 tablespoon snipped parsley
½ teaspoon salt
⅛ teaspoon pepper
1 pound ground beef
1 teaspoon worcestershire sauce

Combine egg and ¼ *cup* of the soup. Stir in the uncooked rice, onion, parsley, salt, and pepper; add meat. Mix well; shape into 20 small balls, referring to tip at right. Place in 10-inch skillet. Mix remaining soup, worcestershire, and ½ cup *water*; add to skillet. Bring to boiling; reduce heat. Cover; simmer 35 to 40 minutes; stir often. Serves 4 or 5.

32

Cranberry Lamb Chops

2 cups whole cranberries, chopped
⅓ cup sugar
6 lamb shoulder chops, cut ¾ inch thick
Cooking oil
½ cup chopped celery
¼ cup chopped onion
½ cup butter or margarine
1 8-ounce package herb-seasoned stuffing mix
2 medium oranges, peeled, sectioned, and chopped
½ cup chopped pecans

Combine cranberries and sugar; set aside. Brown lamb chops in a little oil for 10 to 15 minutes; drain off fat. Cook celery and onion in butter till tender. Combine celery mixture with stuffing mix and 1 cup *water*; mix well. Stir in cranberries, oranges, and pecans. Turn into a 13×9×2-inch baking dish. Top with lamb chops. Sprinkle with salt and pepper. Cover; bake in 350° oven for 45 minutes. Uncover; bake about 15 minutes. Serves 6.

Meat Loaf Florentine

1 10-ounce package frozen chopped spinach, thawed and drained
2 beaten eggs
½ cup milk
1½ cups soft bread crumbs (2 slices)
2 tablespoons soy sauce
1½ teaspoons salt
¼ teaspoon bottled hot pepper sauce
2 pounds ground beef
Mushroom Sauce

Refer to: Combining and shaping ground meat mixtures, steps 1 and 2, and tip, page 26. Combine spinach, eggs, and milk. Stir in crumbs, soy, salt, and hot pepper sauce; add beef and mix. Pat into a 9×5×3-inch loaf pan. Bake in 350° oven for 1½ hours. Pass Mushroom Sauce. Serves 8.

Mushroom Sauce: In saucepan combine one 3-ounce can *chopped mushrooms*, undrained, and 1 tablespoon all-purpose *flour*. Stir in 1 cup *dairy sour cream* and 2 tablespoons *snipped chives*. Cook and stir just till thickened; *do not boil*.

Swedish Meatballs

½ cup chopped onion
3 tablespoons butter or margarine
1 beaten egg
1 cup light cream
1½ cups soft bread crumbs
¼ cup finely snipped parsley
1¼ teaspoons salt
Dash pepper
Dash ground nutmeg
Dash ground ginger
1½ pounds ground beef or ¾ pound ground beef, ½ pound ground veal, and ¼ pound ground pork
2 tablespoons all-purpose flour
1 teaspoon instant beef bouillon granules
½ teaspoon instant coffee crystals
1¼ cups water

Cook onion in *1 tablespoon* of the butter or margarine till tender. In mixing bowl combine egg and cream; stir in cooked onion, bread crumbs, parsley, salt, pepper, nutmeg, and ginger. Add meats. Mix well by hand or on medium speed of electric mixer. Shape into ¾- to 1-inch balls, referring to tip at right (mixture will be soft; for easier shaping, wet hands or chill mixture first).

In large skillet brown meatballs, half at a time, in the remaining 2 tablespoons butter; remove from skillet. Stir flour, bouillon granules, and coffee crystals into pan juices; add water.

Cook and stir till thickened and bubbly. Add meatballs. Cover; simmer about 30 minutes, basting meatballs occasionally. Makes about 60 appetizer meatballs.

Deviled Blade Steak Broil

2 1-pound beef blade steaks, cut ¾ inch thick
Instant unseasoned meat tenderizer
2 tablespoons dry mustard
2 tablespoons worcestershire sauce
2 tablespoons catsup
2 tablespoons water
2 tablespoons butter or margarine
2 teaspoons sugar
1½ teaspoons salt
¾ teaspoon paprika

Refer to: Broiling steaks, page 22. Sprinkle meat with tenderizer according to label directions. For sauce, combine remaining ingredients and ¼ teaspoon *pepper*. Heat and stir till butter is melted; keep warm. Place steaks on unheated rack in broiler pan.

Broil meat 3 to 5 inches from heat for 6 to 7 minutes; brush with sauce and turn. Broil 6 to 7 minutes more, brushing with sauce after 4 minutes. Transfer meat to platter; spoon remaining sauce atop. Makes 4 servings.

33

TIP To shape meatballs to uniform size, *try one of these two methods. Form meat into a roll of desired diameter. Slice, as shown above, round into balls. (For 1-inch meatballs, use a 1-inch roll cut into 1-inch slices.)*

Or, pat meat to a square; cut in cubes, rounding each into a ball. (For 1-inch balls, use a 1-inch-thick square cut into 1-inch cubes.)

POULTRY

Stuffed, stewed, fried, or fricasseed, poultry makes wonderful eating. Because they are also economical and easy to fix, chicken, turkey, and other birds are popular with families everywhere.

Roast Turkey with Bread Stuffing

Techniques: Stuffing and roasting a turkey

½	**cup chopped onion**
½	**cup butter** *or* **margarine**
1	**teaspoon poultry seasoning** *or* **ground sage**
½	**teaspoon salt**
⅛	**teaspoon pepper**
8	**cups dry bread cubes**
1	**cup chicken broth (see recipe on page 103)**
	***or* water**
1	**10-pound turkey**
	Cooking oil

1 Cook onion in butter or margarine till tender. Stir in poultry seasoning or sage, the salt, and pepper. **2** For stuffing, in large bowl add onion mixture to bread cubes; drizzle with broth or water. **3** Toss to mix.

4 Rinse turkey; pat dry. Rub cavities with salt, if desired. Spoon some stuffing into neck cavity. **5** Pull neck skin to back; secure. **6** Spoon remaining stuffing into body cavity; do not pack. **7** Tuck drumsticks under band of skin at tail, or tie legs to tail. **8** Twist wing tips under back.

9 Place bird, breast side up, on rack in shallow roasting pan. Brush with oil. **10** Insert thermometer; cover bird loosely with foil. Roast in 325° oven for a total of 4 to 4½ hours.

11 After about 2½ hours (when bird is ⅔ done), cut band or string between legs. About 45 minutes before bird is done, remove foil. **12** Turkey is done when the thermometer registers 185° and legs move easily in sockets. Let stand 15 minutes before carving. Makes about 10 servings.

1 In saucepan cook chopped onion in butter or margarine over medium-low heat about 5 minutes or till onion is tender but not brown. Stir in poultry seasoning or sage, the salt, and pepper.

2 For stuffing, place the dry bread cubes in a large mixing bowl. Add the onion mixture; drizzle with the broth or water.

Be sure to use a bowl that is large enough to allow for tossing butter mixture with bread cubes.

To make your own dry bread cubes, cut bread into cubes. Spread out in a single layer and let stand to dry for a day or two, turning several times.

7 If turkey has a band of skin across the tail, tuck the drumsticks under it to hold them in place, as shown.

If this band is not present, tie the legs together with a piece of string, then tie the legs to the tail to secure them.

8 Place turkey on its back. Twist the tips of the wings under the back of the bird, as shown. This makes a more compact roast that is easier to carve. It also helps keep the wings from over-browning during cooking.

3 Using a spoon, toss the stuffing mixture together to combine thoroughly. The mixture should be evenly moist throughout.

If you prefer a moister stuffing, add a little extra broth or water.

To avoid a potential food spoilage problem, do not stuff turkey till right before cooking it. If you want to make the stuffing ahead of time, chill it separately from the bird.

4 Remove giblets from turkey's body cavity; reserve for another use. (One good use for giblets is Southern Giblet Gravy, page 114). Rinse the turkey in cold running water and pat dry with paper toweling.

Rub inside of neck and body cavities with salt, if desired. Loosely spoon some of the stuffing into the neck cavity of the bird.

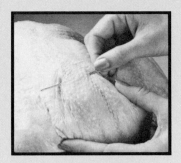

5 Pull the neck skin over the stuffing in the neck cavity. Secure the skin to the back of the turkey with a small skewer, as shown.

6 Place the turkey, neck side down, in a mixing bowl (for larger birds, you may need to place the turkey in a sink rather than a bowl). Lightly spoon the remaining stuffing into the body cavity of the turkey. Holding the bird by its legs, gently shake down the stuffing.

Do not pack stuffing in tightly or it will become too compact and firm when cooked.

35

9 Place the stuffed turkey, breast side up, on a rack in a shallow roasting pan. Use an adjustable or flat rack that holds the entire bird off the bottom of the pan.

Brush the skin of the bird with a little cooking oil.

10 Insert a meat thermometer in the center of the inside thigh muscle, making sure the bulb does not touch the bone. The thermometer is placed here because this part requires the most cooking time.

Cover bird loosely with foil. Press lightly at the ends of drumsticks and neck; leave an air space between bird and foil.

Roast in 325° oven for 4 to 4½ hours. Baste occasionally with juices, if desired.

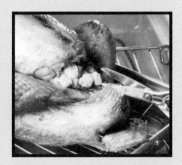

11 When turkey is about ⅔ done (after 2½ to 3 hours of roasting for this size bird), cut the band of skin or string between the legs, as shown. This helps ensure that the thighs will cook evenly.

About 45 minutes before the turkey is done, remove foil from bird to assure even browning.

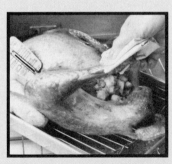

12 When the turkey is done, the meat thermometer will register 185°. Press the thickest part of a drumstick between fingers protected with paper toweling. The meat should feel very soft and tender. The drumsticks should move up and down and twist easily in their sockets, as shown.

Remove bird from oven; cover loosely with foil to keep warm. Let stand 15 minutes to make carving easier.

Poultry

Fried Chicken (pictured on page 6)

Technique: Cutting up and pan-frying chicken

1	2½- to 3-pound broiler-fryer chicken
¼	cup all-purpose flour
1½	teaspoons salt
1	teaspoon paprika
¼	teaspoon pepper
2	tablespoons cooking oil *or* shortening

36

1 To cut chicken into serving pieces, slit skin at hips. **2** Break hip joints. **3** Cut thighs from body. **4** Separate thighs from drumsticks. **5** Cut wings from body. **6** Separate breast from back. **7** Break back in half. **8** Divide chicken breast into 2 pieces.

9 Rinse chicken pieces; pat dry. In a plastic or paper bag combine flour, salt, paprika, and pepper. Add a few chicken pieces at a time; shake to coat. **10** In a 12-inch skillet heat oil or shortening. Add chicken, with meaty pieces toward center of skillet. **11** Cook over medium heat for 15 minutes, turning to brown evenly. Reduce heat; cover tightly. Cook 30 minutes. Uncover; cook 5 to 10 minutes more. **12** Chicken is done when it is easily pierced with a fork. Makes 4 servings.

Crisp Fried Chicken: Prepare chicken as directed in steps 1–10. Cook chicken, uncovered, over medium-low heat for 55 to 60 minutes or till chicken is tender. Turn occasionally; drain on paper toweling.

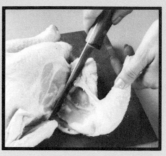

1 Cut chicken into serving pieces. Begin by slitting the skin at a hip joint in preparation for removing thigh from body.

2 With one hand, firmly grasp the body of the chicken. With the other hand, hold thigh; bend back the thigh till the bone pops out of the hip joint and is exposed, as shown.

7 Grasp back piece firmly at both ends and bend toward the skin side to break into 2 pieces. Cut back in half at break. Cut off the tail, if desired.

8 Divide chicken breast into 2 lengthwise pieces, shown at back of cutting board, by cutting along the breastbone.

Or, divide chicken breast into 2 crosswise pieces by grasping the breast as for the back and bending the breast between the wishbone and breastbone. Cut between these bones to make two pieces, as shown.

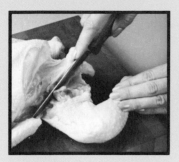 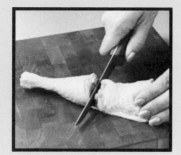  

3 Using the broken hip joint as a guide, and cutting as close to the backbone as possible, cut the thigh away from the body of the chicken with a sharp knife. Repeat steps 1, 2, and 3 on other hip joint and thigh.

4 Using steps 1, 2, and 3 as a guide, separate thigh from drumstick. First, slit the skin, break the joint, then cut the pieces apart, as shown. Repeat with other leg.

5 Slit the skin, break the joint, and cut the wing away from the body of the chicken, referring to steps 1, 2, and 3. Repeat with other wing.

If desired, tuck the wing tip behind the first joint of the wing to make a more compact piece, as shown in step 10.

6 With a sharp knife or kitchen shears, cut along the breast end of the ribs toward the neck of the chicken to separate the breast from the back, as shown. Repeat on other side.

37

9 Rinse chicken pieces under cold running water and pat dry with paper toweling. In a plastic or paper bag combine flour, salt, paprika, and pepper. Add a few chicken pieces at a time; shake to coat with flour mixture.

Or, place flour mixture in a shallow dish; roll chicken pieces in mixture to coat.

10 In a 12-inch skillet heat the cooking oil or shortening. Add flour-coated chicken pieces, with meaty pieces (breasts and thighs) toward the center where the heat is most intense, and bony pieces (wings and backs) toward the edge.

Be careful when adding chicken to the hot fat, as it is likely to spatter. It may continue to spatter occasionally during cooking.

11 Cook chicken over medium heat for 15 minutes, turning with tongs as needed to brown evenly. Reduce heat. Cover tightly and cook for 30 minutes. Uncover; cook 5 to 10 minutes longer or till chicken is tender.

Or, for crisper chicken, cook, uncovered, over medium-low heat for 55 to 60 minutes or till tender. Turn occasionally.

12 Chicken is done when it feels tender and is easily pierced with a fork. Test the thigh or breast at a point near the bone, as these parts require the most cooking time.

Don't be concerned if the meat nearest the bone darkens or is still pink after chicken tests done. This coloring is caused by natural reactions which occur as the chicken cooks, and does not affect flavor.

Poultry

Oven-Fried Chicken

Technique: Oven-frying chicken

- **2 cups cornflakes** *or* **½ cup fine dry bread crumbs**
- **¼ cup butter** *or* **margarine**
- **½ teaspoon salt**
- **¼ teaspoon pepper**
- **1 2½- to 3-pound broiler-fryer chicken, cut up (refer to steps 1–8 on page 36)**

38

1 Crush cornflakes to make 1 cup crumbs; set aside. **2** In small saucepan melt butter or margarine. Remove from heat; stir in salt and pepper.

3 Rinse chicken pieces; pat dry. Brush with butter mixture. **4** Place crushed cornflakes or fine dry bread crumbs on a sheet of waxed paper; roll chicken in crumbs to coat. **5** Arrange chicken, skin side up and so pieces don't touch, in a shallow baking pan. Bake in 375° oven for 50 to 60 minutes. Do not turn. **6** Chicken is done when it is easily pierced with a fork. Season to taste. Makes 4 servings.

1 Place cornflakes in a plastic bag or between 2 pieces of waxed paper. Crush cornflakes with a rolling pin. Set aside.

4 Place crushed cornflakes or bread crumbs on a piece of waxed paper or in a shallow dish. Roll the butter-coated chicken pieces in the crumbs to coat evenly.

2 In a small saucepan melt the butter or margarine. Remove pan from heat; stir in the salt and the pepper.

3 Rinse chicken pieces in cold running water; pat dry with paper toweling. Place chicken pieces on waxed paper. Brush chicken pieces on all sides with the butter mixture, as shown.

TIP *Change the character of Oven-Fried Chicken simply by changing the crumb coating you use.*

Potato Chip Chicken: *Use 1 cup crushed potato chips or barbecue-flavored potato chips for the crumbs in the recipe at left.*

Parmesan Chicken: *Combine ¼ cup fine dry bread crumbs, ¼ cup grated parmesan cheese, 2 tablespoons snipped parsley, and ¼ teaspoon dried oregano, crushed. Substitute this mixture for the crumbs in the recipe at left.*

Coconut and Curry Chicken: *Combine 1 cup coarsely crushed bran flakes, ½ cup shredded coconut, 2 teaspoons curry powder, and 1 teaspoon salt. Substitute this mixture for the crumbs in the recipe at left.*

39

5 Arrange chicken pieces, skin side up, in a shallow baking pan. For best browning, be sure the pieces do not touch each other. Bake in a 375° oven for 50 to 60 minutes or till chicken is tender. Do not turn chicken pieces during cooking.

6 Chicken is done when it feels tender and is easily pierced with a fork. Test the thigh or breast at a point near the bone, as these parts require the most cooking time.

Don't be concerned if the meat nearest the bone darkens or is still pink after cooking. This coloring is caused by natural reactions which occur as the chicken cooks, and does not affect flavor.

Poultry

1 In a large skillet heat the cooking oil. Add the sliced onions and minced garlic. Cook over medium heat till onions are tender but not brown, stirring occasionally.

Chicken Cacciatore

Technique: Braising chicken

2	tablespoons cooking oil
2	medium onions, cut in ¼-inch slices
2	cloves garlic, minced
1	2½- to 3-pound broiler-fryer chicken, cut up (refer to steps 1–8 on page 36)
1	16-ounce can tomatoes, cut up
1	8-ounce can tomato sauce
1	teaspoon salt
1	teaspoon dried oregano *or* basil, crushed
½	teaspoon celery seed
¼	teaspoon pepper
1	or 2 bay leaves
¼	cup dry white wine
	Hot cooked rice

40

1 In a large skillet heat oil; add onions and garlic. Cook over medium heat till onions are tender. **2** Remove onions; set aside. **3** Rinse chicken pieces; pat dry. Add more cooking oil to skillet, if needed. In same skillet over medium heat, brown chicken pieces for 15 minutes, turning as necessary.

4 Return the cooked onions to the skillet. **5** Combine *undrained* tomatoes, tomato sauce, salt, oregano or basil, celery seed, pepper, and bay leaves. Pour over chicken in skillet. Cover; simmer 30 minutes. **6** Stir in wine; cook, uncovered, over low heat 15 minutes longer, turning occasionally. **7** Chicken is done when it is easily pierced with a fork. **8** Skim fat; remove bay leaves. Transfer chicken and sauce to a serving dish. Serve with hot cooked rice. Makes 4 servings.

5 In a bowl combine the *undrained* tomatoes, tomato sauce, salt, oregano or basil, celery seed, pepper, and bay leaves. Pour mixture over chicken and onions in skillet. Cover and simmer over low heat for 30 minutes.

2 Use a slotted spoon to remove the cooked onion slices and garlic from the skillet. Transfer to a bowl and set aside while cooking chicken.

3 Rinse chicken pieces and pat dry. Add more cooking oil to the skillet, if needed, to make about 2 tablespoons. Add chicken pieces to skillet, with meaty parts toward the center of the pan where the heat is most intense. Cook over medium heat for 15 minutes, turning with tongs as necessary to brown evenly.

4 When the chicken pieces are well-browned, use a large spoon to return the cooked onions and garlic to the skillet.

6 Stir in the white wine. Cook chicken pieces, uncovered, over low heat 15 minutes longer or till tender, turning occasionally.

7 Chicken is done when it feels tender and is easily pierced with a fork. Test the thigh or breast at a point near the bone, as these parts require the most cooking time.

Don't be concerned if the meat nearest the bone darkens or is still pink after cooking. This coloring is caused by natural reactions which occur as the chicken cooks, and does not affect flavor.

8 Use a wide shallow spoon to skim the fat from the skillet, as shown. The fat is the oily-looking part of the liquid that rises to the top.

Remove bay leaves. Transfer chicken and sauce to a serving dish. Serve with hot cooked rice.

Poultry

Chicken Kiev

Techniques: Boning, pounding, breading, and deep-fat frying chicken

- **4   whole large chicken breasts, halved lengthwise**
- **2   tablespoons snipped parsley**
- **1   tablespoon chopped green onion**
- **1   ¼-pound stick of butter, well chilled**
- **2   beaten eggs**
- **2   tablespoons water**
- **½   cup all-purpose flour**
- **½   cup fine dry bread crumbs**
-    **Shortening *or* cooking oil for deep-fat frying**

1 Skin chicken breasts. **2–3** Remove and discard bones from chicken. **4** Place each piece of chicken between two pieces of clear plastic wrap; pound to ⅛-inch thickness, working from center. **5** Remove plastic wrap; sprinkle each piece of chicken with some parsley and onion. Season with salt.

6 Cut butter into 8 sticks. **7** Place one stick on each chicken piece. Fold in sides; roll up jelly roll-style, pressing ends to seal.

8 In shallow dish combine eggs and water. Place flour in another shallow dish. Roll chicken in flour to coat, then dip in egg mixture. **9** Coat with crumbs. Cover; chill at least 1 hour.

10 Heat shortening or oil to 375°. Add a few chicken rolls. **11** Fry for 5 minutes or till golden. Remove from fat with tongs; drain on paper toweling. Repeat with remaining rolls. Makes 8 servings.

Oven Chicken Kiev: Make Chicken Kiev according to steps 1–9. Heat ¼ cup *butter or margarine* in a large skillet. Fry chicken rolls on all sides till brown. Transfer to a 12×7½×2-inch baking dish. Bake in 400° oven for 15 to 18 minutes.

1 Place one chicken breast half on cutting board, skin side up. Pull the skin away from the meat; discard skin. Repeat with remaining chicken breast halves.

2 Hold chicken breast half with bone side down, as shown. Starting from the breastbone side of chicken breast, use a sharp knife to begin cutting the meat away from the bone. Cut as close to the bone as possible.

7 Place 1 stick of the butter on each piece of chicken. Fold in the sides. Roll up chicken jelly roll-style, as shown. Make sure the folded sides are included in roll. Press all edges together gently with fingers to seal.

8 In a shallow dish such as a pie plate, combine eggs and water. Place flour in another shallow dish. Roll chicken rolls first in flour to coat. Then dip in egg mixture on all sides, using your fingers, as shown, or tongs.

42

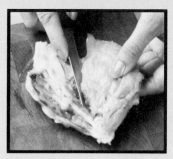

3 Continue cutting the meat from the bone. Use a sawing motion, pressing the flat side of the knife blade against the rib bones. With the other hand, gently pull the meat away from the rib bones. Repeat steps 2 and 3 with remaining chicken; discard the bones.

4 Place each breast half, boned side up, between two pieces of clear plastic wrap to prevent perforating the chicken. Using the fine-toothed side of a meat mallet, pound each piece of chicken to ⅛-inch thickness, working from center to edges.

If a meat mallet is not available, pound the chicken with the flat side of a French knife or cleaver.

5 Remove top piece of plastic wrap. Sprinkle each piece of chicken with some of the snipped parsley and chopped green onion, as shown. Season with a little salt.

Whenever you use green onions, be sure to include the delicately flavored tops to add color and interest to the dish.

6 Cut the stick of butter lengthwise in quarters, then cut each quarter in half crosswise to form 8 sticks of butter.

Be sure butter is well chilled so that it will not melt and run out before the outside of the chicken roll is cooked.

43

9 Place the fine dry bread crumbs on a piece of waxed paper or in a shallow dish. Roll egg-coated chicken in the crumbs to coat, as shown. Arrange chicken rolls on a tray or in a baking dish; cover and chill for at least 1 hour or up to 24 hours.

10 Fill a saucepan or deep-fat fryer one-third to half full of shortening or cooking oil. Heat to 375° using a deep-fat frying thermometer to monitor the temperature of the fat. (For more information on deep-fat frying, see the tip on page 63.)

Use a metal spatula or slotted spoon to add chicken rolls to the hot fat, a few at a time.

11 Fry chicken rolls about 5 minutes or till golden brown. Remove from fat using tongs or a slotted spoon; drain on paper toweling. Keep hot in a 250° oven while frying remaining chicken rolls.

Poultry

Stewed Chicken

Technique: Stewing chicken

---

2 3-pound broiler-fryer chickens, cut up, *or* **1 5- to 6-pound stewing chicken, cut up (refer to steps 1–8 on page 36)**
   Water
4 stalks celery with leaves, cut up
1 carrot, sliced
1 small onion, cut up
2 sprigs parsley
1 bay leaf
2 teaspoons salt
¼ teaspoon pepper

1 Place chicken pieces in a large kettle or Dutch oven; add enough water to cover (about 8 cups). **2** Add celery, carrot, onion, parsley, bay leaf, salt, and pepper. Cover and bring to boiling. Reduce heat and simmer 1 hour for broiler-fryers, or 2 to 2½ hours for stewing chicken. **3** Chicken is done when it is easily pierced with a fork.

   4 Remove chicken; set aside. **5–6** Strain broth; discard vegetables and bay leaf. **7** When cool enough to handle, pull chicken from bones; discard skin and bones. Cut up chicken. **8** Store meat and broth in separate airtight containers; refrigerate at once. Makes about 5 cups cooked chicken and about 8 cups broth.

Crockery-Stewed Chicken: Use ingredients as listed above *except* substitute one 3½- to 4-pound stewing chicken for birds listed; use only 4 cups water and 1 teaspoon salt. Combine all ingredients in electric slow crockery cooker. Cover and cook on low-heat setting for 8 hours, or on high-heat setting for 4 hours. Proceed as described in steps 4–8 above. Makes about 4 cups cooked chicken and 4 cups broth.

44

1 Place chicken pieces in a large kettle or Dutch oven. Add enough water to cover the chicken completely, about 8 cups.

5 Place a colander or sieve over a large mixing bowl or other large container. Carefully strain broth from kettle through colander or sieve.

2 Add the celery, carrot, onion, parsley, bay leaf, salt, and pepper. Cover and bring to boiling. Reduce heat and simmer broiler-fryer chickens for 1 hour, or stewing chicken for 2 to 2½ hours.

Broiler-fryers require less cooking time because they are tender young birds—usually less than 9 weeks old. Stewing chickens may be up to 1½ years old and are tougher.

3 Chicken is done when it feels tender and is easily pierced with a fork. Test the thigh or breast at a point near the bone, as these parts require the most cooking time.

Don't be concerned if the meat nearest the bone darkens or is still pink after cooking. This coloring is caused by natural reactions which occur as the chicken cooks, and does not affect flavor.

4 Use tongs or a slotted spoon to remove the cooked chicken pieces from the hot liquid. Set aside on a plate or other dish to cool.

45

TIP To make chicken with dumplings, *prepare Stewed Chicken according to recipe at left, steps 1–2. When chicken is nearly done, prepare dumplings. Mix 1 cup all-purpose flour, 2 teaspoons baking powder, and ½ teaspoon salt; stir in 2 tablespoons snipped parsley. Beat 1 egg; stir in ¼ cup milk and 2 tablespoons butter, melted. Add to flour mixture; stir just till blended. Drop 6 to 8 dumplings from a tablespoon onto chicken in boiling broth, as shown. Cover tightly; return to boiling. Reduce heat; do not lift cover. Simmer for 12 to 15 minutes or till done. Remove dumplings and chicken to serving dish; keep warm.*

Strain broth. Bring 4 cups of the broth to boiling. Stir 1 cup cold water into ½ cup all-purpose flour; gradually add to boiling broth, mixing well. Cook and stir till bubbly. Stir in 1½ teaspoons salt and ⅛ teaspoon pepper; pour over chicken and dumplings. Serves 6 to 8.

6 Lift colander or sieve from bowl; hold over bowl to let broth drip back into bowl. Discard the cooked vegetables and the bay leaf.

7 When cool enough to handle, pull chicken from bones, cutting when necessary. Discard the skin and bones. Cut the chicken meat into the desired-size pieces.

8 Store meat and broth in separate airtight containers so they can be used separately in recipes. Refrigerate at once; store in refrigerator no longer than 2 days.

When freezing chicken, be sure to label contents and date. If you freeze chicken separately, keep it only 1 month for best quality. Chicken can also be frozen in broth, and will keep for up to 6 months since it will not dry out as quickly.

Poultry

1 In a saucepan melt the butter or margarine. Add the chopped onion; cook over medium-low heat about 5 minutes or till onion is tender but not brown, stirring occasionally.

Individual Chicken Pies

Technique: Making pot pies

6	tablespoons butter *or* margarine
½	cup chopped onion
7	tablespoons all-purpose flour
1	teaspoon salt
¼	teaspoon dried rosemary, crushed, *or* poultry seasoning
⅛	teaspoon pepper
3	cups chicken broth
3	cups cubed cooked chicken *or* turkey
1	10-ounce package frozen peas and carrots, cooked and drained
¼	cup chopped pimiento
1	package (6) refrigerated biscuits

1 In saucepan melt butter or margarine. Add onion; cook till tender. **2** Stir in flour, salt, rosemary or poultry seasoning, and pepper. **3** Add broth; stir to mix well. **4** Cook and stir till thickened and bubbly. **5** Stir in cubed chicken, vegetables, and pimiento; heat till bubbly.

6 Divide mixture into 6 individual casseroles. **7** Cut each biscuit in quarters. **8** Place 4 pieces of biscuit on the *hot* chicken mixture in each casserole. **9** Place casseroles on a shallow baking pan. Bake in 450° oven for 8 to 10 minutes or till biscuits are lightly browned. Makes 6 servings.

6 Use a large spoon or dry measuring cup with a handle to transfer the mixture to 6 individual casseroles. Divide mixture among casseroles, using about 1 cup for each.

2 To the cooked onion add flour, salt, rosemary or poultry seasoning, and pepper. Stir together till well blended.

3 Add the chicken broth all at once; stir till mixture is well blended.

If the broth is freshly made and still hot, add it gradually while stirring to prevent lumps.

Use broth from Stewed Chicken (see recipe on page 44) or canned chicken broth. Or, mix 1 tablespoon instant chicken bouillon granules with 3 cups hot water to make 3 cups broth.

4 Stir constantly with a wooden spoon or wire whisk while cooking over medium heat. When sauce bubbles across entire surface, it is thickened to the proper consistency, as shown.

5 Add the cubed chicken, the drained peas and carrots, and the chopped pimiento to the thickened sauce. Stir in. Heat the mixture till bubbly, stirring occasionally.

For this recipe, you need 3 cups of cooked chicken. You can use meat from Stewed Chicken (see recipe on page 44). Or, substitute leftover meat from a roast turkey.

47

7 Open the package of refrigerated biscuits. Separate into individual biscuits. Use kitchen shears or a sharp knife to cut each biscuit in quarters, as shown.

8 Place 4 biscuit quarters on the *hot* chicken mixture in each individual casserole. It is important to keep the filling hot so that the undersides of the biscuits will not remain doughy.

9 Place individual casseroles on a shallow baking pan. This makes carrying the casseroles easier and, if the pies bubble over, it keeps the filling from running onto the oven floor.

Bake pies in 450° oven for 8 to 10 minutes or till biscuits are lightly browned.

Poultry

Bran Batter Chicken

1 2½- to 3 pound broiler-fryer chicken, cut up (refer to steps 1–8 on page 36)
1 beaten egg
1 cup milk
½ cup whole bran cereal
¼ cup cooking oil
¾ cup all-purpose flour
1 teaspoon baking powder
1 teaspoon onion salt
   Shortening *or* cooking oil for deep-fat frying

In large saucepan simmer chicken in lightly salted water for 20 minutes; drain. Sprinkle chicken pieces with a little salt; set aside.

For batter, combine egg, milk, cereal, and oil; let stand 5 minutes. Mix flour, baking powder, and onion salt. Add egg mixture; stir to blend.

Referring to tip on page 63, heat fat to 350°. Dip chicken pieces into batter. Fry, 2 or 3 at a time, for 4 to 5 minutes, regulating heat so chicken fries at 325°. Drain; keep warm. Serves 4.

Peanut-Chicken Stew

1 2½- to 3-pound broiler-fryer chicken, cut up (refer to steps 1–8 on page 36)
2 tablespoons shortening
1 large onion, chopped (1 cup)
2 medium carrots, sliced
1 medium green pepper, cut into strips
1¾ cups water
1 6-ounce can tomato paste
½ cup peanut butter
1 small bay leaf
1 tablespoon snipped parsley
¾ teaspoon salt

Refer to: Braising chicken, page 40. Cut each breast half into 2 pieces.

In large skillet cook chicken in hot shortening about 15 minutes, turning as necessary to brown evenly. Add onion, carrots, and green pepper.

Stir together water, tomato paste, peanut butter, bay leaf, parsley, and salt. Pour over chicken in skillet. Simmer, covered, 35 to 45 minutes or till chicken is done. Spoon off fat; serve chicken and sauce over hot cooked rice, if desired. Serves 6.

Chicken Croquettes

1½ cups coarsely chopped cooked chicken
¼ of a small onion
3 tablespoons butter *or* margarine
¼ cup all-purpose flour
½ cup chicken broth
⅓ cup milk
1 tablespoon snipped parsley
1 teaspoon lemon juice
¼ teaspoon salt
   Dash nutmeg
   Dash paprika
   Dash pepper
¾ cup fine dry bread crumbs *or* finely crushed saltine crackers (21 crackers)
1 beaten egg
2 tablespoons water
   Shortening *or* cooking oil for deep-fat frying

Put the chopped cooked chicken and onion through the coarse blade of a food grinder; set aside.

Make a thick white sauce, referring to Making white sauce on page 98. In saucepan melt butter or margarine; blend in flour till smooth. Add chicken broth and milk all at once; cook and stir till thickened and bubbly. Cook and stir 1 minute more. Remove from heat.

Stir in parsley, lemon juice, salt, nutmeg, paprika, and pepper. Add the ground chicken mixture. Mix well; cover and chill thoroughly.

With wet hands, shape a scant ¼ cup of the chilled mixture into a ball. Repeat with remaining mixture to form 8 balls. Roll each in fine bread or cracker crumbs. Carefully shape each ball into a cone.

Mix beaten egg and water in a shallow dish. Dip each cone into egg mixture; roll again in crumbs.

Referring to tip on page 63, fry 2 or 3 croquettes in deep hot fat (365°) for 2½ to 3 minutes or till golden. Drain on paper toweling. Keep croquettes hot in a warm oven while frying remaining. Makes 4 servings.

Saucy Chicken Skillet

3 tablespoons butter *or* margarine
¾ teaspoon dried thyme, crushed
1 clove garlic, minced
1 2½- to 3-pound broiler-fryer chicken, cut up (refer to steps 1–8 on page 36)
1 2½-ounce jar sliced mushrooms, drained
3 tablespoons dry white wine
2 tablespoons lemon juice
1 teaspoon instant chicken bouillon granules
1 teaspoon paprika
1 tablespoon all-purpose flour

Refer to: Braising chicken, page 40. In skillet melt butter or margarine. Stir in thyme and garlic. Add chicken; cook slowly about 20 minutes or till brown, turning once. Add mushrooms.

Meanwhile, in small saucepan combine wine, lemon juice, bouillon granules, paprika, and ¾ cup *water*. Bring to boiling; pour over chicken. Cover and simmer 30 to 40 minutes or till chicken is tender. Remove chicken to warm serving platter. Season with salt and pepper.

Skim fat from pan juices; bring juices to boiling. Stir 2 tablespoons cold *water* into flour; stir into boiling juices. Cook and stir till bubbly. Serve over chicken. Serves 4.

Apple-Spiced Chicken

1 2½- to 3-pound broiler-fryer chicken, quartered
   Cooking oil
¼ cup apple jelly
1 tablespoon lemon juice
½ teaspoon ground allspice

Refer to tip at right. Break joints of chicken. Brush chicken with oil; season with salt and pepper. Place in broiler pan, skin side down. Broil 5 to 6 inches from heat about 20 minutes or till lightly browned. Turn; broil 15 to 20 minutes or till done.

Meanwhile, for glaze, melt jelly; stir in lemon juice and allspice. Brush chicken with *half* the glaze; broil 1 to 2 minutes more. Remove to platter; brush with remaining glaze. If desired, serve with Honeyed Apple Rings (see recipe on page 153). Serves 4.

Turkey Teriyaki

- 1 32-ounce frozen white meat turkey roast
- ½ cup packed brown sugar
- ½ cup water
- ½ cup soy sauce
- ¼ cup dry sherry
- 2 tablespoons cooking oil
- 2 teaspoons vinegar
- 1 teaspoon ground ginger
- 1 clove garlic, minced
- 1 fresh pineapple

Partially thaw turkey roast; cut into 12 slices. Arrange in shallow dish. For marinade, mix brown sugar, water, soy sauce, sherry, oil, vinegar, ginger, and garlic; pour over turkey slices. Cover; chill about 1 hour. Drain, reserving marinade.

Meanwhile, referring to steps 7–10 on page 144, remove crown, peel, and eyes from pineapple. Wash, quarter lengthwise, and remove core. Cut fruit lengthwise into spears.

Referring to steps 3–4 on page 24, grill turkey slices over *medium* coals about 25 minutes; turn and baste often with marinade. Grill pineapple about 10 minutes; turn and baste often with marinade. Serve pineapple with turkey. Makes 6 servings.

Chicken with Mushrooms

- 4 whole large chicken breasts, halved lengthwise
- ¼ cup all-purpose flour
- 2 beaten eggs
- 2 tablespoons milk
- 1 cup fine dry bread crumbs
- ¼ cup cooking oil
- ½ cup sliced fresh mushrooms
- ¼ cup chopped onion
- 2 tablespoons butter *or* margarine
- 1 tablespoon all-purpose flour
- ½ teaspoon salt
- ¼ teaspoon pepper
- 1 cup milk
- ½ cup dairy sour cream

Referring to steps 1–4 on page 42, remove skin and bones from chicken breasts. Place chicken between two pieces of clear plastic wrap. Pound to ½-inch thickness; remove wrap.

Coat chicken with the ¼ cup flour. Mix eggs and the 2 tablespoons milk; dip chicken in mixture to coat. Coat with crumbs. In a skillet fry the chicken in hot oil about 5 minutes per side or till golden brown. Remove to platter; cover and keep warm.

Meanwhile, cook mushrooms and onion in butter till tender. Stir in the 1 tablespoon flour, salt, and pepper. Add the 1 cup milk; cook and stir till thickened and bubbly. Stir in sour cream. Heat through; *do not boil*. Pass with chicken. Serves 8.

Crab-Chicken Rolls

- 6 whole medium chicken breasts
- ¼ cup chopped onion
- ¼ cup chopped celery
- 2 tablespoons butter *or* margarine
- 4 teaspoons all-purpose flour
- ¼ teaspoon salt
    Dash white pepper
- ½ cup milk
- 1 7½-ounce can crab meat, drained, flaked, and cartilage removed
- ½ cup snipped parsley
- ¼ cup dry sherry
- ¼ cup butter *or* margarine, melted
- 1 teaspoon paprika

Remove skin and bones from chicken. Referring to step 4 on page 43, place chicken between 2 pieces of plastic wrap and pound to ⅛-inch thickness. Remove wrap; season both sides of chicken with some salt and pepper. Cook onion and celery in the 2 tablespoons butter. Blend in flour, salt, and pepper. Add milk; cook and stir till thickened and bubbly. Stir in crab, parsley, and sherry. Divide mixture around chicken pieces. Fold in sides and roll up, referring to step 7 on page 42. Secure with wooden picks. If desired, wrap and chill up to 24 hours.

Referring to tip below, place rolls in broiler pan. Mix melted butter and paprika; brush over chicken. Broil 5 to 6 inches from heat 20 minutes or till golden; turn and brush with butter mixture. Broil about 15 minutes longer or till done. Serves 6.

49

Apple-Spiced Chicken

TIP Broil chicken *far enough from heat so it browns evenly and cooks to desired doneness.*

Place chicken on rack in a broiler pan; place under broiler unit with surface of chicken 5 to 6 inches from the heat. If the broiler compartment does not allow enough distance, remove rack and place chicken directly in broiler pan.

Remember to preheat broiler unit before cooking, but not broiler pan or rack.

Poultry

Cranberry Cornish Hens

- ⅔ cup chopped cranberries
- 2 tablespoons sugar
- 1 teaspoon finely shredded orange peel
- ½ teaspoon salt
- ⅛ teaspoon ground cinnamon
- 3 cups toasted raisin bread cubes
- ¼ cup butter *or* margarine, melted
- 4 teaspoons orange juice
- 4 1- to 1½-pound cornish game hens
  Cooking oil
- ¼ cup orange juice

Refer to: Stuffing and roasting a turkey, page 34. Combine cranberries, sugar, peel, salt, and cinnamon. Add bread cubes; sprinkle with *half* the melted butter or margarine and the 4 teaspoons orange juice. Toss to mix.

Rinse hens and pat dry; rub cavities with salt. Stuff with cranberry mixture. Skewer neck skin to back. Tie legs to tail; twist wings under back. Place hens, breast side up, on rack in roasting pan. Brush with oil; cover loosely with foil. Roast in 375° oven for 30 minutes.

Combine the ¼ cup orange juice and remaining melted butter. Uncover birds; baste with orange juice mixture. Roast, uncovered, about 1 hour longer or till done; baste once or twice with orange juice mixture. Garnish with parsley, cranberry-centered kumquat roses, and a lemon twist, if desired. Makes 4 servings.

Roast Tarragon Chicken

- 1 3-pound broiler-fryer chicken
- 2 tablespoons lemon juice
- 2 tablespoons butter *or* margarine
- 1½ teaspoons dried tarragon, crushed

Refer to: Roasting a turkey, steps 5 and 7–12, page 34. Brush chicken with lemon juice inside and out; rub with ½ teaspoon *salt.* Skewer neck skin to back; tie legs to tail. Twist wings under back. Place, breast up, on rack in roasting pan. Melt butter; stir in tarragon. Brush over chicken. Roast, uncovered, in 375° oven for 1¼ to 1½ hours or till done. Baste occasionally with drippings. Serves 4.

Chicken Fricassee

- ½ cup all-purpose flour
- 1 teaspoon salt
- ⅛ teaspoon pepper
- 1 3- to 3½-pound broiler-fryer chicken, cut up (refer to steps 1–8 on page 36)
- 2 tablespoons shortening
- ½ cup chopped celery
- ¼ cup chopped onion
- 1 10¾-ounce can condensed cream of mushroom soup
- ¾ cup water
- 2 tablespoons chopped pimiento
  Hot cooked rice

In plastic or paper bag combine flour, salt, and pepper. Add chicken; shake to coat, referring to step 9 on page 37. In large skillet cook chicken in hot shortening for 15 minutes, turning as necessary to brown evenly. Transfer chicken to 3-quart casserole. In same skillet cook celery and onion till tender; drain off fat. Stir in soup, water, and pimiento; pour over chicken. Cover and bake in 350° oven 1 hour or till tender. Serve with rice. Serves 6.

Apricot-Glazed Turkey

- 1 8- to 10-pound turkey
  Melted butter *or* margarine
- ¼ cup apricot preserves
- ¼ cup honey
- 1 tablespoon bottled steak sauce
- 1 tablespoon lemon juice
- 2 teaspoons cornstarch

Refer to: Roasting a turkey, steps 5 and 7–12, page 34. Rub neck and body cavities of turkey with salt and pepper. Skewer neck skin to back. Tuck legs under band of skin or tie legs to tail. Twist wings under back.

Place bird, breast side up, on rack in shallow roasting pan; brush with melted butter. Insert meat thermometer. Cover bird with foil tent. Roast in 325° oven about 4 hours or till thermometer registers 185°.

Meanwhile, in saucepan combine preserves, honey, steak sauce, lemon juice, and cornstarch. Cook and stir till slightly thickened and bubbly. Uncover bird and brush with honey mixture during last 30 minutes of roasting. Makes 8 to 10 servings.

50

Cranberry Cornish Hens

Oyster-Stuffed Turkey

1 10- to 12-pound turkey
1 pint shucked oysters
1 cup chopped onion
6 tablespoons butter *or* margarine
6 cups dry bread cubes
¼ cup snipped parsley
1 teaspoon dried thyme, crushed
½ teaspoon salt
¼ teaspoon pepper
   Cooking oil

Refer to: Stuffing and roasting a turkey, page 34. Simmer turkey giblets in enough water to cover for 1½ to 2 hours or till tender. Drain and chop giblets; reserve liquid. Drain and chop oysters; reserve liquid. Cook onion in butter till tender. Combine giblets, oysters, onion, bread, parsley, thyme, salt, and pepper. Toss with oyster liquid and enough giblet liquid to moisten.

Salt neck and body cavities of turkey; stuff loosely. Skewer neck skin to back; tie legs to tail. Twist wings under back. Place, breast up, on rack in pan; brush with oil. Cap with foil. Roast in 325° oven about 4½ hours or till done. Serves 10 to 12.

Curry-Stuffed Chicken

½ cup chopped onion
½ cup chopped celery
¼ cup butter *or* margarine
1 teaspoon curry powder
½ teaspoon salt
⅛ teaspoon pepper
5 cups dry bread cubes
1 cup chicken broth
1 4- to 5-pound roasting chicken
   Cooking oil

Refer to: Stuffing and roasting a turkey, page 34. Cook onion and celery in butter. Stir in curry, salt, and pepper. Combine with bread cubes; toss with enough of the broth to moisten. Rub neck and body cavities of chicken with salt; stuff loosely. Skewer neck skin to back. Tie legs to tail. Twist wings under back.

Place, breast up, on a rack in roasting pan. Brush with oil. Roast, uncovered, in 375° oven for 2 to 2½ hours or till done. Baste occasionally with pan drippings. Serves 4.

Chicken Florentine

3 whole large chicken breasts, halved lengthwise
1 cup water
1 stalk celery, cut up
½ medium onion, cut up
½ teaspoon salt
2 10-ounce packages frozen chopped spinach
¼ cup butter *or* margarine
¼ cup all-purpose flour
   Dash white pepper
1 cup light cream
½ cup grated parmesan cheese
   Dash ground nutmeg

Remove skin and bones from chicken breasts, referring to steps 1–3 on page 42. In saucepan place chicken breasts, water, celery, onion, and salt. Bring to boiling; reduce heat and simmer about 20 minutes or till chicken is tender, referring to steps 1–6 on page 44. Remove chicken from broth. Strain broth, reserving 1 cup. Discard celery and onion.

Meanwhile, cook the frozen chopped spinach according to package directions; drain well.

In saucepan melt butter or margarine; blend in flour and white pepper. Stir in the 1 cup reserved broth and the cream. Cook and stir over medium heat till thickened and bubbly. Remove from heat; stir *½ cup* of the cream mixture, *¼ cup* of the cheese, and the nutmeg into drained spinach.

Spread spinach mixture in a 10×6×2-inch baking dish. Arrange cooked chicken breasts atop. Pour remaining cream mixture over all. Top with remaining ¼ cup cheese; sprinkle with more nutmeg, if desired.

Bake casserole in a 375° oven for 25 to 30 minutes or till lightly browned. Makes 6 servings.

Sausage-Stuffed Duckling

½ pound bulk pork sausage
4 cups dry bread cubes
1 cup chopped peeled apple
1 cup chopped celery
½ cup chopped onion
¼ cup snipped parsley
½ teaspoon dried thyme, crushed
½ teaspoon dried marjoram, crushed
1 4- to 5-pound duckling

Refer to: Stuffing and roasting a turkey, page 34. Brown sausage; drain well. Transfer to bowl; stir in bread, apple, celery, onion, parsley, thyme, marjoram, ½ teaspoon *salt,* and dash *pepper.* Toss with 2 tablespoons *water.* Rub cavity of duckling with salt; stuff with sausage mixture (reserve any remaining).

Tie legs to tail; twist wing tips under back. Place bird, breast up, on rack in a roasting pan. Prick skin all over with a fork. Roast, uncovered, in 375° oven for 1½ to 2 hours or till tender. Spoon off fat as necessary. Place any reserved stuffing in a 1-quart casserole; sprinkle with 2 tablespoons *water.* Cover; bake casserole last 30 minutes. Serve with duckling. Makes 4 servings.

Spiced Chicken

2 tablespoons cooking oil
2 tablespoons butter *or* margarine
2 large onions, thinly sliced and separated into rings
¼ teaspoon powdered saffron
⅛ teaspoon cayenne
1 2½- to 3-pound broiler-fryer chicken, cut up (refer to steps 1–8 on page 36)
½ cup raisins
½ cup blanched whole almonds, toasted
2 teaspoons lemon juice

In Dutch oven heat oil and butter. Stir in onions, saffron, cayenne, ¾ teaspoon *salt,* and ¼ teaspoon *pepper.* Add chicken; turn to coat. Cover; simmer 45 to 60 minutes or till done, turning occasionally. Remove chicken.

Cook and stir onion mixture over high heat 3 minutes or till thickened. Stir in remaining ingredients; heat through. Pour over chicken. Serves 4.

FISH AND SEAFOOD

Baked, poached, fried, or broiled, fish and seafood have a versatility that makes them ideal for any kind of menu. In this section, you'll learn how to prepare many delicious fish and shellfish specialties.

Corn-Stuffed Whitefish

Technique: Baking a stuffed fish

1	3-pound fresh *or* frozen dressed whitefish *or* other fish, boned
1	tablespoon butter *or* margarine
¼	cup chopped onion
3	tablespoons chopped green pepper
1	12-ounce can whole kernel corn, drained
1	cup soft bread crumbs (1½ slices)
2	tablespoons chopped pimiento
½	teaspoon salt
⅛	teaspoon dried thyme, crushed
2	tablespoons cooking oil

1 Thaw fish, if frozen; pat dry with paper toweling. **2** Place fish in a well-greased shallow baking pan; sprinkle cavity generously with salt.

3 To make stuffing, in a medium saucepan melt butter or margarine. Add onion and green pepper; cook about 5 minutes or till onion is tender. Stir in drained corn, bread crumbs, pimiento, salt, and thyme; mix well.

4 Stuff fish cavity loosely with the corn mixture. **5** Brush skin with the cooking oil. **6** Cover fish loosely with foil. Bake in 350° oven for 45 to 60 minutes. **7** Fish is done when it flakes with a fork. **8** Use two large spatulas to transfer the whole fish to a serving platter. Makes 6 servings.

1 Thaw fish, if it is frozen. Lay fish on paper toweling and gently pat dry with more paper toweling.

A "dressed" fish is one that has been eviscerated and scaled. The head, tail, and fins are usually removed. For this recipe, buy one that has the bones removed to form a cavity for stuffing.

Although whitefish is recommended for this recipe, you may use any other fish that is about the same size.

5 With cooking oil in a custard cup, use a pastry brush to coat the fish with oil. If you prefer, you can apply the oil with folded paper toweling.

2 Generously grease a shallow baking pan using a pastry brush or folded paper toweling. Place the fish in the pan. Open the cavity of the fish and sprinkle it generously with salt.

3 To make stuffing, melt butter or margarine in a medium saucepan. Add onion and green pepper; cook over medium heat about 5 minutes or till onion is tender, stirring occasionally. Stir in the drained corn, bread crumbs, pimiento, salt, and thyme. Mix well.

4 Lightly spoon the corn stuffing into the cavity of the fish. Gently fold the top part of the fish back over the stuffing.

53

6 Cover the stuffed fish loosely with a sheet of aluminum foil. Bake in a 350° oven for 45 to 60 minutes or till fish is done.

7 When fish is done, it will become opaque, white, and tender. To test fish for doneness, remove foil and insert fork tines into fish at a 45-degree angle. Twist the fork gently. Fish is done if it flakes as shown.

If fish resists flaking and still has a translucent quality, it is not done; if it is dry and mealy, it is overdone.

8 When fish tests done, use two large spatulas or serving utensils to transfer the whole fish from the baking pan to a serving platter.

Fish and Seafood

1 Thaw the salmon, if it is frozen. Lay salmon on a large single layer of cheesecloth; bring edges of cloth up to overlap atop the fish.

A "dressed" fish is one that has been eviscerated and scaled. Usually the head, tail, and fins are removed.

Poached Salmon (pictured on page 64)

Technique: Poaching fish

- **1** **4- to 5-pound fresh *or* frozen dressed salmon**
- **2** **cups water**
- **1** **stalk celery, cut up**
- **1** **slice lemon**
- **1** **slice onion**
- **1** **bay leaf**
- **1** **teaspoon salt**
-     **Egg Sauce (optional)**

1 Thaw fish, if frozen; wrap salmon in cheesecloth. **2** Place the wrapped fish on rack of pan (or on strips of foil—see tip at right); place in pan. Add water, celery, lemon, onion, bay leaf, and salt. **3** Cover and simmer for 25 to 30 minutes. **4** Fish is done when it flakes easily when tested with a fork. **5** Remove salmon from pan; wrap in foil to keep warm.

6 If making Egg Sauce, strain cooking liquid, reserving 1 cup. Make Egg Sauce; keep warm.

7 Pull foil and cloth away from fish; carefully remove skin. Discard skin. **8** Transfer fish to serving platter using two large spatulas. Top with Egg Sauce; sprinkle with dried dillweed, if desired. Makes 8 to 10 servings.

Egg Sauce: Refer to Making white sauce, page 98. In saucepan melt ¼ cup *butter or margarine;* blend in 3 tablespoons all-purpose *flour,* ½ teaspoon *salt,* and ⅛ teaspoon *white pepper.* Add reserved *fish stock* and 1 cup light *cream* all at once. Cook and stir till thickened and bubbly. Stir in 2 chopped *hard-cooked eggs;* heat through.

54

5 When the salmon tests done, remove it from the poaching pan by lifting out the rack or foil strips. Place the cheesecloth-wrapped fish on a sheet of aluminum foil and wrap foil around fish to keep warm.

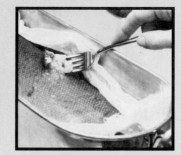

2 Place the wrapped fish on the rack of a poaching pan (or on strips of foil—see tip at right). Carefully lower fish into the pan. Pour in the water; add the celery, lemon, onion, bay leaf, and salt.

3 Cover the poaching pan with the lid or a loose cover of aluminum foil. Bring water in pan to boiling (it probably will be necessary to use two burners of your range); reduce heat and simmer for 25 to 30 minutes.

4 When fish is done, it will become opaque, white, and tender. To test fish for doneness, pull cheesecloth away from fish and place fork tines into the fish at a 45-degree angle. Twist the fork gently. Fish is done if it flakes as shown.

If fish resists flaking and still has a translucent quality, it is not done; if it is dry and mealy, it is overdone.

55

TIP If a poaching pan and rack are not available, *you can poach the salmon in a large roasting pan. Wrap the fish in cheesecloth as directed at left. Lay the wrapped fish on two wide strips of doubled foil to transfer the fish to and from the pan, then proceed as directed in the recipe.*

6 If making Egg Sauce, line a sieve with a small piece of cheesecloth. Pour the cooking liquid through the sieve into a large liquid measure. Reserve 1 cup of the liquid for sauce. Discard vegetables and remaining fish stock.

Make Egg Sauce (see recipe at left). Cover pan and keep warm over low heat.

7 Pull foil and cheesecloth away from salmon. With a sharp knife, carefully peel back the skin from the fish, being sure to preserve the shape of the fish. Discard the skin.

8 Using 2 large spatulas or serving utensils, transfer whole salmon to a serving platter. Garnish with curly endive and cooked tiny whole carrots, if desired (see picture on page 64). Pour Egg Sauce atop fish; sprinkle with dried dillweed, if desired.

Fish and Seafood

1 Thaw fish, if frozen. Rinse fish and pat dry with paper toweling.

A "pan-dressed" fish is a small "dressed" fish; that is, one that has been eviscerated and scaled. The head, tail, and fins may have been removed, but in this case they have been left attached.

Although trout is recommended for this recipe, you may use any other fish of the same approximate size.

Pan-Fried Fish

Technique: Pan-frying fish

- **3** **10- to 12-ounce fresh *or* frozen pan-dressed trout *or* other fish**
- **1** **beaten egg**
- **2** **tablespoons water**
- **¾** **cup fine dry bread crumbs *or* finely crushed saltine crackers (21 crackers) *or* cornmeal**
- **½** **teaspoon salt**
- **Dash pepper**
- **Shortening *or* cooking oil for frying**

1 Thaw fish, if frozen. Rinse and pat dry. **2** In a shallow dish beat egg; blend in water. Dip fish in egg mixture to coat on both sides. **3** Combine bread crumbs or crushed crackers or cornmeal with the salt and pepper. Roll fish in crumb mixture, coating evenly.

4 In large skillet heat ¼ inch shortening or cooking oil. Add fish in single layer to hot oil. Fry fish on one side 4 to 5 minutes or till brown. **5** Turn and fry fish 4 to 5 minutes longer. **6** Fish is done when both sides are brown and crisp, and when it flakes easily when tested with a fork. **7** Drain fish on paper toweling. Makes 3 servings.

5 Using a fork and a spatula or two spatulas, turn fish carefully. Continue to fry over medium heat 4 to 5 minutes longer or till done.

2 In a shallow baking dish such as a pie plate, beat egg with a fork just long enough to break up the yolk. Add water; mix well. Dip fish in the egg-water mixture, turning to coat both sides evenly.

3 Combine bread crumbs or crushed crackers or cornmeal with the salt and pepper. Place on a sheet of waxed paper or in a shallow baking dish. Roll the egg-coated fish in the crumbs to coat evenly.

4 In a large heavy skillet heat about ¼ inch shortening or cooking oil. Add fish in a single layer; avoid crowding (you'll need at least a 12-inch skillet). Fry fish on one side over medium heat 4 to 5 minutes or till brown.

TIP Pan-fry fish fillets or steaks *as well as whole fish, following the recipe at left. Use 2 pounds fresh or frozen fillets or steaks; cut in 6 portions. If fillets have skin on, fry the skin side last.*

Be sure to refer to step 6 at left to determine if fish is done. Thin fillets may require less total cooking time. Two pounds of pan-fried fish steaks or fillets will make 6 servings.

57

6 When fish is done, both sides will be brown and crisp, and the flesh will be opaque, white, and tender. To test fish for doneness, insert fork tines into fish at a 45-degree angle. Twist the fork gently. Fish is done if it flakes as shown.

If fish resists flaking and still has a translucent quality, it is not done; if it is dry and mealy, it is overdone.

7 With a large slotted spatula, lift fish from pan to a baking sheet lined with paper toweling. Set on paper toweling to remove excess fat (don't take fish off slotted spatula or coating may stick to paper); place on serving platter.

If you wish to cook more fish, place the fried fish on an ovenproof platter; keep hot in a warm oven while frying more. Or, use 2 skillets to fry twice as many fish at one time.

Fish and Seafood

Broiled Fish

Technique: Broiling fish

**2 pounds fresh *or* frozen trout *or* other fish fillets,
  or halibut *or* other fish steaks**
2 tablespoons butter *or* margarine, melted

1 Thaw fish, if frozen. Cut into 6 serving-size pieces. **2** Arrange fish in a single layer on greased, unheated rack in a broiler pan or in a greased baking pan. Tuck under any thin edges. **3** Brush *half* the melted butter or margarine over the fish. **4** Season to taste with salt and pepper.

5 Place fish 4 inches from the heat. **6** Broil for 5 to 8 minutes; turn thick pieces. **7** Brush fish with the remaining melted butter or margarine. Broil 5 to 8 minutes longer. **8** Fish is done when it flakes easily when tested with a fork. Makes 6 servings.

58

1 Thaw fillets or steaks, if frozen. Cut into 6 serving-size pieces with a sharp knife.

Fish fillets are pieces cut lengthwise from the sides and away from the backbone. They are boneless and may or may not be skinned.

Steaks are crosswise slices of a fish, cut ⅝ to 1 inch thick. A cross-section of the backbone is the only bone present.

5 Place pan under broiler so that the top surface of the fish is 4 inches from the heat. Follow manufacturer's directions on whether to leave the door slightly open or closed. Most electric ranges require the door to be ajar, while gas ranges should be closed.

2 Place fish pieces in a single layer on the greased, unheated rack in a broiler pan. Tuck under any thin edges so fish will be uniform in thickness and cook evenly.

If broiler compartment does not allow enough distance from heat, remove the rack from pan and cook fish directly on the greased broiler pan or a greased baking pan.

3 Using *half* of the melted butter or margarine, brush over the uncooked fish. Use a pastry brush or a piece of folded paper toweling for this step.

4 Sprinkle the fillets or steaks lightly with salt and pepper. For some recipes, you will add other seasonings at this point, such as crushed dried herbs.

59

TIP To remove the skin from a fish fillet, *place the fillet on a table or cutting board with the skin side down. Begin by cutting skin away from fish at the tail. With one hand, firmly hold skin in place at the tail. Move knife in a sawing motion to separate skin from flesh.*

6 Broil the fish for 5 to 8 minutes. Turn fish, if necessary. Turning is optional if fillets or steaks are thin—less than ¾ inch thick. When fish pieces are this thin, they will cook through without being turned, and turning them may cause them to fall apart.

If fish pieces are thicker, use a spatula to turn them at this point for more even cooking.

7 Whether or not the fish were turned, brush them with the remaining melted butter or margarine. Continue to broil 5 to 8 minutes longer or till fish is done.

8 When fish is done, it will become opaque, white, and tender. To test fish for doneness, insert fork tines into fish at a 45-degree angle. Twist the fork gently. Fish is done if it flakes as shown.

If fish resists flaking and still has a translucent quality, it is not done; if it is dry and mealy, it is overdone.

Fish and Seafood

Boiled Lobster

Technique: Boiling lobster.

12 **cups water**
1   **tablespoon salt**
2   **1- to 1½-pound live lobsters**

1 In large kettle combine water and salt. Bring to boiling. Choose active live lobsters. Holding one lobster just behind the eyes, rinse it in cold running water. Plunge it headfirst into boiling salted water. Repeat with other lobster. **2** Return to boiling; reduce heat and simmer over low heat for 20 minutes. Remove lobster at once.

3 Place each lobster on back. With a sharp knife, cut lobster in half lengthwise. **4** With kitchen shears or a knife, cut away the membrane on the tail. **5** Remove black vein and body organs except red coral roe and liver. **6** Crack open the large claws; break away from body. **7** Serve in the shell with melted butter, if desired (or use meat for salads or other main dishes). Use a seafood fork to remove meat from claws, tail, and body. Pull smaller claws away from body and gently suck out the meat. Makes 2 servings or about 2 cups meat.

Court bouillon *is a seasoned broth that is traditionally used for poaching or boiling seafood. You can substitute this liquid for water and salt when cooking lobster or other seafood. Make it in the kettle you'll use for cooking the seafood.*

Combine 12 cups water; ½ cup vinegar; 1 onion, sliced; 1 lemon, sliced; 1 cup sliced celery; 1 cup sliced carrot; 1 tablespoon salt; 6 whole cloves; 3 whole peppercorns; and 3 bay leaves. Bring to boiling; simmer, covered, for 30 minutes. When cooking smaller pieces, such as scallops, you may want to strain the bouillon before cooking the seafood.

60

1 In a large kettle, combine water and salt. Bring to boiling. (Or, bring court bouillon to boiling.)
Choose active, live lobsters. Take a firm hold on the lobster just behind the eyes, as shown. Rinse it under cold running water. Plunge the lobster headfirst into the boiling salted water or court bouillon.

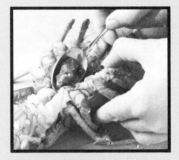

5 Using the tip of a sharp knife, scrape out the black vein that runs the length of the lobster, if present. Remove and discard all the organs that are in the body cavity near the head (except the red coral roe found only in females) and the brownish-green liver (tomalley). Both the roe and the liver are delicacies.

2 Return to boiling; reduce heat and simmer the lobsters, uncovered, over low heat for 20 minutes. Grasp each lobster with large tongs and remove from kettle to a cutting board.

3 Place each cooked lobster on its back on the cutting board as shown. With a sharp knife, cut lobster in half lengthwise up to the tail section, leaving shell back intact, if desired.

4 With shears or a sharp knife, cut away the membrane on the tail of the lobster. This step will expose the tail meat.

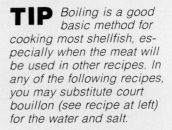

TIP *Boiling is a good basic method for cooking most shellfish, especially when the meat will be used in other recipes. In any of the following recipes, you may substitute court bouillon (see recipe at left) for the water and salt.*

To boil shrimp: Heat 6 cups water and 2 tablespoons salt to boiling. Add 2 pounds fresh or frozen shelled or unshelled shrimp; simmer 1 to 3 minutes or till shrimp turn pink. Drain.

To boil scallops: Heat 4 cups water and 2 teaspoons salt to boiling. Add 2 pounds fresh or thawed frozen scallops. Simmer for 1 minute or till scallops are opaque. Drain.

To boil frozen lobster tails: Heat to boiling enough salted water to cover lobster tails. Simmer the 3-ounce tails for 3 to 4 minutes; 6-ounce tails for 8 minutes; or 8-ounce tails for 11 minutes. Drain.

To boil crabs: Heat to boiling enough salted water to cover crabs. Plunge live, scrubbed dungeness or hard-shell blue crabs into boiling water. Simmer dungeness crabs 8 minutes per pound; simmer blue crabs 15 minutes in all. Drain.

6 Use a nutcracker or lobster cracker to crack open the large claws of the lobster as shown. Break the claws away from the body.

7 Serve lobster in the shell with melted butter, or cut up the meat to use in salads or other dishes.

With a small fork or seafood fork, remove the meat from the claws, the tail, and the body. The smaller claws may be pulled from the body and the meat gently sucked out.

Fish and Seafood

French-Fried Shrimp

Techniques: Deveining, batter-coating, and deep-fat frying shrimp

1 **cup all-purpose flour**
½ **teaspoon sugar**
½ **teaspoon salt**
1 **beaten egg**
1 **cup cold water**
2 **tablespoons cooking oil**
2 **pounds fresh *or* frozen shrimp in shells**
All-purpose flour
Shortening *or* cooking oil for deep-fat frying

1 For batter, stir together the 1 cup flour, the sugar, and salt. Make a well in center. **2** Combine egg, water, and the 2 tablespoons oil; pour into the well. **3** Beat with a rotary beater till smooth.

4 Peel shrimp, leaving last section and tail intact. **5** With a sharp knife, remove the sandy black vein. **6** Butterfly the shrimp. **7** Pat dry with paper toweling. **8** Dip shrimp in flour to coat. **9** Dip flour-coated shrimp into batter.

10 In a saucepan or deep-fat fryer, heat shortening or cooking oil to 375°. Fry a few shrimp at a time in the hot fat for 2 to 3 minutes or till golden. Remove from fat with a slotted spoon; drain on paper toweling. Makes 6 to 8 servings.

1 To make batter, in mixing bowl stir together the 1 cup flour, the sugar, and salt to combine completely. Gently push flour mixture against edges of bowl to make a well in the center.

2 Stir together the beaten egg, water, and the 2 tablespoons cooking oil. Pour mixture into the well in the dry ingredients.

6 After removing the vein, make a deeper slit in the shrimp's back, cutting almost all the way through the shrimp to butterfly it. The sides of the shrimp will open out to resemble a butterfly, as shown.

7 Lay the butterflied shrimp on paper toweling; pat the shrimp dry with more paper toweling, so that the batter will coat the shrimp more evenly.

3 Beat the liquid and dry ingredients together with a rotary beater or a wire whisk till the batter is well mixed and very smooth.

4 Holding shrimp in one hand, carefully peel back the shell, as shown. Leave the last section of the shell and the tail intact.

5 With a sharp knife, make a shallow slit along the back of the shrimp; look for a sandy black vein. If present, use the tip of the knife to scrape out the vein.

TIP *Deep-fat fried foods should have a moist interior and a crisp, golden exterior. The process is the same whether you fry doughnuts or shrimp. For information about the type of fat to use, see page 364.*

• Fill saucepan or deep-fat fryer one-third to half full of cooking oil or shortening.

• Heat oil to temperature indicated in recipe. For best results, use a deep-fat frying thermometer. Be sure to place it so the bulb doesn't touch the pan.

• Add the food in quantities small enough to keep the temperature of the fat from dropping drastically.

• Keep temperature of fat as constant as possible. Too low a temperature will allow food to become greasy; too high a temperature will give a dark exterior and an underdone center.

• Remove food from fat as it finishes cooking. Drain on paper toweling.

• Between batches of frying, remove any food particles from the fat. Wait for fat to return to frying temperature before adding more food.

• After frying, allow fat to cool. Strain through doubled cheesecloth into storage containers; cover and keep in refrigerator. Before next use, add fresh shortening or oil to help used fat regain its freshness.

63

8 Dip each shrimp into a shallow pan of flour, turning to coat all sides. The flour helps the batter cling to the shrimp.

9 Holding the tail as shown, dip the flour-coated shrimp into the batter. Hold shrimp over bowl for a few seconds to allow excess batter to drip back into the bowl.

Coat only enough shrimp to fry at one time, and fry immediately after coating.

10 Referring to tip at right, in a saucepan or deep-fat fryer, heat about 2 inches of shortening or cooking oil to 375°. Carefully lower a few shrimp into the hot fat. Cook for 2 to 3 minutes or till shrimp are golden brown. Remove from fat with a slotted spoon; drain well on paper toweling.

Keep fried shrimp hot in a warm oven while frying remaining shrimp.

Fish and Seafood

Mint-Stuffed Striped Bass

    1 4-pound fresh or frozen dressed
         striped bass, boned
    3 cups dry bread cubes (4 slices)
    1 tablespoon snipped fresh mint
    ¼ teaspoon salt
    ¼ teaspoon dried basil, crushed
    ¼ cup water
    ¼ cup butter or margarine, melted
    2 tablespoons lemon juice

Refer to: Baking a stuffed fish, page 52. Thaw fish, if frozen; pat dry. Place in greased shallow baking pan; sprinkle cavity with salt. Combine bread cubes, mint, salt, basil, and dash *pepper.* Add water and *half* the butter; toss lightly. Stuff fish loosely with mixture. Combine remaining butter and lemon juice; brush over fish. Bake in 350° oven 50 to 60 minutes or till fish flakes easily with a fork; baste occasionally with juice mixture. Serves 6 to 8.

Shrimp-Stuffed Fish

    1 3-pound fresh or frozen dressed
         whitefish, boned
    ½ cup chopped celery
    ¼ cup chopped green pepper
    ¼ cup chopped onion
    6 tablespoons butter or margarine
    2 cups corn bread stuffing mix
    ⅓ cup water
    1 4½-ounce can shrimp, drained
         and deveined
    ¼ cup mayonnaise
    1 tablespoon snipped parsley
       Dash cayenne
    1 tablespoon cooking oil

Refer to: Baking a stuffed fish, page 52. Thaw fish, if frozen. Pat dry. Place in greased shallow baking pan; sprinkle cavity with salt.

Cook celery, green pepper, and onion in butter or margarine till tender. Stir in stuffing mix and water. Add shrimp, mayonnaise, parsley, and cayenne; mix well.

Stuff fish loosely with mixture; brush fish with oil. (Bake any extra stuffing in covered casserole last 30 minutes.) Cover fish with foil; bake in 350° oven 45 to 60 minutes or till fish flakes easily when tested with a fork. Serves 8.

Lemon-Marinated Salmon

    2 pounds fresh or frozen salmon or
         other fish steaks
       Lemon Marinade

Thaw fish, if frozen. In 10-inch skillet bring 1 cup *water* to boiling. Sprinkle salmon with salt. Place *half* of the fish on greased rack in pan, not touching water. Cover tightly; steam 5 to 7 minutes or till fish is done, referring to step 7 on page 53. Remove to shallow dish; repeat with remaining fish. Pour Lemon Marinade over; cover. Chill 2 hours; spoon liquid over fish often. Drain; spoon vegetables over. Serves 6.

Lemon Marinade: In screw-top jar combine ½ cup *lemon juice,* ⅓ cup sliced *green onion,* ¼ cup *cooking oil,* 3 tablespoons snipped *parsley,* 3 tablespoons finely chopped *green pepper,* 1 tablespoon *sugar,* 2 teaspoons *dry mustard,* ¾ teaspoon *salt,* and ⅛ teaspoon *cayenne.* Shake well.

Orange-Glazed Halibut

    1½ pounds fresh or frozen halibut or
          other fish steaks
     2 tablespoons chopped green onion
     1 tablespoon butter or margarine
     4 teaspoons cornstarch
     1 cup orange juice
     1 teaspoon instant chicken bouillon
          granules
     ½ teaspoon salt
     1 orange, peeled, sectioned, and
          diced

Thaw fish, if frozen. Arrange in single layer in 12×7½×2-inch baking dish. In small saucepan cook onion in butter till tender. Blend in cornstarch. Add orange juice, bouillon, and salt. Cook and stir till thickened and bubbly. Stir in diced orange; pour over fish. Bake in 350° oven for 20 minutes or till fish is done, referring to step 7 on page 53. Spoon sauce over fish. Serves 4 to 6.

Poached Salmon (see recipe on page 54)

Trout Amandine

4 to 6 8-ounce fresh *or* frozen
    pan-dressed trout
1 slightly beaten egg
¼ cup light cream *or* milk
¼ cup all-purpose flour
2 tablespoons cooking oil
2 tablespoons butter *or* margarine
¼ cup slivered almonds
¼ cup butter *or* margarine, melted
2 tablespoons lemon juice

Refer to: Pan-frying fish, page 56.
Thaw fish, if frozen; rinse and pat dry.
Season trout with salt and pepper.
Combine egg and cream. Dip trout in
flour, then in egg mixture.

In large skillet heat oil and the 2
tablespoons butter. Fry fish 8 to 10
minutes or till golden, turning once.
Drain; transfer to platter.

In another skillet cook almonds in
the ¼ cup melted butter till golden.
Remove from heat; stir in lemon juice.
Pour almond mixture over fish; serve at
once. Makes 4 to 6 servings.

Crispy Fried Fish

1 pound fresh *or* frozen skinless
    fish fillets
1 cup all-purpose flour
½ teaspoon sugar
1 beaten egg
¾ cup cold water
2 tablespoons cooking oil
    Shortening *or* cooking oil for
      deep-fat frying
    Sweet-Sour Sauce

Thaw fish, if frozen. Cut diagonally in
2-inch pieces; season with salt. Combine flour, sugar, and ½ teaspoon *salt*.
Combine egg, water, and oil; add to
flour mixture. Beat smooth. Dip fish in
batter. Fry a few pieces at a time, in
deep hot fat (375°) for 5 minutes or till
golden (refer to tip on page 63). Drain.
Keep warm in oven while frying remainder. Pass Sweet-Sour Sauce.
Serves 4.

Sweet-Sour Sauce: In saucepan
combine ¼ cup *sugar,* 2 teaspoons
cornstarch, and dash *salt.* Stir in 3
tablespoons cold *water,* 2 tablespoons
vinegar, 1 tablespoon *soy sauce,* and
1 tablespoon dry *white wine.* Cook and
stir till bubbly.

Halibut in Wine Sauce

1½ pounds fresh *or* frozen halibut *or*
    other fish steaks
¼ cup chopped onion
1 clove garlic, minced
2 tablespoons butter *or* margarine
1 small tomato, chopped (½ cup)
⅓ cup dry white wine
1 tablespoon snipped parsley
½ teaspoon salt
    Dash pepper
⅓ cup milk
2 teaspoons cornstarch

Thaw fish, if frozen. In 10-inch skillet
cook onion and garlic in butter. Add
fish, tomato, wine, parsley, salt, and
pepper. Cover; cook over low heat 10
to 12 minutes or till fish is done, referring to step 7 on page 53. Remove fish;
keep warm. Blend milk and cornstarch; add to skillet. Cook and stir till
thickened and bubbly. Cook 1 to 2
minutes more. Pour over fish. Serves 4
to 6.

Skipper's Linguine

6 slices bacon, cut in ½-inch strips
¼ cup sliced green onion
2 cloves garlic, minced
6 tablespoons butter *or* margarine
2 7½-ounce cans minced clams
1 6½- *or* 7-ounce can tuna
½ cup sliced pitted ripe olives
¼ cup snipped parsley
⅛ teaspoon pepper
12 ounces linguine *or* spaghetti

In skillet cook bacon till crisp; drain,
reserving ¼ cup drippings. Set bacon
aside. Cook onion and garlic in reserved drippings till tender. Stir in
butter till melted. Drain clams and
tuna; break tuna into chunks. Add to
skillet along with reserved bacon, olives, parsley, and pepper; heat
through. Keep hot. Cook linguine or
spaghetti according to package directions; drain. To serve, add hot clam
mixture to cooked pasta; toss to mix.
Pass grated parmesan cheese, if desired. Serves 6.

Fish and Seafood

Spicy Crawfish Boil

6 pounds live crawfish
3 gallons water
4 stalks celery, cut in quarters
2 onions, cut in quarters
2 lemons, cut in quarters
½ cup salt
8 whole cloves
4 cloves garlic, minced
4 bay leaves
2 tablespoons crushed red pepper
1 teaspoon dried thyme, crushed
½ teaspoon cayenne
  Melted butter *or* margarine

Refer to: Boiling lobster, page 60. Rinse crawfish well in fresh water. In large kettle combine water, celery, onions, lemons, salt, cloves, garlic, bay leaves, red pepper, thyme, and cayenne. Bring to boiling; add crawfish. Return to boiling; cook about 5 minutes or till crawfish turn deep red. Cool in cooking water; drain. Serve with melted butter. Garnish with lemon slices, if desired. Makes 4 servings.

Delaware Crab Cakes

1 beaten egg
½ cup finely crushed saltine
  crackers (14 crackers)
⅓ cup milk
½ teaspoon dry mustard
⅛ teaspoon white pepper
⅛ teaspoon cayenne
1 7½-ounce can crab meat,
  drained, flaked, and cartilage
  removed
1 tablespoon snipped parsley
3 tablespoons lard *or* shortening
  Lemon wedges

In a bowl combine egg, crushed crackers, milk, mustard, white pepper, and cayenne. Stir in crab meat and parsley. Shape into patties using ⅓ cup mixture for each. Cover and chill patties at least 30 minutes.

In skillet heat lard or shortening. Add patties and cook over medium heat 6 to 8 minutes or till golden brown, turning once. Drain and serve at once with lemon wedges. Makes 5.

Spicy Crawfish Boil

66

Oysters Lafitte

2 cups chopped fresh mushrooms
1 cup chopped cooked shrimp
¼ cup chopped green onion
¼ cup snipped parsley
1 clove garlic, minced
6 tablespoons butter, melted
24 fresh oysters, shucked *or*
  1 pint shucked oysters *or*
  2 8-ounce cans oysters
½ cup dry white wine
½ teaspoon salt
  Dash cayenne
1 cup light cream
¼ cup all-purpose flour
  Rock salt
⅓ cup fine dry bread crumbs
⅛ teaspoon paprika

In skillet cook mushrooms, shrimp, onion, parsley, and garlic in *4 tablespoons* of the butter for 1 minute. Drain oysters, reserving liquid; add water if needed to make ¾ cup. Add oyster liquid, wine, salt, and cayenne to skillet. Bring to boiling; simmer 1 minute. Blend cream into flour; stir into wine mixture. Cook and stir till thickened and bubbly.

Arrange 24 oyster shells on a bed of rock salt in shallow baking pan. Place 1 oyster in each shell; spoon about 2 tablespoons sauce over each. Combine bread crumbs, paprika, and remaining butter; sprinkle atop. Bake in 450° oven for 10 to 12 minutes. Makes 4 main dish or 8 appetizer servings.

Lemon Shrimp Oriental

2 tablespoons cornstarch
1 teaspoon sugar
1 teaspoon salt
1 teaspoon instant chicken bouillon
  granules
⅛ teaspoon pepper
1 cup water
½ teaspoon finely shredded lemon
  peel
3 tablespoons lemon juice
2 tablespoons cooking oil
1 medium green pepper, cut in
  strips
1½ cups bias-sliced celery
¼ cup sliced green onion
2 cups sliced fresh mushrooms
1 6-ounce package frozen pea pods
1 pound fresh *or* frozen shelled
  shrimp

Refer to: Stir-frying vegetables, page 134. Combine cornstarch, sugar, salt, bouillon, and pepper; blend in water, peel, and juice. Set aside. Heat wok or large skillet over high heat; add oil. Add green pepper, celery, and onion; stir-fry 3 minutes. Add mushrooms and pea pods; stir-fry 2 minutes more or till crisp-tender. Remove vegetables. (Add more oil to pan, if needed.) Stir-fry shrimp 7 to 8 minutes or till done. Stir lemon mixture; add to pan. Cook and stir till bubbly. Stir in vegetables. Cover; cook 1 minute. Serve over hot cooked rice, if desired. Serves 6.

Scallops En Brochette

1 pound fresh *or* frozen scallops
¼ cup Italian salad dressing
¼ cup dry white wine
12 small whole mushrooms
½ cup fine dry bread crumbs
4 slices partially cooked bacon, cut in 1-inch squares
1 large green pepper, cut in 1-inch squares (1 cup)

Thaw scallops, if frozen. Cut up large pieces. For marinade, in bowl combine salad dressing and wine. Add scallops and mushrooms. Cover; let stand at room temperature 1 hour. Drain, reserving marinade. Coat scallops with bread crumbs. Alternate scallops with bacon, green pepper, and mushrooms on 4 long skewers, ending with a mushroom. Referring to step 4 on page 24, grill scallops over *medium* coals 8 to 10 minutes or just till tender. Turn often and baste vegetables with marinade. Serves 4.

Shrimp Cocktail

(pictured on page 6)

4 cups water
1 tablespoon salt
1½ pounds fresh *or* frozen shelled shrimp
¾ cup chili sauce
¼ cup lemon juice
2 tablespoons prepared horseradish
1 tablespoon worcestershire sauce
Dash bottled hot pepper sauce
Lettuce
Lemon wedges

Refer to tip on page 61. In saucepan bring water and salt to boiling. Add shrimp; return to boiling. Reduce heat and simmer for 1 to 3 minutes or till shrimp turn pink. Drain; cover and chill.

Stir together chili sauce, lemon juice, horseradish, worcestershire, and bottled hot pepper sauce. Chill.

To serve, pour chilled sauce into a small lettuce-lined bowl set in a larger bowl of ice. Arrange chilled shrimp around edge of larger bowl; garnish with lemon wedges. Makes 8 to 10 appetizer servings.

Glazed Creole Shrimp

¼ cup chopped onion
1 clove garlic, minced
1 tablespoon butter *or* margarine
¼ cup chopped celery
¼ cup chopped green pepper
¼ teaspoon salt
Dash pepper
Dash cayenne
1 bay leaf
½ cup water
½ of an 8-ounce can (½ cup) tomato sauce
¼ cup catsup
2 tablespoons tomato paste
1 tablespoon dry white wine
2 teaspoons light molasses
2 tablespoons butter *or* margarine
2 tablespoons dry white wine
2 tablespoons light molasses
2 tablespoons prepared mustard
1 tablespoon worcestershire sauce
1 pound fresh *or* frozen large shrimp, shelled and deveined
Hot cooked rice

To make sauce, in small saucepan cook onion and garlic in the 1 tablespoon butter or margarine for 5 minutes; add celery, green pepper, the ¼ teaspoon salt, the pepper, cayenne, and bay leaf. Stir in water, tomato sauce, catsup, tomato paste, the 1 tablespoon wine, and the 2 teaspoons molasses. Simmer, covered, for 20 to 25 minutes.

Meanwhile, in medium skillet melt the 2 tablespoons butter. Add the 2 tablespoons wine, the 2 tablespoons molasses, the mustard, and worcestershire. Bring to boiling; reduce heat. Cover and simmer 5 minutes. Add shrimp; cook over medium-high heat, stirring constantly, for 5 to 6 minutes or till shrimp are done and have a glazed appearance.

To serve, pour the vegetable sauce over bed of hot cooked rice; top with glazed shrimp. Serve immediately. Makes 4 servings.

Egg-Stuffed Fish Rolls

4 fresh *or* frozen flounder fillets (about 1 pound)
3 hard-cooked eggs, chopped
2 tablespoons snipped parsley
2 tablespoons mayonnaise *or* salad dressing
1½ teaspoons dijon-style mustard
1 10-ounce package frozen chopped broccoli, thawed
2 cups cooked long grain rice
1 10¾-ounce can condensed cream of shrimp soup
½ cup dry white wine

Thaw fish, if frozen. Sprinkle fillets with a little salt and pepper. Combine eggs, parsley, mayonnaise, and mustard. Spoon 3 to 4 tablespoons of the egg mixture atop each fillet; roll up, referring to tip below.

Combine broccoli and cooked rice. In bowl stir together soup and wine. Stir *1 cup* of the soup mixture into rice mixture. Turn rice mixture into 10×6×2-inch baking dish. Place fish rolls atop rice. Pour remaining soup mixture over rolls. Cover with foil; bake in 375° oven for 25 minutes. Uncover; bake 20 to 25 minutes more or till fish flakes easily when tested with a fork. Makes 4 servings.

67

TIP To stuff fish fillets, *lay fish flat on table. Place filling near one end of the fillet. Starting at filling end, roll fish around filling. Continue rolling to form a compact package. Secure with wooden picks, if necessary.*

Clockwise from left: Asparagus spears topped with Classic Hollandaise (see recipe, page 112); Caramel Floating Island (see recipe, page 96); Huevos Rancheros (see recipe, page 82); Strawberry Meringues (see recipe, page 96); and Fresh Mushroom Omelet (see recipe, page 82).

EGGS

Eggs are one food staple that can be a meal by themselves as well as the basis for a side dish or dessert. On the following pages, we'll explain the hows and whys of poaching, scrambling, frying, and cooking eggs. We'll also show how to use eggs in custards, soufflés, and meringues.

Poached Eggs

Technique: Poaching eggs

> **Cooking oil *or* shortening**
> **4   eggs**
> **Boiling water**

1 Lightly grease a 10-inch skillet. **2** Break egg into sauce dish. **3** Into the skillet heat about 1½ inches of water; bring to boiling. Reduce heat to simmer. Carefully slide egg into water. **4** Add remaining eggs so that each has about equal space. Simmer, uncovered, over low heat for 3 to 5 minutes. Do not let water boil. **5** Smooth edges of eggs during cooking by using a spoon to gently pull away the strings of egg white. **6** When eggs are cooked to the desired doneness, lift out with a slotted spoon. If desired, serve on buttered toast or on an English muffin that has been split and toasted.

If poaching only 1 egg, break egg into sauce dish, referring to step 2 at right. Fill a saucepan with 3 to 4 inches of water. Bring to boiling; reduce to simmering. Carefully slide egg into simmering water, referring to step 3 at right.

If desired, stir the water to swirl before adding the egg. Slip egg into center of swirl, following direction of swirl with motion of dish. This helps prevent the egg white from trailing. Simmer, uncovered, over low heat for 3 to 5 minutes or till desired doneness. Do not let water boil.

1 Lightly grease a 10-inch skillet. Use a pastry brush to evenly spread cooking oil or shortening over the bottom of the skillet. This helps prevent the eggs from sticking while they cook.

Make sure that the skillet is deep enough to hold about 1½ inches of boiling water. If desired, a saucepan may be used instead.

4 Add remaining eggs so each has about one-fourth of the space. Simmer, uncovered, over low heat for 3 to 5 minutes or till desired doneness. Do not let water boil. Eggs cooked at high temperatures will have tough whites and mealy yolks.

Eggs cooked for 3 minutes will have a soft center. Eggs cooked for 5 minutes will have a firm center.

2 Break egg into a sauce dish or custard cup. Breaking the egg into a dish instead of directly into the water eliminates the possibility of starting to cook a less attractive egg with a broken yolk.

If the yolk breaks while putting the egg in the dish, transfer the egg to a jar or plastic container to save for another use, such as in scrambled eggs or baked products.

3 In the greased skillet heat 1½ inches of water to boiling. Reduce heat to simmer. Holding lip of dish as close to water as possible, carefully slide egg into water.

Poached eggs will be more attractive if grade AA or A eggs are used. These have a thicker white than grade B eggs and will hold their shape better during cooking.

71

5 During cooking, smooth the edges of eggs by using a spoon to gently pull away any strings of trailing cooked egg white.

For perfectly round eggs, place a metal egg ring in the simmering water. Slip egg into center of ring. As soon as egg white sets, remove ring. Continue cooking egg till done.

6 When eggs are cooked to the desired doneness, lift out with a slotted spoon, as shown.

If desired, use a kitchen shears to trim any ragged edges from cooked eggs.

TIP To cook eggs in poacher cups, *first grease each cup. Use a pastry brush to lightly spread bottom and sides of cups with cooking oil or shortening, as shown in top photo. Insert each cup into poacher.*

Place poacher in pan of boiling water so that water level is below bottom of poacher. Reduce heat to simmer water. Add eggs; cover and cook for 3 to 5 minutes or till desired doneness.

To serve, lift out egg cups with a fork, as shown in bottom photo. Use a spatula to loosen egg from cup. Carefully slide out egg onto plate.

Eggs

Scrambled Eggs

Technique: Scrambling eggs

1 In mixing bowl combine the eggs, milk or light cream, the salt, and pepper. If desired, also add other seasonings as suggested in the recipe variations.

If you have extra egg whites or yolks, or eggs with broken yolks, substitute them for part of the 6 eggs.

---

6 **eggs**
⅓ **cup milk** *or* **light cream**
¼ **to ½ teaspoon salt**
   Dash pepper
2 **tablespoons butter** *or* **margarine**

72

1 In bowl combine the eggs, milk or light cream, salt, and pepper. **2** Stir with fork to mix. **3** In 10-inch skillet melt the butter or margarine. **4** Pour egg mixture over hot butter in skillet; reduce heat. **5** Cook without stirring till mixture begins to set on bottom and around edges.

6 Lift and fold the partially cooked eggs so uncooked portion flows underneath. Continue cooking about 4 minutes or till eggs are cooked throughout, but are still glossy and moist. Remove from heat immediately. Serves 3 or 4.

Herb Scrambled Eggs: Prepare as above, *except* add 1 tablespoon snipped *parsley or chives* and a dash dried *thyme*, crushed, to the egg mixture in step 1.

Cheese Scrambled Eggs: Prepare as above, *except* cut up one 3-ounce package *cream cheese with chives*; add to egg mixture in step 1.

Deviled Scrambled Eggs: Prepare egg mixture as above, adding one 2-ounce can chopped *mushrooms*, drained; 1 tablespoon snipped *parsley*; ½ teaspoon *dry mustard*; and ¼ teaspoon *worcestershire sauce* in step 1. In skillet cook 1 tablespoon chopped *onion* in 2 tablespoons *butter or margarine.* Pour egg mixture over hot onion and butter; cook as directed in steps 4–6.

4 Carefully pour the egg mixture over the hot butter or margarine in skillet. Eggs will bubble as they hit the hot butter. Reduce the heat.

Eggs should be cooked over low to medium heat to ensure the best eating quality. If the heat is too high, there's a tendency for whites to become tough and yolks to become mealy.

2 Using a fork, stir egg mixture to blend. For scrambled eggs with streaks of yellow and white, stir only slightly. For scrambled eggs with a uniform yellow color, stir till well blended.

3 In a 10-inch skillet melt the butter or margarine (bacon drippings or cooking oil may be substituted). To determine if the pan is hot enough, sprinkle with 1 or 2 drops of water; it should sizzle and hop across the surface.

TIP To bake eggs, you'll need custard cups and a shallow baking pan. Butter the number of cups needed. Break one egg into each; sprinkle with salt and pepper. To each egg add 1 teaspoon light cream or milk.

Set cups in a 13×9×2-inch baking pan; place on oven rack. Pour hot water around cups to a depth of 1 inch, as shown. Bake in 325° oven about 20 minutes or till eggs are firm.

If desired, after 15 minutes of baking, top each egg with some shredded sharp American cheese. Continue baking for 5 to 10 minutes or till eggs are cooked and cheese is melted.

Baked eggs are also called shirred. If desired, they may be baked in ramekins, which are individual baking dishes.

5 Let egg mixture cook, without stirring, till it begins to set on the bottom and around the edges. As it sets the egg mixture will pull slightly away from the sides of the skillet.

6 Using a metal spoon or spatula, lift and fold the partially cooked eggs, as shown. This allows the uncooked portion to flow underneath. For the most attractive appearance, avoid breaking up eggs any more than necessary.

Continue cooking for 4 minutes more or till eggs are cooked throughout. They should still appear glossy and moist. Remove from heat immediately.

Eggs

Fried Eggs

Technique: Frying eggs

Butter *or* **margarine**
4 eggs
Salt
Pepper
2 teaspoons water

74 **1** In a 10-inch skillet melt a small amount of butter or margarine. Add eggs. **2** Sprinkle eggs with salt and pepper. **3** When the whites are set and the edges cooked, add the water. **4** Cover the skillet and continue cooking till eggs are desired doneness.

5 If "over-easy" eggs are desired, carefully lift egg with wide metal spatula and flip over; cook briefly. **6** When eggs are cooked to desired doneness, lift out with a wide metal spatula; transfer to serving plate.

1 In a 10-inch skillet melt a small amount of butter or margarine (bacon drippings may be used instead of butter, if desired).

Carefully break the eggs, one at a time, into the hot butter. If desired, eggs may be broken into a sauce dish first, as described in step 2 on page 71.

A high-quality egg, such as grade AA or A, will hold its shape better during frying than will a grade B egg.

4 Cover the skillet and continue cooking till eggs are desired doneness. Adding the water and covering the skillet allows the eggs to steam and cook more evenly.

2 Sprinkle eggs with salt and pepper. Eggs are easily overcooked, so make sure the skillet does not become too hot. Maintain low to medium heat.

3 When the egg whites are set and the edges are cooked, add the 2 teaspoons water. (Or, add ½ teaspoon water per egg if you're frying more or fewer than four).

TIP Buying eggs *is something most of us don't spend much time thinking about. But planned buying can save grocery money.*

Eggs are sold by grade and size. Grade is an indication of quality, with AA being the highest. Eggs range in size from jumbo to peewee, but the most commonly available sizes are extra large, large, and medium. Size is measured by minimum weight per dozen.

Price is determined by the number of eggs available on the market. If there is less than a 7-cent difference in the per-dozen price between two sizes of the same grade, the larger size usually is the better buy.

75

5 If "over-easy" eggs are desired, carefully lift the egg with a wide metal spatula; flip egg over so yolk is down. Cook briefly to set yolk.

Leave yolk up for "sunny side up" eggs.

6 When eggs are cooked to the desired doneness, lift out with a wide metal spatula; transfer to serving plate.

Eggs

Soft-Cooked or Hard-Cooked Eggs

Technique: Soft-cooking or hard-cooking eggs

6 eggs
Water
Ice cubes

1 Place eggs in shell in saucepan; add water to cover eggs. Bring water to rapid boil over high heat. Water will have large rapidly breaking bubbles, as shown.

1 Place eggs in shell in saucepan; add water to cover eggs. Bring to rapid boil over high heat. **2** Reduce heat so that water is just below simmering. **3** Cover the saucepan. For soft-cooked eggs, continue cooking 4 to 6 minutes. For hard-cooked eggs, cook 15 to 20 minutes.

4 Pour off the hot water. For soft-cooked eggs, add cold water just till eggs are cool enough to handle. Cut off tops and serve in egg cups. For hard-cooked eggs, fill saucepan with cold water; and let stand at least 2 minutes. To quickly cool, add a few ice cubes, if desired.

5 To remove shell of hard-cooked eggs, gently tap egg on counter top; roll egg between palms. **6** Peel off shell, starting at large end. Use in recipes or serve as main dish.

4 Pour off the hot water. For soft-cooked eggs, add cold water just till eggs are cool enough to handle. Cut off tops and serve in egg cups.

For hard-cooked eggs, fill saucepan with cold water and let stand at least 2 minutes. To cool quickly, add a few ice cubes, if desired.

Hard-cooked eggs may be refrigerated to chill completely, but the shells will be slightly more difficult to remove.

76

2 Reduce heat so that water is just below simmering. Water will have bubbles on the bottom of the pan, with only a few rising to the top, as shown.

Eggs used to be termed hard- or soft-boiled, indicating that they were cooked in boiling water. Research has since proved that eggs become tough and overcooked when boiled. Lowering the heat reduces the possibility of overcooking.

3 Cover the saucepan. For soft-cooked eggs, continue cooking 4 to 6 minutes. For hard-cooked eggs, cook 15 to 20 minutes.

If soft-cooking only one egg, you needn't continue to cook as above. Instead, remove pan from heat but do not drain. Cover and leave egg in water for about 2 minutes. If soft-cooking 2 or 3 eggs, remove pan from heat and leave covered for 3 to 4 minutes.

TIP A greenish ring around the yolk *of a hard-cooked egg is a common, harmless occurrence caused by the formation of iron sulfide.*

To lessen the possibility of such rings forming, carefully watch the cooking time and immediately cool the hard-cooked eggs in cold water as described in step 4 at left.

77

5 To remove shell from a hard-cooked egg, gently tap egg on counter top; roll egg between palms. This cracks the shell so that it can be removed more easily.

To crack the shells more thoroughly and uniformly, pour all water from the saucepan. Then gently roll the eggs around by shaking the pan from side to side.

6 Remove shell by starting to peel from the largest end of the egg. The shell should come off easily. If it doesn't, try holding the egg under running water while pulling away the shell.

Eggs

French Omelet

Technique: Making a plain omelet

2 **eggs**
1 **tablespoon water**
⅛ **teaspoon salt**
Dash pepper
1 **tablespoon butter** *or* **margarine**
Mushroom Filling, Cheese Filling, *or* **Vegetable Filling**

78

1 Beat together the eggs, water, salt, and pepper with a fork till blended but not frothy. **2** In a 6- or 8-inch skillet with flared sides, heat the butter till it sizzles and browns slightly. Lift and tilt the pan to coat the sides. **3** Add egg mixture; cook over medium heat. **4** As eggs set, run a spatula around edge of the skillet, lifting the eggs to allow uncooked portion to flow underneath. **5** When eggs are set but still shiny, remove from heat. Spoon filling across center (use Mushroom, Cheese, or Vegetable Filling, as desired).

6 Fold one-third of omelet over center. Overlap remaining third atop filling. **7** Slide omelet to edge of pan. **8** Tilt skillet, then invert to roll omelet out onto warm serving plate. Top with a cheese sauce, if desired (see tip on page 99). Makes 1 serving.

Mushroom Filling: For each omelet cook about ⅓ cup sliced fresh *mushrooms* (or drained, canned mushrooms) in 1 tablespoon *butter or margarine.*

Cheese Filling: For each omelet shred about ¼ cup cheddar, Swiss, monterey jack, mozzarella, or American *cheese.* If desired, top filled omelet with additional shredded cheese and snipped *parsley.*

Vegetable Filling: Using *green onion, asparagus, zucchini, celery, green pepper,* or *bean sprouts,* slice any one or a combination to make ⅓ cup for each omelet. Cook in *butter* till tender. Sprinkle top with grated *parmesan cheese.*

1 In a bowl beat together the eggs, water, salt, and pepper with a fork till blended but not frothy.

If desired, add about ⅛ teaspoon dried, crushed herbs. Try basil, chives, marjoram, oregano, parsley, sage, savory, or thyme.

5 When eggs are set but still slightly shiny on the top surface, remove the skillet from heat. Spoon filling across center of omelet (use Mushroom, Cheese, or Vegetable Filling, as desired).

2 In a 6- or 8-inch skillet with flared sides, heat the butter or margarine over medium heat till it sizzles and browns slightly. Lift and tilt the skillet to coat sides.

Using a skillet with flared sides makes it easier to roll out the cooked omelet. However, straight-sided skillets also may be used.

3 Pour egg mixture into heated skillet. Cook over medium heat. Do not let skillet become too hot or the eggs will be overcooked and tough.

4 As eggs set, run a spatula around the edge of the skillet, lifting the eggs to allow the uncooked portion to flow underneath, as shown. If desired, tip pan slightly so eggs flow easier. The total cooking time for steps 3 and 4 should be about 1 minute.

TIP 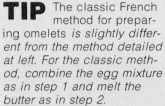 The classic French method for preparing omelets *is slightly different from the method detailed at left. For the classic method, combine the egg mixture as in step 1 and melt the butter as in step 2.*

Add egg mixture to melted butter, leaving the heat at medium. Using a fork, rapidly stir just through the top of uncooked egg in a zigzag pattern.

During stirring, cooked portions will come to center. Shake skillet constantly to keep egg mixture moving, but shake carefully so that omelet remains a constant depth. Cook 1 to 2 minutes.

Fill and roll omelet as described in steps 5–8.

79

6 Using a metal spatula, carefully lift one-third of the cooked omelet and fold over filling in center. Repeat with remaining one-third to overlap, as shown.

7 Gently slide filled omelet to the edge of skillet farthest from the handle. Hold skillet at an angle to a warmed serving plate in preparation for rolling out the filled omelet.

8 Tilt skillet, then invert so that omelet rolls out onto plate. If desired, top the omelet with shredded cheese, a dollop of sour cream, or a cheese sauce (for recipe, see tip on page 99).

Eggs

Puffy Omelet

Technique: Making a puffy omelet

- 4 **egg whites**
- 2 **tablespoons water**
- ¼ **teaspoon salt**
- 4 **egg yolks**
- 1 **tablespoon butter** or **margarine**

1 Beat egg whites till frothy. **2** Add water and salt; continue beating about 1½ minutes or till stiff peaks form. **3** Beat egg yolks at high speed of electric mixer about 5 minutes or till thick and lemon-colored. **4** Fold egg yolks into egg whites.

5 In a 10-inch skillet with an oven-proof handle, heat the butter or margarine till a drop of water sizzles. **6** Pour in egg mixture, mounding it slightly higher at the sides. **7** Cook over low heat, uncovered, for 8 to 10 minutes or till eggs are puffed and set, and bottom is golden brown.

8 Place skillet in a 325° oven; bake for 10 minutes or till knife inserted near center comes out clean. **9** Loosen sides of omelet with a metal spatula. Make a shallow cut across the omelet, cutting slightly off-center. **10–11** Fold the smaller (upper) portion of omelet over the larger portion. Slip omelet onto platter. Makes 2 or 3 servings.

Ham and Cheese Special: To make filling, heat 1 cup diced fully cooked *ham* and one 3-ounce can sliced *mushrooms*, drained, in 1 tablespoon *butter or margarine*; keep warm.

To make sauce, blend one 3-ounce package *cream cheese*, softened, and ⅓ cup *milk*. Blend in 1 beaten *egg yolk*. Add 1½ teaspoons *lemon juice*, 1 teaspoon prepared *mustard*, and dash *salt*; beat well. Cook and stir over low heat till slightly thickened. Add the filling and sauce after transferring omelet to platter.

80

1 Beat egg whites till frothy. Use a large non-plastic bowl with deep, straight sides. Use an electric mixer, rotary beater, or wire whisk to beat air into the whites. This slight whipping forms large air bubbles in the egg whites as the mixture becomes a fluid, transparent foam, as shown.

To obtain the greatest volume, bring egg whites to room temperature before beating.

2 Add the water and salt. Using an electric mixer at medium speed or a rotary beater, continue beating about 1½ minutes or till stiff peaks form. Peaks should look glossy, not dry.

During this beating, the foam becomes whiter and forms stiff peaks that stand straight when beaters are removed, as shown. The whites now contain all of the air they can hold.

7 Cook, uncovered, over low heat for 8 to 10 minutes or till eggs are puffed and set. To check, lift an edge of the omelet with a metal spatula, as shown. The bottom should be golden brown.

Do not use excessive heat; eggs are easily overcooked, giving them a tough, rubbery texture.

8 Place skillet in a 325° oven; bake for 10 minutes or till a knife inserted near the center comes out clean, as shown.

3 Place egg yolks in small mixer bowl; beat at high speed of electric mixer about 5 minutes or till very thick and lemon-colored.

When yolks are sufficiently beaten, they will flow in a thick stream from the lifted beaters, as shown.

The beaten egg yolks and whites tend to act like leavening agents, causing the omelet to rise slightly as the incorporated air heats and expands.

4 Pour beaten egg yolks over egg whites. Fold in by cutting down through mixture with a rubber spatula; scrape across bottom of bowl and bring spatula up and over mixture close to the surface. Repeat this down-up-and-over motion, turning the bowl as you work. Do not stir; this breaks down the air-retaining structure and fluffy consistency of the carefully beaten whites.

5 In a 10-inch skillet with an oven-proof handle, heat the butter or margarine till a drop of water sizzles when sprinkled atop, as shown.

6 Pour in egg mixture, spreading evenly with a rubber spatula, then mound the mixture slightly higher around the edges of the skillet, as shown.

81

9 Loosen the sides of the omelet from the skillet with a metal spatula. Holding the skillet at a slight angle, make a shallow cut across the omelet, cutting slightly off-center so that the two portions are unequal.

10 Using a wide metal spatula, carefully lift the smaller portion of the omelet in preparation for folding it over the larger portion, as shown.

11 Fold smaller portion of omelet over larger portion. Using a wide metal spatula, carefully slip the folded omelet onto a heated platter.

If desired, unfold and spoon in a filling. You may also add a favorite sauce. Try topping filled or unfilled omelets with creamed vegetables or meat, or a cheese, tomato, or wine sauce.

Eggs

Fresh Mushroom Omelets

(pictured on page 68)

- 1½ cups sliced fresh mushrooms
- 2 tablespoons finely chopped onion
- ¼ teaspoon dried basil, crushed
- 3 tablespoons butter *or* margarine
- 1 tablespoon all-purpose flour
- ⅛ teaspoon salt
  Dash cayenne
- ½ cup milk
- ½ cup shredded sharp cheddar cheese (2 ounces)
- 6 eggs
- 2 tablespoons water
- ½ teaspoon salt
- ⅛ teaspoon pepper
- 4 teaspoons butter *or* margarine

Refer to: Making a plain omelet, page 78. To make filling, cook mushrooms, onion, and basil in *2 tablespoons* of the butter or margarine till mushrooms and onion are tender and liquid is nearly evaporated. Remove from heat. Cover; keep warm.

Make sauce, referring to page 98. Melt remaining 1 tablespoon butter or margarine. Stir in flour, ⅛ teaspoon salt, and cayenne. Add milk all at once. Cook and stir till mixture is thickened. Remove from heat; stir in cheese till melted. Cover and keep warm.

To make omelet, beat together eggs, water, ½ teaspoon salt, and pepper with a fork till mixture is blended but not frothy. In a 10-inch skillet melt *2 teaspoons* of the butter; heat till butter sizzles and browns slightly. Tilt pan to grease sides. Add *half* of the egg mixture (⅔ cup). Cook over medium-high heat. As eggs set, run a spatula around edge and lift eggs to allow uncooked portion to flow underneath. When eggs are set but still shiny, remove pan from heat.

Reserve a few mushrooms for garnish. Spoon half of the remaining mushrooms down center of the omelet; fold both sides over filling. Tilt pan to roll out omelet onto plate. Repeat to make second omelet. Spoon *half* of the cheese sauce over each. Garnish with reserved mushrooms. Serves 4.

Deviled Eggs

- 6 eggs
- ¼ cup mayonnaise
- 1 tablespoon chopped sweet pickle
- 1 teaspoon prepared horseradish
- 1 teaspoon prepared mustard
- ¼ teaspoon salt

Hard-cook the eggs, referring to page 76. Peel off shells; cut eggs in half lengthwise. Remove yolks and mash; combine yolks with mayonnaise, pickle, horseradish, mustard, and salt. Refill egg whites. Sprinkle with paprika, if desired. Makes 12.

Huevos Rancheros

(pictured on page 68)

- ¼ cup cooking oil
- 4 8-inch flour tortillas
- ½ cup chopped onion
- 1 clove garlic, minced
  Cooking oil
- 4 large tomatoes, peeled, cored, and chopped (3 cups)
- 1 4-ounce can green chili peppers, rinsed, seeded, and chopped
- ¼ teaspoon salt
- 8 eggs
- 1½ cups shredded monterey jack cheese (6 ounces)

In 12-inch skillet heat the ¼ cup cooking oil. Dip the tortillas in oil for a few seconds on each side or just till limp; add more oil, if necessary. Drain tortillas; keep warm. In the same skillet cook the onion and garlic till tender but not brown; add more oil, if necessary. Stir in tomatoes, chili peppers, and salt. Simmer, uncovered, for 7 to 8 minutes.

Break eggs, one at a time, into sauce dish, referring to step 2 on page 71. Slide each egg into the hot tomato mixture, taking care not to break the egg yolks. Season eggs with salt and pepper. Cover skillet and cook over low heat 8 to 10 minutes for medium-soft yolks or till desired doneness.

Place 2 eggs with some of the tomato mixture on each tortilla. Top each serving with the shredded cheese. Makes 4 servings.

Eggs Florentine

- 1 10-ounce package frozen chopped spinach, cooked and drained
- 1 11-ounce can condensed cheddar cheese soup
- 4 eggs
- 1 tablespoon milk
- 2 teaspoons minced dried onion
- 1 teaspoon prepared mustard
- ½ cup plain croutons

Combine spinach and *half* of the soup. Spoon into 4 individual casseroles, spreading evenly on bottom and up sides. Break one egg into each casserole. Bake in 350° oven for 20 to 25 minutes or till eggs are set.

In saucepan heat and stir remaining soup, milk, onion, and mustard. Spoon over eggs. Garnish with croutons. Makes 4 servings.

Denver Scramble

- 1 cup finely chopped, fully cooked ham
- 1 2-ounce can mushroom stems and pieces, drained
- ¼ cup chopped onion
- 2 tablespoons chopped green pepper
- 2 tablespoons butter *or* margarine, melted
- 8 beaten eggs
- ⅓ cup milk

Refer to: Scrambling eggs, page 72. In skillet cook ham, mushrooms, onion, and green pepper in butter or margarine about 5 minutes or till vegetables are tender but not brown. Combine eggs and milk; add to skillet. Cook without stirring till mixture starts to set on bottom and sides. Lift and fold the partially cooked eggs so that the uncooked portion flows to the bottom of the pan. Continue cooking for 5 to 8 minutes or till eggs are set throughout but still glossy and moist. Immediately remove from heat. Makes 6 servings.

82

Apple Omelet

Apple Omelet

- ¼ cup packed brown sugar
- 1 tablespoon cornstarch
- ⅔ cup cold water
- 2 teaspoons lemon juice
- 3 apples, peeled, cored, and cut in ½-inch-thick wedges
- 2 tablespoons butter *or* margarine
- 3 fully cooked smoked sausage links, sliced diagonally (optional)
- 4 egg whites
- 2 tablespoons water
- ¼ teaspoon salt
- 4 egg yolks
- 1 tablespoon butter *or* margarine

Refer to: Making a puffy omelet, page 80. To prepare sauce, combine brown sugar and cornstarch in saucepan. Stir in the ⅔ cup cold water and lemon juice. Cook quickly, stirring constantly, till thickened and bubbly. Add apples; stir gently. Cover and simmer gently for 3 to 5 minutes or till apples are tender. Add the 2 tablespoons butter and sausage, if desired. Stir till butter melts and sausage is hot; keep warm.

To prepare omelet, beat egg whites till frothy; add water and salt. Beat egg whites till stiff peaks form. Beat egg yolks till very thick and lemon-colored. Gently fold yolks into whites.

Heat the 1 tablespoon butter in 10-inch oven-proof skillet till a drop of water sizzles when dropped atop. Pour in egg mixture and spread evenly with spatula, mounding higher at sides. Cook over low heat for 8 to 10 minutes or till lightly browned.

Bake in 325° oven for 8 to 10 minutes or till knife inserted near center comes out clean. Loosen sides of omelet with spatula. Make a shallow cut across omelet, cutting slightly off-center so that the two portions are unequal. Fold smaller portion over larger portion. Using spatula, slip omelet onto hot serving platter.

Set aside ½ cup of the apple mixture. Unfold omelet and spoon remaining apple mixture across center; refold. Pour the reserved apple mixture atop. Serves 4.

83

Egg Foo Yung

- 8 eggs
- 1 teaspoon salt
- ¼ teaspoon pepper
- 1 16-ounce can bean sprouts, well drained
- 1 cup finely chopped fully cooked ham
- ½ cup finely chopped onion
- ¼ cup finely chopped celery
  Cooking oil
- ½ cup thinly sliced fresh mushrooms
- 1 tablespoon cooking oil
- 4 teaspoons cornstarch
- 1½ cups water
- 1 teaspoon instant beef bouillon granules
- 1½ teaspoons soy sauce
- 1 teaspoon catsup

Beat eggs, salt, and pepper. Stir in bean sprouts, ham, onion, and celery. Heat about 2 tablespoons oil till hot. Using about ¼ cup mixture for each, fry patties in hot oil about 1 minute per side or till golden; keep warm. Repeat till all mixture is used, stirring each time before measuring; add oil as needed.

For sauce, cook mushrooms in 1 tablespoon oil till tender. Blend in cornstarch. Add water, bouillon granules, soy, and catsup. Cook and stir till thick and bubbly. Serve sauce with egg patties. Serves 4 or 5.

Zucchini Frittata

- 1 small zucchini, thinly sliced
- 1 medium leek, thinly sliced
- 1 tablespoon butter *or* margarine
- 6 eggs
- 2 tablespoons snipped parsley
- 2 tablespoons water
- ½ teaspoon snipped fresh rosemary *or* ⅛ teaspoon dried rosemary, crushed
- ½ teaspoon salt
- ⅛ teaspoon pepper
- 4 to 6 wedges camembert cheese

Cook zucchini and leek, covered, in a small amount of boiling salted water about 5 minutes or till just tender; drain well. Melt butter in 10-inch skillet with oven-proof handle. Spread vegetables over bottom of pan.

Prepare omelet, referring to steps 1, 3, and 4 on page 78. Beat eggs, parsley, water, rosemary, salt, and pepper; pour over vegetables. Cook over medium heat. As eggs set, run a spatula around the edge of the skillet, lifting the eggs to allow uncooked portion to flow underneath. When top is almost set, transfer pan to 400° oven. Bake, uncovered, for 4 to 5 minutes or till top is set. Place cheese atop. Cut frittata in wedges. Makes 4 to 6 servings.

Eggs

Baked Custard   (pictured on page 274)

Technique: Making a baked custard

4	**eggs**
2½	**cups milk**
½	**cup sugar**
1	**teaspoon vanilla**
¼	**teaspoon salt**
	Ground nutmeg (optional)

84

1 In a medium bowl lightly beat the eggs. Stir in the milk, sugar, vanilla, and salt. **2** Place six 6-ounce custard cups in a 13×9×2-inch baking pan on oven rack. Divide custard mixture among the custard cups. Sprinkle with ground nutmeg, if desired. **3** Pour boiling water into pan around custard cups to depth of 1 inch. **4** Bake in 325° oven for 30 to 40 minutes or till knife inserted near the center comes out clean. **5** Serve warm or chilled. To unmold chilled custard, first loosen edge with spatula or knife; slip point of knife down side to let air in. **6** Invert onto serving plate. Makes 6 servings.

Large custard: Prepare custard mixture as in step 1. Place a 1-quart casserole in 13×9×2-inch baking pan; pour in the custard mixture. Pour hot water into pan around casserole to a depth of 1 inch. Bake in 325° oven 50 to 60 minutes or till done.

1 In a medium bowl lightly beat the eggs to blend the yolks and whites. Stir in the milk, sugar, vanilla, and salt. The eggs should be well blended throughout since they are the thickening agent in baked custard.

If desired, transfer the mixture to a measuring cup for easier pouring into the custard cups.

4 Bake in a 325° oven for 30 to 40 minutes or till a knife inserted near the center comes out clean. Make a short cut, about ½ inch deep; if custard remains on knife, bake a few minutes longer.

For large custard, bake 50 to 60 minutes. Use same doneness test.

An overcooked custard will have a watery texture, so remove the custard from the pan of water as soon as it's done.

2 Place six 6-ounce custard cups in a 13×9×2-inch baking pan on oven rack. Divide custard mixture among the custard cups.

For one large custard, place a 1-quart casserole in a 13×9×2-inch baking pan. Add the custard mixture.

If desired, sprinkle the custard with a little nutmeg.

3 Pour boiling water into pan around custard cups to a depth of about 1 inch. The water helps to evenly distribute the heat so that the edges won't become over-cooked before the center is done.

5 Serve warm custard in individual baking dishes, or spoon into serving dishes. Or, chill thoroughly.

To unmold chilled custard, first loosen the edge of each custard cup with a spatula or knife, as shown; slip the point of the knife down the side of the cup to let air in.

6 Place a plate over the custard cup. Invert both together and lift off custard cup. Serve large custard by spooning into individual dishes.

If desired, top each serving with fresh fruit, jelly, or fluffs of whipped cream or sour cream.

Eggs

Stirred Custard

Technique: Making a stirred custard

---

  3   **slightly beaten eggs**
  2   **cups milk**
 ¼   **cup sugar**
      Dash salt
  1   **teaspoon vanilla**

86

1 In a heavy saucepan combine the eggs, milk, sugar, and salt. **2–3** Cook and stir over medium heat. **4** Continue cooking egg mixture till it coats a metal spoon. **5** Pour custard mixture into a medium bowl; set inside a larger bowl filled with ice. Stir in the vanilla. **6** Cover with clear plastic wrap; chill. Makes 6 servings.

1 In a heavy saucepan combine the eggs, milk, sugar, and salt. Use a rotary beater to thoroughly blend the ingredients.

If desired, use 2 egg yolks or 2 egg whites for one of the whole eggs. This is a good way to use extra yolks or whites.

Because controlling the heat is very important, stirred custard is sometimes made in a double boiler. This is not necessary if medium heat is used.

4 Continue cooking the egg mixture till it starts to thicken and coats a metal spoon (the coating won't be as visible on your wooden stirring spoon).

Dip the spoon into the egg mixture; it should drip off, leaving a coating slightly thicker than milk. The coating should hold its shape when you wipe a finger across the spoon. Use a clean spoon for each test.

2 Cook egg mixture over medium heat. Eggs are easily overcooked, so be sure heat is kept at medium (overcooked eggs will not thicken the custard as they should). This stirred custard should be cooked in about 12 minutes.

To speed preparation, cook the first 3 to 4 minutes over high heat, then reduce heat to medium and cook till thickened. Be sure to stir constantly and watch carefully.

3 Stir the egg mixture constantly with a figure-8 motion to ensure even cooking. This helps prevent sticking or burning on the bottom. Use a wooden spoon for stirring.

TIP Making custard sauce *is similar to making stirred custard, as shown in steps 1–6 at left.*

In heavy saucepan stir together 4 slightly beaten egg yolks, 1¾ cups milk, ¼ cup sugar, and dash salt. Cook and stir over medium heat for 12 to 15 minutes or till mixture starts to thicken and coats a metal spoon. If desired, speed preparation by cooking over high heat for 3 to 4 minutes, then reduce heat to medium and cook till thickened. Be sure to stir constantly and watch carefully to avoid sticking.

Remove from heat; pour into bowl and set in a larger bowl of ice water to cool. Stir in 1 teaspoon vanilla and continue stirring for 1 to 2 minutes to hasten cooling. Chill till ready to serve over cake or fruit. Makes about 1¾ cups.

87

5 Pour custard into a medium bowl; set inside a larger bowl filled with ice. Stir in the vanilla; continue stirring gently for 1 to 2 minutes to hasten cooling.

Pouring the custard out of the saucepan speeds cooling and helps prevent the custard from curdling.

6 To keep a "skin" from forming on the top of the custard, carefully place a piece of clear plastic wrap or waxed paper directly on the surface of the custard, as shown. Chill till serving time.

Eggs

Strawberry Trifle

- ¼ cup granulated sugar
- 2 tablespoons cornstarch
- 1 16-ounce package frozen strawberries, thawed
- 1 tablespoon lemon juice
- 2 eggs
- 1 egg yolk
- 1¾ cups milk
- ¼ cup granulated sugar
- 8 cups cubed sponge cake*
- ¾ cup cream sherry
- 1 egg white
- 1 tablespoon sifted powdered sugar
- 1 cup whipping cream
- ¼ teaspoon vanilla
- ¼ cup slivered almonds

In saucepan stir together ¼ cup granulated sugar and cornstarch. Add berries with their syrup. Cook and stir over medium heat about 10 minutes or till thick and bubbly. Stir in lemon juice. Cover surface with waxed paper; cool.

Prepare custard, referring to Making a stirred custard, page 86. In heavy saucepan combine eggs, egg yolk, milk, and ¼ cup granulated sugar. Cook and stir about 10 minutes or till custard coats a metal spoon; remove from heat. Pour custard into medium bowl; set inside a larger bowl filled with ice. Stir for 1 to 2 minutes to hasten cooling.

Place 3 cups of the cake cubes in a 2-quart serving dish. Sprinkle with ¼ cup sherry. Reserve ¼ cup strawberry mixture for garnish. Top cake cubes with half the remaining strawberry mixture and half of the custard. Repeat layers using another 3 cups cake cubes, ¼ cup sherry, remaining strawberry mixture, and remaining custard. Add remaining cake cubes; sprinkle with remaining sherry.

Beat egg white to soft peaks. Add powdered sugar; beat till stiff peaks form. Whip cream and vanilla to soft peaks; fold into egg white. Spread mixture atop cake cubes. Refrigerate 6 hours or overnight. Just before serving, dot with reserved strawberry mixture and sprinkle with almonds. Makes 10 to 12 servings.

*Note: Use about ¾'s of a 10-inch sponge cake (see recipe, page 234).

Crème Brûlée

- 3 slightly beaten eggs
- 2 cups light cream
- ¼ cup granulated sugar
- ¼ teaspoon salt
- ½ teaspoon vanilla
- ½ cup packed brown sugar

Refer to: Making a stirred custard, page 86. In heavy 2-quart saucepan combine first four ingredients; cook and stir over medium heat about 10 minutes or till custard coats a metal spoon. Remove from heat; pour into 1-quart baking dish and place in pan of ice water. Stir in vanilla; stir 1 to 2 minutes. Refrigerate at least 2 hours.

Press brown sugar through sieve over custard. Set baking dish in pan of ice cubes and cold water. Broil 4 to 5 inches from heat for 1 to 2 minutes or till sugar turns golden brown and bubbly crust forms. Serve warm or chilled. Makes 6 servings.

Baked Chocolate Custard

- 2 cups milk
- ½ cup semisweet chocolate pieces
- 3 slightly beaten eggs
- ¼ cup sugar
- 1 teaspoon vanilla
- ⅛ teaspoon salt

Refer to: Making a baked custard, page 84. In heavy saucepan cook and stir milk and chocolate over low heat till chocolate melts; cool slightly. Mix eggs, sugar, vanilla, and salt; gradually stir in chocolate mixture. Beat just till chocolate is blended. Place six 6-ounce custard cups in 13×9×2-inch pan on oven rack. Divide custard among cups. Pour hot water into pan to depth of 1 inch. Bake in 325° oven for 40 to 45 minutes or till knife inserted near center comes out clean. Chill. Invert into serving dishes (a chocolate layer will form). Garnish with whipped cream, if desired. Serves 6.

Strawberry Trifle

88

Crème Caramel

- 3 slightly beaten egg yolks
- 2 slightly beaten eggs
- ⅓ cup sugar
- 1⅔ cups milk
- ½ teaspoon vanilla
- ⅓ cup sugar
  Whipped cream
  Strawberries

Refer to: Making a baked custard, page 84. In bowl combine egg yolks, eggs, and ⅓ cup sugar; stir in milk and vanilla. Set aside. In heavy skillet stir ⅓ cup sugar over low heat for 8 to 9 minutes or till melted and golden brown; remove from heat. Pour melted sugar into 3-cup metal ring mold; quickly swirl to coat bottom and sides. Pour egg mixture into mold. Set in 9×9×2-inch baking pan on oven rack; pour hot water around mold to depth of 1 inch. Bake in 325° oven for 50 to 55 minutes or till knife inserted near center comes out clean. Chill 2 to 3 hours. Unmold onto serving platter. Garnish with whipped cream and strawberries, if desired. Makes 6 servings.

Coconut Custard Sauce

- 3 beaten eggs
- 2 cups milk
- ¼ cup sugar
  Dash salt
- 1 teaspoon vanilla
- ½ cup flaked coconut, toasted (see tip at right)

Refer to tip on page 87. In a heavy saucepan combine the beaten eggs, milk, sugar, and salt. Cook and stir over medium heat about 15 minutes or till mixture coats a metal spoon.

Remove from heat and pour sauce into a bowl; set in a larger bowl filled with ice. Stir in the vanilla; continue stirring for 1 to 2 minutes more. Cover and chill thoroughly.

Just before serving, stir in the coconut. Serve over cake or fruit. If desired, sprinkle with additional toasted flaked coconut. Makes about 2½ cups.

Broccoli Strata

- 1 10-ounce package frozen chopped broccoli
- 6 slices rye *or* whole wheat bread
- 4 slices American cheese (4 ounces)
- 1 2-ounce jar (¼ cup) pimiento, drained and chopped
- 4 slices Swiss cheese (4 ounces)
- 4 eggs
- 2 cups milk
- 1 tablespoon chopped onion
- 1 teaspoon salt
- ½ teaspoon prepared mustard
  Dash pepper
- 2 tablespoons butter *or* margarine, melted

Cook broccoli, covered, in boiling salted water for 3 minutes. Drain well. Toast *four* of the slices of bread; arrange in ungreased 9×9×2-inch baking pan. Top with the American cheese, then broccoli and pimiento. Place the Swiss cheese atop. Beat eggs; blend in milk, onion, salt, mustard, and pepper. Pour over casserole. Cover; refrigerate at least 1 hour.

Tear remaining 2 slices of bread into blender container. Cover and blend at low speed to make crumbs. In small bowl combine bread crumbs and melted butter or margarine.

About an hour before serving, sprinkle crumbs over chilled casserole. Bake, uncovered, in 325° oven for 60 to 65 minutes or till knife inserted halfway between center and edge comes out clean. Let stand 10 minutes. Makes 6 servings.

Classic Quiche Lorraine

- 1 unbaked 9-inch pastry shell (see steps 1–9 on page 276)
- 8 slices bacon
- 1 medium onion, thinly sliced
- 4 beaten eggs
- 1 cup light cream
- 1 cup milk
- 1 tablespoon all-purpose flour
- ½ teaspoon salt
  Dash ground nutmeg
- 1½ cups shredded Swiss cheese

Line the unpricked pastry shell with foil; fill with dried beans, referring to step 11 on page 277. Bake in 450° oven for 5 minutes. Carefully remove the beans and foil. Bake 5 to 7 minutes longer or till pastry is nearly done. Remove from oven; reduce oven temperature to 325°. (Pie shell should still be hot when filling is added; do not partially bake pastry shell ahead of time.)

Meanwhile, in skillet cook the bacon till crisp; drain, reserving 2 tablespoons drippings. Crumble bacon finely and set aside. Cook sliced onion in reserved drippings till tender; drain.

In bowl thoroughly stir together the eggs, cream, milk, flour, salt, and nutmeg. Stir in the bacon, onion, and cheese; mix well. Pour into warm pastry shell. If necessary, cover edge of crust with foil to prevent overbrowning.

Bake in 325° oven for 45 to 50 minutes or till set in center; test, referring to step 4 on page 84. Let stand 10 minutes. Makes 6 servings.

89

TIP Toasting coconut *is easy. Place a thin layer of coconut in a shallow baking pan. Bake in 350° oven for 6 to 7 minutes or till lightly browned, stirring the coconut once or twice to prevent overbrowning. Sprinkle atop sauces or puddings, but wait until just before serving so that the toasted coconut stays crunchy.*

Eggs

Cheese Soufflé

Technique: Making a soufflé

- 4 **eggs**
- ¼ **cup butter** *or* **margarine**
- ¼ **cup all-purpose flour**
- ¼ **teaspoon salt**
- **Dash cayenne**
- 1 **cup milk**
- 2 **cups shredded sharp American cheese (8 ounces)**

1 Separate the eggs; set aside. **2** In a heavy saucepan melt the butter or margarine; blend in the flour, salt, and cayenne. **3** Add the milk all at once; cook and stir over medium heat till mixture thickens and bubbles. **4** Turn heat to low; add cheese, stirring to melt. Remove from heat. **5** In small mixer bowl beat the egg yolks till thick and lemon-colored. **6** Slowly add cheese mixture to egg yolks, stirring constantly; cool about 5 minutes while beating egg whites.

7 Using clean beaters and large mixer bowl, beat the egg whites to stiff peaks. **8** Gradually pour the yolk mixture over beaten whites; fold to blend. **9** Pour into an ungreased 2-quart soufflé dish or casserole with straight sides. **10** For a top hat that puffs in the oven, use a knife to trace a 1-inch-deep circle through the mixture about 1 inch from edge. **11** Bake in 300° oven for about 1¼ hours or until knife inserted near center comes out clean. **12** Serve immediately by breaking apart with two forks. Makes 4 servings.

90

1 Separate eggs while they are still chilled. Gently crack the egg in the center with a knife. Hold over a custard cup, as shown; slip the egg yolk back and forth from one shell half to the other, allowing the egg white to fall into the cup.

Drop yolk into small mixer bowl. Transfer egg white to large mixer bowl. Repeat with remaining eggs, making sure whites contain no trace of yolk.

2 In a heavy saucepan melt the butter or margarine. Add the flour, salt, and cayenne, stirring to blend well so that there are no lumps.

7 Using clean beaters and large mixer bowl, beat egg whites till stiff peaks form. Eggs should still appear moist and glossy, not dry. Using an electric mixer or rotary beater, beat the egg whites till the tips of peaks stand straight when lifted out, as shown. This will take about 1½ minutes at medium speed.

Do not use a plastic bowl, since oils retained in the plastic prevent the egg whites from forming peaks.

8 Gradually pour the yolk mixture over the beaten whites, folding to blend. To fold, cut down through the mixture with a rubber spatula, as shown. Scrape across the bottom of bowl, then bring spatula up and over mixture, close to the surface. Repeat this circular down-up-and-over motion, turning bowl as you work. Do this as quickly and carefully as possible to keep batter fluffy.

3 Add the milk all at once. Cook and stir over medium heat till the mixture thickens and bubbles. This is a thick white sauce.

4 Turn heat to low. Add the cheese, stirring constantly to melt. Remove saucepan from heat.

American cheese is a process cheese, and melts more smoothly than natural cheese. Do not substitute natural cheese.

5 In small mixer bowl beat egg yolks at high speed about 5 minutes or till thick and lemon-colored.

When yolks are sufficiently beaten, they will flow in a thick stream from the lifted beaters.

6 Slowly add the cheese mixture to the egg yolks. Start by stirring in just a spoonful at a time, as shown; the last quarter or so may be poured in. This combining is done in small amounts so the heavy cheese mixture won't destroy the fluffiness of the beaten egg yolks. Slow addition also helps prevent the hot cheese mixture from cooking the egg yolks. Let mixture cool about 5 minutes while beating egg whites.

91

9 Carefully pour the egg-cheese mixture into an ungreased 2-quart soufflé dish. A 2-quart casserole with straight sides also may be used.

10 If you want the soufflé to have a top hat that puffs in the oven, as shown in step 11, use a knife to trace a 1-inch-deep circle through the mixture about 1 inch from the edge.

11 Bake in a 300° oven for about 1¼ hours or until a knife inserted near center comes out clean. When inserting the knife, enlarge the hole slightly by moving knife from side to side. Otherwise the soufflé crust may "clean" the knife as it is pulled out. Test at the end of the suggested time; do not open oven door during baking.

Test while soufflé is still in oven, as shown. If you try to lift it out before it is done, it will fall.

12 Soufflés should be served immediately after they are removed from the oven, before they have a chance to fall. It's true that it's better to have guests wait for the soufflé because the soufflé won't wait for the guests.

To serve, insert two forks, back to back as shown, and gently pull apart. Cut into servings in this manner. Use a spoon to transfer to individual plates.

Eggs

Poached Meringues

Technique: Making poached meringues

1 Separate eggs while they are still chilled. Gently crack egg in center with a knife. Holding over a custard cup, slip yolk back and forth from one shell half to the other, allowing the white to fall into the cup. Drop yolk into another bowl; set aside for another use. Transfer the white to small non-plastic mixer bowl. Repeat with second egg, making sure whites contain no trace of yolk.

2   **eggs**
¼   **teaspoon cream of tartar**
     Dash salt
¼   **cup sugar**
3   **cups milk**

1 Separate eggs; reserve whites, saving yolks for another use. **2** Let the egg whites stand for about 1 hour or till they come to room temperature. Add the cream of tartar and salt. **3** Beat to soft peaks. **4–5** Gradually add the sugar, beating to stiff peaks. **6** In skillet heat milk to simmering. Drop meringue onto milk in 6 mounds. Cook slowly, uncovered, about 5 minutes or till set. Lift from milk; drain on paper toweling. Cover and chill till ready to serve. Meringues are best when served the same day.

If desired, cool the milk and use part of it to make stirred custard as directed on page 86. Spoon the cooled custard over fruit and top each serving with a poached meringue. Makes 6.

If egg yolks will not be used immediately, *seal by covering with a layer of cold water; refrigerate. Drain and use within 1 or 2 days. Good uses for extra egg yolks include scrambled eggs, see page 72; and stirred custard, see page 86.*

4 Continue beating at high speed of electric mixer; add the sugar gradually, about a tablespoon at a time. The sugar also helps incorporate air and adds stability.

If desired, you may sweeten this soft meringue with honey, corn syrup, or jelly. But use only 2 tablespoons (1 tablespoon per egg white).

92

2 Let egg whites stand for about 1 hour or till they come to room temperature; this will allow them to incorporate more air during beating, thus giving them greater volume.

Sprinkle the cream of tartar and salt across surface. The cream of tartar acts as a stabilizer to help the beaten egg whites hold their shape.

3 Beat to soft peaks. Use an electric mixer at medium speed; this will take about 1 minute.

Use a rubber spatula to guide the egg whites into the beaters. This helps ensure that the foam has uniformly sized air bubbles.

At this stage, the egg white foam turns white and gets stiffer. Soft peaks form when the beaters are lifted out. The tips of the peaks will bend over in soft curls, as shown.

TIP *Eggs can be frozen if you won't be able to use them right away (suggested refrigerator storage is 5 weeks in the carton).*

Whole eggs and egg yolks become lumpy unless sugar, corn syrup, or salt is added. Whites freeze satisfactorily without any additions; stir, then strain and freeze.

Break eggs into a bowl, separating yolks and whites, if desired. Stir to blend but do not beat. Strain through a medium strainer or put through a food mill.

To each cup of whole eggs add 1 tablespoon sugar or corn syrup or 1 teaspoon salt.

To each cup of yolks add 2 tablespoons sugar or corn syrup or 1 teaspoon salt.

Freeze in usable portions, allowing room for expansion. Use within 9 to 12 months.

Thaw completely in the unopened container in the refrigerator (a one cup container will thaw overnight). Use within 24 hours. Sweetened eggs can be used in desserts; salted eggs can be used in main dishes. Do not use in uncooked foods, such as eggnog.

For 1 fresh whole egg substitute 3 tablespoons frozen whole egg, thawed.

For 1 fresh egg yolk substitute 1 tablespoon frozen egg yolk, thawed.

For 1 fresh egg white substitute 2 tablespoons frozen egg white, thawed.

93

 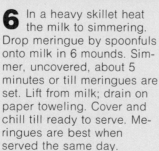

5 Beating to stiff peaks will take about 3 minutes at high speed of electric mixer.

At this stage, the foam becomes even whiter and forms stiff peaks that stand straight when beaters are removed, as shown.

The whites now contain all of the air they are capable of holding.

6 In a heavy skillet heat the milk to simmering. Drop meringue by spoonfuls onto milk in 6 mounds. Simmer, uncovered, about 5 minutes or till meringues are set. Lift from milk; drain on paper toweling. Cover and chill till ready to serve. Meringues are best when served the same day.

Eggs

Meringue Shells

Technique: Making meringue shells

 3 **egg whites**
 1 **teaspoon vanilla**
 ½ **teaspoon cream of tartar**
   Dash salt
 1 **cup sugar**

94

1 Cover baking sheets with brown paper. Draw one 9-inch circle or eight 3-inch circles. Set prepared baking sheets aside. **2** Separate eggs; reserve whites, saving yolks for another use. Place whites in a small mixer bowl. **3** Let egg whites stand about 1 hour or till they come to room temperature. Add the vanilla, cream of tartar, and salt. **4** Beat to soft peaks. **5–7** Gradually add the sugar, beating till very stiff peaks form.

8–9 Spread meringue over circles on paper to make one 9-inch meringue shell *or* 8 individual shells. Bake either size in 275° oven for 1 hour. For large meringue, turn off oven and let dry in oven (with door closed) for at least 2 hours. Individual meringue shells may be used after the 1-hour baking. For crisper meringues, turn off oven and let dry in oven (with door closed) for about 1 hour. Peel off paper.

To serve, fill meringue shells with ice cream or pudding and top with fruit or sauce. If it is necessary to store meringue shells before serving, place in plastic bag or airtight container. Makes 8 servings.

1 Cover baking sheets with plain ungreased brown paper. Using a 9-inch round cake pan as a guide, draw a circle on paper.

Or, for individual meringue shells, draw eight circles about 3 inches in diameter and about 2 inches apart.

Other sizes may also be used, as well as other shapes such as a Valentine heart or a Christmas tree.

If desired, lightly grease the baking sheet instead of using brown paper.

6 Beating egg whites to very stiff peaks will take about 7 minutes. At this stage the foam becomes even whiter and forms stiff peaks that stand straight when beaters are removed, as shown. The whites now contain all of the air they are capable of holding.

2 Separate eggs while they are still chilled. Gently crack egg in center with a knife. Holding over a custard cup, slip yolk back and forth from one shell half to the other, allowing the white to fall into the cup. Drop yolk into another bowl; set aside for another use. Transfer the white to small non-plastic mixer bowl. Repeat with remaining eggs, making sure whites contain no trace of yolk.

3 Let egg whites stand for about 1 hour or till they come to room temperature; this will allow them to incorporate more air during beating, thus giving them greater volume.

Sprinkle the cream of tartar and salt across surface. The cream of tartar acts as a stabilizer to help the beaten egg whites hold their shape.

4 Beat to soft peaks. Use an electric mixer at medium speed; this will take about 1 minute.

Use a rubber spatula to guide the egg whites into the beaters. This helps ensure that the foam has uniformly sized air bubbles.

At this stage, the egg white foam turns white and becomes stiffer. Soft peaks form when the beaters are lifted out. The tips of the peaks will bend over in soft curls, as shown.

5 Continue beating at high speed of electric mixer; add the sugar gradually, about a tablespoon at a time. The sugar also helps incorporate air and adds stability.

95

7 Sugar is added gradually so that it will dissolve completely. To check, rub a little of the meringue between thumb and finger, as shown. It should feel quite smooth. If it feels very grainy, continue beating till all sugar is dissolved. The proportion of sugar to egg whites in this recipe lessens the possibility of overly beaten egg whites.

8 To make a large meringue shell, spread meringue over 9-inch circle drawn on paper. Shape into shell with back of spoon, as shown. Make the bottom ½ inch thick and the sides 1¾ inches high.

Bake in 275° oven for 1 hour. Turn off oven; let dry in oven (with door closed) at least 2 hours. Peel off paper.

If desired, bake in 300° oven for 35 to 45 minutes; color will be light beige rather than white.

9 To make individual meringue shells, spread each of the small circles with about ⅓ cup meringue. Use a spoon to shape into shells, *or* pipe through a pastry tube, as shown.

Bake in 275° oven for 1 hour. If crisper meringues are desired, turn off oven and let dry in oven (with door closed) for about 1 hour. Peel off paper.

If desired, bake in 300° oven for 35 to 45 minutes; color will be light beige.

Strawberry Meringues

(pictured on page 68)

- 3 egg whites
- 1 teaspoon vanilla
- ½ teaspoon cream of tartar
- ¼ teaspoon almond extract
  Dash salt
- 1 cup granulated sugar
- 1 quart fresh strawberries
- 1 cup whipping cream
- 2 tablespoons sifted powdered sugar
- 2 tablespoons brandy

Refer to: Making meringue shells, page 94. Cover baking sheets with brown paper. Draw eight 3-inch-diameter circles spaced 2 inches apart on paper.

Bring egg whites to room temperature. Add vanilla, cream of tartar, almond extract, and salt. Beat to soft peaks. Gradually add granulated sugar, beating to very stiff peaks.

Divide among the 8 circles, using about ⅓ cup for each. Using back of spoon, shape into shells.

Bake in 300° oven for 35 to 45 minutes or till light beige. Cool. Peel off paper. (If not to be used immediately, wrap in waxed paper; store in cool, dry place.)

Set aside 8 whole berries. Hull and slice remaining berries; sweeten, if desired. In chilled bowl combine cream, powdered sugar, and brandy; whip till soft peaks form.

To serve, fill meringue shells with sliced berries. Top with the whipped cream mixture. Garnish with the whole strawberries. Makes 8 servings.

Swiss Corn Soufflé

- 6 ears fresh corn *or* 1 10-ounce package frozen whole kernel corn
- 6 slices bacon
- ¼ cup all-purpose flour
- ¼ teaspoon salt
  Dash pepper
- 1 cup milk
- 1 cup shredded process Swiss cheese (4 ounces)
- 4 egg yolks
- 4 egg whites

Refer to: Making a soufflé, page 90. Cut kernels from cob (you should have about 2 cups cut corn); cook, covered, in small amount of boiling salted water for 6 to 8 minutes or till done (*or* cook frozen corn according to package directions). Drain and set aside.

In skillet cook bacon till crisp. Drain, transferring ¼ cup drippings to saucepan. Crumble bacon and set aside. Blend flour, salt, and pepper into reserved drippings. Add milk. Cook and stir till thickened and bubbly. Stir in cheese till melted. Remove from heat.

Beat egg yolks till thick and lemon-colored. Slowly add cheese mixture, stirring constantly. Stir in corn and bacon. Beat egg whites till stiff peaks form. Fold cheese mixture into egg whites. Turn into ungreased 1½-quart soufflé dish.

Bake in 350° oven for 45 minutes or till knife inserted near center comes out clean. Garnish with bacon curl, if desired. Makes 4 to 6 servings.

Caramel Floating Island

(pictured on page 68)

- 3 egg whites
- ⅓ cup sugar
- 3 cups milk
- 3 egg yolks
- 2 eggs
- ½ cup sugar
  Dash salt
- 1½ teaspoons vanilla
- ¼ cup sugar

Refer to: Making poached meringues, page 92, and Making a stirred custard, page 86. Beat egg whites till soft peaks form. Gradually add the ⅓ cup sugar, beating till stiff peaks form.

In 10-inch skillet heat milk to simmering. Drop egg white mixture onto milk in 8 portions; simmer, uncovered, about 5 minutes or till set. Lift meringues from milk; drain on paper toweling. Chill. Cool milk for custard.

In a 2-quart saucepan slightly beat the egg yolks with the 2 eggs. Stir in the slightly cooled milk. Add the ½ cup sugar and salt. Cook and stir over medium heat till mixture coats a metal spoon. Remove from heat; cool quickly by setting saucepan in bowl of ice. Stir in vanilla. Turn into serving bowl; chill. Arrange meringues atop.

Melt the ¼ cup sugar in a small heavy skillet over low heat, stirring constantly till golden. Remove from heat. Immediately drizzle melted sugar over meringues in a thin, thread-like pattern. Makes 8 servings.

Almond Macaroons

- 2 egg whites
- 1 cup sugar
- 1 8-ounce can almond paste, crumbled

Refer to: Making meringue shells, steps 4–7, page 95. Beat egg whites till soft peaks form. Gradually add sugar, beating till very stiff peaks form. Beat about ½ cup of the egg whites into the crumbled almond paste. Fold almond paste mixture into remaining egg whites. Drop rounded teaspoonfuls onto lightly greased cookie sheet. Bake in 350° oven for 15 to 18 minutes. *Immediately* remove to wire rack. Makes about 36.

96

Surprise Meringue Kisses

3 egg whites
1 teaspoon vanilla
¼ teaspoon cream of tartar
¼ teaspoon peppermint extract (optional)
  Dash salt
1 cup granulated sugar
44 milk chocolate kisses
  Green sugar crystals

Refer to: Making meringue shells, steps 1–6, page 94. In small mixer bowl beat egg whites with vanilla, cream of tartar, peppermint extract, and salt till soft peaks form. Gradually add 1 cup granulated sugar, about 1 tablespoon at a time. Beat till very stiff peaks form. Drop from a tablespoon 1½ inches apart onto lightly greased cookie sheet. Press a chocolate kiss into each cookie. With knife or narrow spatula, bring meringue up and over candy; swirl top. Sprinkle with green sugar. Bake in 275° oven for 30 minutes or till set. Immediately remove cookies to rack; cool. Makes 44.

Blue Cheese Soufflés

6 tablespoons butter *or* margarine
⅓ cup all-purpose flour
1 teaspoon salt
  Dash freshly ground pepper
  Dash freshly ground nutmeg
1½ cups milk
¾ cup crumbled blue cheese (3 ounces)
6 egg yolks
6 egg whites

Refer to: Making a soufflé, page 90. Melt butter or margarine; blend in flour, salt, pepper, and nutmeg. Add milk all at once; cook and stir till mixture thickens and bubbles. Stir in blue cheese. Remove from heat. Beat egg yolks on high speed of electric mixer about 6 minutes or till very thick and lemon-colored. Slowly stir cheese mixture into yolks. Let cool while beating egg whites to stiff peaks (tips stand straight); fold in yolk-blue cheese mixture. Pour into six ungreased 12-ounce soufflé dishes.

Bake in 325° oven for 30 to 35 minutes or till knife inserted near center comes out clean. Serve immediately. Serves 6.

Lemon Meringue Pudding

6 egg whites
½ teaspoon finely shredded lemon peel
1 tablespoon lemon juice
½ teaspoon vanilla
¼ cup granulated sugar
4 egg yolks
1 tablespoon all-purpose flour
5 tablespoons butter *or* margarine
  Powdered sugar

In large mixer bowl combine egg whites, lemon peel, lemon juice, and vanilla; beat at medium speed till soft peaks form. Referring to steps 3–5 on page 93, gradually add granulated sugar; beat at high speed till stiff peaks form. Referring to step 5 on page 91, beat egg yolks at high speed about 5 minutes or till thick and lemon-colored; fold in flour. Referring to step 8 on page 90, fold yolk mixture into whites.

In 350° oven melt butter or margarine in 12×7½×2-inch baking dish; remove from oven. Spoon egg mixture into baking dish, forming 5 or 6 even mounds. Bake in 350° oven for 20 to 22 minutes or till outside is light golden brown. Sift powdered sugar lightly over top. Serve immediately; spoon on some of the melted butter. Makes 5 or 6 servings.

97

Surprise Meringue Kisses

Filbert Macaroons

¾ cup whole unblanched filberts (about 3½ ounces)
2 egg whites
1 teaspoon lemon juice
1 cup sifted powdered sugar
¼ teaspoon ground cinnamon

Refer to: Making meringue shells, steps 4–7, page 95. Grind filberts, using coarse blade of food grinder; set aside. Beat egg whites with lemon juice till soft peaks form. Gradually add sugar and cinnamon, beating till very stiff. Fold in nuts. Drop by rounded teaspoonfuls onto lightly greased cookie sheet. If desired, top each with a whole filbert. Bake in 350° oven for 10 to 15 minutes. Immediately remove to rack. Makes 24.

SAUCES AND SOUPS

Sauces are the starting point for a great number of dishes, and thus are an important part of the basics of cooking. In this section, you'll learn to make a variety of sauces, gravies, stocks, and soups.

White Sauce

Technique: Making white sauce

THIN
- 1 tablespoon butter *or* margarine
- 1 tablespoon all-purpose flour
- ¼ teaspoon salt
- Dash pepper
- 1 cup milk

MEDIUM
- 2 tablespoons butter *or* margarine
- 2 tablespoons all-purpose flour
- ¼ teaspoon salt
- Dash pepper
- 1 cup milk

THICK
- 3 tablespoons butter *or* margarine
- ¼ cup all-purpose flour
- ¼ teaspoon salt
- Dash pepper
- 1 cup milk

1 In a heavy saucepan melt the butter or margarine. Blend in the flour, salt, and pepper. **2** Add the milk all at once. **3** Cook and stir over medium heat. **4** Continue cooking till mixture is thickened and bubbly. Cook and stir 2 minutes more. Makes 1 cup.
5 Thin White Sauce is pourable and is used for soups and creamed vegetables. **6** Medium White Sauce is thicker and is used for sauces, scalloped dishes, and creamed dishes. **7** Thick White Sauce is used for croquettes and soufflés.

1 In a heavy saucepan melt the butter or margarine over low heat. Blend in the flour, salt, and pepper, stirring with a wooden spoon till no lumps remain.
This fat-flour mixture is often called a roux. Combining the ingredients in this way allows the fat to coat the flour particles. This prevents lumps from forming when the liquid is added.
To avoid black specks in the sauce, use white pepper.

5 Thin White Sauce is made with a low proportion of butter and flour to milk, and can be poured rapidly, as shown. Use it as a base for soups and creamed vegetables.

2 With the saucepan over low heat, add the milk all at once. Stir constantly to evenly distribute the fat-flour mixture throughout the total amount of cool milk. It's easier than blending it with a small amount of milk at a time. The fat-flour mixture and the milk must be well blended to avoid a lumpy sauce.

3 Cook over medium heat, stirring constantly in a figure-8 motion so that the sauce is heated evenly throughout. Vigorous beating or stirring will break down the starch particles in the flour, making the sauce slick rather than smooth and velvety. Use a wooden spoon for more comfortable stirring.

4 Continue cooking till the mixture bubbles across its entire surface, as shown. Thickening results when heat expands starch particles in the flour.

Cook 2 minutes more to ensure that the flour is fully cooked and will not taste starchy. Add cheeses or other flavorings at this point.

TIP To make cheese sauces, *start by making Medium White Sauce, following steps 1–4. Add 1 cup shredded sharp American cheese, stirring to melt.*

Or, add ½ cup shredded American cheese and ½ cup shredded Swiss cheese, stirring to melt. Stir in an additional ¼ cup milk, if needed.

Or, prepare Medium White Sauce using 1 teaspoon instant chicken bouillon granules instead of the salt. When sauce thickens and bubbles, stir in ¼ cup dairy sour cream and ¼ cup crumbled blue cheese. Heat through but do not boil.

When a cheese is available as natural or process, choose the process cheese for a smooth sauce. Using natural cheese will give the sauce a grainy texture and a stringy appearance.

99

6 Medium White Sauce—the type most commonly made—is thicker but still pourable, as shown. It's used as a base for sauces, and for scalloped and creamed dishes.

7 Thick White Sauce has the highest proportion of butter and flour to milk. Use it in soufflés, or mix with chopped cooked meat to make a base for croquettes.

Sauces and Soups

Pan Gravy

Technique: Making pan gravy

Hot drippings (from roast meat or poultry)
¼ cup all-purpose flour
Milk *or* water *or* broth
Salt and pepper
Dash dried thyme, crushed (optional)
Few drops Kitchen Bouquet (optional)

100

1 After removing roasted meat to platter, pour the meat juices and fat into a 2-cup glass measure. **2** Skim off the fat, reserving 3 to 4 tablespoons. Return the reserved fat to pan. **3** Stir in the flour. **4** Cook and stir over low heat till bubbly. Remove pan from heat. **5** Add enough milk, water, or broth to reserved meat juices to make 2 cups. **6** Add liquid all at once to the fat-flour mixture; blend well. Add some salt and pepper. If desired, add thyme and Kitchen Bouquet. **7** Cook and stir till thickened and bubbly. Cook 2 minutes more. Season to taste. Makes 2 cups.

1 After removing the roasted meat to a platter, pour the meat juices and fat into a 2-cup glass measure. Leave the crusty bits in the pan so they can be stirred into the gravy.

5 Add enough milk, water, or broth to the reserved meat juices to measure 2 cups liquid.

If desired, wine may be used for part of the liquid.

To make 1 cup gravy, use only 1 cup liquid.

2 To skim the fat from the meat juices, tilt the measuring cup and spoon off the oily liquid that rises to the top. Measure 3 to 4 tablespoons of the fat and return it to the roasting pan. Discard any remaining fat.

To make 1 cup gravy, reserve only 2 tablespoons fat.

3 Blend the flour into the fat in roasting pan. Combining the ingredients in this way allows the fat to coat the flour particles. This prevents lumps from forming when the liquid is added.

To make 1 cup gravy, use only 2 tablespoons flour.

4 Cook and stir over low heat till mixture is bubbly, as shown. Stir in the crusty bits from the bottom of the pan; these help give the gravy a browner color and also add flavor.

If you're using an electric range, remove the pan from the burner. On gas ranges, turn off heat.

101

6 Add the 2 cups liquid all at once to the fat-flour mixture in the roasting pan; stir to blend. Distribute the fat-flour mixture evenly throughout the total amount of liquid. It's easier than blending it with a small amount of the liquid at a time. It must be well blended to avoid a lumpy gravy.

Add some salt and pepper, and the thyme and Kitchen Bouquet (to add color), if desired.

7 Cook, stirring constantly, over medium heat till mixture is thickened and bubbly. Cook 2 minutes longer to ensure that the flour is fully cooked and will not taste starchy. Add salt and pepper to taste.

Stir with a wooden spoon in figure-8 motion so that the sauce is evenly heated throughout. Vigorous stirring will break down starch particles in the flour making the gravy slick rather than smooth and velvety.

TIP When you have meat juices but no drippings, *such as with pot roast or stewed meat or poultry, shake together the flour and part of the liquid. This distributes the flour, preventing lumps.*

For about 2 cups gravy, measure the juices and add enough water to make 1½ cups liquid. In a shaker or screw-top jar, combine ⅓ cup cold water and 3 tablespoons all-purpose flour; shake well. In saucepan stir flour mixture into the juice liquid. Cook, stirring constantly, till thickened and bubbly. Season with salt and pepper. Simmer 2 minutes more, stirring occasionally.

Sauces and Soups

Beef Stock

Technique: Making beef stock

6	**pounds beef soup bones (cut into pieces)**
10	**cups cold water**
1	**cup sliced onion**
½	**cup chopped celery**
8	**whole black peppercorns**
4	**sprigs parsley**
1	**large bay leaf**
2	**teaspoons salt**
1	**egg**
¼	**cup water**

1 Place soup bones and the 10 cups water in large kettle. Bring to boiling; reduce heat. Simmer, uncovered, for 3 hours. **2** Remove meat and bones. Cut meat from bones; discard bones. **3** Return meat to kettle. **4** Add the onion, celery, peppercorns, parsley, bay leaf, and salt. Simmer, uncovered, for 2 hours. **5** Strain stock. Discard meat, vegetables, and seasonings.

6 To clarify stock, separate the egg; set yolk aside for another use. Crush the shell; mix with egg white and the ¼ cup water. Stir into hot stock. Bring to boiling; remove from heat and let stand 5 minutes. **7** Strain stock. **8** If using the stock while hot, skim fat. **9** *Or*, chill stock; lift off fat. Use the stock in recipes calling for beef broth or stock. Makes about 6 cups.

Crockery-Cooked Beef Stock: Use ingredients as above, *except* use only *4 pounds* beef soup bones, and only *5 cups* water. Combine all ingredients except egg in electric slow crockery cooker. Cover; cook on low-heat setting for 12 to 14 hours. Remove meat and bones. Continue as directed in steps 5–9 above. Makes about 4 cups.

102

1 Place soup bones and the 10 cups water in large kettle. Bring to boiling; reduce heat. Simmer, uncovered, for 3 hours.

If desired, instead of using beef soup bones, you may use chuck roast bones left from cutting your own beef cubes.

For chicken broth, use bony chicken pieces, referring to tip at right.

2 Use a slotted spoon or tongs to lift out the meat and bones. Cut meat from bones, as shown. Discard the bones and any pieces of fat or gristle.

6 To clarify or clear the stock, first separate one egg, referring to page 371. Set yolk aside for another use.

Crush the egg shell; mix with the egg white and the ¼ cup water. Stir into hot stock. Bring to boiling; remove from heat and let stand 5 minutes.

7 To strain the stock, line a sieve with 1 or 2 layers of cheesecloth; set over a large bowl. Pour stock mixture through. Discard the cooked egg and any other small particles.

3 Return meat to kettle of stock. Use a knife to push the meat off cutting board into kettle, as shown. Meat may be chopped, if desired.

4 Add the sliced onion, chopped celery, whole peppercorns, parsley, bay leaf, and salt. If desired, include celery leaves in the ½ cup measure. If peppercorns aren't available, add some ground pepper; taste again when cooked, adding more if needed.

Simmer the mixture, uncovered, for 2 hours.

5 Strain meat and vegetables from stock. To strain, line a sieve with 1 or 2 layers of cheesecloth; set over a large bowl. Pour stock mixture through.

Discard meat, vegetables, and seasonings.

103

TIP To make chicken broth, *use the bony pieces (backs, necks and wings) from 2 chickens.* Discard the fat and skin, if desired. Place chicken pieces in Dutch oven. Add 4 cups water; 3 stalks celery with leaves, cut up; 1 carrot, quartered; 1½ teaspoons salt; and ¼ teaspoon pepper. Cut 1 large onion into thirds; insert a whole clove in each third. Add to pan.

Cover tightly and bring to boiling; reduce heat and simmer about 1 hour or till meat is tender. Remove chicken. Strain broth, referring to step 5 at left. Discard the vegetables. Cut chicken meat from bones; discard skin and bones. Chill chicken meat and use in recipes calling for cooked chicken.

Clarify broth and skim fat, referring to steps 6–9 at left.

To make chicken broth in a crockery cooker, *use ingredients as listed above;* place in electric slow crockery cooker. Cover and cook on low-heat setting for 8 to 10 hours. Remove chicken and vegetables with a slotted spoon.

Strain broth, referring to step 5 at left. Discard vegetables. Cut chicken meat from bones; discard skin and bones. Chill chicken meat and use in recipes calling for cooked chicken. Clarify broth and skim fat, referring to steps 6–9 at left.

8 If using the stock while hot, skim off fat. To skim, use a metal spoon to spoon off the oily liquid (fat) that rises to the top, as shown. A bulb baster also may be used to remove fat.

9 *Or,* transfer the broth to straight-sided jars or a bowl; cover and chill. The fat—the oily liquid floating atop the hot broth—will solidify during chilling so that it can easily be lifted off with a fork, as shown.

Sauces and Soups

Brown Sauce

Technique: Making brown sauce

2 tablespoons butter *or* margarine
2 tablespoons all-purpose flour
1½ cups Beef Stock (see recipe, page 102) *or*
canned beef broth *or* 1½ teaspoons instant
beef bouillon granules dissolved in 1½ cups
hot water

1 In heavy saucepan melt the butter or margarine. **2** Blend in the flour. **3** To brown flour, cook and stir mixture over medium-low heat for 15 to 20 minutes. **4** Add Beef Stock or canned broth or bouillon. **5** Bring to boiling, stirring constantly. Boil for 3 to 5 minutes. **6** Reduce heat and simmer about 30 minutes or till reduced to 1 cup; stir frequently. Consistency of sauce should be slightly thinner than gravy. Serve with meat, instead of gravy, or use as a base for Sauce Diable or other sauces. Makes about 1 cup.

Sauce Diable: Combine ¼ cup sliced *green onion*, 3 tablespoons dry *white wine*, and 8 to 10 whole black *peppercorns*, crushed. Boil till mixture is reduced to half volume. Add ½ cup *Brown Sauce*, ½ teaspoon *worcestershire sauce,* and ½ teaspoon snipped *parsley*, heat through. Serve with broiled chicken or steak. Makes about ⅔ cup.

1 In a heavy saucepan melt the butter or margarine over low heat. If you're in a hurry, use higher heat, but be sure to stir often so that the butter doesn't burn.

4 Add the Beef Stock or canned beef broth or bouillon, stirring constantly. If you buy condensed broth, be sure to dilute it with an equal amount of water before using.

2 Leave the saucepan on the burner; add the flour and stir till the mixture is well blended with no lumps. Combining the ingredients in this way allows the fat to coat the flour particles. This prevents lumps from forming when the liquid is added. Use a wooden spoon for more comfortable stirring.

This fat-flour mixture is often called a roux.

3 To brown the flour, cook and stir mixture over medium-low heat for 15 to 20 minutes.

Browning the flour decreases its thickening power. Thus, you must later boil the sauce mixture to further thicken it.

5 Bring mixture to boiling, stirring constantly in a figure-8 motion so that the sauce is heated evenly throughout. Vigorous stirring breaks down the starch particles in the flour, making the sauce slick rather than smooth.

Boil for 3 to 5 minutes, stirring once or twice.

6 Reduce heat and simmer about 30 minutes or till total mixture is reduced to 1 cup; stir frequently. When sauce begins to look thickened, pour into liquid measuring cup. If necessary, return to saucepan and continue cooking till sauce measures 1 cup.

The consistency of this sauce should be slightly thinner than gravy, or about the same as for a thin white sauce, as shown.

Sauces and Soups

Tomato Spaghetti Sauce

Technique: Making sauce from fresh tomatoes

- **2 cloves garlic**
- **1 large onion, chopped**
- **2 tablespoons cooking oil**
- **2 pounds tomatoes (6 medium)** *or* **1 28-ounce can tomatoes**
- **1½ cups water**
- **1 6-ounce can tomato paste**
- **1 tablespoon sugar**
- **2 teaspoons instant beef bouillon granules**
- **1 teaspoon dried oregano, crushed**
- **½ teaspoon salt**
- **½ teaspoon dried basil, crushed**
- **⅛ teaspoon pepper**
- **1 large bay leaf**
- **1 4-ounce can sliced mushrooms**
- **Hot cooked spaghetti**

1 Peel and mince the garlic. **2** In a 3-quart saucepan cook the garlic and onion in hot oil till onion is tender. **3–4** Peel fresh tomatoes. **5** Core fresh tomatoes; cut up tomatoes and add to onion mixture. **6** Add the water, tomato paste, sugar, bouillon granules, oregano, salt, basil, pepper, and bay leaf. **7** Bring to boiling. Reduce heat and simmer, uncovered, for 1¼ to 1½ hours, stirring occasionally. Remove the bay leaf. **8** Stir in the *undrained* mushrooms; simmer 15 to 30 minutes more or till sauce is of the desired consistency. **9** Serve over hot cooked spaghetti; pass grated parmesan cheese, if desired. Makes 6 servings.

1 To peel and mince the garlic, place the garlic cloves on cutting board. Smash with flat edge of chef's knife or cleaver, as shown. This loosens the skins, making the garlic easier to peel. Remove the peel and mince the garlic by finely chopping into very small pieces.

2 In a 3-quart saucepan heat oil; cook the garlic and onion in hot oil over medium-low heat about 5 minutes or till onion is tender but not brown. Remove saucepan from heat.

If desired, cook the garlic and onion in 2 tablespoons shortening, butter, or margarine instead of oil.

6 Add the water, tomato paste, sugar, beef bouillon granules, crushed oregano, salt, basil, pepper, and bay leaf. Stir to mix.

7 Bring tomato mixture to boiling. Reduce heat and simmer, uncovered, for 1¼ to 1½ hours, stirring occasionally. Remove and discard the bay leaf.

The tomato mixture is cooked uncovered so it will "boil down" and thicken, as shown.

3 To peel fresh tomatoes, first loosen the skins as follows. Fill a saucepan with water; bring to boiling. Spear tomato with a fork; plunge into the boiling water for 30 seconds. Skin will split.

Use this method of peeling only when you're going to cook the tomatoes as it softens the flesh.

4 Immediately dip tomato into cold water. Using a sharp paring knife, pull off the tomato skin. Start pulling at one end, as shown, or at the split. Repeat steps 3 and 4 with remaining tomatoes.

5 Core fresh tomatoes. On cutting board, cut fresh tomatoes in quarters. Occasionally scrape tomatoes and accumulated juice into mixing bowl. Add tomatoes with their juice to onion mixture in saucepan.

If using canned instead of fresh tomatoes, cut up as directed in tip at right.

107

TIP To cut up canned tomatoes quickly, *pour tomatoes into a bowl. (You can cut up the canned tomatoes right in the can, if desired.) Using kitchen shears, snip tomatoes, cutting into pieces.*

Most recipes call for using both the cut-up tomatoes and the juice, so do not drain tomatoes unless specifically directed to do so.

8 Stir in the *undrained* mushrooms; simmer sauce 15 to 30 minutes more or till sauce is the consistency you like for serving over spaghetti.

9 Spoon the tomato sauce over hot cooked spaghetti. If desired, pass grated parmesan cheese to sprinkle atop.

Sauces and Soups

1 Using a sharp knife, cut tips off corn kernels. Hold the ear of corn at an angle so that one end rests on a cutting board. Cut down across tips of kernels toward the board, as shown. Repeat with remaining ears of corn.

2 Scrape cobs. Holding the ear of corn at the same angle, scrape ear with knife, as shown. This 2-step method of removing the kernels releases the milky substance in the corn.

Fresh Corn Chowder

Technique: Making egg-thickened soup

6	**medium ears corn**
⅓	**cup water**
¼	**cup chopped onion**
½	**teaspoon salt**
4	**cups milk**
2	**tablespoons butter** *or* **margarine**
1	**teaspoon salt**
¼	**teaspoon pepper**
3	**tablespoons all-purpose flour**
1	**slightly beaten egg**
	Snipped chives (optional)
	Paprika (optional)

1 Using a sharp knife, cut tips off corn kernels. **2** Scrape cobs. **3** In saucepan combine the corn, water, onion, and the ½ teaspoon salt. Bring to boiling; reduce heat and simmer, covered, about 15 minutes or till corn is barely done, stirring occasionally. **4** Stir in *3½ cups* of the milk, the butter or margarine, the 1 teaspoon salt, and the pepper.

5 In a bowl combine the remaining ½ cup milk and the flour; stir till blended. **6** Add milk-flour mixture to corn mixture. **7** Cook and stir till mixture is thickened and bubbly. **8** Gradually stir about 1 cup of the hot mixture into the beaten egg. **9** Return to hot mixture in saucepan. **10** Cook over low heat for 2 minutes more, stirring constantly. If desired, garnish soup with chives and paprika. Makes 6 servings.

6 Gradually add the milk-flour mixture to the hot corn mixture. Stir to blend. The milk-flour "paste" helps to thicken the chowder.

7 Cook over medium heat about 10 minutes or till thickened and bubbly, as shown. Stir constantly to prevent corn from sticking to bottom of pan.

3 In a saucepan combine the corn (including the milky substance), the water, onion, and the ½ teaspoon salt.

Bring to boiling; reduce heat and simmer, covered, about 15 minutes or till corn is barely done. Stir occasionally to prevent sticking.

4 Stir in *3½ cups* of the milk, butter or margarine, the 1 teaspoon salt, and the pepper. If desired, use white pepper to avoid black flecks in the chowder.

5 In a bowl or cup combine the remaining ½ cup *cold* milk and the flour; stir till well blended with no lumps.

Another easy way to combine this mixture is to shake the milk and flour together in a screw-top jar, referring to tip on page 101.

109

8 With the slightly beaten egg in a bowl, gradually stir about 1 cup of the hot corn mixture into the egg. Adding a small amount of the hot mixture to the egg warms the egg, making it less likely to cook too quickly and form lumps when it's combined with the rest of the mixture.

9 Return the egg mixture to the hot corn mixture. Stir while adding to distribute the egg throughout the chowder. The egg also helps to thicken the chowder.

10 Cook over low heat for 2 minutes more, stirring constantly. The finished chowder will have a medium-thick consistency, as shown. If desired, garnish each serving with some snipped chives or a sprinkle of paprika.

Sauces and Soups

Cream of Tomato Soup

Technique: Making cream of tomato soup

2	**cups chopped ripe tomatoes (about 2 tomatoes)**
¼	**cup chopped onion**
1	**small bay leaf**
½	**teaspoon sugar**
½	**teaspoon salt**
	Dash pepper
2	**tablespoons butter *or* margarine**
2	**tablespoons all-purpose flour**
¼	**teaspoon salt**
2	**cups milk**

1 In a saucepan combine the tomatoes, onion, bay leaf, sugar, the ½ teaspoon salt, and the pepper. Bring to boiling; reduce heat and simmer about 10 minutes. **2** Sieve the tomato mixture to make about 1 cup; set aside. **3** In the same saucepan melt the butter or margarine; stir in the flour and the ¼ teaspoon salt. **4** Add milk all at once. **5–6** Cook and stir till thickened and bubbly. Cook 2 minutes more. **7** Slowly add hot tomato mixture, stirring to blend. Serve immediately.

If desired, garnish soup with sliced green onion, crumbled crisp-cooked bacon, dairy sour cream, or seasoned croutons. Makes 4 servings.

1 In a saucepan combine the tomatoes, onion, bay leaf, sugar, the ½ teaspoon salt, and the pepper. Bring to boiling; reduce heat and simmer about 10 minutes.

It is not necessary to peel the tomatoes, since the skins will be removed as the mixture is sieved.

5 Cook over medium heat, stirring constantly in a figure-8 motion so that the sauce is heated evenly throughout. Vigorous beating or stirring will break down the particles in the flour, making the sauce slick rather than smooth and velvety. Use a wooden spoon for more comfortable stirring.

2 Place a sieve over a bowl. Add the tomato mixture to the sieve; press the tomato mixture through with a wooden spoon or rubber spatula to strain the juice, as shown. Discard the pulpy mass left in the sieve.

Or, process the mixture in a blender or food processor, referring to the tip at right.

Set the hot strained mixture aside (you should have about 1 cup).

3 In the same saucepan you used for cooking the tomatoes, melt the butter or margarine over low heat. Blend in the flour and the ¼ teaspoon salt. Stir with a wooden spoon till no lumps remain.

This is the first step in making a white sauce, which is the base for this soup.

4 With the saucepan over low heat, add the milk all at once. Stir constantly to distribute the fat-flour mixture throughout the total amount of cool milk. This is easier than blending it with a small amount of milk at a time. The fat-flour mixture and the milk must be well blended to prevent lumps from forming.

111

TIP Blending the tomato mixture *instead of sieving it is an alternate method for making the tomato puree. However, more seeds will be left in the tomato mixture with blending than with sieving.*

To blend, pour tomato mixture into blender container or food processor; cover and process until smooth.

For a smoother soup from the blender or food processor, be sure to peel the tomatoes before cooking them. For easy peeling refer to steps 3 and 4 on page 107.

6 Continue cooking till the mixture thickens and bubbles across its entire surface. This thickening results when heat expands the starch particles in the flour. Cook 2 minutes longer to ensure that the flour is fully cooked and will not taste starchy.

7 Slowly add the hot tomato mixture to the white sauce, stirring to blend. Heat through, if necessary. Do not heat mixture too long or allow it to boil. The acidity of the tomatoes can cause the milk to curdle when overcooked. Serve immediately.

Sauces and Soups

Classic Hollandaise (pictured on page 68)

Technique: Making hollandaise sauce

 4 **egg yolks**
 ½ **cup butter** *or* **margarine, cut in thirds and**
     softened
 2 **to 3 teaspoons lemon juice**
     Salt and pepper

112 **1** Place egg yolks and *a third* of the butter in top of double boiler. Cook over boiling water till butter melts, stirring rapidly (water in bottom of double boiler should not touch top pan). **2** Add *a second third* of the butter and continue stirring. **3** As butter melts and mixture thickens, add the remaining butter. Stir constantly.

4 When last piece of butter is melted, remove pan from water; stir rapidly 2 minutes. **5** Stir in the lemon juice, 1 teaspoon at a time. Season with salt and pepper. **6** Heat again over boiling water, stirring constantly, for 2 to 3 minutes or till thickened. Remove from heat at once. Serve over hot cooked vegetables, fish, or poultry.

If sauce curdles, immediately beat in 1 to 2 table-spoons boiling water. Makes 1 cup.

1 Place the egg yolks and *one third* of the butter in top of double boiler. Cook over boiling water till butter melts, stirring rapidly. Water in bottom of double boiler should boil, as shown, but should not touch the top pan.

Since hollandaise is easily curdled by excessive heat, it should be made in a double boiler rather than in a sauce-pan over direct heat.

4 When the last piece of butter is melted, remove the top pan from the double boiler.

Using a wooden spoon, rapidly stir the butter mixture for 2 minutes.

2 Add *the second third* of the butter and continue stirring. As the butter melts, it forms fat globules that are held in suspension by the egg yolks. Classic hollandaise is traditionally made with butter; however, margarine may be substituted.

At this stage, the consistency of the sauce should be somewhat runny, as shown.

3 As butter melts and mixture thickens, add the remaining butter. Stir constantly to help melt the butter and distribute it evenly throughout the sauce. After all butter is added and melted, the consistency of the sauce should be quite thick, as shown.

113

TIP To make Blender Hollandaise, *place 3 egg yolks in a blender container. Add 2 tablespoons lemon juice and a dash cayenne. Cover; quickly turn blender on and off to mix ingredients.*

Heat ½ cup butter till melted and almost boiling. Place lid on blender but remove the cover of the center opening. Turn blender on low speed. SLOWLY pour in the melted butter, as shown. (If your blender cover doesn't have a center opening, lift one edge of the lid slightly and pour in butter while blender is running.) Turn blender to high speed. Blend about 30 seconds or till thick and fluffy, scraping blender sides as necessary. Serve immediately or keep warm in a double boiler. Makes 1 cup.

This variation is somewhat thinner than the Classic Hollandaise; it also has a stronger lemon flavor.

5 Stir in the lemon juice, about 1 teaspoon at a time. Season with salt and pepper. If desired, use white pepper to avoid black flecks in the sauce.

6 Replace top pan over boiling water. Heat, stirring constantly, for 2 to 3 minutes or till thickened. Remove from heat at once. The finished sauce should be thick but pourable, as shown, making it a suitable topping for cooked vegetables, fish, and poultry. In this sauce, the egg yolks act as a thickening agent as well as an emulsifier or binder.

If the sauce curdles, immediately beat in 1 to 2 tablespoons boiling water.

Sauces and Soups

Southern Giblet Gravy

½ pound turkey *or* chicken giblets and neck
3 cups water
1 small onion, sliced
1 teaspoon salt
 Few celery leaves
½ cup all-purpose flour
 Dash pepper
2 hard-cooked eggs, chopped

Remove liver from giblets and set aside. In saucepan combine neck and remaining giblets, water, onion, salt, and celery leaves. Cover; simmer 1½ hours. Add the liver; simmer 20 to 30 minutes more. Cool giblets and neck in broth; remove from broth and chop meat. Add enough broth to turkey roasting drippings to make 3 cups. (If making gravy when not roasting a turkey, use 3 cups giblet broth.)

In screw-top jar combine *1 cup* of the cooled broth mixture, the flour, and pepper; shake well, referring to tip on page 101. In saucepan combine the flour mixture and remaining 2 cups broth. Cook and stir till thickened and bubbly. Cook and stir 2 minutes more. Stir in chopped meat and eggs; heat through. Makes 4 cups.

Oyster Stew

1 tablespoon all-purpose flour
1 teaspoon salt
 Dash pepper
 Dash ground mace (optional)
1 tablespoon cold water
1 pint shucked oysters
1 cup light cream
½ cup milk
2 tablespoons butter *or* margarine
 Paprika
 Oyster crackers

In a 2-quart saucepan combine flour, salt, and pepper; stir in mace, if desired. Stir in cold water. Add *undrained* oysters. Cook and stir over medium-high heat till hot. Reduce heat; simmer, stirring gently, 3 to 4 minutes or till edges of oysters curl. Stir in the cream and milk; heat through. Ladle into soup bowls; float butter or margarine atop and sprinkle with paprika. Serve immediately. Pass crackers. Serves 6 to 8.

Turkey Frame Soup

1 meaty turkey frame
5 quarts water
1 onion, quartered
4 teaspoons salt
3 tomatoes, quartered
1 teaspoon dried thyme, crushed
½ teaspoon dried oregano, crushed
8 cups fresh vegetables (any combination of uncooked sliced celery, sliced carrot, chopped onion, chopped rutabaga, sliced mushrooms, chopped broccoli, and cauliflowerets)
3 cups uncooked Homemade Noodles (see recipe, page 218)

Refer to: Making beef stock, page 102. Place turkey frame in large Dutch oven with water, onion, and salt. Bring to boiling; reduce heat and simmer, covered, 1½ hours. Remove turkey frame; cool till it can be handled. Remove meat from bones; discard bones. Remove onion from broth. Add turkey meat, tomatoes, thyme, and oregano to broth. Stir in fresh vegetables. Bring to boiling. Reduce heat; cover and simmer for 45 minutes. Add uncooked Homemade Noodles; simmer, uncovered, 8 to 10 minutes or till noodles are done. Makes 12 servings.

Mushroom Sauce

3 tablespoons butter *or* margarine
1½ cups sliced fresh mushrooms
2 tablespoons all-purpose flour
1 cup chicken broth (see tip, page 103)
1 tablespoon snipped parsley
1 teaspoon lemon juice
1 slightly beaten egg yolk
2 tablespoons milk

Refer to: Making white sauce, page 98. In saucepan melt butter. Add mushrooms; cook over medium-high heat about 5 minutes or till tender. Blend in flour. Add chicken broth. Cook, stirring constantly, till thickened and bubbly. Cook and stir 2 minutes more. Add parsley and lemon juice. Combine egg yolk and milk; stir egg yolk mixture into sauce. Cook and stir over low heat 2 minutes more. Season with salt and pepper. Serve with meat; garnish with snipped parsley, if desired. Makes about 1½ cups.

Mushroom Sauce on broiled steak

Bouillabaisse

- 1 pound small fresh *or* frozen lobster tails
- 1 pound fresh *or* frozen red snapper fillets *or* sole fillets
- 1 pound fresh *or* frozen cod fillets *or* haddock fillets
- 12 ounces fresh *or* frozen scallops
- 12 clams in shells
- 2 large onions, chopped (2 cups)
- ⅓ cup olive oil *or* cooking oil
- 6 cups fish stock* *or* water
- 1 28-ounce can tomatoes, cut up
- 2 small cloves garlic, minced
- 1 tablespoon salt
- 2 sprigs parsley
- 2 bay leaves
- 1½ teaspoons dried thyme, crushed
- ½ teaspoon thread saffron, crushed
- ⅛ teaspoon pepper
  French bread slices

Thaw shellfish and fish, if frozen. When lobster is partially thawed, split tails in half lengthwise; cut in half crosswise, to make 6 to 8 portions. Cut fish fillets into 2-inch pieces. Cut large scallops in half. Wash clams well.

In large saucepan or Dutch oven cook onions in hot oil till tender but not brown. Add the fish stock or water, the *undrained* tomatoes, garlic, salt, parsley, bay leaves, thyme, saffron, and pepper. Simmer, covered, for 30 minutes. Strain the seasoned stock into a large kettle, referring to step 5 on page 103. Discard the vegetables and herbs.

Bring the strained stock to boiling; add lobster and fish and cook 5 minutes. Add scallops and clams; boil about 5 minutes or till clams open. Serve in shallow bowls with French bread. Makes 6 to 8 servings.

*Note: To make fish stock, combine 6 cups water and one 1½-pound fresh *or* frozen dressed fish (with head and tail). Bring to boiling; reduce heat and simmer for 30 minutes. Strain; reserve the cooked fish for another use.

Golden Béchamel Sauce

- ¼ cup finely chopped onion
- 1 tablespoon butter *or* margarine
- 1 tablespoon all-purpose flour
- ½ teaspoon salt
  Dash white pepper
- 1¾ cups milk
- 3 slightly beaten egg yolks

Refer to: Making white sauce, page 98. Cook onion in butter till tender. Blend in flour, salt, and pepper. Add milk all at once. Cook and stir till thickened and bubbly. Cook and stir 2 minutes more. Stir *half* of the hot mixture into egg yolks, referring to steps 8 and 9 on page 109. Return all to pan. Cook and stir over low heat for 2 to 3 minutes. Serve immediately on cooked vegetables or poultry. Makes about 2¼ cups.

Wine Mornay Sauce

- 3 tablespoons butter *or* margarine
- 3 tablespoons all-purpose flour
- ½ teaspoon salt
- ⅛ teaspoon ground nutmeg
  Dash pepper
- 1¼ cups light cream
- ¼ cup dry white wine
- ⅓ cup shredded Swiss cheese

Refer to: Making white sauce, page 98. In saucepan melt butter; blend in flour, salt, nutmeg, and pepper. Add cream all at once. Cook and stir till thickened and bubbly; cook and stir 2 minutes more. Stir in wine. Add cheese; stir till melted. Serve with cooked chicken or poached eggs. Makes about 1¾ cups.

Velouté Sauce

- 2 tablespoons butter *or* margarine
- 3 tablespoons all-purpose flour
- 1 cup chicken broth (see tip, page 103)
- ⅓ cup light cream

Refer to: Making white sauce, page 98. In saucepan melt butter; blend in flour. Add broth and cream all at once. Cook and stir till thickened and bubbly; cook and stir 2 minutes more. Serve with cooked veal, poultry, or fish. Makes about 1⅓ cups.

Classic Béarnaise Sauce

- 3 tablespoons white wine vinegar
- 1 teaspoon finely chopped shallot *or* onion
- 4 whole black peppercorns, crushed
  Dash dried tarragon, crushed
  Dash dried chervil, crushed
- 1 tablespoon cold water
- 4 egg yolks
- ½ cup butter, softened
- 1 teaspoon snipped fresh tarragon *or* ¼ teaspoon dried tarragon, crushed

Refer to: Making hollandaise sauce, page 112. In saucepan mix vinegar, shallot or onion, peppercorns, the dash tarragon, and chervil. Bring to boiling; reduce heat and simmer till reduced to half. Strain, discarding solids; add the cold water to herb liquid.

Beat egg yolks in top of double boiler (not over water). Slowly add herb liquid. Add *2 tablespoons* of the butter to egg yolks; place over simmering water (upper pan should not touch water). Cook and stir till butter melts and sauce begins to thicken. Continue adding remaining butter, 2 tablespoons at a time, while stirring constantly. Cook and stir till sauce is the consistency of thick cream. Remove from heat. Stir in the 1 teaspoon fresh tarragon or ¼ teaspoon dried tarragon; salt to taste. Serve with cooked meat, poultry, or fish. Makes about ¾ cup.

115

TIP Many sauces are only variations of the basic sauces: *White Sauce, Brown Sauce, or Hollandaise (emulsified sauce).*

For example, Velouté Sauce is a white sauce made with chicken, fish, or veal stock instead of all milk. Mornay Sauce is a white sauce with cheese. Béarnaise Sauce is similar to Hollandaise but with added tarragon, shallots, and vinegar. Bordelaise is a brown sauce flavored by red wine, garlic, and shallots.

Sauces and Soups

Cream of Mushroom Soup

- 1 cup sliced fresh mushrooms
- 2 tablespoons chopped onion
- 2 tablespoons butter or margarine
- 2 tablespoons all-purpose flour
- 2 cups chicken broth, (see tip, page 103)
- 1 cup whipping cream
- ¼ teaspoon salt
- ¼ teaspoon ground nutmeg
- ⅛ teaspoon white pepper

Refer to: Making white sauce, page 98. Cook mushrooms and onion in butter or margarine about 5 minutes or till onion is tender but not brown. Stir in flour; add broth. Cook and stir till thickened and bubbly. Cook and stir 2 minutes more. Stir in cream, salt, nutmeg, and pepper. Heat through. Makes 4 to 6 servings.

116

Curried Vegetable Sauce

- 1 medium onion, finely chopped (½ cup)
- 1 small green pepper, finely slivered (½ cup)
- 2 tablespoons butter or margarine
- 1 tablespoon all-purpose flour
- 2 to 3 teaspoons curry powder
- ¼ teaspoon salt
- ½ cup milk
- ½ cup water
- 1 teaspoon instant chicken bouillon granules
- ½ teaspoon worcestershire sauce
- 2 tablespoons chopped pimiento

Refer to: Making white sauce, page 98. In a 1½-quart saucepan cook onion and green pepper in butter or margarine till tender but not brown. Stir in flour, curry powder, and salt. Add milk, water, chicken bouillon granules, and worcestershire sauce all at once. Cook over medium heat, stirring constantly, till mixture is thickened and bubbly. Stir in pimiento. Heat through. Serve over cooked pork, lamb, fish, green beans, or cauliflower. Makes 1½ cups sauce.

French Onion Soup

- 1½ pounds onions, thinly sliced (6 cups)
- ¼ cup butter or margarine
- 3 10½-ounce cans *condensed* beef broth
- 1 teaspoon worcestershire sauce
- ¼ teaspoon salt
  Dash pepper
- 6 to 8 slices French bread or hard rolls, toasted
  Grated parmesan cheese

In a covered 3-quart saucepan cook onions in butter about 20 minutes or till tender. Add *condensed* beef broth, worcestershire, salt, and pepper; bring to boiling.

Sprinkle toasted bread with parmesan; place under broiler till cheese is lightly browned. Ladle soup into bowls and float bread atop. (*Or,* place a bread slice on soup in each broiler-proof soup bowl; sprinkle with parmesan. Broil till cheese is lightly browned.) Serves 6 to 8.

Split Pea Soup

- 1 pound dry split peas
- 8 cups water
- 1 meaty ham bone *or* 2 ham hocks
- 1 large onion, chopped
- 1 teaspoon instant chicken bouillon granules
- ½ teaspoon salt
- ¼ teaspoon pepper
- 1 cup sliced carrot
- 1 cup chopped celery
- 2 slices bacon
- ½ cup light cream
- 2 tablespoons butter *or* margarine

Rinse peas; place in kettle. Add water, ham bone or hocks, onion, bouillon granules, salt, and pepper. Bring to boiling. Reduce heat; cover and simmer 1½ hours, stirring often.

Remove ham bone or hocks; remove and chop meat, referring to step 2 on page 102; discard bones. Return meat to soup; add carrot and celery. Simmer 30 minutes. Cook bacon till crisp; drain and crumble, referring to page 370. Stir bacon, light cream, and butter or margarine into soup; heat through. Makes 8 servings.

Cold Cucumber Soup

- 3 medium cucumbers
- 1 medium onion, chopped (½ cup)
- 2 bay leaves
- 3 cups chicken broth (see tip, page 103)
- 1 tablespoon all-purpose flour
- 1 teaspoon salt
- 1 cup light cream
- ⅓ cup dairy sour cream
- 2 tablespoons lemon juice
  Dash dried dillweed

Peel cucumbers; cut *two* of the cucumbers into slices. In saucepan combine the sliced cucumbers, onion, and bay leaves. Combine broth, flour, and salt; add to saucepan. Simmer, covered, for 20 to 30 minutes. Sieve mixture, referring to step 2 on page 111; chill well. Scoop out and discard seeds of remaining cucumber. Finely shred cucumber and add to chilled mixture. (*Or to use blender,* seed all cucumbers. Cut up two; cook as directed. Place cooked mixture and remaining cucumber in blender container; cover and blend till smooth. Chill.)

Stir light cream into sour cream; stir into chilled mixture along with lemon juice and dillweed. Garnish with additional dried dillweed, if desired. Makes 6 servings.

Cheese Chowder

- ¼ cup finely chopped onion
- 2 tablespoons butter *or* margarine
- ¼ cup all-purpose flour
- 2 cups milk
- 1 13¾-ounce can chicken broth *or* 1¾ cups chicken broth (see tip, page 103)
- 1 cup finely chopped carrot
- ¼ cup finely chopped celery
  Dash salt
  Dash paprika
- ½ cup cubed sharp American cheese (2 ounces)

Refer to: Making white sauce, page 98. In 2-quart saucepan cook onion in butter till tender. Blend in flour; add milk, chicken broth, carrot, celery, salt, and paprika. Cook and stir till bubbly. Cook and stir 2 minutes. Reduce heat; add cheese, stirring to melt. Simmer 15 minutes. Serves 4.

Broccoli Bisque

1¼ to 1½ pounds fresh broccoli, trimmed and cut up, *or* 2 10-ounce packages frozen chopped broccoli
2 13¾-ounce cans chicken broth *or* 3½ cups chicken broth (see tip, page 103)
1 medium onion, quartered
2 tablespoons butter *or* margarine
1 to 2 teaspoons curry powder
1 teaspoon salt
Dash pepper
2 tablespoons lime juice

In large saucepan combine fresh or frozen broccoli, broth, onion, butter or margarine, curry, salt, and pepper. Bring to boiling. Reduce heat; simmer, covered, 8 to 12 minutes or till broccoli is just tender.

Place half the broccoli-broth mixture in blender container. Cover; blend till smooth. Repeat with remaining. Stir in lime juice. Cover; refrigerate at least 4 hours. If desired, garnish each serving with lemon slice, dairy sour cream, and snipped chives. Serves 8.

Gazpacho

2½ cups tomato juice
1 10½-ounce can *condensed* beef broth
3 tablespoons lemon juice
2 tablespoons chopped onion
½ teaspoon salt
¼ teaspoon bottled hot pepper sauce
Dash freshly ground pepper
1 clove garlic, sliced lengthwise
1 small green pepper, finely chopped
1 medium cucumber, finely chopped
1 large tomato, peeled and finely chopped

In a 1-quart screw-top jar combine tomato juice, *condensed* broth, lemon juice, onion, salt, hot pepper sauce, and pepper; spear garlic on wooden pick and add to mixture in jar. Cover; shake well. Pour into bowl; stir in green pepper, cucumber, and tomato. Cover and chill 4 hours *or* place in freezer for about 1 hour (do not freeze).

Remove garlic. Stir, then spoon into soup bowls. Serves 8 to 10.

Broccoli Bisque

Borscht with Dumplings

1 ounce *dried* mushrooms (¾ cup)
3½ cups boiling water
2 pounds beets, peeled, thinly sliced, and quartered
4 cups water
1 cup chopped carrot
1 cup chopped celery
1 medium onion, chopped (½ cup)
2 bay leaves
1 teaspoon salt
2 tablespoons vinegar
1 teaspoon sugar
1 teaspoon salt
⅛ teaspoon pepper
Mushroom Dumplings

In saucepan combine mushrooms with boiling water. Let soak 2 hours at room temperature. Simmer, uncovered, 7 to 10 minutes or till tender. Drain; reserve liquid. Set mushrooms aside for Mushroom Dumplings.

In large saucepan combine beets, the 4 cups water, carrot, celery, onion, bay leaves, and the first 1 teaspoon salt. Cover and cook for 40 to 45 minutes or till vegetables are tender. Meanwhile, prepare Mushroom Dumplings. Remove bay leaves from vegetable mixture. Stir in reserved mushroom liquid, the vinegar, sugar, the remaining 1 teaspoon salt, and pepper. Bring to boil. Ladle into bowls; add hot Mushroom Dumplings to each serving. Makes 10 servings.

Mushroom Dumplings: Mix 1 cup all-purpose *flour,* 1 beaten *egg,* 2 to 3 tablespoons *water,* and ¼ teaspoon *salt.* Knead on floured surface till smooth and elastic. Cover; let stand 10 minutes. Meanwhile, cook 2 tablespoon chopped *onion* in 1 tablespoon *butter or margarine.* Chop the cooked dried mushrooms; stir into onion mixture with 1 *egg white,* 1 tablespoon *fine dry bread crumbs,* ¼ teaspoon *salt,* and dash *pepper.* Divide dough in half. Roll *each* half to ⅛-inch thickness; cut in 1½-inch squares. Top each square with ½ teaspoon of the mushroom mixture; fold the square in half diagonally to form a triangle. Seal. Cook in large amount of boiling salted water for 5 minutes.

Sauces and Soups

Asparagus-Potato Soup

- 3 medium potatoes, peeled and chopped (3 cups)
- 1 13¾-ounce can chicken broth *or* 1¾ cups chicken broth (see tip, page 103)
- ⅓ cup chopped onion
- 1 teaspoon salt
- ⅛ teaspoon ground nutmeg
- 1 10-ounce package frozen cut asparagus
- 1½ cups light cream
- 1 5-ounce jar neufchâtel cheese spread with pimiento *or* 1 4-ounce container whipped cream cheese with pimiento

In saucepan combine potatoes, chicken broth, onion, salt, and nutmeg. Bring to boiling. Reduce heat and simmer, covered, for 5 to 8 minutes or till potatoes are barely tender. Add frozen asparagus; return to boiling. Reduce heat; cover and simmer 5 minutes more or till vegetables are tender. Combine light cream and cheese; stir into soup mixture till melted (*do not boil*). Makes 4 to 6 servings.

Cream of Chicken Soup

- ¼ cup butter *or* margarine
- ⅓ cup all-purpose flour
- 2 10¾-ounce cans *condensed* chicken broth
- 2 cups milk
- 1 cup finely chopped cooked chicken *or* turkey
- Dash pepper
- Snipped chives, snipped parsley, *or* toasted slivered almonds (optional)

Refer to: Making white sauce, page 98. In 3-quart saucepan melt butter or margarine; blend in flour. Add *condensed* broth and milk all at once. Cook and stir till slightly thickened and bubbly; cook and stir 2 minutes longer. Stir in chicken or turkey and pepper; heat through. Serve immediately. If desired, garnish with snipped chives, parsley, or toasted slivered almonds. Makes 4 or 5 servings.

Horseradish-Mustard Sauce

- 1 tablespoon butter *or* margarine
- 2 tablespoons dijon-style mustard
- 1 tablespoon all-purpose flour
- 1 tablespoon prepared horseradish
- ¼ teaspoon salt
- Several drops bottled hot pepper sauce
- Dash pepper
- ½ cup chicken broth (see tip, page 103)
- ½ cup milk *or* light cream
- 2 teaspoons snipped chives
- 1 teaspoon lemon juice

Refer to: Making white sauce, page 98. In saucepan melt the butter or margarine; stir in the mustard, flour, horseradish, salt, hot pepper sauce, and pepper. Add the broth and milk or cream all at once. Cook and stir till thickened and bubbly; cook and stir 2 minutes more. Remove from heat; stir in the chives and lemon juice. Serve with beef. Makes about 1¼ cups.

Mulligatawny

- 4 cups chicken broth (see tip, page 103)
- 2 cups chopped cooked chicken
- 1 16-ounce can tomatoes, cut up
- 1 tart apple, peeled and chopped
- ¼ cup finely chopped onion
- ¼ cup chopped carrot
- ¼ cup chopped celery
- ¼ cup chopped green pepper
- 1 tablespoon snipped parsley
- 2 teaspoons lemon juice
- 1 teaspoon sugar
- 1 teaspoon curry powder
- 2 whole cloves
- ¾ teaspoon salt
- Dash pepper

In a 3-quart saucepan combine broth, chicken, *undrained* tomatoes, apple, onion, carrot, celery, green pepper, parsley, lemon juice, sugar, curry, cloves, salt, and pepper. Bring to boiling. Reduce heat; simmer, covered, for 20 minutes, stirring occasionally. Remove cloves. Makes 6 to 8 servings.

Sweet-and-Sour Sauce

- ½ cup packed brown sugar
- 1 tablespoon cornstarch
- ⅓ cup red wine vinegar
- ⅓ cup chicken broth (see tip, page 103)
- ¼ cup finely chopped green pepper
- 2 tablespoons chopped pimiento
- 1 tablespoon soy sauce
- ¼ teaspoon garlic powder
- ¼ teaspoon ground ginger

In saucepan combine brown sugar and cornstarch. Stir in vinegar, broth, green pepper, pimiento, soy, garlic powder, and ginger. Cook and stir till thickened and bubbly. Serve hot with meat or poultry. Makes about 1¼ cups.

Herbed Tomato Soup

- 2 tablespoons butter *or* margarine
- 2 tablespoons olive oil *or* cooking oil
- 2 medium onions, thinly sliced
- 2 pounds tomatoes (6 medium)
- 1 6-ounce can tomato paste
- 2 tablespoons snipped fresh basil *or* 2 teaspoons dried basil, crushed
- 4 teaspoons snipped fresh thyme *or* 1 teaspoon dried thyme, crushed
- 3 cups chicken broth (see tip, page 103)
- 1 teaspoon salt
- ⅛ teaspoon pepper

Refer to: Making sauce from fresh tomatoes, steps 2–7, page 106. In large saucepan heat butter and oil till butter melts. Add onions; cook till tender but not brown. Peel, core, and quarter tomatoes; add to saucepan. Stir in tomato paste, basil, and thyme; mash tomatoes slightly. Stir in chicken broth; bring to boiling. Reduce heat; cover and simmer for 40 minutes. Press through a food mill. (Or, place about 2 cups in blender container; cover and blend till pureed, referring to the tip on page 111. Repeat with remaining mixture.) Return to saucepan; stir in salt and pepper. Heat through. Garnish with celery leaves, if desired. Makes 8 servings.

118

Vegetable-Beef Soup

Vegetable-Beef Soup

- 3 pounds beef shank crosscuts
- 8 cups water
- 4 teaspoons salt
- ½ teaspoon dried oregano, crushed
- ¼ teaspoon dried marjoram, crushed
- 5 whole black peppercorns
- 2 bay leaves
- 4 ears corn *or* 1 10-ounce package frozen whole kernel corn
- 3 tomatoes, peeled and cut up
- 2 medium potatoes, peeled and cubed (2 cups)
- 1 cup fresh *or* frozen cut green beans
- 2 medium carrots, sliced (1 cup)
- 2 stalks celery, sliced (1 cup)
- 1 medium onion, chopped (½ cup)

Refer to: Making beef stock, page 102. In large kettle or Dutch oven combine beef crosscuts, water, salt, oregano, marjoram, peppercorns, and bay leaves. Bring mixture to boiling. Reduce heat; cover and simmer for 2 hours. Remove the beef. Cut meat from bones; chop meat. Strain broth; skim excess fat. Return broth to kettle. Cut fresh corn from cobs, referring to steps 1 and 2 on page 108. Add the chopped meat, fresh or frozen corn, tomatoes, potatoes, green beans, carrots, celery, and onion to broth. Simmer, covered, for 1 hour. Season to taste with salt and pepper. Serves 10 to 12.

119

Vichyssoise

- 4 leeks, sliced (without tops)
- 1 medium onion, sliced (½ cup)
- ¼ cup butter *or* margarine
- 5 medium potatoes, peeled and thinly sliced
- 4 cups chicken broth (see tip, page 103)
- 1 tablespoon salt
- 2 cups milk
- 2 cups light cream
- 1 cup whipping cream
  Snipped chives

In saucepan cook leeks and onion in butter or margarine till tender but not brown. Add potatoes, broth, and salt. Cook for 35 to 40 minutes. Referring to step 2 and the tip on page 111, rub through very fine sieve. (Or, place in blender container; cover and blend till smooth.)

Return to heat; add milk and light cream. Season to taste with salt and pepper. Bring to boiling; cool. Stir in whipping cream. Chill thoroughly before serving. Garnish with snipped chives. Makes 8 servings.

Sausage-and-Beef Chili

- 1½ pounds ground beef
- ½ pound bulk pork sausage
- 1 large onion, chopped (1 cup)
- 2 15½-ounce cans red kidney beans, drained
- 1 28-ounce can tomatoes, cut up
- 1 cup chopped green pepper
- 1 cup thinly sliced celery
- 1 6-ounce can tomato paste
- 2 cloves garlic, minced
- 2 teaspoons salt
- 2 teaspoons chili powder

In Dutch oven cook beef, sausage, and onion till meats are brown; drain off excess fat, referring to step 7 on page 28. Stir in beans, *undrained* tomatoes, green pepper, celery, tomato paste, garlic, salt, and chili powder. Cover; simmer 1 to 1½ hours, stirring occasionally. (For thinner chili, substitute one 8-ounce can tomato sauce for the tomato paste and do not drain the kidney beans.) Serves 10 to 12.

Sour Cream Gravy

- Hot meat or poultry drippings
- 1 tablespoon all-purpose flour
- ½ teaspoon salt
- ½ cup dairy sour cream

Refer to: Making pan gravy, page 100. After removing roasted meat or poultry to platter, pour the juices and fat into a glass measure. Skim off fat; return 2 tablespoons fat to pan. Blend flour into fat in pan. Cook 2 minutes. Add water to drippings to make 1 cup; stir into fat-flour mixture along with salt. Cook and stir till thickened and bubbly; cook and stir 2 minutes. Stir in sour cream. Heat through over low heat (*do not boil*). Makes about 1¼ cups.

Clockwise from left: New England Baked Beans (see recipe, page 132); Vegetable Stir-Fry (see recipe, page 142); Special Baked Potatoes, and Crumb-Topped Broccoli (see recipes, page 138).

VEGETABLES

Learn how to prepare tasty vegetables, from artichokes to zucchini, plus many favorites in between. The range of techniques in this section will show you how to simmer, bake, steam, scallop, stir-fry, and deep-fat fry some delicious vegetable specialties.

Preparing Fresh Vegetables

Technique: Preparing fresh vegetables

Tomatoes: 1 To peel tomatoes, dip tomato in boiling water about 30 seconds. Then plunge the tomato into cold water. **2** When cool, remove the loosened peel with knife. **3** To make tomato cups, cut a thin slice from top of tomato and scoop out seedy portion.

Asparagus: 4 Remove woody bases from asparagus stalks by breaking stalks instead of cutting. Stalk will snap easily where tender part begins.

Potatoes: 5 Before baking or cooking potatoes with the skins on, scrub them well with a vegetable brush. Remove any sprouts and green areas.

Corn: 6 To prepare corn on the cob, pull off the green husks. **7** Remove silks by hand, as shown, or scrub corn with stiff brush. Rinse with water to loosen silks.

Acorn Squash: 8 Wash squash and cut in half lengthwise. Remove seeds and strings with a spoon.

Cauliflower: 9 Rinse head of cauliflower under cold water and remove outer leaves. Cut out woody stem. **10** Break into flowerets, if desired. A knife may be needed to help loosen flowerets.

Green and Wax Beans: Wash beans in cold water; cut off ends and remove strings, if present. **11** To cut French-style, use the special cutter attached to vegetable peeler and pull bean through. *Or,* use a knife to cut beans end to end. **12** For smaller pieces, snap or cut fresh beans into 1-inch pieces.

1 An easy way to peel a tomato is to spear it with a fork and dip it into a pan of boiling water for about 30 seconds.

Immediately plunge the tomato into a pan of cold water to cool.

2 When tomato is cool, remove the loosened peel with a knife, as shown, or slip off the skin.

An alternate method of peeling tomatoes is to spear the tomato in stem end with a fork and rotate it over an open flame until the skin wrinkles slightly; cool and peel.

7 Remove the silks from the husked corn, using either your fingers or a stiff brush. Rinse with water to help loosen the silks.

8 Wash the squash and cut in half lengthwise. Use a spoon to remove the seeds and strings in the center cavity.

Squash also can be baked whole. After baking, cutting the squash and removing seeds and strings is easier.

3 To make tomato cups for filling, cut a thin slice from top of tomato and scoop out the center seedy portion with a spoon.

Tomatoes may be peeled before removing centers, if desired. Invert on paper toweling to drain.

4 Wash asparagus spears and scrape off scales with a knife. Remove woody base by breaking stalks. Stalk will snap easily where tender part begins.

5 When baking or cooking potatoes with the skins on, use a vegetable brush to scrub them well. Remove any sprouts and green areas. For baked potatoes, use fork tines to prick into the potato.

6 If corn on the cob must be stored, keep it, unhusked, in the coolest part of the refrigerator. When ready to prepare corn, pull off the green husks and silks, as shown.

123

9 Rinse the head of cauliflower under cold water and remove the outer green leaves. Using a knife, remove the woody stem.

10 Cook whole head of cauliflower or break into small pieces called flowerets. If necessary, use a knife to help loosen the flowerets.

11 Wash green or wax beans in cold water. Cut off ends and remove strings, if present. Leave beans whole or cut French-style using the special cutter attached to the vegetable peeler, as shown, or using a knife to slice beans end to end.

12 Another way to prepare green or wax beans is to snap fresh beans into 1-inch pieces. *Or,* use a knife to slice the beans into 1-inch lengths.

Vegetables

Broccoli

Technique: Simmering fresh vegetables

Broccoli
Salt
Water

1 Wash broccoli and remove the outer leaves and tough part of stalks. Cut broccoli stalks lengthwise into uniform spears, following branching lines. **2** Add salt to 1 inch of water in saucepan. Bring water to boiling. **3** Add broccoli spears to the boiling salted water. **4–5** Cover the saucepan and cook broccoli spears 10 to 15 minutes or till crisp-tender. **6** Drain broccoli in colander. Serve immediately, allowing about 1 pound fresh broccoli for 3 or 4 servings.

124

1 Wash broccoli and remove the outer leaves and tough part of stalks. Cut broccoli stalks lengthwise into uniform spears, following branching lines.

2 Pour about 1 inch of water into a saucepan that can be covered. Add salt to the water and bring the water to boiling.

Steamed Vegetables

Technique: Steaming fresh vegetables

2   cups thinly sliced carrots
2   large onions, cut in wedges
2   cups thinly sliced zucchini
16   ounces fresh mushrooms, halved
6   tablespoons butter *or* margarine
2   tablespoons lemon juice
¹/₂   teaspoon salt
¹/₂   teaspoon dried marjoram, crushed
¹/₈   teaspoon freshly ground pepper

1 Place carrots and onion wedges in steamer basket. **2** Place basket over boiling water. Cover and steam for 8 minutes. **3–4** Add sliced zucchini; cover and steam 8 to 10 minutes more or till tender. **5** Meanwhile, in large skillet cook mushrooms in butter or margarine about 5 minutes or just till tender. Add lemon juice, salt, marjoram, and pepper. **6** Add steamed vegetables to mushrooms in skillet and stir gently to mix. Turn into serving bowl; spoon juices over vegetables. Makes 12 servings.

1 Place the thinly sliced carrots and onion wedges in a steamer basket. The steamer basket will prevent the vegetables from coming in contact with the liquid.

2 Place the basket of vegetables over (but not touching) boiling water in a saucepan. Cover the saucepan and steam vegetables for 8 minutes.
Since carrots and onions need the longest cooking time, they are started first.

3 When water is boiling, add the broccoli spears to the salted water.

If desired, broccoli can be cut up and cooked. For cut-up broccoli, cut off the buds and set aside. Cut the remaining part of the stalk into 1-inch pieces. Add the pieces to boiling salted water.

4 Cover the saucepan and cook the whole spears 10 to 15 minutes or till crisp-tender.

For cut-up broccoli, cook the stalks 5 to 8 minutes. Then add the reserved broccoli buds and cook about 5 minutes longer.

5 To test broccoli for tenderness, insert a fork in the stalk portion of the broccoli. When done, the broccoli will be crisp, but tender.

6 Turn broccoli and cooking liquid into a colander placed in the sink. Drain thoroughly to remove any liquid. Serve immediately while hot. Add butter, salt, and pepper, if desired.

125

3 Add the sliced zucchini to the partially cooked carrots and onions in the steamer basket. Replace the cover and steam 8 to 10 minutes more or till tender.

4 To test vegetables for tenderness, insert a fork in several of the slices. Vegetables still should be slightly crisp.

5 While vegetables are steaming, in a large skillet cook mushrooms in butter or margarine about 5 minutes or just till tender, stirring occasionally. Add the lemon juice, salt, marjoram, and pepper.

6 When both the steamed vegetables and mushrooms are tender, add the steamed vegetables to the mushrooms in skillet and stir gently to mix. Turn mixture into a serving bowl and spoon juices from the skillet over the vegetables.

If desired, this recipe can be easily cut in half.

COOKING FRESH VEGETABLES

VEGETABLE	PREPARATION	COOKING DIRECTIONS	COOKING TIME
Artichokes	Wash; trim stems; cut off 1 inch of top. Remove loose outer leaves; snip off sharp leaf tips. Brush lemon juice on cut edges.	In large covered kettle simmer in large amount boiling salted water till leaf pulls out easily. Drain upside down.	20–30 min.
Asparagus	Wash and scrape off scales. Break off woody bases where spears snap easily. Leave whole.	Cook whole spears, covered, in a small amount of boiling salted water. Prop tips up out of water with crumpled foil. Or, fasten spears in bundle; stand upright in deep kettle so tips extend 2 to 3 inches above boiling salted water.	10–15 min. (whole)
	Or, cut up asparagus spears.	Cook, covered, in a small amount of boiling salted water.	8–10 min. (cut up)
Beans, Green and Wax	Wash; remove ends and strings. Leave whole or cut in 1-inch pieces. Or, slice end to end for French-style beans.	Cook, covered, in a small amount of boiling salted water till crisp-tender.	20–30 min. (whole or cut up) 10–12 min. (French-style)
Beets	Cut off all but 1 inch of stems and root. Wash. Do not peel whole beets.	Cook, covered, in boiling salted water till tender. Cool slightly; slip off skins.	35–50 min. (whole)
	Or, peel beets; slice or cube.	Cook, covered, in a small amount of boiling salted water.	15–20 min. (sliced or cubed)
Broccoli	Wash; remove outer leaves and tough part of stalks. Cut lengthwise into uniform spears, following the branching lines.	Cook, covered, in 1 inch of boiling salted water till crisp-tender.	10–15 min. (spears)
	Or, cut off buds; set aside. Cut remaining stalk into 1-inch pieces.	Cook, covered, in boiling salted water for 5 to 8 minutes. Add reserved buds and cook about 5 minutes longer.	10–13 min. total (cut up)
Brussels Sprouts	Trim stems. Remove wilted leaves; wash. Cut large sprouts in half lengthwise.	Cook, covered, in a small amount of boiling salted water till crisp-tender.	10–15 min.
Cabbage	Remove wilted outer leaves; wash. Cut into wedges; remove center core. Or, shred.	Cook, uncovered, in a small amount of boiling salted water for first few minutes. Cover; cook till crisp-tender.	10–12 min. (wedges) 5–7 min. (shredded)
Carrots	Wash, trim, and peel or scrub. Leave tiny ones whole; for larger carrots, slice, dice, shred, or cut in strips.	Cook, covered, in 1 inch of boiling salted water just till tender.	10–20 min. (whole or cut up) 5 min. (shredded)
Cauliflower	Wash. Remove leaves and woody stem. Leave whole or break into flowerets.	Cook, covered, in a small amount of boiling salted water till just tender.	20 min. (whole) 10–15 min. (flowerets)
Celery	Cut off leaves. Separate stalks. Slice.	Cook, covered, in a small amount of boiling salted water till just tender.	10–15 min.
Corn	Remove husks. Remove silks with stiff brush. Rinse. Cook whole.	Cook, covered, in a small amount of boiling salted water till done.	6–8 min.
	Or, cut off the tips of kernels. Scrape cobs with dull edge of knife.	Cook, covered, in a small amount of boiling salted water till done.	12–15 min.

126

VEGETABLE	PREPARATION	COOKING DIRECTIONS	COOKING TIME
Eggplant	Wash; cut off cap. Peel, if desired. Cut into ½-inch-thick slices.	Sauté on both sides in hot cooking oil.	About 2 min. per side
Kohlrabi	Cut off leaves; wash, peel, and chop or slice.	Cook, covered, in a small amount of boiling salted water till tender.	About 25 min.
Mushrooms	Rinse gently; pat dry. Leave whole, chop, or slice through cap and stem.	Add to melted butter in skillet. Cover and cook slowly; stir occasionally.	About 5 min. (sliced)
Okra	Wash pods. Cut off stems.	Cook, covered, in a small amount of boiling salted water till tender.	8–15 min.
Onions	Peel; cut in quarters. Or, leave small onions whole; cut off ends.	Cook, covered, in boiling salted water till tender.	25–30 min.
Parsnips	Wash; peel or scrape. Leave whole, cut in half, slice, or cut in strips.	Cook, covered, in a small amount of boiling salted water till tender.	25–40 min. (whole) 15–20 min. (cut up)
Peas	Shell and wash.	Cook, covered, in a small amount of boiling salted water till just tender.	10–12 min.
Potatoes	Scrub thoroughly; remove any sprouts or green areas. Cook with skin. Or, wash and peel. Cook whole, quartered, or cubed.	Cook, covered, in boiling salted water till tender.	25–40 min. (whole) 20–25 min. (quartered) 10–15 min. (cubed or tiny new potatoes)
	To bake, prick unpeeled potatoes.	Bake in 425° oven till done. Or, wrap in foil and bake in 350° oven till done.	40–60 min. (425°) 1½ hours (350°, wrapped)
Rutabagas	Wash; peel. Slice or cube.	Cook, covered, in a small amount of boiling salted water till just tender.	20–35 min.
Spinach	Wash several times in pan of lukewarm water, lifting out of water each time and discarding water.	Cook, covered, in very small amount of water. Reduce heat when steam forms. Turn with fork frequently.	3–5 min. after steam forms.
Squash, Winter **Summer (cook as Zucchini)**	Wash; cut in half; remove seeds and strings. Cut each half into serving-size pieces.	Place, cut side down, in baking pan. Cover; bake in 350° oven for 30 minutes. Turn cut side up; bake, covered, 20 to 30 minutes more for acorn, buttercup, or butternut squash; 45 to 50 minutes more for hubbard, banana, or spaghetti squash.	50–80 min. total
Sweet Potatoes	Scrub. Cut off woody portions and ends. Peel, or cook in jackets, depending on use.	Cook, covered, in enough boiling salted water to cover until tender. Or, bake whole potatoes in jackets in 375° oven.	30–40 min. (boiled) 40–45 min. (baked)
Tomatoes	Wash; remove stems. Peel. Cut up or cook whole.	In tightly covered pan cook slowly without added water. Season.	10–15 min.
Turnips	Wash; peel. Slice or cube.	Cook, covered, in a small amount of boiling salted water till just tender.	10–20 min.
Zucchini	Wash; do not peel. Cut off ends. Slice.	Cook, covered, in a small amount of boiling salted water till crisp-tender.	5–10 min.

Vegetables

Twice-Baked Potatoes

Technique: Baking potatoes

4	**medium baking potatoes**
2	**tablespoons butter** *or* **margarine**
	Milk
	Salt and pepper
1	**2-ounce can chopped mushrooms, drained**
2	**slices American cheese, halved diagonally**
	Paprika

128

1 Scrub potatoes thoroughly and use fork tines to prick into the potatoes. Bake in 425° oven for 40 to 60 minutes or till done. **2** Cut a lengthwise slice from top of each potato. **3** Discard skin from the slice. **4** Reserving potato shells, scoop out the insides with a spoon and add to potato portions from top slices. **5** Mash potato. Add butter. Beat in enough milk to make a stiff consistency. Season to taste with salt and pepper. **6** Stir in mushrooms. **7** Pile mashed potato mixture into potato shells. Place in 10×6×2-inch baking dish. Return to 425° oven and bake for 20 to 25 minutes or till lightly browned. **8** Place cheese atop potatoes; sprinkle with paprika. Bake 2 to 3 minutes longer or till cheese melts. Makes 4 servings.

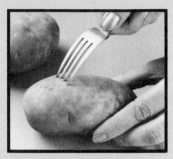

1 Scrub potato skins thoroughly with a vegetable brush. Remove any sprouts and green areas. Use fork tines to prick into the potatoes. Bake potatoes in 425° oven for 40 to 60 minutes or till done.

5 Mash potato mixture with a potato masher. Add the 2 tablespoons butter or margarine. Beat in enough milk to make a stiff consistency. Season to taste with salt and pepper.

2 Let potatoes cool, if desired. Then cut a lengthwise slice from the top of each potato, as shown. Be sure to protect your fingers if you are working with potatoes straight from the oven.

3 Carefully peel the skin off the slice cut from the top of each potato. Discard skin and place potato in bowl.

4 Using a spoon, scoop out the inside of the potato and add to potato portion from top slices. Set the potato shells aside while preparing filling mixture.

TIP To bake potatoes in foil, *scrub potatoes thoroughly with a vegetable brush. Remove any sprouts and green areas. Use fork tines to prick into the potatoes. Wrap potatoes in foil. Bake in a 350° oven for 1½ hours or till done. This method gives a moist, almost steamed potato.*

129

6 Stir the drained, chopped mushrooms into the seasoned mashed potato mixture. Use a wooden spoon and stir carefully to avoid breaking mushrooms.

7 Pile the mashed potato-mushroom mixture into the reserved potato shells. Place filled potatoes in 10×6×2-inch baking dish. Return to 425° oven and bake for 20 to 25 minutes or till potato filling is lightly browned.

8 Place a cheese triangle atop each filled potato. Sprinkle paprika over the cheese. Bake in 425° oven 2 to 3 minutes longer or just till the cheese melts. Serve immediately.

Vegetables

Scalloped Potatoes

Technique: Making scalloped potatoes

  6 **to 8 medium potatoes**
  ¼ **cup finely chopped onion**
  ⅓ **cup all-purpose flour**
1½ **teaspoons salt**
  ⅛ **teaspoon pepper**
  2 **cups milk**

130

1 Peel potatoes. **2** Thinly slice potatoes; measure 6 cups. **3** Place *half* of the potatoes in a greased 2-quart casserole. Add *half* the onion. **4** Sift *half* the flour over vegetables in casserole; sprinkle with *half* the salt and pepper. Repeat layers. **5** Pour milk over all. **6–7** Cover and bake in a 350° oven for 1¼ hours. Uncover and continue baking 15 to 30 minutes longer or till potatoes are done. Makes 6 servings.

1 Peel the medium potatoes using a vegetable peeler or sharp knife. Remember to cut in a direction away from your hands when using sharp utensils. Remove all sprouts and green areas.

  If desired, peel potatoes onto a piece of waxed paper or paper toweling to catch peelings and make clean-up easier.

5 Pour the 2 cups milk evenly over potatoes, onion, flour, and seasonings in casserole. Mixture will thicken as it cooks.

2 Immerse the peeled potatoes in a bowl of cold water until you are ready to slice them. This helps prevent darkening of the cut surfaces.

Cut potatoes into thin slices using a sharp knife on a wooden cutting board. You'll need about 6 cups sliced potatoes.

3 For easier cleanup, grease a 2-quart casserole with shortening. Place half of the potatoes in casserole. Sprinkle half of the onion over top.

4 Although the flour does not have to be sifted before measuring, a sifter is a good way to evenly distribute it over the vegetables in the casserole. If you don't have a sifter, use a sieve or spoon.

Sprinkle with half the flour, salt, and pepper. Repeat layers, beginning with potatoes and onion, and ending with flour, salt, and pepper.

TIP To prepare au gratin potatoes, *in sauce-pan melt 3 tablespoons butter or margarine; blend in 2 tablespoons all-purpose flour, 1½ teaspoons salt, ½ teaspoon dry mustard, ½ teaspoon worcestershire sauce, and ⅛ teaspoon pepper. Add 3 cups milk. Cook and stir till slightly thickened and bubbly. Remove from heat. Stir in 1 cup shredded Swiss cheese till melted.*

Stir in 6 cups thinly sliced potatoes; one 4-ounce jar sliced pimiento, chopped; and ¼ cup finely chopped onion. Bake, covered, in 2½-quart casserole in 350° oven for 45 minutes.

Melt 2 tablespoons butter. Toss with 1½ cups soft bread crumbs. Sprinkle crumbs atop potatoes. Bake, uncovered, 30 minutes more. Makes 6 servings.

For crumb-topped scalloped potatoes, *prepare recipe at left. Sprinkle top with 3 tablespoons buttered fine, dry bread crumbs when cover is removed in step 6.*

131

6 Cover casserole and bake in a 350° oven for 1¼ hours. (Use foil if the casserole does not have a lid.) Uncover and continue baking 15 to 30 minutes longer or till potatoes are done.

7 To test for doneness, insert a fork into potatoes. Potatoes are done when fork can be easily inserted, but does not break potatoes apart.

Vegetables

1 Rinse beans by shaking, half at a time, in strainer under cold running water. In heavy 3-quart saucepan combine beans and 8 cups cold water; cover and soak overnight.

To speed preparation, bring beans in water to boiling; boil 2 minutes. Remove from heat; cover. Soak 1 hour.

New England Baked Beans   (pictured on page 120)

Technique: Making baked beans

- **1   pound dry navy beans *or* dry northern beans (2⅓ cups)**
- **8   cups cold water**
- **½   teaspoon salt**
- **4   ounces salt pork, cut up**
- **1   large onion, chopped**
- **½   cup molasses**
- **⅓   cup packed brown sugar**
- **1   teaspoon dry mustard**
- **½   teaspoon salt**
- **⅛   teaspoon pepper**

1–2 Rinse beans. In heavy 3-quart saucepan combine beans and 8 cups water. Cover; soak overnight. (*Or,* bring to boiling; boil 2 minutes. Remove from heat; cover and let soak 1 hour.) Add ½ teaspoon salt to beans and soaking water. Bring to boiling. Reduce heat and simmer, covered, 1 hour or till tender.

3 Drain beans, reserving liquid. **4** In 2½-quart bean pot or casserole combine the beans, salt pork, and onion. **5** Stir in *1 cup* of the reserved bean liquid, molasses, brown sugar, mustard, ½ teaspoon salt, and pepper. **6** Cover and bake in 300° oven for 2½ hours or to desired thickness, stirring occasionally. Add additional reserved bean liquid, if necessary. Makes 6 to 8 servings.

132

4 Pour the well-drained beans into a 2½-quart bean pot or casserole. Add the cut-up salt pork and the chopped onion.

2 *Do not drain beans.* Add ½ teaspoon salt to beans and water. Bring to boiling. Reduce heat; simmer, covered, 1 hour or till tender. To test beans for doneness, remove a few beans from the saucepan. Press bean between thumb and forefinger. Bean will feel soft when it is done.

3 To drain, pour beans and liquid through a colander or strainer placed over a bowl to reserve the cooking liquid.

133

5 Stir in *1 cup* of the reserved bean liquid, the molasses, brown sugar, mustard, ½ teaspoon salt, and the pepper. Save remaining bean liquid.

6 Cover bean pot or casserole and bake in 300° oven for 2½ hours or till beans cook to desired thickness. Stir the mixture occasionally. If necessary, add additional reserved bean liquid during baking to keep beans from drying out.

TIP To prepare beans in an electric slow crockery cooker, *use ingredients as listed at left. Rinse beans. In saucepan bring beans, water, and ½ teaspoon salt to boiling; reduce heat. Simmer, covered, 1½ hours. Pour into bowl; cover, as shown in top photo. Chill overnight.*

Drain beans, reserving 1 cup liquid; place in an electric slow crockery cooker. Add reserved cooking liquid, as shown in bottom photo. Stir in salt pork, onion, molasses, brown sugar, mustard, ½ teaspoon salt, and pepper. Cover and cook on low-heat setting for 12 to 14 hours. Stir before serving.

Vegetables

Asparagus-Tomato Stir-Fry

Technique: Stir-frying vegetables

- **1   pound fresh asparagus**
- **1   tablespoon cold water**
- **1   teaspoon cornstarch**
- **2   teaspoons soy sauce**
- **¼   teaspoon salt**
- **1   tablespoon cooking oil**
- **4   green onions, bias-sliced into 1-inch lengths**
- **1½ cups sliced fresh mushrooms**
- **2   small tomatoes, cut in thin wedges**

Snap off and discard woody bases from asparagus. Bias-slice asparagus crosswise into 1½-inch lengths; set aside. (If asparagus stalks are not slender and young, cook pieces in small amount of boiling salted water for about 5 minutes; drain well.) **1** Blend water into cornstarch. **2** Stir soy sauce and salt into cornstarch mixture; set aside. **3** Preheat a wok or large skillet (see tip at right) over high heat; add cooking oil.

4–5 Stir-fry asparagus and green onions in hot oil for 4 minutes. **6** Add mushrooms; stir-fry 1 minute more. **7** Push vegetables from center of wok. **8** Stir soy mixture again. **9** Add soy mixture to wok; stir into vegetables. Cook and stir till mixture is thickened and bubbly. **10** Add tomatoes and heat through. Serve at once. Makes 6 servings.

134

1 In a small bowl or custard cup stir together the 1 tablespoon cold water and the cornstarch till thoroughly blended.

2 Stir the soy sauce and salt into the cornstarch-water mixture. Set mixture aside.

To ensure that it will be ready to use when needed, this seasoning mixture is prepared before any of the vegetables are cooked.

6 Add the sliced fresh mushrooms to the other vegetables in the wok. Stir-fry mixture 1 minute longer, frequently lifting and turning food for even cooking.

7 Using the long-handled spoon or spatula, push the stir-fried vegetable mixture from the center of the wok or skillet, as shown.

3 Place the wok ring stand over the largest burner on your range. *For gas ranges,* place the ring with wide end down. *For electric ranges,* place the ring with wide end up. Set the wok securely on the ring stand and warm over high heat. Add cooking oil and heat a few minutes more.

If desired, use a large skillet, as directed in tip at right.

4 Add bias-sliced asparagus and green onions to hot oil in wok. When using green onions, be sure to include the green tops.

5 Stir-fry the mixture for 4 minutes over high heat. To stir-fry, use a long-handled spoon or spatula to turn and lift the food with a folding motion.

This quick cooking is the secret to achieving the desired crisp-tender texture.

135

TIP Use a skillet if you don't own a traditional Oriental cooking wok. *Choose a large heavy skillet for even heating. A skillet with deep sides will make stirring easier.*

Use a wide spatula to stir the mixture and to keep the food moving constantly for more even cooking.

8 Stir the soy-cornstarch mixture to recombine the ingredients. This is necessary to evenly distribute the cornstarch, which will have settled to bottom of the bowl.

9 Add the soy-cornstarch mixture to the center of the wok. Let mixture bubble slightly before stirring it into vegetables. Cook and stir till mixture is thickened and bubbly.

10 Add the thin tomato wedges to thickened mixture in wok. Heat mixture through. Serve at once, since vegetables will overcook if allowed to stand.

Vegetables

French Fries

Technique: Deep-fat frying vegetables

Baking potatoes
Shortening or cooking oil for deep-fat frying

1 Peel potatoes. **2** Cut potatoes lengthwise into ⅜-inch-wide strips. **3** Heat shortening or oil in saucepan or deep-fat fryer to 360°. **4** Dry potatoes with paper toweling. **5** Fry potatoes, a few at a time, in deep hot fat (360°) for 6 to 7 minutes or till crisp and golden brown. **6** Drain on paper toweling.

7 For crisper French fries, fry potatoes at 360° about 5 minutes or till lightly browned. Drain on paper toweling and cool. Just before serving, return French fries to fat at 360° for 2 minutes more; drain again. **8** Sprinkle potatoes immediately with salt. Serve the potatoes at once.

1 Peel the baking potatoes using a vegetable peeler or sharp knife. Cut in a direction away from your hands when using sharp utensils. Remove all sprouts and spots.

If desired, peel potatoes onto a piece of waxed paper or paper toweling to catch peelings and make clean-up easier.

5 Place potatoes, a few at a time, in a frying basket and lower into the deep hot fat. Fry potatoes at 360° for 6 to 7 minutes or till crisp and golden brown. Adjust heat to maintain fat temperature of 360°.

If a frying basket is not available, carefully drop potatoes directly into fat; remove with a slotted spoon.

2 Immerse the peeled potatoes in a bowl of cold water until you are ready to cut them. This helps prevent darkening of cut surfaces.

Cut potatoes lengthwise into ⅜-inch-wide strips using a knife or French fry cutter. Return potato strips to bowl of cold water till ready to fry.

3 Melt shortening in a deep saucepan or deep-fat fryer. Heat shortening or oil to 360° using a deep-fat frying thermometer to check the temperature.

For more information on deep-fat frying, see tip on page 63.

4 Before frying in the hot fat, drain potatoes thoroughly and pat dry with paper toweling.

If potatoes are wet when added to fryer or skillet, the fat will splatter. To avoid this, pat potatoes as dry as possible.

137

TIP To make fried onion rings, *cut 6 medium Bermuda or mild white onions into slices ¼ inch thick. Separate slices into rings.*

In a bowl combine 1 slightly beaten egg, 1 cup milk, and 2 tablespoons cooking oil; add 1 cup plus 2 tablespoons all-purpose flour and ½ teaspoon salt. Beat mixture together just till dry ingredients are well moistened.

Using a fork, dip onion rings in batter; drain off excess. Add to deep hot fat (375°), as shown above. Fry rings, a few at a time, stirring once with fork to separate rings. When onions are golden brown, remove from fat and drain on paper toweling. Sprinkle with salt just before serving.

6 When potatoes are golden brown, remove basket from deep hot fat. Spread potatoes on a pan or baking sheet that is lined with paper toweling. Drain thoroughly. Sprinkle potatoes with salt while hot.

7 For crisper French fries, fry potatoes at 360° only 5 minutes or till lightly browned. Drain on paper toweling and cool. Just before serving, return French fries to 360° fat for 2 minutes more or till potatoes are crisp and golden brown.

8 Remove potatoes from hot fat and spread them out on a pan or baking sheet that is lined with paper toweling. Drain thoroughly. Sprinkle potatoes with salt and serve at once.

Vegetables

Crumb-Topped Broccoli
(pictured on page 120)

4 slices bread
1½ pounds broccoli *or* 2 10-ounce
    packages frozen broccoli
    spears
6 tablespoons butter *or* margarine
¼ cup grated parmesan cheese
½ teaspoon lemon juice

Process bread slices in blender or food processor just till coarse crumbs are formed. Spread crumbs in shallow baking pan. Bake in 350° oven for 15 minutes or till toasted.

Meanwhile, prepare and cook broccoli spears as directed in chart on page 126. (Or, cook frozen broccoli according to package directions.) Drain well. Toss with *2 tablespoons* of the butter or margarine. Place broccoli on serving platter; keep warm.

Melt the remaining *4 tablespoons* butter; stir in the toasted bread crumbs, parmesan cheese, and the lemon juice. Spoon crumb mixture around broccoli on serving platter. Makes 6 servings.

Special Baked Potatoes
(pictured on page 120)

4 medium baking potatoes
½ cup dairy sour cream
½ teaspoon salt
1 tablespoon snipped chives *or*
    sliced green onion tops

Refer to: Baking potatoes, page 128. Scrub; prick into the potatoes with a fork. Bake in 425° oven for 40 to 60 minutes or till done. Cut a lengthwise slice from the top of each potato; discard skin from slice. Reserving potato shells, scoop out the insides and add to potato portions from top slices. Mash potato. Beat in sour cream, salt, and dash *pepper* till fluffy.

Pile mashed potato mixture into potato shells. Place in 10×6×2-inch baking dish. Bake in 425° oven 20 to 25 minutes or till heated through. Sprinkle with paprika, if desired; garnish each potato with chives or green onion tops. Makes 4 servings.

Note: If made ahead and chilled, add 5 to 10 minutes to baking time.

Cheddar-Squash Bake

2 pounds yellow crookneck summer
    squash *or* zucchini
1 cup dairy sour cream
2 beaten egg yolks
2 tablespoons all-purpose flour
2 stiff-beaten egg whites
1½ cups shredded cheddar cheese
4 slices bacon, crisp-cooked,
    drained, and crumbled
⅓ cup fine dry bread crumbs
1 tablespoon butter *or* margarine,
    melted

Scrub squash; cut off ends. Do not peel. Slice to make 6 cups. Cook, covered, in small amount of boiling salted water 15 to 20 minutes or till tender. Drain well; sprinkle with salt.

Mix sour cream, egg yolks, and flour; fold in egg whites. In a 12× 7½×2-inch baking dish layer *half* the squash, *half* the egg mixture, and *half* the cheese; sprinkle bacon atop. Repeat layers of squash, egg, and cheese. Combine crumbs and butter or margarine; sprinkle atop. Bake, uncovered, in 350° oven for 20 to 25 minutes. Top with additional bacon and parsley, if desired. Makes 8 to 10 servings.

Baked Bean Quintet

6 slices bacon
1 cup chopped onion
1 clove garlic, minced
1 18-ounce jar baked beans in
    brown sugar sauce
1 17-ounce can lima beans, drained
1 16-ounce can dark red kidney
    beans, drained
1 16-ounce can butter beans,
    drained
1 15-ounce can garbanzo beans,
    drained
¾ cup catsup
¼ cup packed brown sugar
½ teaspoon dry mustard
¼ teaspoon pepper

In 12-inch skillet cook bacon till crisp; drain, reserving 2 tablespoons drippings. Crumble bacon and set aside. In same skillet cook onion and garlic in reserved drippings till onion is tender but not brown. Stir in crumbled bacon, baked beans in sauce, lima beans, kidney beans, butter beans, garbanzo beans, catsup, brown sugar, dry mustard, and pepper. Turn into a 2-quart casserole. Bake, covered, in 375° oven 1 to 1¼ hours or till heated through. Makes 12 to 14 servings.

Green Beans
Amandine

Broccoli-Zucchini Deluxe

2 cups chopped fresh broccoli (8 ounces)
2 cups chopped unpeeled zucchini (8 ounces)
½ cup chopped onion
1 clove garlic, minced
2 tablespoons butter *or* margarine
3 tablespoons all-purpose flour
2 tablespoons snipped parsley
½ teaspoon salt
½ teaspoon dried oregano, crushed
¾ cup milk
1½ cups ricotta *or* cream-style cottage cheese
8 ounces spinach noodles, cooked, drained, and buttered
Grated parmesan cheese

In medium saucepan combine broccoli and zucchini; cook, covered, in a small amount of boiling salted water about 8 to 10 minutes or till tender. Drain well.

In large saucepan cook onion and garlic in butter or margarine till onion is tender but not brown. Blend in flour, parsley, salt, and oregano. Add milk all at once. Cook and stir till thickened and bubbly. Add ricotta cheese. Cook and stir till cheese is nearly melted. Stir in cooked vegetables; heat through. Serve over hot cooked noodles. Pass parmesan. Makes 4 to 6 servings.

Green Beans Amandine

1 pound green beans
2 tablespoons slivered almonds
2 tablespoons butter *or* margarine
1 teaspoon lemon juice

Cut green beans French-style, referring to step 11 on page 123. Cook as directed in chart on page 126; drain.

Meanwhile, in saucepan cook slivered almonds in butter or margarine over low heat, stirring occasionally, till golden. Remove from heat; add lemon juice. Pour over beans. Serves 4.

Springtime Peas

3 to 6 lettuce leaves
2 cups shelled peas *or* 1 10-ounce package frozen peas
¼ cup sliced green onion
1 teaspoon sugar
½ teaspoon salt
Dash pepper
Dash dried thyme, crushed
1 tablespoon butter *or* margarine

Moisten lettuce leaves, leaving a few drops of water clinging. Line bottom of a 10-inch skillet with lettuce leaves. Top with fresh or frozen peas and green onion. Sprinkle with sugar, salt, pepper, and thyme.

Cover tightly and cook over low heat 18 to 20 minutes or till peas are tender. Remove lettuce. Drain peas well; dot with butter or margarine. Serves 4.

Cranberry-Potato Boats

3 large sweet potatoes
½ cup cranberry-orange relish
¼ cup raisins
⅓ cup packed brown sugar
½ teaspoon salt
3 tablespoons butter *or* margarine
¼ cup broken walnuts

Prepare sweet potatoes and cook in jackets in boiling salted water as directed in chart on page 127. Remove skins. Cut potatoes in half lengthwise. Scoop out centers; set the potato shells aside.

Combine the scooped-out potato with the relish; whip till fluffy. Stir in raisins. Pile into shells. Combine sugar and salt; cut in butter or margarine. Stir in nuts. Sprinkle sugar mixture over filled potatoes. Bake in 350° oven about 30 minutes or till hot. Makes 6 servings.

Asparagus Supreme

4 cups fresh asparagus, cut up, *or* 2 8-ounce packages frozen cut asparagus
1 10¾-ounce can condensed cream of shrimp soup
½ cup dairy sour cream
2 tablespoons coarsely shredded carrot
1 teaspoon grated onion
⅛ teaspoon pepper
½ cup herb-seasoned stuffing mix
1 tablespoon butter *or* margarine, melted

Cook fresh asparagus as directed in chart on page 126. (Or, cook frozen asparagus according to package directions.) Drain well. Combine soup, sour cream, carrot, onion, and pepper; fold in asparagus. Turn into a 1-quart baking dish.

Combine the stuffing mix and melted butter or margarine; sprinkle around edge of asparagus mixture. Bake, uncovered, in 350° oven for 30 to 35 minutes. Makes 4 to 6 servings.

139

TIP Cooking vegetables in a microwave oven *is an excellent way to retain their color, flavor, and nutritional content. Not only can you micro-cook fresh vegetables, but frozen and canned vegetables are easily prepared, too. Consult your owner's manual for specific cooking times and directions. Remember to cook vegetables till they are almost done, since their stored heat will finish the cooking.*

You also can save time when micro-cooking certain vegetables, such as potatoes. Two 8-ounce baking potatoes take 6 to 8 minutes; four potatoes take 13 to 15 minutes. Prick into potatoes with fork and arrange on paper toweling. Rearrange halfway through cooking.

Vegetables

Vegetable Skillet

- 4 ears corn *or* 1 10-ounce package frozen whole kernel corn
- 2 tablespoons butter *or* margarine
- 1 pound zucchini, sliced (4½ cups)
- ½ cup chopped onion
- ⅓ cup chopped green pepper
- ¾ teaspoon salt
- ½ teaspoon dried dillweed

Prepare fresh corn referring to steps 6–7 on page 123. Cut corn from cob; do not scrape cob.

In skillet melt butter or margarine; stir in corn, zucchini, onion, green pepper, salt, and dillweed. Cook, covered, 12 to 15 minutes or till vegetables are tender. Makes 6 servings.

Garden Pepper Boats

- 3 medium green peppers
- ¼ cup chopped onion
- 2 tablespoons butter *or* margarine
- 1 medium tomato, chopped (about ¾ cup)
- ½ cup cooked baby lima beans
- ½ cup whole kernel corn
- ½ cup soft bread crumbs
- 1 tablespoon butter *or* margarine

Cut peppers in half lengthwise; remove seeds and membrane. Precook for 5 minutes in boiling salted water; drain. Sprinkle inside of peppers with salt.

Cook onion in 2 tablespoons butter or margarine till tender. Add tomato, lima beans, and corn; mix well. Fill peppers; place in 10×6×2-inch baking dish. Combine bread crumbs and the 1 tablespoon butter; sprinkle over top of filling. Bake in 350° oven for 30 minutes. Makes 6 servings.

Mustard-Sauced Artichokes

- Artichokes
- 1 tablespoon all-purpose flour
- 1 tablespoon dry mustard
- 1 teaspoon salt
- ½ teaspoon dried dillweed
- ¼ teaspoon white pepper
- ¾ cup skim milk
- 4 beaten egg yolks
- 3 tablespoons lemon juice

Prepare and cook artichokes as directed in chart on page 126.

In top of double boiler combine flour, mustard, salt, dillweed, and pepper. Stir in milk and egg yolks. Place over (but not touching) boiling water. Cook, stirring constantly, till mixture thickens. Stir in lemon juice.

Serve the sauce hot with cooked artichokes. Refrigerate any remaining sauce, reheat slowly, and serve with vegetables at another meal. Makes 1 cup sauce.

Eggplant Julienne

- 5 slices bacon
- 1 medium onion, chopped (½ cup)
- 1 medium eggplant, peeled and cut into ¼-inch julienne strips (1 pound)
- 1 8-ounce can tomatoes, cut up
- 1 teaspoon sugar
- ¾ teaspoon dried basil, crushed
- ½ teaspoon salt
- Dash pepper
- 2 tablespoons snipped parsley

In skillet cook bacon till crisp. Remove from skillet, reserving 2 tablespoons drippings. Crumble bacon; set aside.

In skillet drippings, cook onion about 5 minutes or till tender but not brown. Stir in bacon, eggplant, undrained tomatoes, sugar, basil, salt, and pepper. Cover; simmer 10 minutes. Turn eggplant into serving dish. Top with parsley. Makes 6 servings.

Mustard-Sauced Artichokes

Cheesy Cauliflower

- 1 medium head cauliflower
- 1½ cups sliced fresh mushrooms (4 ounces) *or* 1 4-ounce can sliced mushrooms, drained
- 2 tablespoons butter *or* margarine
- 2 tablespoons all-purpose flour
- ¼ teaspoon salt
- Dash white pepper
- 1 cup milk
- 1 cup shredded sharp American cheese (4 ounces)
- 1 teaspoon prepared mustard
- 1 tablespoon snipped parsley

Prepare cauliflower referring to steps 9–10 on page 123, leaving head whole or breaking into flowerets. Cook cauliflower as directed in chart on page 126. Drain cauliflower thoroughly; keep warm.

Meanwhile, cook fresh mushrooms in butter or margarine about 4 minutes or till tender (if using canned mushrooms, set aside and melt butter). Blend flour, salt, and white pepper into butter. Add milk all at once. Cook, stirring constantly, till thickened and bubbly. Stir in cheese and mustard. (If using canned mushrooms, stir them into sauce.) Heat till cheese melts.

Place head of cauliflower on platter; spoon some of the sauce over. Pass remaining sauce. (Or, pour all sauce over flowerets in a bowl.) Sprinkle with parsley. Makes 6 servings.

140

Cheese-Sauced Potatoes

- 1 cup shredded sharp American cheese (4 ounces)
- ½ cup dairy sour cream
- ¼ cup butter *or* margarine, softened
- 2 tablespoons chopped green onion
- 6 baking potatoes

Bring cheese, sour cream, butter or margarine, and onion to room temperature. Prepare and bake potatoes, referring to step 1 on page 128.

Meanwhile, in small bowl combine cheese, sour cream, butter, and onion; beat till fluffy.

To serve, roll potatoes gently with palms of hands (protect hands with pot holders). Immediately cut crisscrosses in top with fork; press ends, pushing up centers to fluff. Spoon some of the cheese mixture atop each potato. Makes 6 servings.

Scalloped Spinach

- 2 10-ounce packages frozen chopped spinach
- 3 beaten eggs
- ¾ cup milk
- ¾ cup shredded American cheese
- 3 tablespoons chopped onion
- ½ teaspoon salt
  Dash pepper
- 1 cup coarse soft bread crumbs
- 1 tablespoon butter *or* margarine, melted

Cook spinach following package directions; drain well. In bowl combine the eggs, milk, ½ cup of the cheese, onion, salt, and pepper. Stir in drained spinach. Turn into a greased 8×8×2-inch baking pan.

Bake in 350° oven for 25 minutes. Combine crumbs, remaining ¼ cup cheese, and butter; sprinkle atop spinach. Bake 10 to 15 minutes more or till knife inserted off-center comes out clean. Let stand 5 minutes before serving. Serves 6.

Colcannon

- 6 medium potatoes, peeled and quartered
- 4 cups shredded cabbage
- 1 cup chopped onion
- ¼ cup butter *or* margarine
- ½ to ¾ cup milk
- 1 teaspoon salt
- ⅛ teaspoon pepper
- 1 tablespoon snipped parsley

Cook potatoes in water as directed in chart on page 127; drain. Meanwhile, combine cabbage and onion and cook in a small amount of boiling salted water for 15 minutes; drain. Mash potatoes using electric mixer. Beat in butter and as much milk as necessary to make fluffy. Add salt and pepper. Stir in cabbage and onion. Top with parsley. Serves 6.

Succotash

- 2 cups fresh *or* frozen baby lima beans
- 2 ounces salt pork
- ½ cup water
- ½ teaspoon salt
- ½ teaspoon sugar
  Dash pepper
- 2 cups fresh *or* frozen whole kernel corn
- ⅓ cup light cream
- 1 tablespoon all-purpose flour

In saucepan combine beans, salt pork, water, salt, sugar, and pepper. Cover; simmer till beans are almost tender. Stir in corn. Cover and simmer till vegetables are tender. Remove salt pork.

Blend cream with flour. Stir into vegetable mixture. Cook and stir till thickened and bubbly. Makes 6 servings.

Corn-Mushroom Bake

- ¼ cup all-purpose flour
- 1 17-ounce can cream-style corn
- 1 3-ounce package cream cheese, cut into cubes
- ½ teaspoon onion salt
- 1 17-ounce can whole kernel corn, drained
- 1 4-ounce can mushroom stems and pieces, drained
- ½ cup shredded Swiss cheese
- 1½ cups soft bread crumbs
- 2 tablespoons butter *or* margarine, melted

In saucepan stir flour into cream-style corn. Add cream cheese and onion salt; heat and stir till cream cheese melts. Stir in whole kernel corn, mushrooms, and Swiss cheese.

Turn mixture into a 1½-quart casserole. Toss soft bread crumbs with melted butter or margarine; sprinkle crumbs atop casserole. Bake in 350° oven 40 minutes or till heated through. Makes 6 to 8 servings.

141

TIP To add a special touch to your vegetable cookery, *dress up plain vegetables with these simple additions.*

Sprinkle cooked vegetables with buttered bread crumbs, crumbled corn chips or cornflakes, snipped chives or parsley, or plain or flavored croutons.

Or, toss cooked vegetables with a butter-almond sauce. To prepare, brown slivered almonds in butter, and add a teaspoon or two of fresh lemon juice.

Add crunch to cooked vegetables with sliced water chestnuts, celery, green pepper, or chopped peanuts. For a touch of tartness, add a spoonful of dairy sour cream or plain yogurt.

For color contrast, add chopped pimiento, sliced ripe or pimiento-stuffed olives, sliced hard-cooked eggs, or shredded carrot.

Vegetables

Breaded Tomato Slices

2 beaten eggs
1 tablespoon milk
¼ teaspoon seasoned salt
4 firm medium tomatoes
1 cup finely crushed saltine crackers (about 28 crackers)
2 to 3 tablespoons cooking oil
½ cup shredded sharp American cheese (2 ounces)

Combine eggs, milk, seasoned salt, and dash *pepper*. Cut tomatoes into ¾-inch-thick slices. Dip in cracker crumbs, then in egg mixture. Dip again in crumbs. In skillet fry in hot oil till browned on both sides. Sprinkle with cheese. Cover; cook over very low heat till cheese is nearly melted. Makes 4 servings.

Sweet-Sour Red Cabbage

6 cups shredded red cabbage
¼ cup currant jelly
2 tablespoons butter *or* margarine
2 tablespoons vinegar
¾ teaspoon caraway seed
½ teaspoon salt

Shred and cook cabbage as directed in chart on page 126; drain well. In same saucepan combine the jelly, butter or margarine, vinegar, caraway seed, and salt. Heat and stir till butter melts. Return drained cabbage to pan; toss and stir till the cabbage is heated through. Makes 4 or 5 servings.

TIP Flavored butters can enhance cooked vegetables. *Serve corn on the cob drizzled with a mixture of ½ cup softened butter, 1 tablespoon prepared mustard, 1 teaspoon prepared horseradish, ½ teaspoon salt, and dash pepper.*
Serve cooked asparagus or broccoli with a mixture of ¼ cup melted butter, 1 tablespoon lemon juice, 1 tablespoon snipped parsley, and dash pepper.

Stir-Fried Pea Pods

1½ teaspoons instant chicken bouillon granules
⅓ cup hot water
1 tablespoon soy sauce
2 tablespoons cold water
2 teaspoons cornstarch
1 8-ounce can bamboo shoots
1 8-ounce can water chestnuts
1 6-ounce can whole mushrooms
2 tablespoons cooking oil
1 clove garlic, minced
2 6-ounce packages frozen pea pods, thawed

Refer to: Stir-frying vegetables, page 134. Dissolve bouillon granules in hot water; stir in soy sauce. Blend cold water into cornstarch; stir into bouillon mixture. Set aside. Drain bamboo shoots, water chestnuts, and mushrooms; thinly slice water chestnuts.
Preheat a wok or large skillet over high heat; add cooking oil. Stir-fry garlic in hot oil for 30 seconds. Add bamboo shoots, water chestnuts, mushrooms, and pea pods; stir-fry for 2 minutes. Stir chicken broth mixture; stir into vegetables. Cook and stir till thickened and bubbly. Cover and cook 1 minute more. Serve at once. Garnish with cashews, if desired. Makes 8 servings.

Blue-Cheesed Sprouts

2 pints fresh brussels sprouts *or* 2 10-ounce packages frozen brussels sprouts
3 tablespoons butter *or* margarine
¼ cup crumbled blue cheese (1 ounce)

Prepare and cook fresh brussels sprouts as directed in chart on page 126. (Or, cook frozen sprouts according to package directions.) Drain sprouts thoroughly.
Meanwhile, melt butter or margarine; stir in blue cheese just till melted. Toss cheese mixture with hot drained sprouts. Makes 6 servings.

Vegetable Stir-Fry

(pictured on page 120)

¼ cup cold water
1 teaspoon cornstarch
2 tablespoons soy sauce
½ cup water
½ teaspoon salt
2 medium carrots, bias-sliced (1 cup)
1 cup sliced cauliflower
2 tablespoons cooking oil
1 clove garlic, minced
½ pound fresh asparagus, bias-sliced into ½-inch lengths
1 medium zucchini, sliced (1 cup)
1 cup sliced fresh mushrooms

Refer to: Stir-frying vegetables, page 134. Blend the ¼ cup cold water and cornstarch; stir in soy sauce. Set aside. In saucepan bring ½ cup water and the salt to boiling. Add carrots and cauliflower; cover and simmer for 2 minutes. Drain well.
Preheat a wok or large skillet over high heat; add cooking oil. Stir-fry garlic in hot oil for 30 seconds. Add asparagus; stir-fry for 2 minutes. Add zucchini, carrots, and cauliflower; stir-fry for 2 minutes. Add mushrooms; stir-fry for 1 minute more. Stir soy mixture again. Add soy mixture to wok; stir into vegetables. Cook and stir till bubbly. Serve at once. Makes 6 servings.

Beets with Sour Cream

1 pound beets
½ cup dairy sour cream
2 tablespoons milk
1 tablespoon sliced green onion
1 tablespoon vinegar
1 teaspoon sugar
¼ teaspoon salt
Dash cayenne

Peel and slice beets; halve slices. Cook beets as directed in chart on page 126; drain.
Meanwhile, in small saucepan combine sour cream, milk, green onion, vinegar, sugar, salt, and cayenne. Heat through over low heat, but *do not boil*. Turn beets into serving dish; spoon sour cream mixture atop. Stir to combine, if desired. Serves 4.

Golden Carrot Bake

    3   cups shredded carrot (1 pound)
 1½   cups water
    ⅔   cup long grain rice
    ½   teaspoon salt
    2   cups shredded American cheese
         (8 ounces)
    1   cup milk
    2   beaten eggs
    2   tablespoons minced dried onion
    ¼   teaspoon pepper

In saucepan combine carrot, water, rice, and salt. Bring to boiling. Reduce heat and simmer, covered, 25 minutes. *Do not drain.* Stir in *1½ cups* of the shredded cheese, milk, eggs, onion, and pepper. Turn carrot-rice mixture into 1½-quart casserole.

Bake, uncovered, in 350° oven about 1 hour. Top with remaining ½ cup shredded cheese. Return to oven about 2 minutes to melt cheese. Makes 6 servings.

Grilled Corn on the Cob

    ½   cup butter *or* margarine, softened
    1   teaspoon salt
    ½   teaspoon dried rosemary,
         crushed
    ½   teaspoon dried marjoram,
         crushed
    6   ears corn

Cream together butter and salt till fluffy. Add herbs and blend into butter. Keep butter at room temperature for 1 hour to mellow. Turn back husks of corn; remove silks, referring to step 7 on page 122.

Place each ear on a piece of heavy foil. Spread corn with about *1 tablespoon* of the butter. Lay husks back in position. Wrap corn securely.

Grill ears directly on *hot* coals, turning frequently, for 12 to 15 minutes or till corn is tender. (Or, if you have a covered grill with an elevated rack, roast corn according to manufacturer's directions.) Makes 6 servings.

Vegetable Tempura

    ½   pound fresh broccoli
    ½   pound fresh green beans, cut into
         2-inch lengths
    ½   pound fresh asparagus spears,
         cut into 2-inch lengths
    2   medium sweet potatoes, peeled
         and sliced ¼ inch thick
    1   medium onion, sliced and
         separated into rings
    1   small eggplant, peeled and cut
         into 1-inch cubes
    1   cup all-purpose flour
    2   tablespoons cornstarch
    1   cup ice-cold water
    1   egg yolk
    2   stiff-beaten egg whites
         Cooking oil
         Tempura Sauce
         Condiments

Prepare broccoli in spears as directed in chart on page 126; cut off buds and cut remaining stalk into 1-inch pieces. Bring broccoli and other vegetables to room temperature.

To make batter, stir together the flour, cornstarch, and ½ teaspoon *salt*; make a well in center, referring to step 4 on page 209. Combine ice-cold water and egg yolk; add all at once to flour mixture. Slowly stir just till moistened (a few lumps should remain). Fold in the egg whites. Do not allow batter to stand more than a few minutes before using.

Pour oil into deep saucepan to depth of 2 inches (or use deep-fat fryer or electric fondue cooker); refer to tip on page 63. Heat to 400°. Add 1 teaspoon *salt*.

Dip vegetables into batter, swirling to coat. Drain off excess. Fry, a few at a time, for 2 to 3 minutes; drain. Pass Tempura Sauce and Condiments. Makes 6 to 8 servings.

Tempura Sauce: In saucepan mix 1 cup *water*, ½ cup *soy sauce*, ¼ cup *dry sherry*, 1 teaspoon *sugar*, and 1 teaspoon instant *chicken bouillon granules*. Cook and stir till boiling.

Condiments: (1) grated *gingerroot*; (2) equal parts grated *turnip* and *radish*, mixed; (3) ½ cup prepared *mustard* mixed with 3 tablespoons *soy sauce*.

143

Vegetable Tempura

FRUITS

The variety and uses of fruits are almost limitless. They go well in everything from refreshing salads to tempting desserts. This section describes preparation basics for popular fruits and fruit dishes.

Fresh Fruit Preparation

Technique: Preparing fresh fruits

Cherries: 1 Remove the stems from cherries. Place cherries in colander and rinse under cold running water. Drain. Pit cherries.

Strawberries: 2 Place strawberries in a pan of cold water. Swirl berries slowly with your hands. Lift the strawberries from the water and drain thoroughly. Remove caps.

Oranges or grapefruit: 3 To section the fruit, first peel by removing the outer peel and white membrane. **4** Cut into sections over a bowl, catching juices.

Apples: 5 Wash apples. Cut in half and then in quarters. Remove the core and slice fruit. To keep slices from turning brown, dip them in lemon juice.

Melons: 6 Cut melon in half and remove seeds. Scoop out balls of fruit.

Pineapple: 7 Remove the crown from pineapple. **8** Cut off the peel. **9** Remove the eyes from the fruit by cutting diagonal wedge-shaped grooves in the pineapple. **10** Cut into spears or chunks, removing the hard center core.

Peaches: 11–12 Wash and peel peaches. Cut fruit in half and remove pits.

1 Remove the stems from cherries. Place cherries in a colander and rinse under cold running water. Drain.

To pit cherries, hold the fruit in one hand and insert the tip of a paring knife into the cherry with the other hand. Push the pit up and out with the tip of the knife, as shown.

2 Place strawberries in a pan of cold water. Swirl berries slowly with your hands. Lift the fruit from the water. Drain.

To remove strawberry caps, insert the tip of a paring knife into the fruit just under the cap and lift out the cap. *Or,* use a tweezer-like strawberry huller to pull the caps from the fruit.

Strawberries should be washed and hulled just before using.

7 To remove the crown from a pineapple, hold the pineapple in one hand and the crown in the other, then twist in opposite directions. Use a towel or pot holder to protect hands from the sharp sides and top of the fruit, if necessary.

8 Trim the top of the pineapple and cut off the base; set it upright on a cutting board. Cut off wide strips of peel with a knife, starting at the top of the fruit and working toward the bottom, as shown.

3 To section grapefruit or oranges, begin by cutting off the peel and the white membrane. Work on a cutting board and cut down from the top of the fruit, as shown.

If desired, first cut a thin slice from one end of the grapefruit so fruit will sit level on the cutting board.

You'll need a very sharp utility knife or a serrated knife for peeling citrus.

4 Remove the sections by cutting into the center of the fruit between one section and the membrane. Then turn knife and slide the knife down the other side of the section next to the membrane, as shown.

Remove any seeds. Allow grapefruit or orange section to fall into a bowl. Work over a bowl so that you catch the juice.

5 Wash apples. Cut in half and then in quarters. Remove the section of core from each quarter; slice fruit.

To keep apple slices (or any fruit) from turning brown after being cut, dip the fruit into a bowl of lemon juice. Or, use orange juice, grapefruit juice, or an ascorbic acid color keeper. Then drain fruit on paper toweling.

6 Cut melon in half and remove seeds.

An attractive way to serve melon is to scoop the fruit out into balls with a melon baller. Once you've scooped out as many balls as possible, cut the leftover fruit into chunks and store in the refrigerator for snacking.

145

9 To remove the eyes from the fruit, make narrow wedge-shaped grooves into the pineapple. Cut diagonally around the fruit, following the pattern of the eyes. Cut away as little of the fruit as possible.

10 To cut pineapple spears, cut the pineapple vertically into eighths or tenths. Then cut the hard center core from each spear. To make pineapple chunks, cut each spear into fourths or sixths.

11 Wash peaches. Bring a small saucepan of water to boiling. Insert a fork into end of peach. Dip the peach into the boiling water for about 20 seconds, making sure it is completely covered.

12 With the fruit still on the fork, remove the peach from the water and peel off the skin with a paring knife, working from top to bottom, as shown. If the skin is still difficult to peel, return the peach to the boiling water for a few seconds.

Cut fruit in half and remove the pit.

Fruits

Applesauce

Technique: Making applesauce

4 medium cooking apples
¼ to ⅓ cup water
2 inches stick cinnamon
2 to 4 tablespoons sugar

1 With paring knife, cut apples into quarters. **2** Core each of the quarters. **3** Peel each apple quarter. **4** Place apples in a medium saucepan and pour water over fruit. Add stick cinnamon. **5** Bring to boiling. Reduce heat; cover and simmer for 8 to 10 minutes or till tender. Uncover; remove stick cinnamon. **6** Remove from heat; mash apples with potato masher till smooth. **7** Stir in sugar. **8** Spoon applesauce into serving dishes or refrigerate, covered, till ready to serve. Makes 1½ cups.

Chunky Applesauce: Use ingredients as listed above. Prepare apples as directed in steps 1–3. In medium saucepan combine apples, water, cinnamon, and sugar; bring to boiling. Reduce heat; cover and simmer for 8 to 10 minutes or till apples are tender. Remove cinnamon. Mash slightly, if desired. Makes 1½ cups.

Quantity Applesauce: To make a large quantity of Applesauce or Chunky Applesauce, prepare as directed above *except* use a *4-quart* Dutch oven, 4 pounds cooking *apples,* 1 to 1½ cups *water,* 6 inches *stick cinnamon,* and ½ to 1 cup *sugar.* Makes about 5 cups.

1 Start by choosing tart, juicy cooking apples such as jonathan, McIntosh, or winesap. Working on a cutting board, cut each apple in half and then into quarters with a paring knife. If you have extremely large apples, cut them into sixths or eighths so the pieces will cook more evenly.

5 Bring to boiling. Reduce heat; cover and simmer for 8 to 10 minutes. Uncover; check the texture of the apples with a fork. They should fall apart easily. Remove the stick cinnamon.

Applesauce is cooked covered to prevent the apple juices from boiling away.

2 Working with one piece of apple at a time, hold the apple wedge with point upright and remove the core by making a semicircular slice with the paring knife, as shown.

3 Continuing to work with one wedge of apple at a time, cut the peel from each piece, removing as little of the fruit as possible.

4 Place the apple wedges in a medium saucepan. For thick applesauce, add ¼ cup water. For a thinner sauce, add ⅓ cup water. Add the stick cinnamon.

147

TIP To save time when making a large batch of applesauce, *do not peel the apples in step 3. Cook them as in steps 4 and 5, but instead of mashing the apples in step 6, press them through a food mill. Discard the peel. Then continue with steps 7 and 8.*

If you use red apples, cooking the quarters unpeeled will give the applesauce a festive rosy color.

6 Transfer the saucepan to a trivet or hot pad on a table or counter and mash the apples with a potato masher, as shown. Continue mashing until there are no large chunks and the apples have a smooth texture.

7 Stir in 2 tablespoons sugar (if your measuring set includes an ⅛-cup measure, you may use that). Taste applesauce for sweetness. If you prefer sweeter applesauce, add additional sugar, a tablespoon at a time, tasting the sauce after each addition.

8 The consistency of the finished sauce should be fairly smooth, as shown. If you enjoy applesauce warm, spoon it directly into serving dishes and serve at once. For chilled applesauce, spoon the sauce into a refrigerator container; cover and chill for several hours.

Fruits

Fresh Peach Crisp

Technique: Making fresh fruit crisp

½   **cup quick-cooking rolled oats**
½   **cup packed brown sugar**
¼   **cup all-purpose flour**
½   **teaspoon ground cinnamon**
    Dash salt
¼   **cup butter *or* margarine**
2½ **pounds peaches (10 medium)**
    Vanilla ice cream, light cream, *or* whipped
      cream

148

1 In mixing bowl combine oats, brown sugar, flour, cinnamon, and salt. Cut in butter or margarine till mixture is crumbly. **2** Pieces of butter should be the size of coarse crumbs. Set aside. **3** Peel peaches. **4** Halve, pit, and slice fruit; measure 5 cups. **5** Place fruit in a 10×6×2-inch baking dish. Sprinkle the flour mixture over fruit. **6** Bake in 350° oven for about 40 minutes or till fruit tests done with a fork. Serve warm with ice cream, light cream, or whipped cream. Makes 6 servings.

1 In mixing bowl combine oats, brown sugar, flour, cinnamon, and salt. Add butter or margarine. Holding a pastry blender vertically, cut the butter into the oat mixture with an up-and-down motion. Between strokes, use a rubber spatula to remove any butter that sticks to the pastry blender.

4 Cut each peeled peach in half. Remove the pit. Place fruit cut-side down on cutting board and slice each half into 5 or 6 pieces. Measure 5 cups of sliced fruit.

2 Continue cutting the butter into the oat mixture till the pieces of butter are the size of coarse crumbs or small peas, as shown. Set the crumb mixture aside.

3 To peel the peaches, bring a small saucepan of water to boiling. Insert a fork into the end of one peach at a time and dip the peach into the boiling water for about 20 seconds, making sure the fruit is completely covered. Holding the fork handle, peel the fruit with a paring knife, working from top to bottom, as shown.

TIP You also can make delicious fruit crisp with other fruits, such as apples or pears. *To make apple crisp, substitute 2 pounds apples (6 medium) for the peaches. For pear crisp, use 2½ pounds pears (10 medium).*

Peel, core, and slice fruit to make about 5 cups; place in baking dish. Top with crumbs and bake as directed for peach crisp.

149

5 Arrange peach slices in an ungreased 10×6×2-inch baking dish. Using a spoon, sprinkle the flour mixture evenly over the fruit.
  If desired, substitute an 8×8×2-inch baking dish.

6 Bake the crisp, uncovered, in a 350° oven for about 40 minutes or till the fruit is tender when tested with a fork. Serve warm in dessert dishes with ice cream, light cream, or whipped cream.

Fruits

Fruit Royale

Technique: Making fruit sauce

- **1 16-ounce can pear halves**
- **4 teaspoons cornstarch**
- **½ cup strawberry jelly**
- **2 tablespoons lemon juice**
- **¼ teaspoon ground nutmeg**
- **1 11-ounce can mandarin orange sections, drained**
- **Pound cake *or* vanilla ice cream**

1 Drain pears, reserving ½ cup syrup. **2** Slice pears; set aside. **3** In medium saucepan blend reserved pear syrup into cornstarch. **4** Stir in strawberry jelly; stir in lemon juice and nutmeg. **5** Cook, stirring constantly, till mixture is thickened and bubbly. Add pears and drained oranges to sauce. Simmer 5 minutes, stirring occasionally. Remove from heat. **6** Serve warm or chilled over slices of pound cake or scoops of ice cream. Makes 2½ cups.

1 Set a strainer atop a 2-cup measure. Pour pears into the strainer, allowing syrup to drain into measure. Reserve ½ cup of the syrup.

4 Thoroughly blend the strawberry jelly into the cornstarch mixture. Stir in the lemon juice and ground nutmeg.

If desired, raspberry jelly may be substituted for the strawberry jelly.

2 On a cutting board slice each drained pear half into about 5 pieces using a utility knife. Set pear slices aside.

3 Place cornstarch in a medium saucepan. Blend in the reserved pear syrup. Stir well with a wooden spoon to eliminate any lumps of cornstarch.

151

5 Over medium heat cook and stir the cornstarch mixture till thickened and bubbly, as shown. Add the sliced pears and drained oranges to the sauce. Simmer 5 minutes more, stirring occasionally to prevent sticking. Remove saucepan from heat.

6 To serve the sauce warm, spoon the fruit mixture over slices of pound cake or scoops of ice cream. For a chilled sauce, transfer the fruit mixture to a covered container. Chill in the refrigerator for several hours.

TIP To make this sauce into an elegant dessert, serve it flaming.

To flame brandy, *pour ¼ cup brandy into a ladle; warm over a burner till brandy almost simmers. Use a ladle with a protected handle or hold it with a pot holder. Quickly ignite brandy with a long match and pour over sauce (see top photo). Stir; spoon sauce over cake or ice cream.*

To flame sugar cubes, *soak 6 sugar cubes in 1 teaspoon lemon extract. Spoon sauce over cake or ice cream. Place a sugar cube on each serving and ignite (see bottom photo).*

Fruits

Harvest Fruit Compote

- 1 15¼-ounce can pineapple chunks
- 1 12-ounce package pitted, dried prunes
- 1 cup dried apricots
- 2½ cups water
- 1 21-ounce can cherry pie filling
- ¼ cup dry sherry
- ¾ teaspoon ground cardamom

In 3-quart casserole place *undrained* pineapple, prunes, and apricots. Combine water, cherry pie filling, dry sherry, and cardamom; pour over fruit. Cover and bake in a 350° oven for 1½ hours. Serve warm or cold. Makes 8 servings.

Apple-Orange Salad

- 1 11-ounce can mandarin orange sections, chilled
- 2 large apples, cored and cut into bite-size pieces
- ¼ cup broken walnuts
- ½ cup orange yogurt
- 2 tablespoons orange marmalade

Drain the orange sections. Stir together oranges, apple pieces, and walnuts. Combine yogurt and marmalade; toss with fruit. Makes 6 servings.

TIP To cook dried fruit, *place the fruit in a saucepan. Add water to cover, to a level of 1 inch above the fruit. Cover and simmer 20 to 30 minutes for apples, apricots, mixed dried fruits, or prunes. Cook dried peaches or pears for 30 to 35 minutes. If you enjoy sweetened fruit, add 2 to 4 tablespoons sugar per cup of fruit during last 5 minutes of cooking. Serve with the syrup.*

To plump raisins, place them in a saucepan; cover with water. Bring to boiling; remove from heat and let stand for 5 minutes.

Jewish Fruit Kugel

- 4 ounces wide noodles
- 2 beaten eggs
- ¼ cup sugar
- 3 tablespoons cooking oil
- ⅛ teaspoon ground cinnamon
- 1 medium apple, peeled, cored, and diced
- ¼ cup dried apricots, chopped
- ¼ cup raisins

Cook noodles according to package directions; drain well. In a large bowl combine eggs, sugar, cooking oil, and cinnamon; beat well. Stir in apple, apricots, and raisins. Toss fruit mixture with drained noodles. Turn into a greased 1-quart casserole. Cover and bake in a 350° oven for 30 minutes. Stir occasionally. Serve hot as a meat accompaniment or as a dessert. Makes 7 servings.

Banana Crisp

- ½ cup all-purpose flour
- ½ cup quick-cooking rolled oats
- ⅓ cup packed brown sugar
- ½ teaspoon salt
- ¼ teaspoon ground cinnamon
- 6 tablespoons butter *or* margarine
- 4 bananas, sliced (3 cups)
- ¼ cup orange juice
- 1 tablespoon lemon juice
- ¼ cup granulated sugar
   Vanilla ice cream

Refer to: Making fresh fruit crisp, page 148. Combine flour, oats, brown sugar, salt, and cinnamon; cut in butter or margarine till mixture resembles coarse crumbs. Set aside. Arrange banana slices in a 10×6×2-inch baking dish. Combine orange and lemon juices; pour over bananas. Sprinkle with the granulated sugar. Top with flour mixture. Bake in 375° oven for 30 to 35 minutes. Serve with ice cream. Makes 6 servings.

Spicy Pear Cobbler

- ½ cup sugar
- ½ teaspoon ground nutmeg
- 2 tablespoons cornstarch
- 1⅓ cups cranberry juice cocktail
   Few drops red food coloring (optional)
- 2½ pounds pears, peeled, cored, and sliced (10 medium)
- 1 tablespoon butter *or* margarine
- 1½ cups packaged biscuit mix
- ⅓ cup milk

Combine sugar and nutmeg; set aside 3 tablespoons. In saucepan blend the remaining sugar mixture and cornstarch. Referring to steps 3–5 on page 151, stir in the cranberry juice and food coloring. Cook and stir over medium heat till thickened and bubbly. Add pears and butter or margarine; return to boiling. Reduce heat; simmer 5 minutes or till pears are tender. Meanwhile, for topper, combine biscuit mix and *2 tablespoons* of the reserved sugar mixture. Stir in milk.

Turn *hot* pear mixture into a 2-quart casserole. Immediately spoon topper in 8 portions atop pear mixture. Sprinkle with the remaining sugar mixture. Bake in a 400° oven about 20 minutes or till topper is golden brown. Serve warm. Makes 8 servings.

Berry Parfaits

- 1 tablespoon sugar
- 1 teaspoon finely shredded orange peel
- ½ teaspoon finely shredded lemon peel
- ⅛ teaspoon ground cinnamon
   Dash salt
- 1 8-ounce carton plain yogurt
- 1½ cups strawberries, sliced
- 1½ cups blueberries

In bowl combine sugar, peels, cinnamon, and salt. Gently fold in yogurt. Set aside 6 strawberry slices. In 6 parfait glasses layer the remaining strawberries, yogurt mixture, and blueberries, ending with a dollop of yogurt mixture. Top each parfait with a strawberry slice. Serves 6.

Rumtopf

- 3 medium oranges
- 3 medium pears, cored and diced
- 1 cup maraschino cherries
- 1 cup sugar
- 1 cup rum

Peel, section, and cut up oranges over a bowl to catch juice, referring to steps 3 and 4 on page 145. In a nonmetal container combine the oranges, pears, and cherries. Stir in the sugar; add the juice from sectioned oranges and the rum. Cover; refrigerate for 2 weeks. Serve as a compote or as a topping for ice cream or cake. Makes about 4½ cups.

To replenish Rumtopf: For every cup of fruit removed, add 1 cup *fruit,* ⅓ cup *sugar,* and ⅓ cup *rum.* Keep Rumtopf refrigerated.

Rumtopf

Baked Apples in Wine

- 4 large baking apples
- ¼ cup packed brown sugar
- ¼ teaspoon ground nutmeg
- 4 teaspoons butter *or* margarine
- 1 cup rosé wine
- ½ cup dairy sour cream (optional)
  Ground nutmeg (optional)

To core apples, use an apple corer or the rounded tip of a vegetable peeler. Push through apple center, turning to loosen the core. Remove and discard core. Peel a strip from the top of each apple. Place apples in an 8×8×2-inch baking dish. Stir together the brown sugar and the ¼ teaspoon nutmeg; divide among apple centers. Top each apple with *1 teaspoon* of the butter. Pour wine into baking dish. Bake in a 350° oven about 1 hour or till apples are tender. Baste with wine occasionally. Serve apples warm; top with a dollop of sour cream and a dash of additional nutmeg, if desired. Makes 4 servings.

Bananas Foster

- 4 small ripe bananas
  Lemon juice
- ⅔ cup packed brown sugar
- 6 tablespoons butter *or* margarine
  Ground cinnamon
- 3 tablespoons banana liqueur *or* light rum
- 3 tablespoons light rum
  Vanilla ice cream

Peel bananas and cut in half crosswise. Cut in half again lengthwise; brush with lemon juice. In blazer pan of chafing dish cook sugar and butter or margarine over direct heat till melted. Add bananas. Cook 3 to 4 minutes, turning once. Sprinkle lightly with cinnamon. Drizzle the 3 tablespoons liqueur or rum over all. Referring to the tip on page 151, heat the 3 tablespoons rum in a ladle till it *almost* simmers. Ignite the rum and pour over the bananas. Serve over ice cream. Makes 6 servings.

Honeyed Apple Rings

(pictured on page 49)

- 4 medium cooking apples
- ½ cup honey
- 2 tablespoons vinegar
- ¼ teaspoon salt
- ¼ teaspoon ground cinnamon (optional)

Wash and core apples. Cut unpeeled apples into ½-inch thick rings. In saucepan combine the honey, vinegar, salt, and cinnamon. Bring to boiling. Add apple rings. Cook 10 to 12 minutes or till apples are tender, turning often. Serve as a meat or poultry accompaniment. Serves 4.

Apple Dumplings

- 2¼ cups all-purpose flour
- ½ teaspoon salt
- ⅔ cup shortening
- 6 to 8 tablespoons cold water
- 6 small apples, peeled and cored
- ⅔ cup sugar
- ¼ cup light cream
- ⅛ teaaspoon ground nutmeg
- ¾ cup maple-flavored syrup
  Hard Sauce *or* light cream

Make pastry as follows, referring to steps 1–3 on page 276. Mix the flour and salt. Cut in shortening till the mixture resembles coarse crumbs. Sprinkle the water over, a little at a time; mix lightly till all is moistened. Form into a ball. On floured surface, roll out to a 18×12-inch rectangle; cut into six 6-inch squares.

Place an apple in the center of each pastry square. Mix sugar, ¼ cup cream, and nutmeg; spoon equally into the centers of the apples. Moisten the edges of the pastry; fold corners to center atop apple. Pinch the edges together. Place dumplings in an ungreased 11×7×1½-inch baking pan. Bake in a 375° oven for 35 minutes. Pour the syrup over dumplings. Bake 15 minutes longer or till apples are tender. Serve warm topped with Hard Sauce or more cream. Serves 6.

Hard Sauce: Cream 1 cup sifted *powdered sugar* and 6 tablespoons *butter or margarine,* softened, till fluffy. Drop tablespoonfuls onto waxed paper, making 6 mounds. Chill.

153

Clockwise from left: 24-Hour Vegetable Salad (see recipe, page 172); Strawberry Soufflé Salad (see recipe, page 163); a fresh fruit plate with Celery Seed Dressing (see recipe, page 178); and a tossed green salad with French Dressing (see recipe, page 179).

SALADS

Whether you're preparing a gelatin, frozen, tossed, potato, or wilted greens salad, you'll find the technique easy to master if you follow these helpful step-by-step directions.

Tomato Aspic

Technique: Making molded gelatin salad

2	envelopes unflavored gelatin
1	cup cold tomato juice
3	cups tomato juice
⅓	cup chopped onion
¼	cup chopped celery
2	tablespoons brown sugar
1	teaspoon salt
4	whole cloves
2	bay leaves
3	tablespoons lemon juice
	Lettuce leaves

1 To soften the gelatin, add unflavored gelatin to 1 cup cold tomato juice; stir to combine. In medium saucepan combine *2 cups* of the tomato juice, onion, celery, brown sugar, salt, cloves, and bay leaves. Simmer the mixture, uncovered, for 5 minutes. **2** Pour the hot mixture into a sieve set over bowl; strain. **3** Add the softened gelatin to hot juice mixture; stir to dissolve. Stir in the remaining 1 cup tomato juice and lemon juice. Pour mixture into a 5-cup tower mold. Chill till firm. **4–8** Unmold onto a serving plate. **9** Garnish by sliding lettuce leaves under the edges of the unmolded salad. Makes 8 to 10 servings.

1 In a 2-cup glass measure or bowl soften the gelatin by adding the unflavored gelatin to the 1 cup cold tomato juice. Stir to thoroughly combine.

In a medium saucepan combine *2 cups* of the tomato juice, onion, celery, brown sugar, salt, cloves, and bay leaves. Simmer the mixture, uncovered, for 5 minutes.

2 Pour the hot tomato mixture into a sieve set over bowl; strain. Discard the cooked vegetables, cloves, and bay leaves.

6 Place hand over the gelatin and tilt or rotate the mold to let air loosen the gelatin all the way around the salad.

7 Center an upside-down serving plate over the mold. Holding tightly, invert plate and the mold together. Shake the mold gently.

3 Add the softened gelatin to the hot juice mixture. Using a rubber spatula, stir to dissolve the gelatin (there should be no visible gelatin granules remaining). Stir in the remaining 1 cup tomato juice and lemon juice.

Pour the mixture into a 5-cup tower mold. Chill till firm (the gelatin should not be sticky to the touch and should not move when tilted in the mold).

4 To unmold, dip the mold just to the rim in warm water for a *few seconds*. Tilt slightly to ease gelatin away from one side and let air in.

5 With the tip of a small metal spatula, loosen the gelatin from the mold by carefully running the spatula around the edges.

157

TIP Gelatin salads often feature chopped vegetables or fruits and nuts as part of the recipe. *In order for the solid ingredients to remain evenly distributed throughout the salad, the gelatin mixture first must be chilled till partially set, as shown. This "jellying" stage produces a consistency similar to unbeaten egg whites. It's at this stage that any solid ingredients are folded into the gelatin mixture.*

8 Lift off the mold, being careful not to tear the gelatin. If the salad doesn't slide out easily, repeat steps 4 through 7.

9 Use a wide spatula to lift up the edges of the salad, and then slide lettuce leaves under. A simple garnish like this adds an attractive touch to the salad.

Salads

Cran-Raspberry Mold

Technique: Making layered gelatin salad

2   3-ounce packages *or* 1 6-ounce package
     raspberry-flavored gelatin
1¾   cups boiling water
1   20-ounce can crushed pineapple
1   16-ounce can whole cranberry sauce
1   cup dairy sour cream

158

1 In bowl dissolve gelatin in boiling water. **2** Add *undrained* pineapple and cranberry sauce, stirring till cranberry sauce melts. **3** Chill till partially set by placing bowl into a larger bowl of ice water; or chill in refrigerator.

4 Pour *half* of the gelatin mixture into a 6½-cup ring mold. **5** Chill till almost firm. Let the remaining gelatin stand at room temperature. **6–7** In small bowl stir sour cream; spread evenly over the almost-firm gelatin in the mold. **8** Gently spoon the remaining gelatin mixture on top of the sour cream layer. **9** Chill till firm. **10–12** Unmold onto serving plate. Makes 12 servings.

1 In large bowl dissolve raspberry-flavored gelatin in boiling water, stirring constantly with a rubber spatula, as shown.

2 Add the undrained crushed pineapple and whole cranberry sauce to the gelatin. Stir mixture till the cranberry sauce melts.

7 Spread the sour cream evenly over the almost-firm gelatin, sealing all the edges. Be careful not to tear the gelatin while spreading the sour cream.

8 Gently spoon the remaining gelatin mixture on top of the sour cream layer. Avoid spreading the gelatin mixture around, as this will cause the sour cream to mix into the soft gelatin.

3 Chill gelatin till partially set. Place several ice cubes in a large bowl; add some water. Set the bowl of gelatin into the ice water, pressing down to force the ice cubes around the bowl to quick-chill the gelatin, as shown. Or, instead of using ice cubes, place the bowl of gelatin in the refrigerator to chill.

The consistency of the gelatin at this stage is similar to that of unbeaten egg whites.

4 Pour *half* of the gelatin mixture into a 6½-cup ring mold. Spread mixture around the mold to distribute the gelatin evenly.

5 Place the ring mold in the refrigerator. Chill till almost firm. (The gelatin mixture will appear to be set, but should feel sticky to the touch. The mixture also should flow slightly when mold is tipped to one side.)

6 In a small bowl stir the sour cream thoroughly. Stirring helps the sour cream achieve a better spreading consistency.

9 Place the ring mold in the refrigerator. Chill till firm (gelatin should not feel sticky to the touch or move when the mold is tilted). Allow several hours or overnight for the gelatin to set.

10 To unmold, dip the mold just to the rim in warm water for a *few seconds*. Tilt slightly to ease gelatin away from sides of mold and to let in air.

With the tip of a narrow metal spatula, loosen gelatin from the outside and center of the ring mold by running the spatula around the edges.

11 Center an upside-down serving plate over the mold. Holding tightly, invert plate and mold together. Shake mold gently to let in air, loosening the gelatin all the way around.

12 Lift off the mold, being careful not to tear the gelatin. If the salad doesn't slide out easily, repeat steps 10 through 12.

If desired, garnish salad with lettuce. Use a wide spatula to lift up the edges of the salad; slide lettuce leaves under.

Salads

Frozen Fruit Slices

Technique: Making frozen fruit salad

2   3-ounce packages cream cheese, softened
1   cup mayonnaise *or* salad dressing
1   30-ounce can (3½ cups) fruit cocktail,
       well-drained
2½   cups tiny marshmallows
½   cup drained maraschino cherries, quartered
1   cup whipping cream
       Lettuce

160

1 In large mixer bowl, combine cream cheese and mayonnaise or salad dressing; beat with electric mixer till well blended. **2** Stir in the drained fruit cocktail, marshmallows, and maraschino cherries.

3 In small mixer bowl whip the chilled cream till soft peaks form. **4** Fold the whipped cream into the fruit mixture. Tint mixture with maraschino cherry juice, if desired. **5** Pour into a 12×7½×2-inch dish. Cover and freeze till firm. **6–7** To serve, remove salad from freezer and let stand at room temperature about 10 minutes. Cut into squares. **8** Serve on lettuce-lined salad plates. Garnish each serving with fresh mint sprig, if desired. Makes 10 to 12 servings.

1 In large mixer bowl combine softened cream cheese and mayonnaise or salad dressing; beat with electric mixer till well blended. The consistency of the beaten mixture will be smooth and creamy, as shown.

5 Pour the mixture into a 12×7½×2-inch dish, as shown. Using a rubber spatula, spread the mixture to distribute evenly; cover. Place in freezer and freeze till firm. This will take about 6 hours.

2 Add the drained fruit cocktail, marshmallows, and quartered maraschino cherries to the cream cheese-mayonnaise mixture; stir to thoroughly combine.

3 Place chilled whipping cream in small mixer bowl. Using a rotary beater or an electric mixer beat about 2 minutes or till soft peaks form. Peaks will mound slightly when the beaters are removed, as shown. For best results, thoroughly chill the mixer bowl and the beaters before whipping the cream.

4 Fold the whipped cream into the fruit mixture. Tint the mixture a light pink by adding some maraschino cherry juice, if desired.

6 To serve, remove from the freezer and let stand at room temperature about 10 minutes to soften slightly. Cut salad into squares.

7 Using a wide spatula, lift out the salad squares.
　You can freeze salads in a variety of different containers. For round slices, pour the salad mixture into 20- to 30-ounce fruit or vegetable cans. For single servings, spoon the mixture into muffin pans lined with paper bake cups or into individual salad molds. For wedge-shaped slices, pour mixture into ring mold or round pan.

8 Arrange lettuce leaves on individual salad plates. Place the frozen salad squares atop lettuce. Garnish each serving with a fresh mint sprig, if desired.

Salads

Cherry-Cider Salad

2 cups apple cider *or* apple juice
1 6-ounce package cherry-flavored gelatin
1 16-ounce can pitted dark sweet cherries
½ cup thinly sliced celery
½ cup chopped walnuts
1 3-ounce package cream cheese, softened
1 8½-ounce can (1 cup) applesauce
  Leaf lettuce

Refer to: Making layered gelatin salad, page 158. Bring apple cider or juice to boiling. Dissolve gelatin in boiling cider. Drain cherries, reserving syrup. Halve cherries and set aside. Add enough water to reserved syrup to measure 1½ cups liquid; stir into gelatin. Set aside 2 cups of the gelatin mixture; keep at room temperature. Chill remaining gelatin till partially set. Fold cherries, celery, and walnuts into partially set gelatin. Pour into 6½-cup ring mold. Chill till almost firm.

Gradually add reserved gelatin to softened cream cheese, beating till smooth. Stir in applesauce. Spoon cream cheese mixture over cherry layer in mold. Chill till firm. Unmold on lettuce-lined platter. Serve with mayonnaise or salad dressing sprinkled with additional walnuts, if desired. Makes 10 to 12 servings.

Orange-Apricot Freeze

2 8-ounce cartons orange yogurt
½ cup sugar
1 17-ounce can unpeeled apricot halves, drained
⅓ cup coarsely chopped pecans
  Lettuce leaves

In mixing bowl stir together yogurt and sugar to blend. Cut up apricots. Fold apricots and nuts into yogurt mixture. Spoon into a muffin pan lined with 8 to 10 paper bake cups. Cover and freeze till firm. Peel off paper from salads. Serve on lettuce-lined plates. Makes 8 to 10 servings.

Cherry-Cider Salad

Shrimp Mousse

2 envelopes unflavored gelatin
1½ cups cold water
1 cup mayonnaise *or* salad dressing
½ cup chopped seeded cucumber
¼ cup lemon juice
3 tablespoons chopped pimiento-stuffed olives
2 teaspoons sugar
2 teaspoons prepared horseradish
½ teaspoon onion juice
¼ teaspoon salt
¼ teaspoon paprika
½ cup whipping cream
2 4½-ounce cans shrimp, drained and cut in half

Refer to: Making molded gelatin salad, steps 4–9 and tip, page 157. In saucepan soften gelatin in the cold water; heat and stir till gelatin dissolves. Remove from heat. Beat in mayonnaise or salad dressing. Chill till partially set. Combine cucumber, lemon juice, olives, sugar, horseradish, onion juice, salt, and paprika; fold into gelatin. Beat whipping cream till soft peaks form; fold into gelatin mixture. Fold in shrimp. Pour into 5½-cup mold. Chill till firm. Unmold and serve. Garnish with lettuce, if desired. Serves 8.

Tuna Salad Mold

1 envelope unflavored gelatin
1 cup cold water
1 tablespoon lemon juice
1 teaspoon drained capers
1 teaspoon snipped parsley
½ teaspoon salt
¼ teaspoon paprika
2 6½- *or* 7-ounce cans tuna, drained and flaked
1 cup chopped celery
¼ cup mayonnaise *or* salad dressing
1 teaspoon prepared mustard
½ cup whipping cream

Refer to: Making molded gelatin salad, steps 4–9 and tip, page 157. In small saucepan soften gelatin in the cold water; heat and stir till gelatin dissolves. Remove from heat; stir in lemon juice, capers, parsley, salt, and paprika. Chill till partially set. Fold in the tuna and celery. Combine mayonnaise or salad dressing and mustard; fold in. Beat whipping cream till soft peaks form; fold into gelatin mixture. Spoon the mixture into 6 individual molds. Chill till firm. Unmold and serve. Garnish with lettuce, if desired. Makes 6 servings.

162

Strawberry Soufflé Salad

(pictured on page 154)

2 10-ounce packages frozen sliced
    strawberries, thawed
1 6-ounce package strawberry-
    flavored gelatin
½ teaspoon salt
2 cups boiling water
¼ cup lemon juice
½ cup mayonnaise *or* salad
    dressing
½ cup chopped walnuts
    Lettuce leaves

Refer to: Making molded gelatin salad, steps 4–9 and tip, page 157. Drain strawberries, reserving syrup; set strawberries aside. Add enough water to syrup to measure 1¼ cups liquid. In large mixing bowl dissolve gelatin and salt in the boiling water. Add reserved strawberry syrup mixture and lemon juice. Beat in mayonnaise or salad dressing till well blended. Chill till partially set. Beat the gelatin mixture with electric mixer till fluffy. Fold in the reserved strawberries and walnuts. Turn mixture into a 6½-cup tower mold. Chill till firm. To serve, unmold onto a lettuce-lined serving platter. Garnish with fresh strawberries, if desired. Serves 10 to 12.

Frozen Lime-Mint Salad

1 29½-ounce can crushed
    pineapple *or* 1 8¼- *and* 1
    20-ounce can crushed
    pineapple
1 3-ounce package lime-flavored
    gelatin
1 6-ounce bag tiny marshmallows
1 cup butter mints, crushed
1 9-ounce container frozen whipped
    dessert topping
    Lettuce leaves

In large bowl combine the *undrained* pineapple, *dry* lime gelatin, marshmallows, and crushed mints. Cover; refrigerate for several hours or till marshmallows begin to soften.

Thaw dessert topping; fold into pineapple mixture. Spoon into muffin pans lined with 16 paper bake cups. Cover; freeze till firm. Peel off paper. Serve salads on lettuce-lined plates. Makes 16 servings.

Perfection Salad

1 6-ounce package lemon-flavored
    gelatin
¾ teaspoon salt
3¼ cups boiling water
⅓ cup white vinegar
2 tablespoons lemon juice
2 cups finely shredded cabbage
1 cup chopped celery
½ cup chopped green pepper
¼ cup sliced pimiento-stuffed olives
    Lettuce leaves

Refer to: Making molded gelatin salad, steps 4–9 and tip, page 157. In mixing bowl dissolve lemon gelatin and salt in boiling water. Stir in vinegar and lemon juice. Chill till partially set. Fold in shredded cabbage, celery, green pepper, and olives. Turn mixture into a 5½-cup mold or 10 individual molds. Chill till firm. To serve, unmold salad onto a lettuce-lined serving platter or individual salad plates. Serve with mayonnaise or salad dressing, if desired. Makes 10 servings.

Cheesy Coleslaw Mold

1 3-ounce package lime-flavored
    gelatin
1½ cups boiling water
2 tablespoons vinegar
⅓ cup mayonnaise *or* salad
    dressing
½ teaspoon salt
    Dash pepper
1 cup chopped cabbage
½ cup shredded carrot
½ cup shredded sharp American
    cheese (2 ounces)
⅛ teaspoon celery seed
    Lettuce leaves

Refer to: Making molded gelatin salad, steps 4–9 and tip, page 157. Dissolve gelatin in boiling water; stir in vinegar. Add mayonnaise, salt, and pepper; beat smooth with rotary beater. Chill till partially set. Fold cabbage, carrot, cheese, and celery seed into gelatin. Pour into 6 individual molds. Chill till firm. To serve, unmold salads onto lettuce-lined plates. Makes 6 servings.

TIP Recipes for gelatin salads often refer to different "jellying" stages. *Each step in preparing the salad (blending, folding, beating, and layering) should be done while the gelatin is the proper consistency or thickness. Because the consistency of the gelatin changes as it chills, it's important to recognize each stage as it occurs. We've listed the terms used to describe the different stages, plus some helpful hints on how to recognize them.*

Chill till partially set: *The gelatin is the consistency of unbeaten egg whites. At this stage, chopped ingredients are folded in. If whipped at this stage, the mixture will become fluffy and will mound. (Refer to tip on page 157.)*

Chill till almost firm: *The gelatin mixture appears set, but will tend to flow if tipped to one side and is sticky to the touch. This is the desired consistency for preparing a layered salad. (Refer to: Making layered gelatin salad, step 5, page 159.)*

Chill till firm: *The gelatin mixture can now hold a distinctive cut and doesn't move when tilted in the mold. The gelatin is completely set and ready to unmold. (Refer to: Making layered gelatin salad, step 9, page 159.)*

163

Salads

Tossed Salad

Technique: Making tossed salad

- ½ **medium head romaine**
- ½ **medium head iceberg lettuce**
- 1 **small cucumber**
- ½ **green pepper**
- 1 **medium carrot**
  Salad dressing (see recipes, pages 178–179)
- 2 **tomatoes**
  Croutons

164

1 Cut the bottom core from the romaine and discard. Wash romaine leaves under cold running water. **2** Gently pat dry with paper toweling or clean kitchen towel. **3** Place romaine in plastic bag; chill to crisp the leaves. **4** Remove outer leaves of iceberg lettuce. To loosen lettuce core, whack stem end on a counter. **5** Twist the core and lift out. Place the lettuce, bottom side up, under cold running water. Drain thoroughly. Place lettuce in plastic bag; chill to crisp the lettuce.

6 With sharp knife, cut lengthwise along both sides of the heavy midrib of the romaine; remove and discard. Tear romaine and lettuce into bite-size pieces and place in salad bowl.

7 Slice cucumber into thin slices. Slice green pepper into rings. Shred carrot on coarse shredder. Add cucumber, pepper, and carrot to the greens. **8** Pour your choice of salad dressing over salad. **9** Roll-toss salad. Slice tomatoes into wedges; add to the salad. Toss. **10** Sprinkle croutons over salad. Makes 8 to 10 servings.

1 Cut the bottom core from romaine; discard. Wash romaine leaves under cold running water. Discard any discolored or wilted leaves.

2 Transfer drained leaves to paper toweling or clean kitchen towel. Place a second piece of paper toweling over leaves. Gently pat romaine dry.

6 With sharp knife, cut lengthwise along both sides of the heavy midrib of romaine; remove and discard. Tear romaine and lettuce leaves into bite-size pieces; place in salad bowl. Chopping greens with a knife bruises them. Tearing exposes the juicy insides and allows dressing to become absorbed by the greens.

Half of either a romaine head or an iceberg lettuce head will yield about 3 cups.

7 On a cutting board, slice the cucumber into thin slices. Slice the green pepper into thin rings. Using a coarse shredder and holding carrot at 45-angle, shred the carrot. Add cucumber, green pepper rings, and carrot to the greens.

3 Place romaine leaves loosely in plastic bag. Refrigerate romaine at least 8 hours to crisp the leaves.

4 Remove and discard any discolored or wilted outer leaves of iceberg lettuce. To loosen lettuce core, whack stem end sharply on a countertop.

5 Twist the core and lift out. Place the lettuce, bottom side up, under cold running water. Rinse the lettuce well. Invert head lettuce and let water run out. Drain thoroughly. Place lettuce in plastic bag; refrigerate at least 8 hours to crisp the leaves.

TIP A hearty chef's salad makes a welcome late-evening supper or a light but satisfying lunch. *Atop your favorite greens, arrange julienne strips of cooked chicken or turkey, ham, and cheddar or Swiss cheese in spoke-fashion. Arrange hard-cooked egg slices or wedges, tomato wedges, and pitted ripe olives atop. Serve with your favorite salad dressing.*

165

8 Prepare one of the salad dressings from pages 178 or 179, or use one of your favorite bottled salad dressings.

If using an oil-vinegar dressing, shake well just before using. Shaking emulsifies the oil and vinegar and blends the seasonings.

Pour salad dressing in a thin stream over the salad ingredients.

9 Roll-toss salad using two salad servers or two spoons. Gently push downward to bottom of bowl with one server and up and over with the other server.

Cut tomatoes in wedges; add to salad and toss gently. Adding the tomatoes last prevents them from diluting dressing.

10 Just before serving, sprinkle croutons over salad. Use purchased croutons or prepare your own as follows. Brush both sides of white, whole wheat, or rye bread slices with butter or margarine; cut bread into ½-inch cubes. Spread out on baking sheet. Bake in 300° oven for 20 to 25 minutes or till croutons are dry and crisp, stirring frequently. Cool. Store in covered container in refrigerator.

Salads

Perfect Potato Salad

Technique: Making potato salad

3	**medium potatoes**
1	**teaspoon sugar**
1	**teaspoon vinegar**
½	**cup sliced celery**
⅓	**cup finely chopped onion**
¼	**cup chopped sweet pickle**
1	**teaspoon salt**
1	**teaspoon celery seed**
¾	**cup mayonnaise *or* salad dressing**
2	**hard-cooked eggs, sliced**

1 In covered pan cook whole potatoes in enough boiling salted water to cover about 25 minutes or till almost tender. Drain well. Peel the warm potatoes. **2** Quarter and slice potatoes; transfer to mixing bowl. **3** Sprinkle potatoes with sugar and vinegar. **4** Add the sliced celery, onion, sweet pickle, salt, and celery seed to the potatoes; stir the mixture to combine. **5-6** Add mayonnaise or salad dressing; fold into potato mixture. **7** Carefully fold in the sliced eggs. Cover and chill thoroughly. Makes 4 servings.

166

1 In a covered pan cook whole potatoes in enough boiling salted water to cover about 25 minutes or till almost tender. Drain well. Peel potatoes. Using a fork to hold the warm potato upright, use a sharp paring knife to scrape and pull away peel from the cooked potato, as shown.

5 Add the mayonnaise or salad dressing to the potato mixture. For an accurate measure, use a rubber spatula to remove all the mayonnaise from the measuring cup.

2 On a cutting board cut peeled potatoes into quarters. Slice the potatoes into ¼-inch-thick pieces. Transfer potato pieces to a mixing bowl.

3 For even distribution, sprinkle the sugar and vinegar over the entire surface of the potatoes, as shown.

4 Add the sliced celery, finely chopped onion, chopped sweet pickle, salt, and celery seed to the potatoes; stir mixture to combine. A rubber spatula will help you gently lift the ingredients from the sides of the bowl for a thorough mixing.

6 Fold the mayonnaise or salad dressing into the potato mixture. To fold, cut down through the mixture with a rubber spatula. Scrape across bottom of bowl; then bring spatula up and over mixture, close to the surface. Repeat this circular down-up-and-over motion, turning bowl as you work.

7 Carefully fold the hard-cooked egg slices into the potato mixture. Careful handling will prevent the egg slices from breaking into pieces. Cover and chill thoroughly.

Salads

Wilted Spinach Salad

Technique: Making wilted greens salad

½	**pound fresh spinach (6 cups)**
¼	**cup sliced green onion**
	Whole black pepper
2	***or* 3 slices bacon**
1	**tablespoon white wine vinegar**
2	**teaspoons lemon juice**
½	**teaspoon sugar**
¼	**teaspoon salt**
1	**hard-cooked egg, chopped**

1 Wash fresh spinach and pat dry on paper toweling.
2 Tear spinach into bite-size pieces and place in a mixing bowl; add green onion. **3** Grind a generous amount of pepper over the spinach. Cover and chill.

4 Cut bacon into small pieces. In large skillet cook bacon till crisp. **5** Stir in vinegar, lemon juice, sugar, and salt. **6** Gradually add chilled spinach and green onion. **7–8** Toss mixture till spinach is well-coated with bacon mixture. Cook 1 to 2 minutes or till spinach is slightly wilted.

9 Turn the spinach mixture into serving dish. Sprinkle with the chopped hard-cooked egg; serve immediately. Makes 4 servings.

1 Wash spinach leaves well in a large bowl of lukewarm water (rather than washing each leaf separately under cold water). It's important to wash spinach thoroughly to remove sand particles. After a few minutes, lift out and drain leaves; discard the water. Repeat until no sand collects in the bowl. Gently pat clean leaves dry on paper toweling.

2 Tear the spinach leaves into bite-size pieces and place in a mixing bowl. Add sliced green onion. Be sure to include some of the green tops when slicing onion.

6 Gradually add the chilled spinach and green onion to the skillet mixture. Stir constantly to prevent the spinach from cooking too fast.

7 Using two spoons or forks, toss the spinach mixture to coat evenly with bacon mixture. Cook spinach mixture 1 to 2 minutes.

3 Using a pepper mill with whole black pepper, grind a generous amount of pepper over the spinach-onion mixture. Or, sprinkle with ground pepper. Cover and chill spinach mixture.

4 Using kitchen shears or a sharp paring knife and a cutting board, cut the bacon strips into small pieces. Place the bacon pieces in a large skillet; cook over medium heat till crisp and brown.

5 In a 1-cup liquid measure or a small bowl, combine the white wine vinegar, lemon juice, sugar, and salt. Gradually add vinegar mixture to bacon and drippings in skillet, stirring to combine.

169

8 Cook till spinach is slightly wilted and no longer crisp, as shown. The spinach should not be cooked completely.

9 Turn the spinach mixture into a serving dish; sprinkle with chopped hard-cooked egg. Serve immediately while spinach is still warm.

Salads

Sweet-Sour Coleslaw

> 5 cups shredded green *or* red
> cabbage
> ⅓ cup finely chopped onion
> ½ cup mayonnaise *or* salad
> dressing
> 2 tablespoons sweet pickle relish
> 1 tablespoon sugar
> 1 tablespoon vinegar
> ½ teaspoon salt
> ½ teaspoon celery seed

Refer to tip at right. In large bowl combine the shredded cabbage and chopped onion. Set aside. To prepare dressing, stir together the mayonnaise or salad dressing, pickle relish, sugar, vinegar, salt, and celery seed, stirring till the sugar is completely dissolved. Pour the dressing over the cabbage mixture; toss lightly to coat vegetables. To serve, sieve a hard-cooked egg yolk over top of the salad, if desired. Makes 6 servings.

Cheddar-Macaroni Salad

> 3 cups medium shell macaroni
> 2 cups cubed cheddar cheese
> 1 cup chopped celery
> ½ cup chopped green pepper
> ¼ cup chopped onion
> 1 cup dairy sour cream
> 1 cup mayonnaise *or* salad
> dressing
> ¼ cup milk
> ½ cup sweet pickle relish
> 4 teaspoons vinegar
> 1½ teaspoons prepared mustard
> ¾ teaspoon salt

In large kettle cook macaroni in a large amount of boiling salted water till tender; drain. Cool to room temperature. Toss with cheese, celery, green pepper, and onion.

Combine sour cream, mayonnaise or salad dressing, and milk; stir in relish, vinegar, mustard, and salt. Toss with macaroni mixture (salad will appear quite moist). Cover; chill several hours. Serve in lettuce-lined bowl. Garnish with green pepper rings, if desired. Makes 12 servings.

Tossed Egg Salad

> 1 medium head iceberg lettuce, torn
> (6 cups)
> 6 hard-cooked eggs, sliced
> 1 small onion, thinly sliced
> ¼ cup shredded sharp cheddar
> cheese (1 ounce)
> ¼ cup salad oil
> 2 tablespoons vinegar
> 1 tablespoon snipped parsley
> 1 teaspoon worcestershire sauce
> ½ teaspoon salt
> ⅛ teaspoon pepper
> Dash paprika

Refer to: Making tossed salad, steps 4 and 5, page 165. In large salad bowl combine lettuce, egg slices, sliced onion, and shredded cheese. Cover and chill thoroughly. To make dressing, in a screw-top jar combine salad oil, vinegar, parsley, worcestershire sauce, salt, pepper, and paprika; cover and shake well to mix together. Pour dressing over chilled salad. Toss salad lightly to coat vegetables. Makes 6 servings.

Hot Bean and Onion Salad

> 2 9-ounce packages frozen Italian
> green beans
> 1 small onion, sliced and separated
> into rings
> 3 tablespoons olive oil
> 3 tablespoons red wine vinegar
> ½ teaspoon dried oregano, crushed
> ¼ teaspoon salt
> Dash pepper

Cook green beans according to package directions; drain. Mix hot beans with onion. To make dressing, in a screw-top jar combine olive oil, vinegar, oregano, salt, and pepper; cover and shake well to mix together. Pour the dressing over the bean mixture. Toss salad lightly to coat vegetables. Makes 8 servings.

Cheddar-Macaroni Salad

Asparagus Vinaigrette

¾ pound fresh asparagus *or* 1
    8-ounce package frozen
    asparagus spears
½ cup salad oil
2 tablespoons vinegar
2 tablespoons lemon juice
2 teaspoons sugar
½ teaspoon salt
½ teaspoon paprika
½ teaspoon dry mustard
    Dash cayenne
2 tablespoons finely chopped
    pimiento-stuffed olives
1 hard-cooked egg, finely chopped
2 small tomatoes, chilled
    Lettuce leaves

Wash fresh asparagus and scrape off scales. Break off woody bases at point where spears snap easily. Place whole spears in a skillet or saucepan with a small amount of boiling salted water. To avoid overcooked tips, prop them out of water with crumpled foil. (Or, fasten whole spears in a bundle and stand upright in a deep kettle, letting tips extend 2 to 3 inches above boiling salted water.) Cover pan and cook 10 to 15 minutes or till spears are crisp-tender. (Or, cook frozen asparagus according to package directions.) Drain.

To make dressing, in a screw-top jar combine salad oil, vinegar, lemon juice, sugar, salt, paprika, dry mustard, and cayenne. Add the pimiento-stuffed olives and chopped hard-cooked egg; cover and shake well to mix together.

Arrange asparagus in a shallow dish; top with the dressing. Cover asparagus and refrigerate for several hours or overnight, spooning the dressing over asparagus occasionally.

To serve, drain asparagus, reserving the dressing. Slice the tomatoes. On each of 4 salad plates, arrange a few asparagus spears atop lettuce. Top each salad with a few tomato slices. Spoon a little of the reserved dressing over each salad. Makes 4 servings.

Original Caesar Salad

    Garlic Olive Oil
    Caesar Croutons
3 medium heads romaine, chilled
    and torn into bite-size pieces
    (16 cups)
2 to 3 tablespoons wine vinegar
1 lemon, halved
2 eggs
    Dash worcestershire sauce
    Whole black pepper
⅓ cup grated parmesan cheese
    Rolled anchovy fillets (optional)

One or more days before serving the salad, prepare Garlic Olive Oil. Several hours before serving, prepare Caesar Croutons. Chill salad bowl and dinner plates.

Refer to: Making tossed salad, steps 1–3, page 164. At serving time place romaine in chilled salad bowl. Drizzle with about ⅓ *cup* of the Garlic Olive Oil and vinegar; squeeze lemon over.

To coddle eggs, place eggs in shell in boiling water. Remove pan from heat and let stand 1 minute. Remove eggs; let cool slightly. Break over romaine. Add worcestershire; sprinkle with salt. Grind a generous amount of pepper over; sprinkle with cheese. Toss lightly till dressing is combined and romaine is well coated. Add Caesar Croutons; toss once or twice. Serve immediately on chilled dinner plates. Garnish with anchovies, if desired. Makes 6 to 8 servings.

Garlic Olive Oil: Slice 6 cloves *garlic* lengthwise into quarters; combine with 1 cup *olive or salad oil.* Store in covered jar in refrigerator. Remove garlic before using oil.

Caesar Croutons: Brush both sides of 3 slices white *bread* with *Garlic Olive Oil;* cut bread into ½-inch cubes. Spread out on baking sheet. Bake in 250° oven about 1 hour or till croutons are dry and crisp. Sprinkle with grated *parmesan cheese.* Cool. Store croutons in covered jar in refrigerator.

Cottage Cheese-Spinach Salad

½ cup dairy sour cream
2 tablespoons sugar
1 tablespoon prepared horseradish
½ teaspoon dry mustard
¼ teaspoon salt
3 tablespoons tarragon vinegar
7 cups torn fresh spinach
1½ cups cream-style cottage cheese
    (12 ounces)
½ cup chopped walnuts

To prepare dressing, stir together sour cream, sugar, horseradish, mustard, and salt. Gradually blend in vinegar till well-combined. Cover and chill. In salad bowl arrange the spinach; top with cottage cheese and walnuts. To serve, stir the dressing and pour over the salad; toss lightly to coat spinach leaves. Makes 6 to 8 servings.

171

TIP Save time by shredding cabbage in blender. *Remove any wilted outer leaves; rinse cabbage. Cut into wedges; remove center core. Place a few cabbage wedges in the blender container. Cover with cold water. Cover the blender container and blend till coarsely chopped. Remove from blender; drain well. Repeat with the remaining cabbage wedges. Cover and chill. Before serving, drain cabbage again and toss with your favorite coleslaw dressing.*

Salads

Pea-Cheese Salad

    2 cups shelled peas *or* 1 10-ounce
      package frozen peas *or* 1
      17-ounce can peas
    1 cup cubed cheddar cheese (4
      ounces)
    2 hard-cooked eggs, chopped
    ¼ cup chopped celery
    2 tablespoons chopped onion
    2 tablespoons chopped pimiento
    ⅓ cup mayonnaise *or* salad
      dressing
    ½ teaspoon salt
    ¼ teaspoon bottled hot pepper
      sauce
    ⅛ teaspoon pepper
    6 medium tomatoes, cored
      Salt
      Lettuce leaves

In covered pan cook fresh peas in small amount of boiling salted water, 10 to 12 minutes or till tender. (Or, cook frozen peas according to package directions.) Thoroughly drain the cooked or canned peas. Cool cooked peas.

In large bowl combine peas, cheese cubes, hard-cooked eggs, celery, onion, and pimiento. Combine mayonnaise or salad dressing, salt, hot pepper sauce, and pepper. Add to pea mixture; toss to coat. Cover and chill several hours or overnight.

With stem end up, cut each tomato into 6 wedges, cutting to, but not through, base of tomato. Spread wedges apart slightly; sprinkle lightly with salt. Cover and chill.

On 6 salad plates, place tomatoes atop lettuce leaves. Stir the pea mixture well; spoon atop tomatoes. Makes 6 servings.

172

Wilted Lettuce-Orange Salad

    3 slices bacon
    ¼ cup vinegar
    1 tablespoon salad oil
    2 teaspoons sugar
    ¼ teaspoon salt
    ⅛ teaspoon dried tarragon, crushed
      Dash freshly ground pepper
    ¼ cup chopped celery
    1 tablespoon sliced green onion
    1 medium head iceberg lettuce,
      torn (6 cups)
    2 medium oranges, peeled and
      sectioned

Refer to: Making wilted greens salad, steps 4–8, page 169. Cut bacon into small pieces. In large skillet cook bacon till crisp; drain, reserving 2 tablespoons drippings in skillet. Stir vinegar, oil, sugar, salt, tarragon, and pepper into bacon and drippings in skillet; bring to boiling. Add celery and onion.

Gradually add torn lettuce, tossing just till leaves are coated with dressing mixture and are slightly wilted. Add orange sections. Toss lightly to coat; serve immediately. Makes 8 to 10 servings.

Cucumbers in Sour Cream

    2 medium cucumbers, thinly sliced
    1 medium onion, very thinly sliced
    ½ cup dairy sour cream
    1 tablespoon sugar
    1 tablespoon vinegar
    ½ teaspoon salt

In bowl combine the cucumbers and onion. Stir together sour cream, sugar, vinegar, and salt; toss to coat vegetables. Cover and chill; stir occasionally. Makes 3 cups.

24-Hour Vegetable Salad

(pictured on page 154)

    3 cups torn leaf lettuce
    1½ cups shredded Swiss cheese
      (6 ounces)
    1 10-ounce package frozen peas,
      thawed (2 cups)
    4 hard-cooked eggs, sliced
    ½ pound bacon, crisp-cooked,
      drained, and crumbled
      (10 or 11 slices)
    ½ medium head romaine
    ¾ cup mayonnaise *or* salad
      dressing

Place lettuce in bottom of large bowl; sprinkle with a little salt, pepper, and sugar. Top with the cheese. Spoon peas atop, spreading evenly over cheese. Arrange egg slices and bacon over peas. Sprinkle eggs with salt. Prepare romaine, referring to steps 1–3 and 6 on page 164. Arrange romaine atop eggs and bacon.

Spread mayonnaise or salad dressing over top of salad, sealing to edge of bowl. Cover and chill the salad in the refrigerator 24 hours or overnight.

If desired, garnish top of salad with additional crumbled bacon, radish slices, and parsley. Toss before serving to coat the vegetables. Makes 10 to 12 servings.

Bermuda Salad Bowl

    1 small head cauliflower, broken
      into flowerets
    ½ large Bermuda onion, sliced
    ½ cup sliced pimiento-stuffed olives
    ⅔ cup French salad dressing
    1 small head iceberg lettuce, torn
      in bite-size pieces
    ½ cup crumbled blue cheese

Slice cauliflowerets into a large salad bowl. Separate onion slices into rings; add to cauliflower. Add olives. Pour dressing over; toss. Cover; chill 30 minutes. Just before serving, add the lettuce and cheese; toss lightly. Pass additional dressing, if desired. Makes 8 to 10 servings.

Tuna Salad in Tomato Cups

Calico Potato Salad

- 7 medium potatoes
- ½ cup chopped cucumber
- ½ cup chopped onion
- ¼ cup chopped green pepper
- 3 tablespoons chopped pimiento
- 1½ teaspoons salt
- ¾ teaspoon celery seed
- ¼ teaspoon pepper
- 2 hard-cooked eggs
- ⅓ cup mayonnaise *or* salad dressing
- 3 tablespoons vinegar
- 2 tablespoons sugar
- 1 tablespoon prepared mustard
- ½ cup whipping cream

Cook, peel, and slice potatoes, referring to steps 1 and 2 on page 166. In bowl stir together potatoes, cucumber, onion, green pepper, pimiento, salt, celery seed, and pepper. Reserve 1 hard-cooked egg yolk; coarsely chop the white and remaining hard-cooked egg. Add chopped eggs to potato mixture. Cover; chill.

To make the dressing, combine mayonnaise or salad dressing, vinegar, sugar, and mustard. Beat whipping cream till soft peaks form, referring to step 3 on page 161; fold into dressing. About ½ hour before serving, toss the dressing with potato mixture. Sieve the reserved egg yolk; sprinkle over salad. Makes 6 servings.

Tuna Salad in Tomato Cups

- 1 6½- *or* 7-ounce can tuna, drained and flaked
- ½ cup sliced celery
- ¼ cup sliced pimiento-stuffed olives
- ¼ cup sliced green onion
- 1 tablespoon lemon juice
- ¼ teaspoon salt
  Dash pepper
- ½ cup mayonnaise *or* salad dressing
- 2 hard-cooked eggs, chopped
- 4 medium tomatoes, cored
  Salt
  Leaf lettuce

In bowl combine tuna, celery, olives, green onion, lemon juice, salt, and pepper. Gently fold in mayonnaise or salad dressing and chopped eggs; cover and chill.

With stem end up, cut each tomato into 6 wedges, cutting to, but not through, base of tomato. Spread wedges apart slightly; sprinkle lightly with salt. Cover and chill.

To serve, place a chilled tomato on each individual, lettuce-lined plate; fill each tomato with about ½ cup of the tuna mixture. Garnish with additional sliced pimiento-stuffed olives, if desired. Makes 4 servings.

Tossed Fruit Salad

- ½ cup sugar
- ¼ cup tarragon vinegar
- 2 tablespoons water
- 1 teaspoon celery salt
- 1 teaspoon paprika
- 1 teaspoon dry mustard
- 1 cup salad oil
- 2 medium oranges, chilled
- 1 medium grapefruit, chilled
- 1 ripe medium banana
- 4 cups torn iceberg lettuce
- 2 cups torn escarole
- 1 avocado, seeded, peeled, and thinly sliced
- 1 cup red grapes, halved and seeded

To make dressing, heat and stir sugar, vinegar, and water just till sugar dissolves; cool. Combine vinegar mixture, celery salt, paprika, and mustard. Add oil in a slow stream, beating with electric mixer till thick. Cover and chill.

Peel and section oranges and grapefruit, reserving juices. Peel and slice banana; brush with reserved citrus juices. Set aside.

In large salad bowl combine lettuce and escarole. Arrange orange and grapefruit sections, banana, avocado slices, and grapes atop. Pour dressing over; toss to coat fruits. Makes 6 to 8 servings.

Cheese-Anchovy Bowl

- 4 cups torn iceberg lettuce
- 1 cup torn curly endive
- 1 cup torn watercress
- 1 cup Swiss cheese, cut in thin strips (4 ounces)
- 1 2-ounce can anchovy fillets, drained and cut up
- 3 tablespoons bottled Italian salad dressing

In large salad bowl combine lettuce, endive, and watercress. Add cheese strips and anchovy fillets. Toss with Italian salad dressing to coat. Makes 6 to 8 servings.

SALAD DRESSINGS

Many salads rely on their dressing for exciting flavor. Whether tart or tangy, spicy or sweet, or oil-based or creamy, the dressing often determines the success of the salad. Here you'll learn the difference between various types of dressings— including mayonnaise, cooked, and shaken varieties—as well as which salads they complement best.

Mayonnaise

Technique: Making mayonnaise

- **1 teaspoon salt**
- **½ teaspoon dry mustard**
- **¼ teaspoon paprika**
  Dash cayenne
- **2 egg yolks**
- **2 tablespoons vinegar**
- **2 cups salad oil**
- **2 tablespoons lemon juice**

1 In small mixer bowl combine salt, dry mustard, paprika, and cayenne. Add egg yolks and vinegar; beat mixture at medium speed of electric mixer till blended. **2** Add the salad oil, 1 teaspoon at a time, beating constantly. Continue beating mixture till ¼ cup oil has been added. **3–6** While continuing to beat, add the remaining oil in a thin, steady stream, alternating the last ½ cup salad oil with the lemon juice. Store in a tightly covered jar in the refrigerator. Label and date the jar before storing. Since homemade mayonnaise doesn't contain preservatives, you should use it within 4 weeks. Makes 2 cups.

1 In small mixer bowl combine salt, dry mustard, paprika, and cayenne. Add the egg yolks and vinegar; beat mixture at medium speed till blended.

4 Before the lemon juice and the last portion of the oil are added, the mixture will be smooth and creamy, as shown.

2 Add the salad oil to egg mixture, 1 teaspoon at a time, beating constantly. Continue beating mixture till ¼ cup oil has been added.

This step is very important to assure that the desired emulsion forms. If oil is added to the yolk mixture too rapidly, an emulsion will not form. Instead, the oil will separate out.

3 While continuing to beat, add the remaining salad oil in increasing amounts by pouring in a thin, steady stream till all but ½ cup has been added.

175

TIP If your mayonnaise fails to form an emulsion, *the mixture will separate and appear thin or curdled, as shown. If this happens, restore the mayonnaise by very slowly beating the separated mixture into an egg yolk. This remedy will not work if you reverse the procedure by beating the yolk into the separated mayonnaise mixture.*

5 Alternate the last ½ cup of salad oil with the lemon juice, beating at medium speed till thoroughly blended.

6 The consistency of the finished mayonnaise is thick and smooth, as shown. If too much oil is added, the mayonnaise will break down, no matter how patiently you work.

Generally, a proportion of up to 1 cup of oil per egg yolk will ensure a stable mayonnaise mixture.

Salad Dressings

Cooked Dressing

Technique: Making cooked salad dressing

  2 **tablespoons all-purpose flour**
  2 **tablespoons sugar**
  1 **teaspoon salt**
  1 **teaspoon dry mustard**
     Dash cayenne
 ¾ **cup milk**
  2 **egg yolks**
 ¼ **cup vinegar**
1½ **teaspoons butter *or* margarine**

1 In a small saucepan thoroughly combine flour, sugar, salt, dry mustard, and cayenne. **2** Add milk to the dry ingredients all at once; stir to blend. **3** Beat egg yolks slightly; add to saucepan. **4** Cook, stirring constantly, over low heat till thickened and bubbly. **5–6** Add vinegar and butter or margarine; stir till butter or margarine melts and mixture is blended. Remove from heat; cool. Store in a tightly covered jar in the refrigerator. Makes 1 cup.

176

1 In a small saucepan combine the all-purpose flour, sugar, salt, dry mustard, and cayenne. Stir the dry ingredients to mix well.

4 Cook the mixture over low heat till thickened and bubbly, as shown. Stir constantly with a wooden spoon in a figure-8 motion to assure even cooking.

2 Add the milk all at once to the dry ingredients in the saucepan, stirring to thoroughly blend the mixture, as shown.

3 In a custard cup, slightly beat the egg yolks with a fork, as shown. Add the yolks to the saucepan, stirring to blend the mixture.

177

5 Add the vinegar and the butter or margarine. Stir till butter or margarine melts and mixture is blended.

6 Cooked salad dressing should have a thick, creamy consistency, and appear satin-smooth and glossy, as shown.

Remove the cooked dressing from heat and set aside to cool. Store in tightly covered jar in refrigerator.

TIP To make shaken salad dressings, *such as vinaigrette dressing, use a small screw-top jar for both mixing and storing.*

Combine the salad oil and all the herbs and seasonings in the jar, as shown in top photo. Cover the jar and shake to mix the ingredients together, as shown in bottom photo. Refrigerate the salad dressing to chill thoroughly. Shake the dressing again just before serving.

Salad Dressings

Blue Cheese Dressing

⅓ cup crumbled blue cheese (about 1 ounce)
1 tablespoon finely chopped onion
½ clove garlic, minced
½ cup mayonnaise *or* salad dressing
½ cup dairy sour cream
1 tablespoon lemon juice
1 tablespoon vinegar
Dash pepper

In small mixer bowl combine blue cheese, onion, and garlic. Using an electric mixer, mix on low speed for 3 minutes. Add mayonnaise or salad dressing, sour cream, lemon juice, vinegar, and pepper to cheese mixture; mix 2 minutes more or till smooth. Pour into a covered container. Store in refrigerator to chill. Serve with tossed salad. Garnish with more crumbled blue cheese, if desired. Makes about 1½ cups.

Avocado Dressing

1 3-ounce package cream cheese, softened
1 avocado, seeded, peeled, and cut up
1 tablespoon lemon juice
½ cup mayonnaise *or* salad dressing
¼ teaspoon salt
¼ teaspoon garlic powder
¼ cup milk

In mixer bowl combine cream cheese, avocado, lemon juice, mayonnaise or salad dressing, salt, and garlic powder; beat with electric mixer till smooth. Stir in enough milk to achieve desired consistency (about ¼ cup). Serve with tossed salad. Makes about 1½ cups.

Poppy-Lime Dressing

¾ cup sugar
⅓ cup lime juice
¼ cup vinegar
1 teaspoon salt
1 teaspoon dry mustard
1 teaspoon poppy seed
1 teaspoon paprika
1 cup salad oil

In small saucepan combine sugar, lime juice, vinegar, salt, dry mustard, poppy seed, and paprika. Cook and stir over low heat till sugar dissolves. Remove from heat and cool. Gradually add the salad oil, beating with electric mixer till slightly thickened. Store in a tightly covered jar in the refrigerator. Serve with fresh fruit. Makes about 2 cups.

Thousand Island Dressing

1 cup mayonnaise *or* salad dressing (see recipe, page 174)
¼ cup chili sauce
2 hard-cooked eggs, chopped
2 tablespoons chopped green pepper
2 tablespoons chopped celery
1½ tablespoons finely chopped onion
1 teaspoon paprika
½ teaspoon salt

Combine mayonnaise or salad dressing, chili sauce, hard-cooked eggs, green pepper, celery, onion, paprika, and salt; stir together till well mixed. Store in a tightly covered jar in the refrigerator. Serve with tossed salad. Makes about 2 cups.

Celery Seed Dressing

(pictured on page 154)

⅔ cup sugar
1 teaspoon dry mustard
1 teaspoon paprika
1 teaspoon celery seed
¼ teaspoon salt
⅓ cup honey
⅓ cup vinegar
1 tablespoon lemon juice
½ teaspoon grated onion (optional)
1 cup salad oil

In small mixer bowl combine sugar, mustard, paprika, celery seed, and salt. Add honey, vinegar, lemon juice, and onion; beat with electric mixer to thoroughly blend. Gradually add oil in a slow stream, beating constantly with electric mixer till dressing is thick. Serve over fruit or tossed salads. Makes 2 cups.

178

Poppy-Lime Dressing
Avocado Dressing
Blue Cheese Dressing (back)
Thousand Island Dressing

French Dressing

(pictured on page 154)

- ½ **cup salad oil**
- 2 **tablespoons vinegar**
- 2 **tablespoons lemon juice**
- 1 **teaspoon sugar**
- ¾ **teaspoon dry mustard**
- ½ **teaspoon salt**
- ⅛ **teaspoon paprika**
  Dash cayenne

Refer to tip on page 177. In a screw-top jar combine all the ingredients. Cover and shake well to blend thoroughly. Chill. Shake again just before serving. Makes ¾ cup.

Blue Cheese French: Add 2 ounces *blue cheese,* finely crumbled (½ cup).

Garlic French: Add ¼ teaspoon *garlic powder or* 1 small clove *garlic,* minced.

Vinaigrette: Add 2 tablespoons finely chopped pimiento-stuffed *olives,* 1 tablespoon finely chopped *pimiento,* 1 tablespoon finely snipped *chives,* and 1 *hard-cooked egg,* finely chopped.

Zippy Onion Dressing

- ⅔ **cup salad oil**
- ⅓ **cup vinegar**
- ¼ **cup sliced green onion**
- ¼ **cup snipped parsley**
- 2 **tablespoons finely chopped green pepper**
- 1 **tablespoon sugar**
- 2 **teaspoons dry mustard**
- ½ **teaspoon salt**
- ⅛ **teaspoon cayenne**

In a screw-top jar combine salad oil, vinegar, green onion, parsley, green pepper, sugar, dry mustard, salt, and cayenne. Cover; let stand at room temperature for 1 hour. Shake well to blend thoroughly. Serve with seafood or tossed salads. Makes about 1¼ cups.

Italian-Cheese Dressing

- 1⅓ **cups salad oil**
- ½ **cup vinegar**
- ¼ **cup grated parmesan cheese**
- 1 **tablespoon sugar**
- 2 **teaspoons salt**
- 1 **teaspoon celery salt**
- ½ **teaspoon white pepper**
- ½ **teaspoon dry mustard**
- ¼ **teaspoon paprika**
- 1 **clove garlic, minced**

In blender container combine salad oil, vinegar, parmesan cheese, sugar, salt, celery salt, white pepper, dry mustard, paprika, and garlic. Cover and blend ingredients till well combined.

(Or, in a screw-top jar combine all ingredients; cover and shake well to blend thoroughly, referring to tip on page 177.) Chill. Mix again just before serving. Makes about 1¾ cups.

Mayonnaise Variations

Refer to: Making mayonnaise, page 174. Starting with our homemade mayonnaise—or commercial mayonnaise or salad dressing—make any of these delectable creamy dressings.

Creamy Fruit Dressing: Mix 1 cup *mayonnaise or salad dressing,* 1 cup dairy *sour cream,* 2 tablespoons *lemon juice,* 2 tablespoons *orange juice,* and 4 teaspoons *sugar.* Makes 2¼ cups.

Curry Dressing: Mix 3 tablespoons hot *water* into 1½ teaspoons *beef-flavored gravy base;* stir to dissolve. Stir in 1 cup *mayonnaise or salad dressing* and ½ teaspoon *curry powder.* Makes 1¼ cups.

Cranberry Fruit Dressing: Mix 1 cup *mayonnaise or salad dressing,* ⅓ cup *cranberry juice cocktail,* and a dash *salt;* add 2 tablespoons toasted chopped *almonds.* Makes 1⅓ cups.

Chili Mayonnaise: Mix 1 cup *mayonnaise or salad dressing* and ½ cup *chili sauce.* Makes 1½ cups.

Herb Dressing: Mix 1 cup *mayonnaise or salad dressing;* 2 tablespoons finely chopped *onion;* 1 tablespoon *lemon juice;* 1 tablespoon *dry sherry;* 1 clove *garlic, minced;* 1 teaspoon *worcestershire sauce;* and ½ teaspoon dried mixed *salad herbs.* Makes 1¼ cups.

Chive Mayonnaise: Mix 1 cup *mayonnaise or salad dressing,* ¼ cup snipped *chives,* 1 tablespoon *lemon juice,* 2 teaspoons *tarragon vinegar,* and a dash *salt.* Makes 1¼ cups.

Honey Mayonnaise: Mix 1 cup *mayonnaise or salad dressing;* ¼ cup *honey,* 2 tablespoons *lemon juice,* 1 teaspoon *celery seed,* and ½ teaspoon *paprika.* Makes 1½ cups.

Blue Cheese Mayonnaise: Mix 1 cup *mayonnaise or salad dressing* and ¼ cup crumbled *blue cheese* (1 ounce) till smooth; stir in 2 tablespoons *milk* and several drops *bottled hot pepper sauce.* Makes 1 cup.

179

Clockwise from left: Cinnamon Swirl Loaf (see recipe, page 202); Ambrosia Muffins and Orange Doughnuts (see recipes, page 220); Italian Loaves (see recipe, page 199); Biscuit Bubble Ring (see recipe, page 220); Waffles (see recipe, page 214); and Cheese Bread Knots (see recipe, page 203).

BREADS

In the following pages, you'll find two methods for preparing yeast doughs and making rolls, doughnuts, and bagels. Hints and explanations for quick breads begin on page 206. Included are muffins, biscuits, pancakes, waffles, crepes, and noodles.

White Bread

Technique: Using the conventional method for yeast breads

1 package active dry yeast
¼ cup warm water (110° to 115°)
2 cups milk
2 tablespoons sugar
1 tablespoon shortening
2 teaspoons salt
5¾ to 6¼ cups all-purpose flour

1 Soften yeast in water. **2** Heat milk, sugar, shortening, and salt till sugar dissolves; cool to lukewarm. **3** Turn into bowl. Stir in *2 cups* of the flour. **4** Add the softened yeast; stir till smooth. **5** Stir in as much remaining flour as you can mix in with a spoon. **6** Turn out onto floured surface; knead in enough of the remaining flour to make a moderately stiff dough. **7–8** Continue kneading till smooth and elastic (6 to 8 minutes). **9** Shape into a ball. Place in greased bowl; turn once to grease surface.

10–11 Cover; let rise in warm place till double (about 1¼ hours). **12** Punch down; turn out onto lightly floured surface. **13** Divide dough in half. Shape into two smooth balls. Cover; let rest 10 minutes. **14** Grease two 8×4×2-inch loaf pans.

15 Shape each ball of dough into a loaf. (**16–17** *Or* roll each into a 12×8-inch rectangle; roll from shortest end to make a loaf.) Place in pans. **18** Cover; let rise in warm place till double (45 to 60 minutes). **19** Bake in 375° oven about 45 minutes or till done. **20** Remove from pans; cool on rack. Makes 2 loaves.

1 Soften yeast in warm water. For best results, check the water temperature with a candy or roast and yeast thermometer. It should register 110°. If the water is cooler, the yeast won't grow as it should. Hotter water will kill the yeast.

If a thermometer is not available, test a few drops of water on inside of wrist. It should just feel warm.

2 In a saucepan heat together the milk, sugar, shortening, and salt; cool to lukewarm (105° to 110°). Use a thermometer for accurate results.

The mixture must be cooled before adding the yeast or the yeast may be killed.

Using milk instead of water as the liquid gives the bread a softer crust.

6 Turn dough out onto lightly floured surface. Using a well-floured pastry cloth makes the dough easier to knead, so less flour is worked into the dough. This is an advantage, since adding more flour tends to make the bread drier.

Knead in enough of the remaining flour to make a moderately stiff dough. To knead, fold the dough over and push down with the heel of the hand, curving your fingers over the dough.

7 Give the dough a quarter turn, then fold over and push down again. Kneading is important in determining the final structure of the loaf as it develops the gluten of the flour. If the dough is not kneaded enough, the loaf will be more likely to have a coarse texture and will probably not rise as high in the pan.

3 Transfer the cooled milk to a large mixing bowl. Add *2 cups* of the flour and beat well. Batter at this stage should be smooth with no lumps, as shown. Adding the flour before the yeast also helps make the dough temperature right for the yeast.

4 Add the softened yeast to the milk-flour mixture. Stir with a wooden spoon to evenly distribute the yeast throughout the batter.

5 By hand, stir in as much of the remaining 4¼ cups flour as you can mix in with a wooden spoon.

To maintain a smooth dough, add the flour in portions and stir after adding each.

183

TIP *Yeast doughs used for coffee cakes and sweet rolls usually include 1 or more eggs for richness. Add the eggs right after the softened yeast in step 4.*

8 Continue kneading in the fold-push-turn procedure till dough is smooth and elastic, as shown.

To be sure you've kneaded enough, set a timer for the maximum time suggested in the recipe. You may want to stop and rest a bit instead of kneading the dough all at once. Just be sure the total time is as long as the recipe suggests. Cover the dough with a towel if you are interrupted or stop to rest.

9 Shape the dough into a ball and place in a lightly greased bowl that's at least twice as large as the size of the ball of dough. Turn dough over once to grease entire surface. This helps keep it from drying out.

10 Cover the bowl of dough with a cloth. You may first want to cover the dough with lightly greased waxed paper or plastic wrap. This way, the dough won't stick to the cloth if it rises to the top of the bowl.

The oven is a good draft-free place to set the bowl of dough. Place on upper rack with a bowl or pan of hot water on the lower rack. Keep the oven door closed. (*continued next page*)

Yeast Breads

White Bread *Continued*

11 Dough should be allowed to rise until it doubles in size. Times suggested in the recipes are guidelines. The actual time needed may be more or less than that indicated.

The dough is ready to shape when you can lightly and quickly press two fingertips ½ inch into the dough and the indentation remains, as shown.

12 Punch down the dough by pushing your fist into the center of the dough, as shown. Then, pull the edges of the dough to the center, turn dough over, and place on lightly floured surface.

16 To shape dough by rolling, place ball of dough on lightly floured pastry cloth or board. Roll into a 12×8-inch rectangle, rolling to the outer edges to remove all the bubbles. Roll up tightly, starting with narrow edge. Seal with fingertips as you roll. Repeat to make second loaf.

17 Be sure to seal the final edge thoroughly. After rolling up, seal the ends by pressing down on each end to make a thin sealed strip. Fold strips under loaf and place in prepared pan. Repeat for second loaf.

13 Divide dough into two portions. Shape each into a smooth ball. Cover with a towel to keep warm and to help prevent a dried-out surface. Let rest about 10 minutes; this allows the gluten to relax and makes the dough easier to roll.

14 Grease two 8×4×2-inch loaf pans. Use folded paper toweling, waxed paper, or a pastry brush to lightly cover the bottoms and sides of pans with shortening or cooking oil.

15 Shape each ball of dough into a loaf by patting or rolling. To pat, gently pull the dough into a loaf shape, tucking the edges beneath.

185

18 Cover loaves; set in a warm place and let rise (see step 10 on page 183). Dough should rise over top of pan in a rounded shape, as shown. Loaf is ready to bake when an indentation remains after touching lightly with finger. This will probably take 45 to 60 minutes.

19 Bake in 375° oven about 45 minutes or till done. Test by tapping the top with your finger. A hollow sound means that the loaf is properly baked. If top browns too fast, cover loosely with foil the last 15 minutes of baking.

20 Remove bread from pans; cool on wire rack. When completely cooled, wrap in foil or clear plastic wrap or place in plastic bag; store in a cool dry place (refrigerator storage is not recommended since it causes yeast breads to stale). To freeze, wrap cooled bread in moisture-vaporproof wrap. Thaw at room temperature, then warm in 250° to 300° oven.

Yeast Breads

Easy-Mix White Bread

Technique: Using the easy-mix method for yeast bread

5¾ to 6¼ cups all-purpose flour
1 package active dry yeast
2¼ cups milk
2 tablespoons sugar
1 tablespoon shortening
2 teaspoons salt

186

1 Combine *2½ cups* of the flour and the yeast. **2** Heat milk, sugar, shortening, and salt just till warm and shortening is almost melted; stir constantly. **3** Add to flour mixture. **4** Beat at low speed for ½ minute; scrape sides of bowl. **5** Beat 3 minutes at high speed. **6** Stir in as much of the remaining flour as you can mix in with a spoon. **7** Turn out onto lightly floured surface. Knead in enough of the remaining flour to make a moderately stiff dough. **8–9** Continue kneading till smooth and elastic (6 to 8 minutes). **10** Shape into a ball. Place in lightly greased bowl; turn once to grease surface. **11–12** Cover; let rise in warm place till double (about 1¼ hours). **13** Punch dough down; turn out onto lightly floured surface.

14 Divide dough into two portions. Cover; let rest 10 minutes. **15** Lightly grease two 8×4×2-inch loaf pans. **16–18** Shape or roll each half of dough into a loaf. **19** Cover; let rise in warm place till double (45 to 60 minutes). **20** Bake in 375° oven about 45 minutes or till done. **21** Remove from pans; cool. Makes 2 loaves.

Do not use the easy-mix method in Canada. *Differences in the yeast make it impossible to get good results. Instead, here's how to convert recipes to the conventional method. Change ¼ cup of the liquid to warm water; add yeast to dissolve. Heat remaining liquid as directed in step 2 on page 182. Continue as directed for the conventional method.*

1 Place 2½ cups of the flour in large mixer bowl. Sprinkle dry yeast atop. Stir well to evenly distribute the yeast.

2 In saucepan heat the milk, sugar, shortening, and salt just till warm (115° to 120°) and shortening is almost melted. Use a thermometer for accurate results. Stir the milk mixture constantly to melt the shortening as much as possible (it won't melt completely).

6 Stir in as much of the remaining 3¾ cups flour as you can mix in with a spoon. Do not try to use your electric mixer for this step unless it is specially equipped to handle heavy doughs. Otherwise, you may burn out the mixer motor.

It's helpful to measure out the remaining 3¾ cups flour before starting to add it to the dough. This way, you won't lose count if you're interrupted while measuring.

7 Turn dough out onto lightly floured surface. Using a well-floured pastry cloth makes the dough easier to knead, so less flour is worked into the dough. This is an advantage, since adding more flour tends to make the bread drier.

Knead in enough of the remaining flour to make a moderately stiff dough. To knead, fold the dough over and push down with the heel of the hand, curving your fingers over the dough.

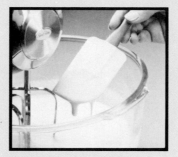

3 Pour milk mixture over flour mixture in mixer bowl. Since the yeast is mixed with the flour, the temperature of the milk mixture can be warmer (115° to 120°) than the water used to dissolve yeast in the conventional method (110° to 115°).

4 Beat milk-flour mixture at low speed of electric stand mixer for ½ minute (most portable mixers should not be used as the heaviness of the mixture may cause their motors to burn out).

Scrape sides of bowl constantly to make sure all flour and yeast are moistened.

5 Beat mixture at high speed for 3 minutes, scraping sides of bowl occasionally. Batter should be smooth and well blended, as shown.

187

TIP *Yeast doughs used for coffee cakes and sweet rolls usually include 1 or more eggs for richness. Add the eggs right after the warm milk in step 3.*

8 Give the dough a quarter turn, then fold over and push down again. Kneading is important in determining the final structure of the loaf, as it develops the gluten of the flour. If the dough is not kneaded enough, the loaf will be more likely to have a coarse texture, and will probably not rise as high in the pan.

9 Continue kneading in the fold-push-turn procedure till dough is smooth and elastic, as shown.

To be sure you've kneaded enough, set a timer for the maximum time suggested in the recipe. You may want to stop and rest a bit instead of kneading the dough all at once. Just be sure the total time is as long as the recipe suggests.

Cover the dough with a towel if you are interrupted or stop to rest.

10 Shape the dough into a ball and place in a greased bowl that's at least twice as large as the size of the ball of dough. Turn dough over once to grease entire surface. This helps keep it from drying out. *(continued next page)*

Yeast Breads

Easy-Mix White Bread *Continued*

11 Cover dough with a cloth. You may first want to cover the dough with lightly greased waxed paper or plastic wrap. This way, the dough won't stick to the cloth if it rises to the top of the bowl.

The oven is a good draft-free place to set the bowl of dough. Place on upper rack with a bowl or pan of hot water on the lower rack. Keep the oven door closed.

12 Dough should be allowed to rise until it doubles in size. Times suggested in the recipes are guidelines. The actual time needed occasionally may be more or less than that indicated. The dough is ready to shape when you can lightly and quickly press two fingertips ½ inch into the dough and the indentation remains, as shown.

17 To shape dough by rolling, place ball of dough on lightly floured pastry cloth or board. Roll into a 12×8-inch rectangle, rolling to the outer edges to remove all the bubbles. Roll up tightly starting with narrow edge. Seal with fingertips as you roll. Repeat to make second loaf.

18 Be sure to seal the final edge thoroughly. After rolling up, seal the ends by pressing down on each end to make a thin sealed strip. Fold strips under loaf and place in prepared pan. Repeat for second loaf.

13 Punch down the dough by pushing your fist into the center of the dough, as shown. Then pull the edges of the dough to the center, turn dough over, and place on lightly floured surface.

14 Divide dough into two portions. Shape each into a smooth ball. Cover with a towel to keep warm and to help prevent a dried-out surface. Let rest about 10 minutes; this allows the gluten to relax and makes the dough easier to roll.

15 Grease two 8×4×2-inch loaf pans. Use folded paper toweling, waxed paper, or pastry brush to lightly cover the bottom and sides of pans with shortening or cooking oil.

16 Shape each ball of dough into a loaf by patting or rolling. To pat, gently pull the dough into a loaf shape, tucking the edges beneath.

189

19 Cover loaves; set in a warm place and let rise (see step 11). Dough should rise over top of pan in rounded shape as shown. Loaf is ready to bake when an indentation remains after touching lightly with finger. This will probably take 45 to 60 minutes.

20 Bake in 375° oven about 45 minutes or till done. Test by tapping the top with your finger. A hollow sound means that the loaf is properly baked. If top browns too fast, cover loosely with foil the last 15 minutes of baking.

21 Remove bread from pans; cool on wire rack. When completely cooled, wrap in foil or clear plastic wrap, or place in plastic bag; store in a cool dry place (refrigerator storage is not recommended since it causes yeast breads to stale). To freeze, wrap cooled bread in moisture-vaporproof wrap. Thaw at room temperature, then warm in 250° to 300° oven.

Breads

Dinner Rolls

Technique: Shaping yeast dough rolls

3½	cups all-purpose flour
1	package active dry yeast
1¼	cups milk
¼	cup sugar
¼	cup shortening
1	teaspoon salt
1	egg

190

Refer to: Using the easy-mix method, page 186. Mix *2 cups* of the flour and yeast. Heat and stir milk, sugar, shortening, and salt till warm. Add to flour mixture; add egg. Beat at low speed for ½ minute. Beat 3 minutes at high speed. Stir in as much of the remaining flour as you can mix in with a spoon. Knead in enough of the remaining flour to make a moderately stiff dough. Knead till smooth (6 to 8 minutes). Shape into ball. Place in greased bowl; turn. Cover; let rise till double (45 to 60 minutes). Punch down; divide in half. Cover; let rest 10 minutes.

1 Shape into simple pan rolls. **2** *Or* shape into shortcut cloverleaves. **3** *Or* shape into cloverleaves. **4–5** *Or* shape into fantans. **6** *Or* shape into butterhorns. **7** *Or* shape into Parker House rolls. **8** *Or* shape into bowknots. **9** *Or* shape into swirls. **10** *Or* shape into rosettes.

Cover; let rise in warm place till double (30 to 45 minutes). Bake in 400° oven for 10 to 12 minutes. Makes 24 to 36 rolls.

1 Simple pan rolls: Lightly grease two 8×1½- or 9×1½-inch round baking pans. Divide each half of dough into 12 pieces. Shape each into a ball, pulling edges under to make a smooth top, as shown. Place 12 balls, smooth side up, in each prepared pan. Let rise again and bake as directed. Makes 24.

2 Shortcut cloverleaves: Lightly grease 24 muffin cups. Divide each half of dough into 12 pieces. Shape each piece into a ball, pulling edges under to make a smooth top. Place one ball in each greased muffin cup, smooth side up.

Using scissors dipped in flour, snip top in half, then snip again, making 4 points, as shown. Let rise again and bake as directed. Makes 24.

6 Butterhorns: Lightly grease baking sheets. Divide dough into *three* equal pieces (instead of two). On lightly floured surface, roll each ball to a 12-inch circle. Brush with melted butter. Cut each circle into 12 wedges.

To shape rolls, begin at wide end of wedge and roll toward point, as shown. Place point down, 2 to 3 inches apart, on prepared baking sheets. Let rise; bake as directed. Makes 36.

7 Parker House rolls: Lightly grease baking sheets. On lightly floured surface, roll out each half of dough to ¼-inch thickness. Cut with floured 2½-inch round cutter. Brush with melted butter. Make an off-center crease in each round. Fold so large half overlaps slightly, as shown (dough crawls back during baking so that top half is shorter). Place 2 to 3 inches apart on baking sheets. Let rise; bake as directed. Makes 36.

3 Cloverleaves: Lightly grease 24 muffin cups. Divide each half of dough into 36 one-inch pieces. Pull edges under, smoothing tops to make balls. Place 3 balls in each greased muffin cup, smooth side up. Let rise and bake as directed. Makes 24.

4 Fantans: Lightly grease 24 muffin cups. Divide dough into *three* equal pieces (instead of two). On lightly floured surface, roll each ball to a 12×9-inch rectangle. Brush with melted butter or margarine.

Using a sharp knife, cut each rectangle of dough lengthwise into 6 strips, each 1½ inches wide, as shown.

5 Pile six strips of dough on top of one another, making ends even. Using sharp knife, cut each stack of strips into 1½-inch lengths, making 8 pieces per stack.

Place pieces in muffin cups, cut side down, as shown. Let rise and bake as directed. Makes 24.

TIP To reheat yeast rolls, *place in a brown paper bag with water (a clothes sprinkler works well) and fold the opening closed.*

Warm the rolls in a 325° oven about 10 minutes or till heated through. You also can wrap and heat the rolls in foil. Sprinkle rolls with water before wrapping.

Or use a countertop microwave oven. *Place rolls on a paper napkin or plate to absorb moisture. Heat 1 roll for 10 to 15 seconds; 2 rolls for 15 to 20 seconds; or 4 rolls for 25 to 30 seconds.*

191

8 Bowknots: Lightly grease baking sheets. Divide each half of dough into 16 equal pieces. On lightly floured surface, roll each piece into a pencil-like strand about 9 inches long.

Form a loose knot, as shown (pull strands gently before tying knots if they shrink). Place 2 to 3 inches apart on prepared baking sheets. Let rise and bake as directed. Makes 32.

9 Swirls: Lightly grease baking sheets. Divide each half of dough into 18 equal pieces. On a lightly floured surface, roll each piece into a pencil-like strand about 8 inches long.

Beginning at center, make a loose swirl with each strand, as shown (if desired, press end under). Place 2 to 3 inches apart on prepared baking sheets. Let rise and bake as directed. Makes 36.

10 Rosettes: Lightly grease baking sheets. Divide each half of dough into 16 pieces. On lightly floured surface, roll each into a pencil-like strand about 12 inches long, referring to step 8.

Form into a loose knot, leaving two long ends. Tuck top end under roll. Bring bottom end up and tuck into center of roll. Place 2 to 3 inches apart on prepared baking sheets. Let rise; bake as directed. Makes 32.

Yeast Breads

Sweet Roll Dough

Technique: Making sweet rolls

3½	to 4 cups all-purpose flour
1	package active dry yeast
1	cup milk
¼	cup sugar
¼	cup shortening
1	teaspoon salt
2	eggs

Refer to: Using the easy-mix method, page 186. Mix *2 cups* of the flour and yeast. Heat and stir milk, sugar, shortening, and salt till warm. Add to flour mixture; add eggs. Beat at low speed for ½ minute. Beat 3 minutes at high speed. Stir in as much of the remaining flour as you can mix in with a spoon. Knead in enough of the remaining flour to make a moderately stiff dough. Knead till smooth (6 to 8 minutes). Shape into ball. Place in greased bowl; turn. Cover; let rise till double (45 to 60 minutes). Punch down; divide in half. Cover; let rest 10 minutes. Roll each into a 12×8-inch rectangle. Use in Creamy Cinnamon Rolls or Caramel-Pecan Rolls.

Creamy Cinnamon Rolls: Grease two 9×1½-inch round baking pans. **1** Brush dough with 3 tablespoons melted *butter*. **2** Sprinkle with mixture of ⅔ cup packed *brown sugar*, ½ cup chopped *walnuts*, and 2 teaspoons ground *cinnamon*. Roll up. **3** Seal. **4** Slice. **5** Place in pans. Cover; let rise till double (about 30 minutes). Pour ¾ cup *whipping cream* over the two pans. Bake in 375° oven for 18 to 20 minutes. **6** Cool slightly; remove. If desired, make Confectioners' Icing, referring to tip on page 249; drizzle atop rolls. Makes 24.

Caramel-Pecan Rolls: 1 In *each* of two 9×1½-inch round baking pans combine ⅓ cup packed *brown sugar*, 2 tablespoons *butter*, and 1 tablespoon *light corn syrup*. Cook and stir till blended. Sprinkle each pan with ¼ cup chopped *pecans*. **2** Brush dough with 3 tablespoons melted *butter*. Sprinkle mixture of ½ cup granulated *sugar* and 1 teaspoon ground *cinnamon* atop. Roll up. **3** Seal. **4** Slice. **5** Place in pans. Cover; let rise till double (about 30 minutes). Bake in 375° oven for 18 to 20 minutes. **6** Cool about 30 seconds. Invert; remove from pans. Makes 24.

192

1 Creamy Cinnamon Rolls
In small saucepan melt 3 tablespoons *butter or margarine*. Brush half over each rectangle of dough.

2 Combine ⅔ cup packed *brown sugar*, ½ cup chopped *walnuts*, and 2 teaspoons ground *cinnamon*. Sprinkle half of mixture atop each rectangle of dough. Roll up, starting from longest end. (To make fewer larger rolls, start rolling the dough from the shortest side.)

1 Caramel-Pecan Rolls
In *each* of two 9×1½-inch round baking pans combine ⅓ cup packed *brown sugar*, 2 tablespoons *butter*, and 1 tablespoon *light corn syrup*. Cook and stir each over medium heat just till butter melts and mixture is blended. (Be sure to use metal pans. If using glass pans, heat mixture in oven.)
Sprinkle ¼ cup chopped *pecans* over each pan; set aside.

2 In small saucepan melt 3 tablespoons *butter*. Brush each rectangle of dough with *half* of the melted butter.
Combine ½ cup *granulated sugar* and 1 teaspoon ground *cinnamon*. Sprinkle *half* atop each piece of dough.
Roll up, starting from longest end. (To make fewer larger rolls, start rolling dough from the shortest side.)

3 Pinch dough together to seal firmly. Moistening the edge of the dough with water makes it easier to seal firmly.

4 Slice each roll of dough into 12 pieces. An easy method uses a piece of ordinary sewing-weight or heavy-duty thread.

Place thread under rolled dough where you want to make the cut; pull thread up around sides. Crisscross thread across top of roll, pulling quickly as though tying a knot. A sharp knife also can be used, but it's much more apt to squash the rolls.

5 Place rolls in prepared pans. Cover; let rise till double (about 30 minutes). Using ¾ cup *whipping cream*, pour half over each pan of rolls. Bake in 375° oven for 18 to 20 minutes.

6 Cool rolls slightly; remove from pans to wire rack set on waxed paper.

If desired, make Confectioner's Icing, referring to tip on page 249.

Drizzle by spooning back and forth across rolls. If desired, sprinkle chopped nuts or candied fruits atop before the icing sets. (If rolls are to be frozen, do not ice until reheated for serving.)

193

3 Pinch dough together to seal firmly. Moistening the edge of the dough with water makes it easier to seal firmly.

4 Slice each roll of dough into 12 pieces. An easy method uses a piece of ordinary sewing-weight or heavy-duty thread.

Place thread under rolled dough where you want to make cut; pull thread up around sides. Crisscross thread across top of roll, pulling quickly as though tying a knot.

A sharp knife also can be used, but it's much more apt to squash the rolls.

5 Place rolls in prepared pans. Cover; let rise till double (about 30 minutes). Bake in 375° oven for 18 to 20 minutes.

6 Cool rolls in pans about 30 seconds. Invert on rack or serving plate and remove pans. Serve warm, or cool completely. Or, if desired, wrap in moisture-vaporproof paper, label, and freeze. To serve, thaw at room temperature, then heat in warm oven.

Yeast Breads

1 On lightly floured surface, roll out each half of dough to ½-inch thickness. Keep dough soft by using as little flour as possible during rolling.

Cut doughnuts with a floured doughnut cutter, pressing straight down.

To reduce the possibility of a tough product with a compact texture, avoid over-handling the dough (rerolled dough will make a tougher doughnut).

Yeast Doughnuts

Technique: Frying yeast doughnuts

3	**to 3½ cups all-purpose flour**
2	**packages active dry yeast**
¾	**cup milk**
⅓	**cup sugar**
¼	**cup shortening**
1	**teaspoon salt**
2	**eggs**
	Cooking oil *or* shortening for deep-fat frying
	Glaze *or* granulated sugar (optional)

194

Refer to: Using the easy-mix method, page 186. Combine *1½ cups* of the flour and the yeast. Heat together milk, sugar, shortening, and salt just till warm (115° to 120°), stirring constantly. Add to flour mixture; add eggs. Beat at low speed of electric mixer for ½ minute, scraping sides of bowl constantly. Beat 3 minutes at high speed.

Stir in as much of the remaining flour as you can mix in with a spoon. Turn out onto a lightly floured surface. Knead in enough of the remaining flour to make a moderately soft dough. Continue kneading till smooth and elastic (3 to 5 minutes). Shape into a ball. Place in greased bowl, turning once. Cover; let rise till double (45 to 60 minutes). Punch dough down; turn out onto a lightly floured surface. Divide in half, let rest 10 minutes.

1 Roll each half of dough to ½-inch thickness. Cut with floured doughnut cutter into doughnuts. **2** Cover and let rise till very light (30 to 45 minutes). **3** Heat cooking oil or shortening to 375°. **4** Add doughnuts, a few at a time. **5** Fry about 1 minute. Turn and fry about 1 minute more or till golden. **6** Drain. **7** For glaze, blend 2 cups sifted *powdered sugar*, ¼ cup *milk*, and 1 teaspoon *vanilla*. Dip warm doughnuts in glaze. **8** Or shake in bag of granulated sugar. Makes 18 to 20.

5 After about 1 minute, when doughnut is golden, turn and fry second side about 1 minute more or till golden.

Use a two-pronged fork for easier turning. A slotted spoon or metal spatula can also be used.

2 Cover doughnuts with a towel and let rise till very light (30 to 45 minutes). During this time, the doughnuts should double in size.

3 Fill saucepan or deep-fat fryer one-third to half full of cooking oil or shortening. (For more information, see tip on page 63.)

Heat till deep-fat thermometer registers 375° *or* till a bread cube dropped into the hot fat is lightly browned within one minute.

Try to keep temperature constant during frying. If it is too hot, the doughnuts will be browned on the outside before the inside is cooked.

4 Gently lower doughnuts into hot fat. Use a metal spatula to avoid spattering, as shown.

Do not try to fry more than two or three at a time. Adding too many at once lowers the temperature of the fat, causing the doughnuts to become fat-soaked.

195

6 When doughnuts are done, remove and drain on paper toweling. Also remove any free food particles. Wait for the fat to return to frying temperature before adding more doughnuts.

After frying, allow fat to cool. Strain through a double layer of cheesecloth into storage containers; cover and keep refrigerated. To reuse, add some fresh oil or shortening to the used fat.

7 To glaze warm doughnuts, combine 2 cups sifted *powdered sugar*, ¼ cup *milk*, and 1 teaspoon *vanilla*. Stir till well blended. Carefully dip warm doughnuts into glaze.

If planning to freeze doughnuts, dip in glaze after thawing and reheating.

8 If desired, shake warm doughnuts in granulated sugar instead of glazing. Place sugar in paper or plastic bag. Add doughnuts, one or two at a time and shake to coat.

You may also add a little ground cinnamon or nutmeg to the sugar.

This sugaring process may also be applied to doughnuts which are to be frozen.

TIP *A doughnut with a jelly center instead of a hole is often called a bismarck.*

To make bismarcks, prepare doughnut dough as directed at left. Roll out to ⅜-inch thickness and cut with a round 2½-inch floured cookie cutter (no hole in center). Let rise, fry, and drain as directed.

With a sharp knife, cut a slit in the side of each cooked bismarck, as shown in top photo.

Using a spoon, fill center with 2 teaspoons jam or jelly, as shown in bottom photo.

Roll bismarcks in granulated or powdered sugar. Makes 18 to 20.

Yeast Breads

Bagels

Technique: Making bagels

___

4¼ to 4½ cups all-purpose flour
2 packages active dry yeast
1½ cups warm water (110° to 115°)
3 tablespoons sugar
1 tablespoon salt
1 tablespoon sugar

Refer to: Using the easy-mix method, page 186. **1** In mixer bowl combine *1½ cups* of the flour and the yeast. Combine warm water, the 3 tablespoons sugar, and salt. Pour over flour mixture. Beat at low speed for ½ minute, scraping sides of bowl constantly. Beat 3 minutes at high speed. **2** Stir in as much of the remaining flour as you can mix in with a spoon.

3–4 Turn out onto lightly floured surface. Knead in enough of the remaining flour to make a moderately stiff dough. Continue kneading till smooth and elastic (6 to 8 minutes). Cover; let dough rest 10 to 15 minutes. **5** Cut into 12 portions; shape into smooth balls. Punch a hole in center of each. **6** Pull gently to enlarge hole. **7** Place on greased baking sheet. Cover; let rise 20 minutes. **8** Broil 5 inches from heat for 1½ to 2 minutes on each side (tops should not brown). **9** Heat 1 gallon *water* and 1 tablespoon sugar to boiling; reduce heat. Cook bagels, 4 or 5 at a time, for 7 minutes, turning once; drain. **10** Place on greased baking sheet. Bake in 375° oven 25 to 30 minutes. Makes 12.

Herb Bagels: Prepare bagels as above, *except* add 2 teaspoons dried *marjoram*, crushed; *or* 1 teaspoon dried *dillweed*, crushed; *or* 1 teaspoon dried *tarragon*, crushed; *or* ½ teaspoon *garlic powder* to the 1½ cups flour and yeast mixture.

Parmesan Bagels: Prepare bagels as above, *except* stir ¼ cup grated *parmesan cheese* into the 1½ cups flour and yeast.

196

1 In mixer bowl combine *1½ cups* of the flour and the yeast. Blend water, 3 tablespoons sugar, and salt; pour over the flour mixture. Beat at low speed for ½ minute, scraping sides of bowl constantly. Beat 3 minutes at high speed.

Since there is no shortening to melt or milk to heat in this recipe, the water mixture doesn't need to be heated as it was in step 2 on page 186.

2 Stir in as much of the remaining flour as you can mix in with a spoon.

Do not try to use your electric mixer for this step unless it is specially equipped to handle heavy dough. Otherwise, you might burn out the mixer motor.

It's helpful to measure out the remaining 3 cups flour before starting to add it to the dough. This way, you'll not lose count if you're interrupted while measuring.

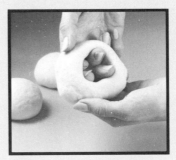

6 Pull dough gently to make a 1½- to 2-inch hole. While pulling, try to keep each bagel in a uniform shape. For mini-bagels, make ¾- to 1-inch holes.

7 Place shaped bagels on a greased baking sheet. Cover and let rise for 20 minutes (same timing for mini-bagels).

3 Turn out onto lightly floured surface. Using a well-floured pastry cloth makes the dough easier to knead, so less flour is worked into the dough. This is an advantage, since adding more flour tends to make the bagels drier.

Knead in enough of the remaining flour to make a moderately stiff dough. To knead, fold the dough over and push down with the heel of the hand, curving your fingers over the dough.

4 Give the dough a quarter turn, then fold over and push down again. Continue kneading with the fold-push-turn procedure till dough is smooth and elastic. This will probably take 6 to 8 minutes.

Cover; let dough rest 10 to 15 minutes. This allows the gluten to relax and makes the dough easier to work with.

5 Cut dough into 12 equal portions; shape into smooth balls. Punch a hole in the center of each with a floured finger.

To make mini-bagels, shape into 24 portions.

197

TIP *Bagels can be varied not only by adding seasonings to the dough, but also by brushing on different toppings during the baking.*

To make onion bagels, prepare bagels as directed at left. Cook ½ cup finely chopped onion or shallots in 3 tablespoons butter or margarine till tender but not brown. Brush or spoon on bagels after first 10 minutes of baking.

8 Broil raised bagels five inches from heat for 1½ to 2 minutes. Turn bagels and broil 1½ to 2 minutes more; the tops should not brown. (Same timing for mini-bagels.) This gives the bagels a glossy surface.

9 In large kettle combine 1 gallon *water* and 1 tablespoon sugar. Bring to boiling; reduce heat to simmering. Cook four or five bagels at a time for 7 minutes, turning once; drain on paper toweling.

(Cook six mini-bagels at a time for 4 minutes, turning once.)

10 Place drained bagels on well-greased baking sheet. Bake in 375° oven for 25 to 30 minutes or till tops are golden brown (same timing for mini-bagels).

This three-step cooking procedure gives bagels their typical chewy texture.

Yeast Breads

Finnish Braid

5 to 5⅓ cups all-purpose flour
2 packages active dry yeast
½ teaspoon ground cardamom
1 cup milk
½ cup butter *or* margarine
½ cup sugar
1 teaspoon salt
2 eggs
1 tablespoon finely shredded
    orange peel
⅓ cup orange juice
1 egg yolk
1 tablespoon milk

Refer to: Using the easy-mix method, page 186. In large mixer bowl combine *2 cups* of the flour, the yeast, and ground cardamom. In saucepan heat the 1 cup milk, the butter or margarine, sugar, and salt just till warm (115° to 120°) and butter is almost melted, stirring constantly. Add to flour mixture in mixer bowl; add the 2 eggs, orange peel, and orange juice.

Beat at low speed of electric mixer for ½ minute, scraping sides of bowl constantly. Beat 3 minutes at high speed. Stir in as much of the remaining flour as you can mix in with a spoon.

Turn out onto floured surface. Knead in enough of the remaining flour to make a moderately stiff dough. Continue kneading till smooth and elastic (6 to 8 minutes). Place in greased bowl; turn. Cover; let rise in warm place till double (about 1 hour). Punch dough down.

Divide in half. Divide each half in thirds; shape into six balls. Cover; let rest 10 minutes. Roll each ball into a 16-inch rope. Line up three ropes, 1 inch apart, on greased baking sheet. Braid loosely, beginning in middle and working toward ends. Pinch ends together and tuck under. Repeat with remaining dough. Cover; let rise in warm place till almost double (about 30 minutes).

Stir together the 1 egg yolk and the 1 tablespoon milk. Brush braids with egg yolk mixture. Bake in 350° oven for 25 to 30 minutes or till golden brown. Cover loosely with foil the last 5 to 10 minutes to prevent overbrowning. Makes 2 braids.

Honey Wheat Bread

3½ to 4 cups all-purpose flour
1 cup cracked wheat
2 packages active dry yeast
1¼ cups water
½ cup milk
⅓ cup honey
3 tablespoons butter *or* margarine
1 tablespoon salt
1 cup whole wheat flour

Refer to: Using the easy-mix method, page 186. Combine *2 cups* of the all-purpose flour, cracked wheat, and yeast. Heat water, milk, honey, butter, and salt just till warm and butter is almost melted; stir constantly. Add to flour mixture. Beat at low speed for ½ minute, scraping sides of bowl. Beat 3 minutes at high speed.

Stir in whole wheat flour and as much of the remaining 2 cups all-purpose flour as you can mix in with spoon. Knead in enough of the remaining flour to make a moderately stiff dough. Knead till smooth and elastic (6 to 8 minutes). Shape into ball. Place in greased bowl; turn once. Cover; let rise till double (about 1 hour). Punch down; divide in half. Cover; let rest 10 minutes. Shape into two loaves; place in two greased 8×4×2-inch loaf pans. Cover; let rise till almost double (about 45 minutes). Bake in 375° oven 35 to 40 minutes. Remove from pans; cool. Makes 2 loaves.

Honey Wheat Bread

Italian Loaves

(pictured on page 180)

   2 packages active dry yeast
   2 cups warm water (110° to 115°)
   2 teaspoons salt
   5 to 5¼ cups all-purpose flour
     Cornmeal

In bowl dissolve yeast in warm water; stir in salt. Add *2 cups* of the flour; beat on low speed of electric mixer for ½ minute, scraping sides of bowl. Beat 3 minutes at high speed. Stir in enough of the remaining 3¼ cups flour to make a very stiff dough. Cover; let rise till double (1 to 1¼ hours).

Turn out onto lightly floured surface; knead 10 to 12 strokes. Halve dough; shape into two balls. Cover; let rise till double (about 1 hour). On floured surface, flatten each ball of dough with palms of hands. Fold over top half; flatten to make an oblong shape. Repeat, lapping top half over lower; press down with palms. Using palms, roll dough on floured surface to a 15-inch length. Place on baking sheet sprinkled with cornmeal; repeat with remaining dough. Cover; let rise till double (about 45 minutes). With sharp knife, make 3 or 4 diagonal cuts about ¼ inch deep across top of loaves. Bake in 375° oven 35 to 40 minutes. Makes 2.

Individual loaves: Cut each half of risen dough into quarters, making 8 pieces; round into balls. Cover; let rest 10 minutes. Shape each into a 6-inch loaf; taper ends. Place 2½ inches apart on greased baking sheet sprinkled with cornmeal. Press down ends of loaves. Cover; let rise till double (about 45 minutes). Make 3 shallow cuts diagonally across top of each. Blend 1 tablespoon *water* into 1 *egg white*; brush atop. Bake in 400° oven 25 to 30 minutes. Makes 8.

Hard rolls: Cut each half of risen dough into eighths, making 16 pieces. Shape into rolls; place 2 inches apart on greased baking sheet sprinkled with cornmeal. Cover; let rise till double (about 45 minutes). Cut a shallow crisscross in tops. Blend 1 tablespoon *water* into 1 *egg white*; brush atop rolls. Bake in 400° oven 25 to 30 minutes. Makes 16.

Rye Pretzels

   1 package active dry yeast
   1½ cups warm water (110° to 115°)
   1 tablespoon malted milk powder
   1 tablespoon caraway seed
   1 tablespoon molasses
   1 teaspoon salt
   4½ cups rye flour
     Coarse salt

Soften yeast in water. Add malted milk powder, caraway seed, molasses, and salt. Stir in rye flour. Knead on floured surface till smooth (about 5 minutes) referring to steps 6–8 on page 182. Cut into 12 pieces; roll each into a 15-inch rope. Shape into pretzels; place on greased baking sheet. (No rising is needed.) Moisten lightly with water; sprinkle with coarse salt. Bake in 425° oven 15 to 20 minutes or till browned. Remove from pan; cool. Makes 12.

Sweet Batter Rolls

   3 cups all-purpose flour
   2 packages active dry yeast
   ½ teaspoon ground cinnamon
   1¼ cups water
   ⅓ cup granulated sugar
   ⅓ cup shortening
   1 teaspoon salt
   1 egg
   2 tablespoons finely shredded
     orange peel
   1 cup raisins
   1 cup sifted powdered sugar
   1 to 2 tablespoons milk

Combine *1½ cups* of the flour, yeast, and cinnamon. Heat water, granulated sugar, shortening, and salt just till warm (115° to 120°) and shortening is almost melted; stir constantly. Add to flour mixture; add egg and peel. Beat at low speed of electric mixer for ½ minute, scraping bowl constantly. Beat 3 minutes at high speed. Add remaining 1½ cups flour and raisins; stir by hand till blended. Cover; let rise in warm place till almost double (40 to 45 minutes). Stir down. Fill greased muffin pans ⅔ full. Let rise till almost double (about 25 minutes). Bake in 425° oven for 10 to 15 minutes. Cool slightly. For icing, combine powdered sugar and milk; dip rolls in icing. Makes 22.

Oatmeal Batter Bread

   3 cups all-purpose flour
   1 cup rolled oats
   1 package active dry yeast
   1¼ cups milk
   ¼ cup shortening
   ¼ cup honey
   2 teaspoons salt
   2 eggs
   3 tablespoons rolled oats

In large mixer bowl combine *1½ cups* of the flour, the 1 cup oats, and yeast. In saucepan heat milk, shortening, honey, and salt just till warm (115° to 120°) and shortening is almost melted; stir constantly. Add to flour mixture. Separate 1 egg; set aside egg white. Add yolk and remaining egg to flour mixture.

Beat at low speed with electric mixer for ½ minute, scraping sides of bowl constantly. Beat 3 minutes at high speed. By hand, stir in remaining 1½ cups flour, making a soft dough. Beat with wooden spoon till smooth. Cover; let rise in warm place till double (1¾ to 2 hours). Stir dough down. Sprinkle a greased 2-quart casserole with *2 tablespoons* of the rolled oats. Turn dough into prepared casserole. Let rise till double (about 45 minutes).

Beat reserved egg white slightly; brush over loaf. Sprinkle with remaining 1 tablespoon oats. Bake in 350° oven for 45 to 50 minutes. Let stand 15 minutes. Remove and cool. Makes 1.

199

TIP Batter breads *are prepared like breads using the easy-mix method, but with one important exception: batter breads are not kneaded. Because of this, they take on the shape of the container in which they are baked. The absence of kneading also gives the final bread a more open, coarse texture than that found in kneaded breads. Batter breads often are almost pourable because they contain more liquid in proportion to flour.*

Yeast Breads

TIP To shape a tea ring, *roll out raised dough to 13×9-inch rectangle. Brush with melted butter; sprinkle evenly with filling. Roll up jelly roll-style, starting from long side. Seal edge. Shape in a ring on greased baking sheet. Pinch to seal ends together.*

Divide ring into quarters, using scissors to snip almost to center. Snip each quarter into thirds, making 12 sections, as shown in top photo.

Gently pull sections apart and twist slightly, as shown in bottom photo. Use your fingers to help turn the filled dough.

English Tea Ring

2¾ to 3 cups all-purpose flour
1 package active dry yeast
¾ cup milk
½ cup sugar
¼ cup shortening
1 teaspoon salt
1 beaten egg
½ teaspoon vanilla
½ cup finely chopped mixed candied fruits and peels
½ cup chopped walnuts
¼ cup sugar
1 teaspoon ground cinnamon
Butter *or* margarine, melted

Refer to: Using the easy-mix method, page 186. In bowl combine *2 cups* of the flour and the yeast. Heat together the milk, the ½ cup sugar, shortening, and salt just till warm (115° to 120°) and shortening is almost melted; stir constantly.

Add to flour mixture; add egg and vanilla. Beat at low speed of electric mixer for ½ minute, scraping sides of bowl. Beat 3 minutes at high speed. Stir in as much of the remaining 1 cup flour as you can mix in with a spoon. Turn out on floured surface. Knead in enough of the remaining flour to make a moderately soft dough. Continue kneading till smooth (3 to 5 minutes). Place in greased bowl; turn once. Cover; let rise till double (1½ to 2 hours).

To prepare filling, mix candied fruits and peels, walnuts, ¼ cup sugar, and cinnamon; set aside.

Shape dough into tea ring, referring to tip at left. Roll out into a 13×9-inch rectangle. Brush with about 1 tablespoon melted butter; sprinkle evenly with filling. Roll up jelly roll-style, starting from long side; seal. Shape in ring on greased baking sheet. Pinch to seal ends together. Divide ring into quarters, using scissors to snip almost to center. Snip each quarter into thirds, making 12 sections. Pull sections apart; twist slightly.

Let rise till double (35 to 45 minutes). Bake in 375° oven 18 to 20 minutes. Brush top while warm with additional melted butter or margarine. Remove from baking sheet; cool on wire rack. Makes 1.

German Stollen

4 to 4½ cups all-purpose flour
1 package active dry yeast
¼ teaspoon ground cardamom
1¼ cups milk
½ cup butter *or* margarine
¼ cup granulated sugar
1 teaspoon salt
1 slightly beaten egg
1 cup raisins
¼ cup chopped mixed candied fruits and peels
¼ cup dried currants
¼ cup chopped blanched almonds
2 tablespoons finely shredded orange peel
1 tablespoon finely shredded lemon peel
1 cup sifted powdered sugar
2 tablespoons hot water
½ teaspoon butter *or* margarine

Refer to: Using the easy-mix method, page 186. Combine *2 cups* of the flour, yeast, and cardamom. Heat milk, the ½ cup butter, granulated sugar, and salt just till warm (115° to 120°) and butter is almost melted; stir constantly. Add to flour mixture; add egg. Beat at low speed for ½ minute; scrape sides of bowl constantly. Beat 3 minutes at high speed. Stir in as much of the remaining 2½ cups flour as you can mix in with a spoon. Stir in raisins, candied fruits and peels, currants, almonds, and orange and lemon peels.

Turn out onto lightly floured surface. Knead in enough of the remaining flour to make a moderately soft dough. Knead till smooth (3 to 5 minutes). Place in a greased bowl; turn once. Cover; let rise in a warm place till double (about 1¾ hours). Punch down; turn out onto a lightly floured surface. Divide into thirds. Cover; let rest 10 minutes.

Roll one third of the dough to a 10×6-inch rectangle. Without stretching, fold the long side over to within 1 inch of the opposite side; seal. Place on greased baking sheet; repeat with remaining dough.

Cover; let rise till almost double (about 1 hour). Bake in 375° oven for 18 to 20 minutes or till golden. Combine the powdered sugar, hot water, and ½ teaspoon butter; brush over warm bread. Makes 3.

Croissants

1½ cups butter *or* margarine
⅓ cup all-purpose flour
2 packages active dry yeast
½ cup warm water (110° to 115°)
¾ cup milk
¼ cup sugar
1 teaspoon salt
1 egg
3¾ to 4¼ cups all-purpose flour
1 egg yolk
1 tablespoon milk

Refer to: Making Danish pastry, steps 1–7, page 304; and Using the conventional method, steps 1–8, page 182. Cream butter with ⅓ cup flour. Roll mixture between two sheets of waxed paper into a 12×6-inch rectangle. Chill at least 1 hour.

Soften yeast in warm water. Heat ¾ cup milk, sugar, and salt till sugar dissolves. Cool to lukewarm; turn into large mixing bowl. Add softened yeast and 1 egg; beat well.

Stir in *2 cups* of the flour; beat well. Stir in as much of the remaining 2¼ cups flour as you can mix in with a spoon. Turn out onto lightly floured surface. Knead in enough of the remaining flour to make a moderately soft dough. Continue kneading till smooth and elastic (3 to 5 minutes). Let rest 10 minutes.

Roll into a 14-inch square. Place *chilled* butter on one half of dough; fold over other half and seal edges. Roll into a 21×12-inch rectangle; seal edges. Fold in thirds. Roll into a 21×12-inch rectangle. Fold and roll twice more; seal edges. Chill after each rolling. Fold in thirds to 12×7 inches. Chill several hours or overnight.

Cut dough crosswise in fourths. Roll each fourth into a 12-inch circle. Cut each into 12 wedges. Roll up each wedge loosely starting from wide edge, referring to step 6 on page 190.

Place on *ungreased* baking sheets, point down; curve ends. Cover; let rise till double (30 to 45 minutes). Beat egg yolk with 1 tablespoon milk; brush on rolls. Bake in 375° oven for 12 to 15 minutes. Remove from baking sheets. Makes 48.

Croissants

201

Rye Bread

3¼ to 3¾ cups all-purpose flour
2 packages active dry yeast
1 tablespoon caraway seed
2 cups warm water (115° to 120°)
½ cup packed brown sugar
1 tablespoon cooking oil
1 teaspoon salt
2½ cups rye flour

Refer to: Using the easy-mix method, page 186. Combine *2½ cups* of the all-purpose flour, yeast, and caraway. Blend water, brown sugar, oil, and salt. Add to flour mixture. Beat at low speed for ½ minute, scraping bowl. Beat 3 minutes at high speed. Stir in rye flour and as much of the remaining 1¼ cups all-purpose flour as you can mix in with a spoon. Turn out onto floured surface. Knead in enough of the remaining flour to make a moderately stiff dough. Knead till smooth (6 to 8 minutes); dough will be sticky. Place in greased bowl; turn once.

Cover; let rise till double (about 1½ hours). Punch down; divide in half. Cover; let rest 10 minutes. Shape into two 4½-inch round loaves on greased baking sheets (or place in greased 8×4×2-inch loaf pans). Cover; let rise till double (about 40 minutes). Bake in 350° oven for 40 to 45 minutes. Remove from pans; cool. Makes 2.

Whole Wheat Bread

4 to 4½ cups whole wheat flour
2 packages active dry yeast
1¾ cups milk
⅓ cup packed brown sugar
2 tablespoons shortening
2 teaspoons salt

Refer to: Using the easy-mix method, page 186. Mix *2 cups* of the flour and yeast. Heat milk, brown sugar, shortening, and salt just till warm (115° to 120°) and shortening is almost melted; stir constantly. Add to flour mixture. Beat at low speed for ½ minute, scraping sides of bowl. Beat 3 minutes at high speed. Stir in as much of the remaining 2½ cups flour as you can mix in with a spoon. Turn out onto lightly floured surface. Knead in enough of the remaining flour to make a moderately stiff dough. Continue kneading till smooth and elastic (6 to 8 minutes). Shape into ball. Place in lightly greased bowl, turning once. Cover; let rise in warm place till double (1 to 1½ hours). Punch down; turn out onto lightly floured surface. Cover; let rest 10 minutes. Shape into a loaf in greased 8×4×2-inch loaf pan. Cover; let rise till double (about 30 minutes). Bake in 375° oven for 35 to 40 minutes. Remove from pan; cool on rack. Makes 1 loaf.

Yeast Breads

Cinnamon Swirl Loaf
(pictured on page 180)

- 7 to 7½ cups all-purpose flour
- 2 packages active dry yeast
- 2 cups milk
- ½ cup sugar
- ½ cup shortening
- 2 teaspoons salt
- 2 eggs
- ½ cup sugar
- 2 teaspoons ground cinnamon
  Confectioners' Icing (see tip on page 249)

Refer to: Using the easy-mix method, page 186. In bowl combine *3½ cups* of the flour and the yeast. In saucepan heat milk, ½ cup sugar, shortening, and salt just till warm (115° to 120°) and shortening is almost melted; stir constantly. Add to flour mixture; add eggs. Beat at low speed with electric mixer for ½ minute, scraping sides of bowl. Beat 3 minutes at high speed. By hand, stir in as much of remaining 4 cups flour as you can mix in with a spoon.

Turn out onto lightly floured surface. Knead in enough of the remaining flour to make a moderately soft dough. Continue kneading till smooth and elastic (3 to 5 minutes). Shape into a ball. Place in lightly greased bowl; turn once.

Cover; let rise in warm place till double (about 1 hour). Punch dough down; turn out onto lightly floured surface. Divide in half. Cover; let rest 10 minutes. Roll *each half* into a 15×7-inch rectangle. Brush entire surface with water.

Combine the ½ cup sugar and the cinnamon. Sprinkle each rectangle with half the sugar-cinnamon mixture. Roll up jelly roll-style, beginning with narrow side. Seal long edge and ends. Place, sealed edge down, in 2 greased 9×5×3-inch loaf pans. Cover; let rise till almost double (35 to 45 minutes).

Bake in 375° oven for 35 to 40 minutes or till done. (If crust browns too quickly, cover with foil last 15 minutes of baking.) Remove from pans; cool on wire racks. Drizzle with Confectioners' Icing. Makes 2.

Hamburger Buns

- 3½ to 4 cups all-purpose flour
- 1 package active dry yeast
- 1 cup warm water (115° to 120°)
- ⅓ cup cooking oil
- ¼ cup sugar
- 1½ teaspoons salt
- 1 egg

Refer to: Using the easy-mix method, page 186. Combine *2 cups* of the flour and the yeast. Blend water, oil, sugar, and salt; add to flour mixture. Add egg. Beat at low speed for ½ minute, scraping sides of bowl constantly. Beat 3 minutes at high speed. Stir in as much of the remaining 2 cups flour as you can mix in with a spoon.

On floured surface, knead in enough of the remaining flour to make a moderately stiff dough; knead till smooth (6 to 8 minutes). Place in greased bowl; turn once. Cover; let rise till double (about 1½ hours). Punch down; divide in thirds. Cover; let rest 5 minutes. Divide each third of dough into 4 balls. Turn each, folding edges under to make even circles. Press flat between hands. Place on greased baking sheet; press to 3½-inch circles. Let rise till double (about 30 minutes). Bake in 375° oven for 13 to 15 minutes. Remove from pans; cool. Makes 12.

Quick Coffee Cake

- 2 cups all-purpose flour
- 1 package active dry yeast
- ½ cup milk
- 6 tablespoons butter *or* margarine
- 5 tablespoons sugar
- ½ teaspoon salt
- 1 egg
- ⅓ cup slivered almonds
- 1 tablespoon butter *or* margarine

Refer to: Tip, page 199. In large mixer bowl combine *1 cup* of the flour and the yeast. Heat milk, 6 tablespoons butter, *4 tablespoons* of the sugar, and salt till warm (115° to 120°) and butter is almost melted; stir constantly. Add to flour mixture; add egg. Beat at low speed for ½ minute, scraping bowl. Beat 3 minutes at high speed. Stir in remaining 1 cup flour. Turn into a greased 8×1½- or 9×1½-inch round baking pan. Top with almonds and remaining 1 tablespoon sugar. Cover; let rise till almost double (about 1 hour). Dot with remaining 1 tablespoon butter. Bake in 375° oven for 18 to 20 minutes. Makes 1.

Caramel-Pecan Rolls
(see recipe on page 192)

202

Sourdough-Rye Buns

Sourdough Starter
3¾ cups warm water
4½ cups whole wheat flour
4 cups rye flour
½ cup cooking oil
1 tablespoon salt
¼ cup all-purpose flour
1 beaten egg white
Coarse salt *or* caraway seed

In large bowl combine *1 cup* Sourdough Starter and warm water. Stir in whole wheat flour. Beat well. Cover; let stand several hours or refrigerate overnight. Stir in rye flour, oil, and salt. Mix well (dough will be slightly sticky). Turn out onto floured surface. Knead, adding the all-purpose flour as necessary to make a moderately soft dough. Knead till smooth (about 5 minutes). Place in greased bowl; turn once. Cover; let rise till double. Punch down. Divide dough into thirds. Cover; let rest 5 minutes. Divide each third into 8 balls. Turn each ball in hands, folding edges under to make an even circle. Press dough flat between hands. Place on greased baking sheet; press each to a 3½-inch circle. Brush with egg white; sprinkle with coarse salt or caraway seed. Let rise till double. Bake in 375° oven for 25 to 30 minutes. Makes 24.

Sourdough Starter: Mix 2½ cups all-purpose *flour*, 2½ cups warm *water*, 1 package *active dry yeast*, and 1 tablespoon *honey*. Let stand, uncovered, in a glass *or* crockery jar at room temperature for 24 hours. Cover; let stand about 5 days or till sour. Stir occasionally. (Time depends on room temperature; dough will sour faster in a warm room.)

To replenish starter, add equal parts all-purpose flour and water to equal total amount removed. Between use, keep covered in refrigerator. To keep several weeks, add 1 teaspoon *sugar* weekly.

Sourdough is indeed "soured dough." *A starter, in which yeast is allowed to grow, gives the characteristic sour flavor. If making loaves, it is usually necessary to use yeast plus starter to ensure proper rising.*

Cheese Bread Knots

(pictured on page 180)

5 to 5½ cups all-purpose flour
2 packages active dry yeast
2 cups milk
1½ cups cubed process Swiss cheese (6 ounces)
½ cup sugar
¼ cup butter *or* margarine
1 tablespoon salt
1 egg

Refer to: Using the easy-mix method, page 186. In large mixer bowl combine *2 cups* of the flour and the yeast. In saucepan heat milk, cheese, sugar, butter or margarine, and salt just till warm (115° to 120°) and butter and cheese are almost melted; stir constantly. Add to flour mixture; add egg.

Beat at low speed of electric mixer for ½ minute, scraping sides of bowl constantly. Beat 3 minutes at high speed. Stir in as much of remaining 3½ cups flour as you can mix in with a spoon.

Turn out onto lightly floured surface. Knead in enough of the remaining flour to make a moderately soft dough. Continue kneading till smooth and elastic (3 to 5 minutes). Shape into a ball. Place in lightly greased bowl, turning once to grease surface. Cover and let rise in warm place till double (about 1½ hours).

Punch dough down; turn out onto lightly floured surface. Divide dough into four equal pieces; shape each into a ball. Cover and let rest 10 minutes. Roll each ball into a 12×6-inch rectangle. Cut crosswise into 6×1-inch strips. Tie each strip into a loose knot, referring to step 8 on page 191. Place 2 to 3 inches apart on greased baking sheet. Cover and let rise till double (about 40 minutes).

Brush with some additional melted butter, if desired. Bake in 375° oven 10 to 12 minutes or till brown. Makes 48 rolls.

Brioche

(pictured on page 224)

1 package active dry yeast
¼ cup warm water (110° to 115°)
½ cup butter *or* margarine
⅓ cup sugar
½ teaspoon salt
4 cups all-purpose flour
½ cup milk
4 eggs

Soften yeast in water. Cream butter, sugar, and salt. Add *1 cup* of the flour and the milk to creamed mixture. Separate one of the eggs; set egg white aside. Blend yolk with remaining 3 eggs. Add eggs and softened yeast to creamed mixture; beat well. By hand, stir in remaining 3 cups flour till smooth. Turn into greased bowl. Cover; let rise in warm place till double (about 2 hours). Refrigerate overnight; stir down. Turn out on floured surface. Divide dough into quarters; set one aside. Divide each of the remaining into 8 pieces, making a total of 24. Form each piece into a ball. With floured hands, tuck under cut edges. Place in greased muffin pans. Divide reserved dough into 24 pieces; shape into balls.

With floured finger, make indentation in each large ball. Press small balls into indentations. Cover; let rise till double (40 to 45 minutes). Blend reserved egg white and 1 tablespoon *water*; brush over rolls. Bake in 375° oven 15 minutes, brushing again after 7 minutes. Makes 24.

203

TIP *Brush loaves before or after baking to achieve the desired type of crust.*

For a crisp, shiny crust, brush unbaked loaf with milk, water, or egg diluted with milk or water. Use egg white, yolk, or the entire egg.

To soften the crust and give it a browner color, brush the loaf, before or after baking, with melted shortening, butter, margarine, or cooking oil.

Yeast Breads

TIP To shape a daisy-style coffee ring, *transfer risen dough to greased baking sheet. Roll out to a 14-inch circle. Place a beverage tumbler in center.*

Make four cuts in dough at equal intervals, from outside of circle to tumbler. In the same manner, cut each section into five strips, making 20 strips.

Twist two strips together, as shown in top photo. Repeat, making 10 twists; pinch ends. Remove tumbler.

Remove one twist; coil and place in center. Coil remaining twists toward center to form daisy design, as shown in bottom photo.

Apricot Daisy Bread

    3 to 3½ cups all-purpose flour
    1 package active dry yeast
    ¾ cup milk
    ¼ cup butter *or* margarine
    2 tablespoons sugar
    1 teaspoon salt
    2 eggs
    ½ cup apricot preserves
    2 tablespoons chopped nuts
      Confectioners' Icing (see tip on page 249)

Refer to: Using the easy-mix method, page 186. In large mixer bowl combine *1½ cups* of the flour and the yeast. In saucepan heat together milk, butter or margarine, sugar, and salt just till warm (115° to 120°) and butter is almost melted; stir constantly. Add to flour mixture; add eggs.

Beat at low speed of electric mixer ½ minute, scraping sides of bowl constantly. Beat 3 minutes at high speed. By hand, stir in as much of the remaining 2 cups flour as you can mix in with a spoon.

Turn out onto lightly floured surface. Knead in enough of the remaining flour to make a moderately stiff dough. Continue kneading till dough is smooth and elastic (6 to 8 minutes). Place in greased bowl, turning to grease surface. Cover; let rise till double (about 1¼ hours). Punch down; cover and let rest 10 minutes. Transfer to greased baking sheet.

Shape into daisy coffee ring, referring to tip at left. Roll dough to 14-inch circle. Place a beverage tumbler in center. Make four cuts in dough at equal intervals, from outside of circle to tumbler. Cut each section into five strips in the same manner, making 20 strips. Twist 2 strips together; continue around circle, making 10 twists. Remove tumbler. Remove one twist; coil and place in center. Coil remaining twists toward center to form daisy design.

Let rise till double (about 45 minutes). Bake in 375° oven for 20 to 25 minutes. Combine apricot preserves and nuts; spread evenly atop bread. Drizzle with Confectioners' Icing. Makes 1.

English Muffins

    5½ to 6 cups all-purpose flour
    2 packages active dry yeast
    2 cups milk
    2 tablespoons sugar
    2 tablespoons shortening
    2 teaspoons salt
      Cornmeal

Refer to: Using the easy-mix method, page 186. In mixer bowl stir together *2 cups* of the flour and the yeast. In saucepan heat milk, sugar, shortening, and salt till warm (115° to 120°) and shortening is almost melted, stirring constantly. Add to flour mixture.

Beat at low speed of electric mixer for ½ minute, scraping sides of bowl constantly. Beat at high speed for 3 minutes. By hand, stir in as much of the remaining 4 cups flour as you can mix in with a spoon.

Turn onto lightly floured surface. Knead in enough of the remaining flour to make a moderately stiff dough. Continue kneading till smooth (6 to 8 minutes). Place dough in greased bowl, turning once to grease surface. Cover; let rise in warm place till double (about 1¼ hours).

Punch down; cover and let rest 10 minutes. On lightly floured surface, roll out dough to about ¼-inch thickness. Cut with a 4-inch round cutter. Dip in cornmeal to coat both sides. Cover; let rise in warm place till very light (about 30 minutes).

Bake muffins all at once, placing 4 on each of 4 ungreased griddles or skillets. Bake over medium heat, for 25 minutes; turn frequently. Cool. Split; toast both sides. Makes 16 muffins.

If you don't have four skillets, bake only half of the dough at a time. Cover the remaining dough and keep refrigerated. If desired, cut the remaining dough before refrigerating. The cut muffins will rise some while in the refrigerator, so they may not need all of the suggested 30 minutes to become light.

Apricot Daisy Bread

Brown-and-Serve Rolls

　5 to 5½ cups all-purpose flour
　1 package active dry yeast
1½ cups warm water (115° to 120°)
　½ cup mashed cooked potatoes
　⅓ cup cooking oil
　¼ cup sugar
　1 teaspoon salt

Refer to: Using the easy-mix method, page 186. In large mixer bowl combine *2 cups* of the flour and the yeast. Combine water, mashed potatoes, oil, sugar, and salt. Add to flour mixture in mixer bowl.

Beat at low speed of electric mixer for ½ minute, scraping sides of bowl constantly. Beat 3 minutes at high speed. By hand, stir in as much of the remaining 3½ cups flour as you can mix in with a spoon.

Turn out on lightly floured surface. Knead in enough of the remaining flour to make a moderately stiff dough. Continue kneading till smooth and elastic (6 to 8 minutes). Shape into ball. Place in greased bowl; turn once. Cover; let rise in warm place till almost double (45 to 60 minutes). Punch down; turn out on lightly floured surface. Cover; let rest 10 minutes.

Shape into rolls, referring to pages 190 and 191. Place on greased baking sheet or in greased muffin pans. Cover; let rise till almost double (30 to 40 minutes). Bake in 325° oven for 10 to 12 minutes; *do not brown.* Remove from pans; cool. Wrap, label, and freeze.

To serve, open packages containing the desired number of rolls. Thaw at room temperature for 10 to 15 minutes. Unwrap completely. Bake on ungreased baking sheets in 450° oven for 5 to 10 minutes or till golden. Makes 24 to 36 rolls.

French Doughnuts

　3 cups all-purpose flour
　1 package active dry yeast
　½ teaspoon ground nutmeg
　1 cup milk
　¼ cup granulated sugar
　¼ cup cooking oil
　¾ teaspoon salt
　1 egg
　　Shortening for deep-fat frying
　　Powdered sugar

Combine *1¾ cups* of the flour, the yeast, and nutmeg. Heat milk, granulated sugar, oil, and salt just till warm (115° to 120°); stir occasionally. Add to yeast mixture; add egg. Beat at low speed for ½ minute, scraping sides of bowl. Beat 3 minutes at high speed. Stir in remaining 1¼ cups flour to make a soft dough. Cover; chill several hours or overnight. Turn out onto well-floured surface; form into ball. Cover; let rest 10 minutes. Roll into an 18×12-inch rectangle. Cut into 3×2-inch rectangles. Cover; let rise 30 minutes (dough will not double). Fry, a few at a time, in deep hot fat (375°); refer to steps 3–6 on page 194. Fry about 1 minute or till golden; turn once. Drain. Sprinkle with powdered sugar. Makes 36.

Cornmeal Batter Rolls

　5 cups all-purpose flour
　1 package active dry yeast
2¼ cups milk
　½ cup sugar
　½ cup shortening
　1 tablespoon salt
　2 eggs
　1 cup cornmeal

Refer to: Tip, page 199. Combine *3½ cups* of the flour and the yeast. Heat milk, sugar, shortening, and salt just till warm (115° to 120°) and shortening is almost melted; stir constantly. Add to flour mixture; add eggs. Beat at low speed with electric mixer for ½ minute, scraping the sides of the bowl. Beat 3 minutes at high speed.

By hand, stir in cornmeal and remaining 1½ cups flour. Cover; let rise in warm place till double (about 45 minutes). Stir batter down; fill 24 greased muffin cups ⅔ full. (If you don't have 24 muffin cups, refrigerate remaining dough till pan is ready to reuse.) Cover; let rise in warm place till double (about 45 minutes). Bake in 400° oven 15 to 20 minutes or till golden. Serve warm. Makes 24 rolls.

Quick Breads

Banana-Nut Loaf

Technique: Using creamed method for quick breads

2	**cups all-purpose flour**
2	**teaspoons baking powder**
¾	**teaspoon salt**
¼	**teaspoon baking soda**
½	**cup shortening**
½	**cup sugar**
2	**eggs**
1	**teaspoon finely shredded orange peel**
2	**ripe medium bananas, cut up**
2	**tablespoons milk**
½	**cup chopped pecans** *or* **walnuts**

1 Lightly grease a 9×5×3-inch loaf pan; set aside. **2** In mixing bowl thoroughly stir together the flour, baking powder, salt, and soda; set aside.

3 In small mixer bowl cream the shortening and sugar till light and fluffy. **4** Add eggs and orange peel; beat well.

5 In small bowl mash bananas with fork (should have about 1 cup); stir in milk. **6–7** Add flour mixture and banana mixture alternately to creamed mixture. **8** Beat till smooth after each addition. **9** Fold in nuts. **10** Pour batter into prepared pan. **11** Bake in 350° oven for 45 to 50 minutes or till wooden pick inserted near center comes out clean. **12** Turn out and cool on wire rack. Makes 1 loaf.

1 Grease a 9×5×3-inch loaf pan. Use folded paper toweling, waxed paper, or pastry brush to cover bottom and sides of pan with shortening or cooking oil. Grease sides only part way up to prevent a ruffled top edge.

2 In mixing bowl thoroughly stir together the flour, baking powder, salt, and soda with a fork or mixing spoon (sifting is not necessary). Set aside.

7 Add about ½ of the banana mixture to the creamed mixture. Beat at low speed just till smooth. Scrape sides of bowl.

Add another ⅓ of the flour mixture; beat till smooth. Add remaining banana mixture, then remaining flour mixture in the same manner.

In recipes using the creamed method, the flour mixture usually is added alternately with the liquid. In this recipe the banana plus the milk are the liquid.

8 Mixture should appear smooth and fluffy after beating in all of the flour and liquid mixtures.

These ingredients are added alternately to help maintain the fluffy quality given by the creaming of the shortening and sugar in step 3. Adding one or the other all at once tends to reduce the fluffiness of the batter.

3 Cream shortening and sugar to incorporate air into the mixture and give the loaf a lighter, more cake-like texture.

In small mixer bowl beat the shortening and sugar at high speed of electric mixer about 5 minutes or till light and fluffy, as shown. Scrape sides of bowl often.

Creaming also may be done by rubbing the mixture against the sides of the bowl with the back of a wooden spoon till fluffy.

4 Add eggs and shredded orange peel. Beat at medium speed of electric mixer about one minute or till smooth and fluffy, as shown. Scrape sides of bowl often with a rubber spatula.

5 In small bowl mash the bananas with a fork. Ripe bananas will mash more easily and also give more flavor to the bread. Stir the milk into the mashed bananas.

6 To add flour mixture and banana mixture alternately, begin by spooning about ⅓ of the flour mixture over the creamed mixture in mixer bowl. Beat at low speed just till smooth. Scrape sides of bowl often with a rubber spatula.

9 Carefully fold the chopped nuts into the batter. A rubber spatula works well for this. Again, remember that the goal is to keep the batter nearly as fluffy as it was when the eggs were added.

10 Turn the batter into the prepared pan, scraping the bowl with a rubber spatula. Lightly spread the batter evenly in the pan.

11 Bake in 350° oven for 45 to 50 minutes. (If using a glass loaf dish, reduce the oven temperature to 325°.)

Test for doneness by inserting a wooden pick near the center of the loaf. If the pick comes out with wet batter sticking to it, the loaf is not done.

A crack atop is typical of many quick bread loaves.

12 Place loaf on wire rack; cool in pan 10 minutes. Turn out bread on its side. Remove pan; turn loaf right-side-up; Cool.

The loaf will be easier to slice if it is tightly wrapped in foil or clear plastic wrap and kept at room temperature overnight.

Or freeze the tightly wrapped loaf. Thaw at room temperature. (Thawing in a warm oven tends to make the outside dry, leaving the inside frozen.)

Quick Breads

Muffins

Technique: Using muffin method for quick breads

    1   egg
    ¾   cup milk
    ⅓   cup cooking oil
    1¾ cups all-purpose flour
    ¼   cup sugar
    2½ teaspoons baking powder
    ¾   teaspoon salt

208

1 Grease 12 muffin cups (or line with paper bake cups). **2** In a small mixing bowl slightly beat egg with fork; beat in milk and cooking oil. Set aside. **3** In large mixing bowl stir together the flour, sugar, baking powder, and salt. **4** Make a well in the center. **5** Add egg mixture all at once. **6** Stir just till moistened (batter should be lumpy). **7** Spoon into prepared muffin cups, filling each about ⅔ full. Bake in 400° oven for 20 to 25 minutes. **8** Remove from pan; serve warm. Makes 12 muffins.

Self-Rise Muffins: Prepare muffins as above *except* use 1¾ cups *self-rising all-purpose flour* instead of all-purpose flour; omit the baking powder and salt.

Enriched Muffins: Prepare Muffins as above *except* stir ⅓ cup nonfat *dry milk powder* into the flour mixture.

Cheese Muffins: Prepare Muffins as above *except* stir ½ cup shredded sharp Swiss or cheddar *cheese* (2 ounces) into flour mixture.

1 Grease two 6-cup muffin pans (or one 12-cup muffin pan). Use folded paper toweling or waxed paper to cover bottoms and sides of cups with shortening or cooking oil.

Instead of greasing, use paper bake cups, if desired.

5 Add egg-milk-oil mixture to flour mixture all at once, pouring into the well.

2 In small mixing bowl beat egg slightly with fork till yolk and white are blended, as shown. Add milk and cooking oil; beat with fork till well blended. Set aside.

3 In large mixing bowl thoroughly stir together the flour, sugar, baking powder, and salt (sifting is not necessary).

To make mixing easier, sprinkle the baking powder and salt over the surface of the flour instead of pouring it all in one spot.

4 Gently push flour mixture against edges of bowl to make a well in the center. Use a wooden spoon for this.

209

TIP When adding berries to muffin batter, *be careful to avoid overmixing. Prepare the batter as directed at left, then combine ¾ to 1 cup fresh blueberries (or frozen berries, thawed and drained) with 2 tablespoons sugar. Fold into batter.*

For cranberry muffins coarsely chop 1 cup fresh cranberries and combine with ¼ cup sugar. Carefully fold into the batter.

6 Stir mixture just till moistened. It should appear lumpy; do not try to beat till smooth. Such overmixing will result in muffins that are peaked and smooth on top; with a tough heavy texture and holes or tunnels.

7 Fill prepared cups only ⅔ full to allow space for rising and to yield perfect-size muffins. An easy way to fill muffin cups is to push the batter from the spoon with a rubber spatula.

Bake in 400° oven for 20 to 25 minutes or till golden brown. Overbaking will result in muffins that are dry and tough. Underbaking results in pale, moist, heavy muffins.

8 Loosen muffins with small metal spatula. Remove, serve warm. If they cannot be served at once tip each muffin to one side in pan. This helps keep them from steaming and becoming soggy.

Store leftover muffins in covered container. Or wrap in moisture-vaporproof material; freeze for up to 2 months.

Thaw, unwrapped, at room temperature for 1 hour or heat in 300° oven 25 minutes or till heated through.

Quick Breads

Biscuits (pictured on page 224)

Technique: Using biscuit method for quick breads

  2   cups all-purpose flour
  1   tablespoon baking powder
½   teaspoon salt
⅓   cup shortening
¾   cup milk

210 **1** In mixing bowl thoroughly stir together the flour, baking powder, and salt. **2–3** Add shortening and cut in till mixture resembles coarse crumbs. **4** Make a well in dry mixture; add milk all at once. **5** Stir just till dough clings together.

  6 On lightly floured surface knead dough gently for 10 to 12 strokes. **7** Pat or roll dough to ½-inch thickness. **8** Cut with 2½-inch biscuit cutter, dipping cutter in flour between cuts. **9** Transfer cut biscuits to ungreased baking sheet. **10** Bake in 450° oven for 10 to 12 minutes or till golden. Serve immediately. Makes 10 biscuits.

Self-Rise Biscuits: Prepare as above *except* use 2 cups *self-rising all-purpose flour* instead of all-purpose flour. Omit the baking powder and salt.

Sour Cream Biscuits: Prepare biscuits as above *except* substitute 1 cup dairy *sour cream* for the milk.

Whole Wheat Biscuits: Prepare biscuits as above *except* use only 1½ cups all-purpose flour and add ½ cup *whole wheat flour.*

1 In mixing bowl thoroughly stir together the flour, baking powder, and salt. Mix well to evenly distribute the leavening (baking powder) and salt.

2 Cut shortening into flour mixture till mixture resembles coarse crumbs. Be sure to use solid shortening instead of cooking oil or melted butter.

  The best utensils to use for cutting in shortening are a pastry blender or a blending fork. Mixing by hand tends to soften the shortening, making a sticky, difficult-to-handle dough.

6 Turn the dough out onto a lightly floured surface. Knead gently 10 to 12 strokes. This helps develop the biscuit's structure and evenly distributes the moisture to make the biscuits more flaky.

  For ease in kneading, curve your fingers over the dough, pull it toward you, then push it down and away from you with the heel of your hand. Give dough a quarter turn; fold toward you, and push it down again.

7 On the lightly floured surface pat the dough to ½-inch thickness (or use a lightly floured rolling pin, if desired).

  Add a little flour to the surface of the dough if necessary to keep the dough from sticking.

3 After cutting in the shortening, the mixture should resemble coarse crumbs, as shown.

Avoid blending the fat completely with the flour or using a liquid shortening. These produce mealy biscuits rather than the flaky, tender ones which are more desirable.

4 Gently push the flour-shortening mixture against the edges of the bowl, making a well in the center. Add the milk all at once, pouring it into the well.

5 Using a fork, stir the mixture quickly. Stir just till the dough follows the fork around the bowl and forms a soft dough. Too much mixing may result in biscuits that are tough and not as light as desired.

211

TIP Make drop biscuits *when time is short and you want a really quick hot bread. These are not kneaded, rolled, or cut. Instead, additional milk is used to make a thick batter which can be dropped from a spoon.*

Use biscuit recipe at left except increase the milk to 1 cup. Combine ingredients as directed but do not knead. Use a knife or narrow spatula to push dough from tablespoon onto ungreased baking sheet. Bake as directed. Makes 12 biscuits.

8 Cut dough with a 2½-inch biscuit cutter. Dip cutter in flour between cuts to prevent sticking. Press the cutter straight down to get straight-sided, evenly shaped biscuits. Be especially careful not to twist the cutter or flatten the cut biscuit edges.

If you do not have a biscuit cutter, pat the dough into a ½-inch thick rectangle. Cut into squares or triangles (pictured on page 224) using a sharp knife.

9 Using a metal spatula, carefully transfer the cut biscuits to an ungreased baking sheet. For crusty-sided biscuits, place about 1-inch apart..For soft-sided biscuits, place biscuits close together in an ungreased baking pan.

Reroll scraps of dough and cut into biscuit shapes.

10 Bake biscuits in 450° oven for 10 to 12 minutes or until biscuits are golden. Serve immediately.

The perfectly baked biscuit is straight-sided and fairly smooth-topped with a golden brown top and a flaky, tender crust. It should have doubled in size during baking.

Quick Breads

1 In small mixing bowl beat egg with fork till frothy. Add milk and cooking oil; beat with fork till well blended. Set aside.

Buttermilk Pancakes

Technique: Making pancakes

1	**egg**
1¼	**cups buttermilk *or* sour milk**
2	**tablespoons cooking oil**
1	**cup all-purpose flour**
1	**tablespoon sugar**
2	**teaspoons baking powder**
½	**teaspoon baking soda**
½	**teaspoon salt**

212

1 In small mixing bowl beat egg with fork. Beat in buttermilk or sour milk and cooking oil. Set aside. **2** In large mixing bowl stir together the flour, sugar, baking powder, soda, and salt. **3** Add egg mixture to flour mixture. **4** Stir mixture till blended but still slightly lumpy.

5 Lightly grease a griddle or heavy skillet. **6** Heat till water sprinkled on the griddle dances across the surface. **7** Pour about ¼ cup batter on griddle for each pancake. **8** When pancakes have a bubbly surface and slightly dry edges, turn to cook other side.

Refrigerate any leftover batter for use the next day; bring to room temperature before using. Makes eight or nine 4-inch pancakes.

To make sour milk: *Place 1 tablespoon vinegar in a 2-cup glass measure. Add enough fresh milk to make 1¼ cups liquid. Stir well and let mixture stand about 5 minutes before using in recipe.*

5 Lightly grease a griddle or heavy skillet. Use a pastry brush to lightly cover the griddle surface with shortening or cooking oil. Grease again as needed during baking.

2 In large mixing bowl thoroughly stir together the flour, sugar, baking powder, soda, and salt (sifting is not necessary).

3 Add egg-milk-oil mixture all at once to flour mixture. Adding liquid ingredients all at once helps prevent overbeating.

4 Stir only till mixture is blended. Batter will be slightly lumpy, but these lumps disappear during the baking.

TIP Adding fruit or nuts *to the pancakes during baking makes them extra special. Use chopped nuts, chopped apple, or rinsed, well-drained berries.*

For best results, do not stir fruit or nuts into batter. Instead, before turning the partially baked pancakes, sprinkle each with 1 to 2 tablespoons fruit or nuts. Turn and brown the other side as usual.

213

6 Heat the griddle or skillet over medium heat till drops of water sprinkled atop dance across the surface of the griddle.

During baking, if the pancakes appear to be baking too slowly, turn up the heat. If the pancakes are baking too quickly, leaving uncooked centers, reduce the heat.

7 When griddle is hot, dip out about ¼ cup batter for each pancake. This amount of batter will make standard-size cakes. For dollar-size pancakes, use a tablespoonful of batter. Be sure to space the batter far enough apart so that the pancakes will not touch as they expand.

8 Pancakes are ready to turn when tops are bubbly all over, with a few broken bubbles. Edges of the pancakes will be slightly dry. Remember to turn the pancakes only once. For easiest turning, use a broad spatula.

Keep baked pancakes warm by piling them on a paper-lined baking sheet in warm oven. Put paper toweling between each layer to absorb the steam that could make them soggy.

Quick Breads

Waffles (pictured on page 180)

Technique: Making waffles

---

  2   **egg yolks**
1¾ **cups milk**
 ½ **cup cooking oil** *or* **melted shortening**
1¾ **cups all-purpose flour**
 1 **tablespoon baking powder**
 ½ **teaspoon salt**
 2 **egg whites**

214

1 In small mixing bowl beat egg yolks with fork. Beat in milk and cooking oil or melted shortening. **2** In large mixing bowl stir together the flour, baking powder, and salt. **3** Add egg mixture to flour mixture all at once. **4** Stir mixture till blended but still slightly lumpy.

    5 In small mixer bowl beat egg whites till stiff peaks form (tips stand straight). **6** Carefully fold egg whites into egg-flour mixture. **7** Leave a few fluffs of egg white. *Do not overmix.*

    8 Lightly grease the waffle baker. Preheat. **9** Pour batter onto grids of preheated baker. Close lid quickly; do not open during baking. **10** Remove waffle from baker with a fork. Makes three 9-inch waffles.

Pecan Waffles: Prepare as above *except* sprinkle about 2 tablespoons broken *pecans* atop waffles before closing lid to bake.

Corn Waffles: Prepare waffles as above *except* reduce milk to 1¼ cups and add 1 cup canned *cream-style corn* to egg-milk mixture.

1 In small bowl slightly beat egg yolks with fork. Add milk and cooking oil or melted shortening; mix well.

2 In large mixing bowl thoroughly stir together the flour, baking powder, and salt (sifting is not necessary).

6 Carefully add beaten egg whites to egg-flour mixture, using a rubber spatula to fold in egg whites.

7 Be careful not to overmix. Some small fluffs of beaten egg white should remain interspersed throughout the batter, as shown.

3 Add egg-milk-oil mixture all at once to flour mixture. Adding liquid ingredients all at once helps prevent overbeating.

4 Stir only till mixture is blended. Batter will be slightly lumpy; however these lumps disappear during the baking.

5 In small mixer bowl beat egg whites till stiff peaks form (tips stand straight). This will take about 1 to 1½ minutes at medium speed of an electric mixer.

8 Lightly grease waffle baker. Use a pastry brush to lightly cover the griddle surface with shortening or cooking oil. Grease again as needed during baking. Heat the waffle baker (check manufacturer's directions) till water sprinkled atop the grid hops across the surface.

9 Pour batter onto grids of preheated waffle baker. Check manufacturer's directions for the recommended amount of batter to use with your waffle baker. Close lid quickly; do not open during baking.

10 Waffles are done when steam stops escaping from sides of baker or when the indicator light comes on.

For crisp waffles, allow the waffle to remain on grid a few seconds after opening lid. Or bake waffles a little longer for extra crispness. Use a fork to help lift the baked waffle off grid.

To keep baked waffles hot for serving, place in single layer on rack placed atop baking sheet in warm oven.

Quick Breads

Crepes

Technique: Making crepes

---

  1 **cup all-purpose flour**
1½ **cups milk**
  2 **eggs**
  2 **tablespoons sugar**
  1 **tablespoon cooking oil**
⅛ **teaspoon salt**

1–2 In mixing bowl combine the flour, milk, eggs, sugar, cooking oil, and salt. Beat with rotary beater till smooth.

3 Lightly grease a 6-inch skillet. **4** Heat pan till water dropped on surface sizzles. **5** Pour in about 2 tablespoons of batter. **6** Lift and tilt skillet to spread the batter. **7** Return to heat and cook on one side only till browned.

8 Loosen crepe by running a small metal spatula around edges of crepe in pan. **9** Invert pan over paper toweling; remove crepe. Repeat with remaining batter, greasing skillet as needed. Makes 16 to 18 crepes.

To freeze crepes: *Stack crepes alternately with two sheets of waxed paper (this makes crepes easier to separate). Place stack in moisture-vaporproof bag; seal. Protect crepes from bending during initial freezing by placing stack in glass or plastic container. When crepes are frozen, container may be removed. For best quality use crepes within four months of freezing.*

To use, remove desired number of crepes; reseal bag. Let crepes thaw at room temperature about 1 hour before filling.

1 In mixing bowl beat together the flour, milk, eggs, sugar, cooking oil, and salt with a rotary beater. Be sure to add the ingredients to bowl in the order listed, with flour first. Adding the milk and eggs to the flour helps reduce the possibility of lumpiness.

2 Beat the ingredients till the mixture is smooth with no lumps, as shown. If you don't have a rotary beater, you can use a wire whisk or electric mixer. Just be certain to beat till batter is very smooth.

6 Lift and tilt skillet, rotating pan so that batter covers bottom in a thin, even layer.

If batter won't swirl to coat, it is probably too thick; thin it by gradually blending in a little additional milk. Or, the pan may be too hot; try reducing the temperature.

If a bubble breaks or if there's a tear in the crepe, simply patch it with a little batter and continue cooking till set.

7 Cook crepe on one side only, for 45 to 60 seconds or till crepe is lightly browned on bottom. Lift edge with a small metal spatula to check for doneness. If crepes have a dark, veined appearance, the pan may be either too hot or not hot enough; adjust the heat. Or the pan may have been oiled too much. If that is the case, wipe off the excess oil.

3 Lightly grease a 6-inch skillet by brushing with cooking oil or shortening. (Pans with sloping sides are easier to use.)

Whether you use a regular metal skillet or a pan with a non-stick coating, make sure it is well seasoned before you begin. For best results, follow manufacturer's directions for seasoning a new pan. (If using an inverted crepe pan or a small round electric skillet, follow manufacturer's directions.)

4 Heat skillet over medium heat till water dropped on surface of pan sizzles.

Check the heat as you cook. If the batter sticks to the pan even though the pan has been properly seasoned, you may need to increase the heat. "Medium heat" on your stove may not be hot enough.

The heaviness of the pan used also affects the amount of heat needed.

5 Pour about 2 tablespoons of the crepe batter into the heated pan. For easy pouring, use a full ⅛-cup coffee measure. Or remember that 2 tablespoons is half of a ¼-cup measure.

217

TIP *Although crepes are sometimes layered like a torte, with filling between, they are usually wrapped or folded around the filling.*

Easy fillings to use with these crepes include canned pie fillings, puddings, and creamed meat mixtures.

To fill a crepe, spoon some of the filling along the center of the unbrowned side of the crepe. Fold the two opposite edges so they overlap atop the filling.

To freeze filled crepes, space them slightly apart on a greased baking sheet. Freeze uncovered. When frozen remove and seal in a moisture-vaporproof bag. Place in a glass or plastic container for protection. Use within two months.

Do not freeze cream-type fillings or those that contain potato, mayonnaise, cooked egg white, or raw vegetables.

8 When crepe is cooked, loosen edge with a small metal spatula. To prevent sticking, you'll probably need to grease the pan after every fourth or fifth crepe.

9 To remove crepe from pan, invert over paper toweling and let the crepe fall, smoothing if necessary so that it lies flat to cool.

If crepes are to be frozen, stack alternately with two sheets of waxed paper to make them easier to separate.

Quick Breads

Homemade Noodles

Technique: Making egg noodles

1   egg
2   tablespoons milk
½   teaspoon salt
1   cup all-purpose flour

1 In mixing bowl beat the egg; stir in milk and salt. **2–3** Add enough of the flour to make a very stiff dough; turn out on floured surface. **4** Roll dough very thin. **5** Let dough rest 20 minutes. Roll up dough loosely. **6** Cut into ¼-inch wide slices; unroll and cut into desired lengths. **7** Spread out cut dough; let dry 2 hours. Place in covered container and store until needed.

8 To cook, drop noodles into large amount of boiling salted water or broth; cook, uncovered, 8 to 10 minutes. Makes 3 cups uncooked or cooked noodles.

218

1 In mixing bowl slightly beat the egg with a fork to blend yolk and white. Stir in milk and salt, mixing well.

5 Let dough rest about 20 minutes to allow dough to "relax".
Roll up dough loosely, making a roll about three inches wide.

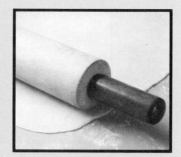

2 Stir in about half of the flour; mix well. Stir in enough of the rest of the flour to make a very stiff dough.

3 When dough has the right consistency it has a rough texture and can be shaped into a ball in the bowl. Turn out onto a lightly floured surface.

4 Using a rolling pin on a floured surface, roll out dough to about ¹⁄₁₆-inch thickness. This will make a rectangle approximately 18×12 inches.

219

6 Cut rolled-up dough crosswise into strips about ¼ inch wide. Be sure to use a sharp knife and try to cut straight down.

7 Unroll strips of dough; cut into desired lengths. Spread out and let dry for 2 hours. Store dried noodles in an airtight container until ready to use.

8 To cook, drop noodles into a large amount of boiling salted water or broth. Cook, uncovered, 8 to 10 minutes or till noodles are tender yet firm to the bite. Drain well; serve with butter or margarine, if desired.

TIP Spaetzle (spet′ zel) is a noodle-like product traditionally served with sauerbraten and other roasts in southern Germany.

To make Spaetzle, stir together 2 cups all-purpose flour and 1 teaspoon salt. In another bowl combine 2 eggs and ¾ cup milk; stir into the flour mixture. Pour batter into a colander with large holes, as shown in top photo. Hold over kettle of boiling salted water.

Press batter through colander as shown in bottom photo. (If dough is too thick to push through, thin it with a little milk.) Cook and stir for 5 minutes; drain. Sprinkle with buttered bread crumbs. Makes 4 cups.

Quick Breads

Biscuit Bubble Ring
(pictured on page 180)

- 1 3-ounce package cream cheese, chilled
- 2 cups all-purpose flour
- 2 tablespoons granulated sugar
- 4 teaspoons baking powder
- ½ teaspoon salt
- ⅓ cup shortening
- ⅔ cup milk
- ¼ cup granulated sugar
- ½ teaspoon ground cinnamon
- 5 tablespoons butter, melted
- ⅓ cup chopped pecans
- ¼ cup light corn syrup
- 2 tablespoons brown sugar
- 2 tablespoons butter

Refer to: Using biscuit method, page 210. Cut cream cheese into 20 pieces. Shape each into a ball; set aside. Stir together the flour, 2 tablespoons granulated sugar, baking powder, and salt. Cut in shortening till mixture resembles coarse crumbs; make a well in center. Add milk all at once. Stir just till dough clings together. On a lightly floured surface knead dough gently for 10 to 12 strokes. Divide dough into 20 pieces. Pat each piece to a 2½- to 3-inch round.

Combine the ¼ cup granulated sugar and cinnamon. Place a cream cheese ball and ¼ *teaspoon* of the cinnamon-sugar mixture on each dough round. Bring up edges of dough around cream cheese; pinch to seal.

Pour *3 tablespoons* of the melted butter into the bottom of a 5½-cup ring mold; rotate mold to coat sides. Sprinkle *half* of the pecans and *half* of the remaining cinnamon-sugar mixture into the mold.

Roll filled biscuits in remaining melted butter; place *half*, seam side up, atop mixture in mold. Sprinkle with remaining pecans and remaining cinnamon-sugar mixture. Top with remaining biscuit balls, seam side down.

Bake in 375° oven about 25 minutes or till browned. Cool 5 minutes. Invert onto serving plate; remove pan.

Meanwhile, in small saucepan combine the corn syrup, brown sugar, and 2 tablespoons butter. Heat and stir till sugar dissolves. Drizzle over warm coffee cake. Serves 10.

Ambrosia Muffins
(pictured on page 180)

- 1 beaten egg
- ½ cup milk
- ⅓ cup cooking oil
- ¼ cup frozen orange juice concentrate, thawed
- 1¾ cups all-purpose flour
- 2 tablespoons sugar
- 2½ teaspoons baking powder
- ¾ teaspoon salt
- ½ cup flaked coconut

Refer to: Using muffin method, page 208. Grease 10 muffin cups; set aside. Combine egg, milk, oil, and juice concentrate. Thoroughly stir together the flour, sugar, baking powder, and salt. Add egg mixture all at once, stirring just till moistened. Fold in coconut. Fill prepared pans ⅔ full.

Bake in 375° oven about 20 minutes. Remove muffins from pans. If desired, lightly brush tops with additional juice concentrate; sprinkle generously with additional sugar. Makes 10 muffins.

Bran Muffins
(pictured on page 224)

- 1½ cups whole bran cereal
- 1 cup buttermilk
- 1 beaten egg
- ¼ cup cooking oil *or* melted shortening
- 1 cup all-purpose flour
- ⅓ cup packed brown sugar
- 2 teaspoons baking powder
- ½ teaspoon baking soda
- ½ teaspoon salt
- ¾ cup raisins *or* snipped pitted dates (optional)

Refer to: Using muffin method, page 208. Grease 10 to 12 muffin cups; set aside. Combine bran and buttermilk; let stand 3 minutes or till liquid is absorbed. Stir in egg and oil or melted shortening; set aside. Stir together the flour, brown sugar, baking powder, soda, and salt. Add bran mixture all at once, stirring just till moistened (batter will be thick). Fold in raisins. Fill prepared pans ⅔ full. Bake in 400° oven 20 to 25 minutes. Makes 10 to 12.

Orange Doughnuts
(pictured on page 180)

- 3¼ cups all-purpose flour
- 2 teaspoons baking powder
- Dash salt
- 2 beaten eggs
- ⅔ cup sugar
- 1 teaspoon vanilla
- 1 teaspoon finely shredded orange peel
- ⅔ cup orange juice
- ¼ cup butter *or* margarine, melted
- Shortening for deep-fat frying
- Orange Glaze

Refer to: Frying yeast doughnuts, page 194. Combine flour, baking powder, and salt. In mixer bowl beat eggs, sugar, and vanilla till thick and lemon-colored. Combine orange peel, juice, and butter.

Set aside ¼ of the flour mixture. Add remaining flour mixture and orange mixture alternately to egg mixture. After each addition beat with electric mixer just till blended. By hand stir in remaining flour mixture. Cover; chill 2 hours.

On lightly floured surface roll dough to ⅜-inch thickness. Cut with floured 2½-inch doughnut cutter. Fry in deep hot fat (375°) about 1 minute; turn and fry about 1 minute more. Drain on paper toweling. While warm, drizzle with Orange Glaze. Makes 16.

Orange Glaze: Mix 2 cups sifted *powdered sugar,* 1 teaspoon finely shredded *orange peel,* and 3 tablespoons *orange juice.*

Chocolate Waffles

- 1 beaten egg
- ¾ cup milk
- ¼ cup chocolate-flavored syrup
- 2 tablespoons cooking oil
- 1 cup packaged pancake mix
- ⅓ cup chopped pecans

Refer to: Making waffles, page 214. Beat together egg, milk, syrup, and oil. Place pancake mix in large bowl. Add egg mixture; beat just till blended.

Pour about half the batter on grid of greased, preheated waffle baker. Sprinkle with half of the nuts. Bake; repeat. Makes two 9-inch waffles.

French Breakfast Puffs

Whole Wheat Soda Bread

    3 cups all-purpose flour
    1 cup whole wheat flour
    2 teaspoons baking powder
 1½ teaspoons baking soda
    1 teaspoon salt
    ½ cup butter or margarine
 1½ cups raisins
    1 tablespoon caraway seed
    2 well-beaten eggs
 1½ cups buttermilk

Refer to: Using biscuit method, page 210. Grease a 2-quart casserole; set aside. Stir together all-purpose flour, whole wheat flour, baking powder, soda, and salt. Cut in butter till mixture is crumbly; stir in raisins and caraway seed. Reserve *1 tablespoon* beaten egg; set aside. Combine remaining egg and buttermilk; add to flour mixture, stirring just till moistened.

Knead gently on lightly floured surface for 10 to 12 strokes. Shape dough into ball; place in prepared casserole. With sharp knife cut a 4-inch cross, ¼ inch deep, across center of loaf. Brush with reserved 1 tablespoon egg.

Bake in 350° oven 70 to 80 minutes or till wooden pick inserted in center comes out clean. Remove from casserole. Cool thoroughly. Slice very thin. Makes 1 round loaf.

221

Two-Corn Bread

    3 eggs
    1 cup cream-style cottage cheese
    1 8-ounce can cream-style corn
    1 cup all-purpose flour
    1 cup yellow cornmeal
    2 tablespoons sugar
    1 tablespoon baking powder
    ¼ teaspoon salt

Refer to: Using muffin method, page 208. Lightly grease a 9×9×2-inch baking pan; set aside. In small bowl beat eggs and cottage cheese till smooth; stir in corn. Set aside. In large bowl stir together flour, cornmeal, sugar, baking powder, and salt. Add egg mixture all at once. Stir just till blended. Turn into prepared pan. Bake in 375° oven for 30 to 35 minutes. Serve warm. Serves 9.

French Breakfast Puffs

 1½ cups all-purpose flour
 1½ teaspoons baking powder
    ½ teaspoon salt
    ¼ teaspoon ground nutmeg
    ½ cup sugar
    ⅓ cup shortening
    1 egg
    ½ cup milk
    ½ cup sugar
    1 teaspoon ground cinnamon
    6 tablespoons butter or margarine, melted

Refer to: Using creamed method, page 206. Lightly grease 12 muffin cups; set aside. Stir together flour, baking powder, salt, and nutmeg; set aside. In mixer bowl cream together ½ cup sugar, the shortening, and egg. Add flour mixture and milk alternately to creamed mixture, beating well after each addition.

Fill prepared muffin cups ⅔ full. Bake in 350° oven for 20 to 25 minutes or till golden. Combine ½ cup sugar and the cinnamon. Remove muffins from oven; immediately dip in melted butter or margarine, then in cinnamon-sugar mixture till coated. Serve warm. Makes 12 muffins.

Lemon Nut Bread

    2 cups all-purpose flour
 2½ teaspoons baking powder
    1 teaspoon salt
    ¾ cup sugar
    ¼ cup butter or margarine
    2 eggs
    1 tablespoon finely shredded lemon peel
    ¾ cup milk
    ½ cup chopped walnuts
    ¼ cup sugar
    2 tablespoons lemon juice

Refer to: Using creamed method, page 206. Lightly grease an 8×4×2-inch loaf pan.

In small mixing bowl stir together flour, baking powder, and salt; set aside. In large mixer bowl cream together the ¾ cup sugar and butter or margarine. Add eggs and lemon peel; beat well. Add flour mixture and milk alternately to creamed mixture, beating just till smooth after each addition. Fold in walnuts. Turn into prepared pan.

Bake in 350° oven 55 to 60 minutes or till done. Let cool in pan 10 minutes. For glaze combine the ¼ cup sugar and the lemon juice. Prick top of loaf well with fork. Spoon glaze over top. Remove from pan; cool. Wrap; store overnight. Makes 1 loaf.

Quick Breads

Cherry-Pecan Bread

- 2 cups all-purpose flour
- 1 teaspoon baking soda
- ½ teaspoon salt
- ¾ cup sugar
- ½ cup butter *or* margarine
- 2 eggs
- 1 teaspoon vanilla
- 1 cup buttermilk
- 1 cup chopped pecans
- 1 10-ounce jar maraschino cherries, drained and chopped (1 cup)

Refer to: Using creamed method, page 206. Lightly grease a 9×5×3-inch loaf pan; set aside.

In mixing bowl thoroughly stir together flour, soda, and salt; set aside. In large mixer bowl cream together sugar, butter or margarine, eggs, and vanilla till light and fluffy. Add flour mixture and buttermilk alternately to creamed mixture. Beat just till blended after each addition. Fold in nuts and cherries. Turn batter into prepared pan.

Bake in 350° oven for 55 to 60 minutes. Remove from pan; cool. If desired, glaze with Confectioners' Icing (see tip on page 249).

Crullers

- 1¾ cups all-purpose flour
- ½ teaspoon salt
- ½ teaspoon ground nutmeg
- ¼ teaspoon ground mace
- ⅓ cup granulated sugar
- ¼ cup butter *or* margarine
- 2 eggs
- 2 tablespoons milk
  Shortening *or* cooking oil for deep-fat frying
  Sifted powdered sugar

Refer to: Using creamed method, page 206; and to Frying yeast doughnuts, page 194.

In bowl stir together flour, salt, nutmeg, and mace; set aside. In mixer bowl cream together granulated sugar and butter or margarine till light and fluffy. Add eggs, one at a time; beat well after each addition. Beat in milk (batter may appear slightly curdled). By hand stir in the flour mixture. Chill at least 1 hour.

On lightly floured surface roll *half* the dough (*rolling in one direction only* so that doughnuts will puff) to a 16×8-inch rectangle. Cut into 2-inch squares (*do not reroll*). (If desired, use pastry wheel for pretty edges.) Repeat with remaining dough.

Fry in deep hot fat (375°) about 1½ minutes or till golden on both sides, turning once. Dust with powdered sugar. Makes 64.

Cocoa Spice Doughnuts

- 4 cups all-purpose flour
- ⅓ cup unsweetened cocoa powder
- 4 teaspoons baking powder
- 1 teaspoon ground cinnamon
- ¾ teaspoon salt
- ¼ teaspoon baking soda
- 2 beaten eggs
- 1¼ cups sugar
- ¼ cup cooking oil
- 1 teaspoon vanilla
- ¾ cup buttermilk
  Shortening *or* cooking oil for deep-fat frying
  Cinnamon Glaze

Refer to: Frying yeast doughnuts, page 194. In bowl stir together the flour, cocoa powder, baking powder, cinnamon, salt, and soda; set aside.

In mixer bowl beat eggs and sugar about 4 minutes or till thick and lemon-colored. Stir in oil and vanilla. Add flour mixture and buttermilk alternately to egg mixture, beginning and ending with flour. Beat just till blended after each addition. Chill about 2 hours. On lightly floured surface roll dough, half at a time, to ½-inch thickness (keep remaining dough chilled). Cut with floured 2½-inch doughnut cutter.

Fry in deep hot fat (375°) about 1½ minutes per side or till golden; drain. Dip warm doughnuts in Cinnamon Glaze. Makes 24.

Cinnamon Glaze: In small mixing bowl combine 4 cups sifted *powdered sugar*, 1 teaspoon *vanilla*, ½ teaspoon *ground cinnamon*, and enough *milk* to make of spreading consistency (see tip on page 249).

222

Cherry-Pecan Bread

Tea Scones

2 cups all-purpose flour
2 tablespoons sugar
1 tablespoon baking powder
½ teaspoon salt
6 tablespoons butter *or* margarine
⅓ cup dried currants (optional)
1 beaten egg
½ cup milk
1 beaten egg

Refer to: Using biscuit method, page 210. Mix flour, sugar, baking powder, and salt. Cut in butter till crumbly; stir in currants. Combine 1 beaten egg and milk. Add to flour mixture; stir just till dough clings together.

On lightly floured surface knead gently for 12 to 15 strokes. Divide dough in half. Shape *each half* into ball; pat or roll to 6-inch circle. Cut each circle into 6 or 8 wedges. Space slightly apart on ungreased baking sheet. Brush with beaten egg.

Bake in 425° oven 12 to 15 minutes or till deep golden. Makes 12 or 16.

Whole Wheat Pancakes

2 beaten eggs
1½ cups milk
1 teaspoon vanilla
4 drops lemon extract
1 cup packaged whole wheat pancake mix
½ cup wheat germ
2 tablespoons nonfat dry milk powder
2 teaspoons baking powder
½ teaspoon salt
1 banana, chopped (½ cup)
½ cup chopped pecans *or* walnuts

Refer to: Making pancakes, page 212. Combine eggs, milk, vanilla, and lemon extract. Stir together the pancake mix, wheat germ, milk powder, baking powder, and salt. Add egg mixture; stir just to moisten.

For each pancake, pour about ¼ cup batter on greased, preheated griddle. Bake till bubbles break on surface and edges are dry. Sprinkle each pancake with some of the banana and nuts; turn. Bake 45 to 60 seconds more. Makes 12 to 14 four-inch pancakes.

Coconut French Toast

2 beaten eggs
½ cup milk
1 tablespoon sugar
½ cup chopped shredded coconut
⅓ cup crushed cornflakes
6 slices white bread
Butter *or* margarine

In shallow dish blend eggs, milk, and sugar. In another shallow dish combine coconut and cornflakes. Dip bread into egg mixture, then into coconut mixture, coating both sides. Heat a little butter in skillet. Add bread; fry till lightly browned on both sides, adding more butter as needed. Serves 6.

Cranberry-Orange Bread

(pictured on page 274)

3 medium oranges
1 beaten egg
2 tablespoons cooking oil
2 cups all-purpose flour
¾ cup granulated sugar
1½ teaspoons baking powder
1 teaspoon salt
½ teaspoon baking soda
1 cup coarsely chopped fresh *or* frozen cranberries
½ cup chopped walnuts
1 cup sifted powdered sugar

Refer to: Using muffin method, page 208. Lightly grease one 8×4×2-inch loaf pan *or* three 6×3×2-inch loaf pans.

Shred peel from 1 orange; reserve. Squeeze juice from all oranges. Measure ¾ cup juice; reserve remaining.

Combine the ¾ cup juice, *1 teaspoon* of the peel, egg, and oil. Stir together the flour, granulated sugar, baking powder, salt, and soda. Add orange mixture; stir just till moistened. Fold in cranberries and walnuts; turn into prepared pans. Bake in 350° oven 50 to 60 minutes for large pan (30 to 40 minutes for smaller pans) or till wooden pick comes out clean. Cool. To prepare glaze, blend *1 tablespoon* of the reserved orange juice with powdered sugar. Add more juice to make of drizzling consistency. Drizzle atop cooled loaves; garnish with reserved shredded orange peel. Makes 1 large or 3 small loaves.

Hush Puppies

1 beaten egg
1 cup buttermilk
½ cup finely chopped onion
¼ cup water
1¾ cups cornmeal
½ cup all-purpose flour
1 tablespoon sugar
2 teaspoons baking powder
1 teaspoon salt
½ teaspoon baking soda
Shortening *or* cooking oil for deep-fat frying

Refer to: Using muffin method, page 208. Blend egg, buttermilk, onion, and water; set aside. Combine cornmeal, flour, sugar, baking powder, salt, and soda. Add egg mixture to cornmeal mixture; stir just to moisten.

Drop batter by tablespoonfuls into deep hot fat (375°). Fry about 2 minutes or till golden brown, turning once. Drain on paper toweling. Serve hot with butter, if desired. Makes about 24.

Apple-Nut Coffee Cake

2 cups all-purpose flour
1 teaspoon baking powder
1 teaspoon baking soda
¼ teaspoon salt
1 cup granulated sugar
½ cup shortening
2 eggs
1 teaspoon vanilla
1 cup dairy sour cream
2 cups finely chopped apple
½ cup chopped nuts
½ cup packed brown sugar
1 teaspoon ground cinnamon
2 tablespoons butter, melted

Refer to: Using creamed method, page 206. Grease a 13×9×2-inch baking pan; set aside. Stir together flour, baking powder, soda, and salt. Cream granulated sugar and shortening. Beat in eggs and vanilla. Add flour mixture and sour cream alternately to creamed mixture. Fold in apple. Spread batter in prepared pan.

Combine nuts, brown sugar, and cinnamon; stir in butter. Sprinkle evenly over batter. Bake in 350° oven for 35 to 40 minutes. Makes 1.

From back left: Biscuits (see recipe, page 210); Bran Muffins (see recipe, page 220); Brioche (see recipe, page 203); Honey-Pumpkin Pie (see recipe, page 284); Apple Pie (see recipe, page 282); Lime Chiffon Pie (see recipe, page 299); Lemon Meringue Pie (see recipe, page 294); and Buttermilk Spice Cake (see recipe, page 232).

CAKES AND FROSTINGS

There's nothing like a homemade cake to top off the perfect dinner for family or guests. And this section abounds with luscious layer cakes, sponge and chiffon cakes, angel cakes, pound cakes, fruitcakes, and jelly rolls. You'll also find delicious recipes for fluffy frostings, as well as tips on how to use them.

Busy-Day Cake

Technique: Using one-bowl method for cakes

- ⅓ **cup shortening**
- 1½ **cups all-purpose flour**
- ¾ **cup sugar**
- 2½ **teaspoons baking powder**
- ½ **teaspoon salt**
- ¾ **cup milk**
- 1 **egg**
- 1½ **teaspoons vanilla**

1–2 Grease and lightly flour a 9×9×2-inch baking pan; set aside. **3** Place shortening in small mixer bowl. Add flour, sugar, baking powder, and salt. **4** Add *half* the milk, the egg, and vanilla. **5** Mix at low speed of electric mixer till blended. Beat 2 minutes at medium speed. **6–7** Scrape sides of bowl. Beat in remaining milk. Beat 2 minutes more at medium speed. **8** Turn into prepared pan. **9** Bake in 375° oven for 25 to 30 minutes or till wooden pick inserted in center comes out clean. **10** Cool on wire rack. Frost with desired frosting. Makes one 9-inch square layer or 9 servings.

1 Grease and lightly flour a 9×9×2-inch baking pan. To grease, use folded paper toweling, folded waxed paper, or a pastry brush to generously apply shortening (about 1 tablespoon) to bottom of pan. (Or, prepare and use pan-coating, referring to the tip on page 230.) If you plan to remove the cake and frost it as a layer, grease the pan sides also.

2 Add about 1 tablespoon flour to the greased pan. Tilt and tap the pan to distribute the flour evenly, as shown. When the greased area is flour-dusted, dump the excess flour.

6 Scrape sides of mixer bowl with a rubber spatula. Beat in remaining milk. Beat 2 minutes more at medium speed of electric mixer. Again, use the spatula to guide the mixture toward the beaters.

7 When the mixing is completed, the cake batter will be smooth and fairly thick, as shown.
   Clean batter from beaters with a rubber spatula. For safety, unplug the mixer or remove the beaters before cleaning.

3 Place shortening in a small mixer bowl. Add the flour, sugar, baking powder, and salt. This easy one-bowl method does not require creaming the shortening.

4 Add *half* the milk, the egg, and vanilla. Use a liquid measuring cup for the milk so you can easily see when you've added half of it.

To avoid getting eggshell into the mixture, first break the egg into a custard cup or small bowl. Then skim off any shell fragments before adding egg to milk mixture.

5 Mix at low speed of electric mixer till blended. Beat 2 minutes at medium speed. Using a rubber spatula, guide mixture toward beaters for thorough mixing. At the end of this time, the mixture will be thick and smooth, as shown.

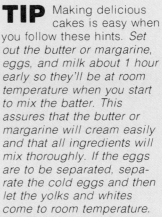

TIP Making delicious cakes is easy when you follow these hints. *Set out the butter or margarine, eggs, and milk about 1 hour early so they'll be at room temperature when you start to mix the batter. This assures that the butter or margarine will cream easily and that all ingredients will mix thoroughly. If the eggs are to be separated, separate the cold eggs and then let the yolks and whites come to room temperature.*

Preheat the oven to the correct temperature before starting to mix the cake. Use an oven thermometer to check the accuracy of the oven.

Place the baking pans as near to the center of the oven as possible. Air should circulate freely around cakes during baking, so make sure pans do not touch each other or the sides of the oven. If the pans won't fit on 1 oven shelf, stagger them on 2 shelves, but avoid placing them directly under each other.

Set the cake on a wire rack to cool thoroughly before frosting. This will take about 4 hours.

227

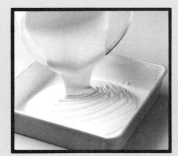

8 Turn batter into prepared pan. Use a rubber spatula to scrape the bowl and smooth the batter in the pan. Be sure to spread batter to all corners of the pan. Lightly tap the bottom of the pan on a countertop to remove large air bubbles.

9 Bake in a 375° oven for 25 to 30 minutes or till a wooden pick inserted in center comes out clean. Avoid opening the oven until the cake has baked about 25 minutes, then test with a wooden pick. If the wooden pick doesn't come out clean, bake cake a few minutes more and test again. When the cake is done, it will have shrunk slightly from the sides of the pan.

10 Cool on wire rack. Elevating the cake by placing it on a wire rack allows air to circulate freely underneath. Cooling a cake without elevating it will result in a gummy bottom layer.

Cakes and Frostings

White Cake Supreme

Technique: Using creamed method for cakes

2¼ **cups sifted cake flour**
5 **egg whites**
1½ **cups sugar**
¾ **cup shortening**
1½ **teaspoons vanilla**
1 **tablespoon baking powder**
1 **teaspoon salt**
1 **cup milk**

1 Grease and lightly flour two 9×1½-inch round baking pans. **2** Sift and measure the cake flour; set aside. **3** Beat egg whites till stiff peaks form (tips stand straight); set aside. **4** Cream sugar, shortening, and vanilla till light, scraping bowl frequently.

5 Sift together cake flour, baking powder, and salt. **6–7** Add sifted dry ingredients to creamed mixture alternately with milk, beating after each addition. **8** Gently fold in stiff-beaten egg whites, half at a time. **9** Pour into prepared pans.

10 Bake in 375° oven for 18 to 20 minutes or till wooden pick inserted in center comes out clean. **11–12** Cool on wire racks for 10 minutes. Remove from pans. Cool thoroughly. Frost with desired frosting. Makes two 9-inch layers or 12 servings.

1 Grease and lightly flour two 9×1½-inch round baking pans. Use folded paper toweling or a pastry brush to generously apply shortening (about 1 tablespoon per pan) to the bottoms and sides. Add about 2 teaspoons flour to each pan, then tilt and tap the pan to distribute the flour evenly. When the pan is completely flour-dusted, dump the excess flour. (Or, prepare and use pan-coating, referring to the tip on page 230.)

2 Sift cake flour, then measure. Since cake flour tends to pack more than all-purpose flour, it should be sifted first to assure accurate measuring.

Sift cake flour onto a piece of waxed paper. (*Or*, place a metal sieve over a bowl. Add cake flour, stirring to press through sieve.)

Lightly spoon the sifted flour into measuring cup and level off with a straight-edged spatula, as shown. Set measured flour aside.

7 Then, add half the milk and beat till thoroughly combined, again guiding mixture toward beaters. Add another ⅓ of the dry ingredients, the remaining milk, and then the remaining dry ingredients, beating after each addition.

8 Add half of the stiff-beaten egg whites. Fold in by cutting down through mixture with a rubber spatula; scrape across bottom of bowl; then bring spatula up and over mixture, close to the surface. Repeat this down-up-and-over motion, turning the bowl as you work. Do not stir; this breaks down the air-retaining structure and fluffy consistency of the carefully beaten whites. Repeat with remaining egg whites.

3 In small mixer bowl beat egg whites till stiff peaks form. Using an electric mixer or rotary beater, beat the egg whites about 1½ minutes or till the tips of peaks stand straight when beaters are removed.

Use a deep, straight-sided glass or metal bowl. Do not use a plastic bowl when beating egg whites since oils retained in the plastic prevent the whites from forming peaks.

4 In a larger mixer bowl cream sugar, shortening, and vanilla till light. Using a rubber spatula, guide toward beaters.

(If using chilled shortening or butter, soften by creaming a few minutes, then gradually add sugar and cream till light.)

Beat on medium speed of electric mixer till well creamed, as shown (this usually takes about 5 minutes). Beating with a portable mixer may take longer.

5 In a sifter or sieve combine the cake flour, baking powder, and salt. Sift into a bowl or onto waxed paper. Sifting assures even distribution of the baking powder and salt.

6 Add sifted dry ingredients to creamed mixture alternately with milk, beating after each addition. First, spoon about ⅓ of the dry ingredients over the creamed mixture, as shown. Beat till thoroughly combined, using a rubber spatula to guide mixture toward beaters.

229

9 Pour batter into prepared pans. Divide batter evenly between the 2 pans, filling each about half full. Smooth the batter with a rubber spatula. Tap the bottom of the pans lightly on a countertop to remove large air bubbles.

10 Bake in 375° oven for 18 to 20 minutes or till a wooden pick inserted in center comes out clean.

To allow air to circulate freely, be sure cake pans don't touch each other or the sides of the oven. Avoid opening the oven door until the cakes have baked 18 minutes, then test each layer with a wooden pick. If the wooden pick doesn't come out clean, continue baking a few minutes, then test again.

11 Cool cakes in pans on wire racks for 10 minutes. Remove cakes from pans by inverting each cake layer on a wire rack, as shown. Lift off the pan. Pans may be hard to remove if cake is cooled in pan longer than 10 minutes.

12 Since the top of a cake is rounded, the cake won't sit securely on the rack when inverted and thus is apt to crack. To prevent the cake from cracking, place a second wire rack atop the cake and invert again, as shown, so that the base rests on the rack.

Cool thoroughly. Frost with desired frosting.

Cakes and Frostings

Milk-and-Honey Cake

⅓ cup sugar
⅓ cup shortening
1 teaspoon vanilla
1 egg
¼ cup honey
1½ cups all-purpose flour
2½ teaspoons baking powder
½ teaspoon salt
⅔ cup milk
 Maple Frosting (see recipe, page 259)
⅓ cup chopped pecans

Grease and lightly flour a 9×9×2-inch baking pan, referring to steps 1 and 2 on page 226. In mixer bowl cream together sugar, shortening, and vanilla, referring to step 4 on page 229. Add egg and honey; beat on medium speed for 1 minute.

Thoroughly stir together flour, baking powder, and salt. Add flour mixture to creamed mixture alternately with milk, beating after each addition till just combined; refer to steps 6 and 7 on pages 228–229. Spread batter evenly in prepared pan. Bake in 350° oven for 30 to 35 minutes or till wooden pick inserted in center comes out clean. Cool on wire rack. Frost with Maple Frosting. Sprinkle with chopped pecans. Makes 9 servings.

TIP Pan-coal greasing *is the one-step way to grease and flour pans to make cakes easy to remove and to give them a smooth, crumb-free surface. To make pan-coating, combine ½ cup shortening and ¼ cup all-purpose flour; mix together well. To use, generously grease bottoms and sides of pans with the mixture. There will be enough mixture to coat several cake pans. Store extra pan-coating mixture in a covered container on the kitchen shelf.*

Banana Cake

1¼ cups sugar
¾ cup butter *or* margarine
2 eggs
1 teaspoon vanilla
½ teaspoon banana flavoring
2 cups sifted cake flour
2 teaspoons baking powder
¼ teaspoon salt
¾ cup milk
1 cup sugar
1 cup water
1 teaspoon vanilla
 Banana Frosting (see recipe, page 258)
1 medium banana

Refer to: Using creamed method for cakes, page 228. Grease and lightly flour two 8×1½-inch round baking pans; set aside.

In mixer bowl cream the 1¼ cups sugar and butter or margarine till light. Add eggs, 1 teaspoon vanilla, and the banana flavoring; beat till fluffy. Sift together cake flour, baking powder, and salt. Add sifted dry ingredients to creamed mixture alternately with milk, beating well after each addition. Spread in the prepared pans.

Bake in 375° oven for 20 to 25 minutes or till wooden pick inserted in center comes out clean. Cool in pans on wire racks for 10 minutes. Remove from pans. Cool thoroughly on wire rack with waxed paper underneath.

In saucepan combine the 1 cup sugar and water; bring to boiling, stirring to dissolve sugar. Boil 3 minutes. Remove from heat; stir in 1 teaspoon vanilla. With fork, liberally prick top of cake layers. Slowly spoon hot sugar mixture over cake layers, allowing it to soak in. Cool well.

To assemble cake, place one cake layer, top side down, on cake plate; spread with *about 1 cup* of the Banana Frosting. Thinly slice banana; arrange on frosted cake. Place second layer, top side up, over frosted layer. Frost top and sides of cake with remaining Banana Frosting. Chill cake. Makes 12 servings.

Mocha Chip Cupcakes

1 tablespoon instant coffee crystals
½ cup milk
2 eggs
½ cup sugar
6 tablespoons butter *or* margarine
1 square (1 ounce) unsweetened chocolate, melted and cooled
1 cup all-purpose flour
1 teaspoon baking powder
¼ teaspoon salt
¼ teaspoon baking soda
1 teaspoon instant coffee crystals, crushed
⅓ cup sugar
½ cup semisweet chocolate pieces
½ cup chopped walnuts

Dissolve the 1 tablespoon coffee crystals in milk. Separate 1 of the eggs; set the egg white aside. Cream together the ½ cup sugar, butter or margarine, the whole egg, and the egg yolk, beating till fluffy. Stir in melted and cooled chocolate. Stir together flour, baking powder, salt, and baking soda; add to creamed mixture alternately with milk mixture, beating after each addition and referring to steps 6 and 7 on page 228.

Fill paper bake cups in muffin pans ⅔ full with batter. Bake in 375° oven for 12 minutes.

Meanwhile, in small mixer bowl beat together the reserved egg white and the 1 teaspoon coffee crystals until soft peaks form (tips curl over) Gradually add the ⅓ cup sugar, beating till stiff peaks form (tips stand straight). Fold in chocolate pieces and walnuts.

Carefully spoon about 1 tablespoon of the egg white mixture atop each partially baked cupcake. Bake 10 to 12 minutes longer or till lightly browned. Makes 12 cupcakes.

Choco-Peanut Butter Cake

1½ cups sugar
½ cup butter, softened
⅓ cup chunk-style peanut butter
3 squares (3 ounces) unsweetened chocolate, melted and cooled
2 eggs
1½ teaspoons vanilla
2½ cups all-purpose flour
2½ teaspoons baking powder
1⅔ cups milk

Grease and lightly flour a 13×9×2-inch baking pan, referring to steps 1 and 2 on page 226. Cream sugar, butter, and peanut butter till light and fluffy, scraping the bowl frequently. Add chocolate, eggs, and vanilla; beat at medium speed of electric mixer till light and fluffy, scraping bowl frequently. Stir together flour, baking powder, and 1 teaspoon *salt*; add to creamed mixture alternately with milk, beating after each addition and referring to steps 6 and 7 on page 228. Turn into prepared pan. Bake in 350° oven for 30 to 35 minutes or till wooden pick inserted in center comes out clean. Cool. Serves 12 to 15.

Gingerbread

Carrot Cake

2 cups all-purpose flour
2 cups sugar
1 teaspoon baking powder
1 teaspoon baking soda
1 teaspoon salt
1 teaspoon ground cinnamon
3 cups finely shredded carrot (9 carrots)
1 cup cooking oil
4 eggs
Cream Cheese Frosting (see recipe, page 259)

Grease and lightly flour a 13×9×2-inch baking pan, referring to steps 1 and 2 on page 226. In large mixer bowl stir together flour, sugar, baking powder, baking soda, salt, and cinnamon; add carrot, oil, and eggs. Mix till moistened; beat at medium speed of electric mixer for 2 minutes. Pour into prepared pan. Bake in 325° oven for 50 to 60 minutes or till wooden pick inserted in center comes out clean. Cool thoroughly on wire rack. Frost with Cream Cheese Frosting. Serves 12 to 15.

Gingerbread

½ cup shortening
¼ cup packed brown sugar
1 egg
½ cup light molasses
1½ cups all-purpose flour
¾ teaspoon ground ginger
¾ teaspoon ground cinnamon
½ teaspoon baking powder
½ teaspoon baking soda
Lemon Sauce

Grease and lightly flour one 9×1½-inch round baking pan, referring to steps 1 and 2 on page 226. Cream shortening and brown sugar till light. Add egg and molasses; beat well. Stir together flour, spices, baking powder, soda, and ½ teaspoon *salt*; add to creamed mixture alternately with ½ cup *boiling water*, beating after each addition and referring to steps 6 and 7 on page 228. Pour into pan. Bake in 350° oven 30 to 35 minutes. Serve with Lemon Sauce. Serves 8.

Lemon Sauce: Mix ½ cup *sugar*, 1 tablespoon *cornstarch*, and ⅛ teaspoon *each salt* and ground *nutmeg*. Add 1 cup *water*. Cook and stir till thick and bubbly. Stir in 2 tablespoons *each butter* and *lemon juice*.

231

Citrus Cake

1¼ cups sugar
½ cup butter, softened
1 egg
½ cup buttermilk
1 teaspoon grated orange peel
⅓ cup orange juice
3 tablespoons lemon juice
1½ cups all-purpose flour
1 teaspoon baking powder
¼ teaspoon baking soda
Citrus Frosting (see recipe, page 259)

Grease and lightly flour a 13×9×2-inch baking pan, referring to steps 1 and 2 on page 226. Cream sugar and butter till light, referring to step 4 on page 229. Beat in egg. Mix in buttermilk, peel, and juices. Stir together dry ingredients and ¼ teaspoon *salt*. Stir into creamed mixture. Pour into pan. Bake in 350° oven 25 to 30 minutes. Frost warm cake with Citrus Frosting. Serves 12 to 15.

Cakes and Frostings

Sweet Chocolate Cake

Spicy Pumpkin Cake

- ½ cup packed brown sugar
- ½ cup butter *or* margarine, softened
- 2 eggs
- ¾ cup buttermilk
- ½ cup canned pumpkin
- ½ cup light molasses
- 2½ cups all-purpose flour
- 2 teaspoons finely shredded orange peel
- 1 teaspoon baking soda
- ½ teaspoon salt
- ½ teaspoon ground cinnamon
- ½ teaspoon ground ginger
  Sifted powdered sugar
  (continued next column)

Grease and lightly flour a 13×9×2-inch baking pan, referring to steps 1 and 2 on page 226. In mixer bowl cream together brown sugar and butter or margarine till light, referring to step 4 on page 229. Add eggs, one at a time, beating well after each. Combine buttermilk, pumpkin, and molasses. Thoroughly stir together flour, orange peel, soda, salt, and spices. Add dry ingredients to creamed mixture alternately with buttermilk mixture, beating after each addition and referring to steps 6 and 7 on page 228. Turn into prepared pan. Bake in 350° oven for 30 to 35 minutes or till wooden pick inserted in center comes out clean. Cool thoroughly on wire rack. Sprinkle with powdered sugar. Makes 12 servings.

Buttermilk Spice Cake

(pictured on page 224)

- ½ cup shortening
- 1¾ cups all-purpose flour
- ¾ cup packed brown sugar
- ½ cup granulated sugar
- 1½ teaspoons ground cinnamon
- 1 teaspoon baking powder
- 1 teaspoon salt
- ¾ teaspoon baking soda
- ¼ teaspoon ground cloves
- 1¼ cups buttermilk
- 3 eggs
  Vanilla Filling
  Sea Foam Frosting (see recipe, page 258)

Refer to: Using one-bowl method for cakes, page 226. Grease and lightly flour three 8×1½-inch round baking pans. Place shortening in large mixer bowl. Add flour, brown sugar, granulated sugar, cinnamon, baking powder, salt, baking soda, and cloves. Add *half* the buttermilk and the eggs. Mix at low speed of electric mixer till blended. Beat 2 minutes at medium speed. Scrape sides of bowl. Beat in remaining buttermilk. Beat 2 minutes more at medium speed. Turn into prepared pans.

Bake in 350° oven about 20 minutes or till wooden pick inserted in center comes out clean. Cool cake in pans on wire rack for 10 minutes. Remove from pans. Cool completely. Spread Vanilla Filling between layers. Frost with Sea Foam Frosting. Makes 16 servings.

Vanilla Filling: Refer to: Making cream pudding, page 338. In saucepan combine ⅓ cup granulated *sugar*, ¼ cup all-purpose *flour*, and ¼ teaspoon *salt*. Stir in 1¼ cups *milk*. Cook and stir over medium heat till mixture is thickened and bubbly. Cook and stir 2 minutes more. Remove from heat. Gradually stir the hot mixture into 1 beaten *egg;* return to saucepan. Cook and stir 2 minutes more. Remove from heat. Stir in 2 tablespoons *butter or margarine* and 1½ teaspoons *vanilla.* Cover surface with clear plastic wrap. Cool. (Do not stir.)

Choco-Cream Cheese Cake

2 3-ounce packages cream cheese, softened
½ cup butter or margarine, softened
1 teaspoon vanilla
6½ cups sifted powdered sugar
⅓ cup milk
4 squares (4 ounces) unsweetened chocolate, melted and cooled
¼ cup butter or margarine, softened
3 eggs
2¼ cups all-purpose flour
1 teaspoon baking powder
1 teaspoon baking soda
1 teaspoon salt
1¼ cups milk

Grease and lightly flour two 9×1½-inch round baking pans, referring to steps 1 and 2 on page 226. In mixer bowl cream together the cream cheese, the ½ cup butter or margarine, and vanilla. Alternately beat in sifted powdered sugar and the ⅓ cup milk. Beat in chocolate. Remove 2 cups of the chocolate mixture; cover and refrigerate this portion to use as frosting.

Cream remaining chocolate mixture and the ¼ cup butter or margarine. Add eggs; beat well. Stir together flour, baking powder, soda, and salt. Add dry ingredients to creamed mixture alternately with the 1¼ cups milk, beating after each addition and referring to steps 6 and 7 on page 228. Pour into the prepared pans.

Bake in 350° oven about 30 minutes or till wooden pick inserted in center comes out clean. Cool cake in pans on wire racks for 10 minutes. Remove cake from pans; cool thoroughly. Remove reserved chocolate frosting mixture from refrigerator; let stand 15 minutes. Frost cake. Serve immediately or chill till serving time. Serves 12.

Sweet Chocolate Cake

1 4-ounce bar sweet cooking chocolate
⅓ cup water
3 egg whites
1 cup sugar
½ cup butter or margarine, softened
1 teaspoon vanilla
3 egg yolks
1⅔ cups all-purpose flour
1 teaspoon baking soda
½ teaspoon salt
⅔ cup buttermilk
Coconut Frosting (see recipe, page 258)

Refer to: Using creamed method for cakes, page 228. Grease and lightly flour two 8×1½-inch round baking pans. Set aside.

In small saucepan combine chocolate and water. Stir over low heat till chocolate melts; cool thoroughly. In small mixer bowl beat egg whites till stiff peaks form (tips stand straight); set aside.

In large mixer bowl cream sugar, butter or margarine, and vanilla till light and fluffy. Add egg yolks, one at a time, beating well after each. Beat in chocolate mixture.

Stir together flour, baking soda, and salt. Add dry ingredients to creamed mixture alternately with buttermilk, beating after each addition. Gently fold in stiff-beaten egg whites. Pour into prepared pans.

Bake in 350° oven for 30 to 35 minutes or till wooden pick inserted in center comes out clean. Cool cake in pans on wire racks for 10 minutes. Remove from pans. Cool thoroughly. Fill and frost top with Coconut Frosting. Makes 12 servings.

Butter Pecan Cupcakes

⅔ cup chopped pecans
2 tablespoons butter or margarine
1¼ cups sugar
½ cup butter or margarine
2 teaspoons vanilla
2 eggs
2 cups all-purpose flour
1½ teaspoons baking powder
¼ teaspoon salt
⅓ cup milk
Toasted Pecan Frosting (see recipe, page 259)

Place nuts in shallow baking pan; dot with 2 tablespoons butter or margarine. Toast in 350° oven about 15 minutes, stirring often. Cream the sugar, ½ cup butter or margarine, and vanilla till light, referring to step 4 on page 229. Add eggs, one at a time, beating well after each. Stir together flour, baking powder, and salt; add to creamed mixture alternately with milk, beating well after each addition and referring to steps 6 and 7 on page 228. Fold in toasted nuts. Fill paper bake cups in muffin pans half full. Bake in 375° oven for 20 to 25 minutes or till done. Cool. Frost with Toasted Pecan Frosting. Makes 18 cupcakes.

233

TIP Make a plain cake fancy by splitting the layers *and spreading a filling or frosting between the halves. As a cutting guide, insert wooden picks halfway up the side of each cake layer, as shown. Then use a sharp, long-bladed knife to slice through the layer.*

Cakes and Frostings

Lemon Sponge Cake

Technique: Making sponge cake

8	**egg yolks**
¼	**cup water**
1	**teaspoon finely shredded lemon peel**
1	**tablespoon lemon juice**
1	**teaspoon vanilla**
¾	**cup sugar**
¾	**teaspoon salt**
1½	**cups all-purpose flour**
8	**egg whites**
1	**teaspoon cream of tartar**
¾	**cup sugar**

1 In small mixer bowl beat egg yolks at high speed about 6 minutes or till thick and lemon-colored. **2** Combine water, lemon peel, lemon juice, and vanilla. Pour mixture into egg yolks. Beat at low speed till blended. **3** Turn mixer to medium speed; beat till thick. **4** Gradually add ¾ cup sugar and the salt, beating till sugar dissolves. **5** Sprinkle about ¼ of the flour over yolk mixture. Gently fold in flour just till blended. Repeat with remaining flour, ¼ at a time.

6 Wash beaters thoroughly. In large mixer bowl beat egg whites with cream of tartar at medium speed about 1 minute or till soft peaks form (tips curl over). Gradually add ¾ cup sugar; continue beating till stiff peaks form (tips stand straight). **7** Stir about 1 cup of the beaten egg whites into yolks. **8** Thoroughly fold yolk mixture into remaining whites. **9** Turn into *ungreased* 10-inch tube pan. **10** Bake in 325° oven 60 to 65 minutes or till cake tests done. **11** Invert cake in pan; cool. **12** Using a spatula, loosen cake from pan; remove.

1 Place egg yolks in small mixer bowl; beat at high speed of electric mixer about 6 minutes or till thick and lemon-colored.

When yolks are sufficiently beaten, they will flow in a thick stream from the lifted beaters, as shown.

2 In a 1-cup glass measure combine water, lemon peel, lemon juice, and vanilla. Pour mixture into egg yolks, as shown. Beat at low speed till thoroughly blended.

7 Stir about 1 cup of the beaten egg whites into egg yolks using a rubber spatula. This helps to lighten the egg yolk mixture before folding it into the egg whites.

8 Fold the egg yolk mixture into the remaining egg whites.

To fold, cut down through the mixture with a rubber spatula; scrape across bottom of bowl; then bring spatula up and over mixture, close to the surface. Repeat this circular down-up-and-over motion, turning bowl as you work.

3 Turn mixer to medium speed and beat egg yolk mixture about 4 minutes more or till thick. Lift the beaters and check consistency, as shown.

4 Gradually add ¾ cup sugar and the salt; continue beating the mixture 5 to 6 minutes or till the sugar dissolves. The egg yolk mixture should feel smooth when rubbed between thumb and index finger. If it feels grainy, continue beating till all sugar is dissolved.

5 Remove bowl from mixer stand. Sprinkle about ¼ of the flour over yolk mixture. Fold in by cutting down through mixture with a rubber spatula; scrape across bottom of bowl and bring spatula up and over mixture close to the surface. Repeat with remaining flour, ¼ at a time. Do not stir; this breaks down the air-retaining structure and fluffy consistency of the carefully beaten whites.

6 Wash beaters thoroughly before beating egg whites. Place egg whites and cream of tartar in large mixer bowl (use a deep, straight-sided glass or metal bowl; do not use a plastic bowl). Beat at medium speed about 1 minute or till soft peaks form (tips curl over).
  Gradually add ¾ cup sugar, 2 tablespoons at a time, as shown. Beat mixture 4 to 5 minutes or till stiff peaks form (tips stand straight).

235

9 Turn the batter into an *ungreased* 10-inch tube pan, as shown. Use the rubber spatula to distribute batter evenly around the pan.

10 Place pan on the rack as near to the center of the oven as possible.
  Bake in 325° oven for 60 to 65 minutes or till the cake springs back and leaves no imprint when lightly touched on the top, as shown. The cake also will shrink slightly from sides of tube pan.

11 Remove cake from oven. Invert cake in pan and place on counter to cool. Inverting the pan prevents the cake from losing volume while cooling.
  If cake pan doesn't have long enough legs, invert pan and set tube over a bottle; cool.

12 With a narrow spatula, loosen cake from pan edges and center tube. Using spatula, gently lift cake off bottom to loosen. Center an upside-down serving plate over cake. Holding tightly, invert plate and pan together. Shake pan gently; carefully lift off. This puts the smooth side up for frosting. If cake "rocks" on plate, invert again. (See step 10 on page 243 if using a pan with removable bottom.)

Cakes and Frostings

Jelly Roll

Technique: Making jelly roll

4 egg yolks
⅓ cup granulated sugar
½ teaspoon vanilla
4 egg whites
½ cup granulated sugar
½ cup all-purpose flour
1 teaspoon baking powder
¼ teaspoon salt
   Sifted powdered sugar
½ cup jelly *or* jam

1 In small mixer bowl beat egg yolks at high speed about 5 minutes or till thick and lemon-colored. Gradually add the ⅓ cup granulated sugar, beating till sugar dissolves. Add vanilla; mix well. **2** Wash beaters thoroughly. In large mixer bowl beat egg whites at medium speed till soft peaks form (tips curl over). Gradually add the ½ cup granulated sugar; continue beating till stiff peaks form (tips stand straight). **3** Fold yolks into whites. **4-5** Combine flour, baking powder, and salt; sprinkle over egg mixture. Gently fold in flour mixture just till blended.

6 Grease and lightly flour a 15×10×1-inch jelly roll pan; spread batter evenly in pan. **7** Bake in 375° oven for 12 to 15 minutes or till done.

8-9 Immediately loosen edges of cake from pan and turn out onto towel sprinkled with sifted powdered sugar. **10** Starting with the narrow end, roll the warm cake and towel together; cool on wire rack.

11 Unroll; spread cake with jelly or jam, leaving a 1-inch rim. **12** Roll up the cake. Makes ten slices.

Note: You can serve jelly rolls with a variety of tasty fillings. Try wrapping up pie filling, pudding, whipped cream (plain or with fruit folded in), or softened ice cream.

1 Place egg yolks in small mixer bowl; beat at high speed of electric mixer about 5 minutes or till thick and lemon-colored.

When yolks are sufficiently beaten, they will flow in a thick stream from the lifted beaters, as shown.

Gradually add the ⅓ cup sugar to the beaten egg yolks. Beat the mixture till the sugar dissolves. Add vanilla; mix well.

2 Wash the beaters thoroughly before preparing the egg whites. Place egg whites in a large mixer bowl (use a deep, straight-sided glass or metal bowl; do not use a plastic bowl). Beat egg whites at medium speed about 1 minute or till soft peaks form (tips curl over).

Gradually add the ½ cup sugar, as shown. Beat egg whites about 4½ minutes or till stiff peaks form (tips stand straight).

7 Adjust oven rack to center position; place pan on the rack as near to the center of oven as possible.

Bake in 375° oven for 12 to 15 minutes or till cake springs back and leaves no imprint when lightly touched on the top.

8 Remove the cake from oven. Using a narrow spatula, immediately loosen edges of the warm cake from the pan, as shown.

3 Fold the egg yolk mixture into the egg whites. To fold, cut down through the mixture with a rubber spatula; scrape across bottom of bowl and bring spatula up and over mixture, close to the surface. Repeat this circular down-up-and-over motion, turning bowl as you work.

4 In small bowl combine the all-purpose flour, baking powder, and salt; sprinkle over egg mixture by spoonfuls, as shown.

5 Using a rubber spatula, gently fold in flour mixture just till blended. Avoid excessive blending, which reduces the air volume incorporated in the eggs.

6 Grease and lightly flour a 15×10×1-inch jelly roll pan, referring to steps 1 and 2 on page 226. Using a pastry brush apply about 1 tablespoon shortening to the bottom and sides of pan. Add about 2 teaspoons flour; tilt and tap pan to evenly distribute flour. When all the pan is flour-dusted, dump the excess flour. (Or, use pan-coating, referring to tip on page 230.) Spread the batter evenly, as shown.

237

9 Holding pan with pot holders, quickly invert and shake gently over a towel sprinkled with sifted powdered sugar (the powdered sugar helps prevent warm cake from sticking to the towel). Lift off the jelly roll pan, being careful not to tear the cake.

10 Starting with the narrow end, roll the warm cake and towel together, as shown.
It's necessary to roll the cake while it's still warm to prevent tearing. The towel prevents the cake from sticking together as it cools.
Place cake roll on a wire rack to cool thoroughly.

11 Carefully unroll the cooled cake and towel. Spoon your favorite jelly or jam on cake; spread over the surface, leaving a 1-inch rim around all four sides, as shown.

12 Again starting with the narrow end, roll up the cake. If desired, trim ends of jelly roll. Place cake on a serving platter, seam side down. If using one of the other fillings, refrigerate or freeze the cake till serving time. To serve, slice cake crosswise into 1-inch slices.

Cakes and Frostings

Dark Fruitcake

Technique: Making fruitcake

- **3** cups all-purpose flour
- **2** teaspoons baking powder
- **2** teaspoons ground cinnamon
- **1** teaspoon salt
- **½** teaspoon ground nutmeg
- **½** teaspoon ground allspice
- **½** teaspoon ground cloves
- **1** 16-ounce package (2½ cups) diced mixed candied fruits and peels
- **1** 15-ounce package (3 cups) raisins
- **1** 8-ounce package (1½ cups) whole candied red cherries
- **1** 8-ounce package (1⅓ cups) pitted dates, snipped
- **1** cup slivered almonds
- **1** cup pecan halves
- **½** cup candied pineapple, chopped
- **4** eggs
- **1¾** cups packed brown sugar
- **1** cup orange juice
- **¾** cup butter *or* margarine, melted and cooled
- **¼** cup light molasses

1 Stir together flour, baking powder, cinnamon, salt, nutmeg, allspice, and cloves. Add fruits and peels, raisins, cherries, dates, almonds, pecans, and pineapple; mix till well coated. **2** Beat eggs till foamy. **3** Gradually add brown sugar. **4** Add orange juice, butter or margarine, and molasses; beat till blended. **5** Stir into fruit mixture.

6 Grease one 6×3×2-inch loaf pan, one 8×4×2-inch loaf pan, *and* one 10×3½×2½-inch loaf pan. Line bottom and sides of pans with brown paper; grease paper. **7** Turn batter into pans, filling each about ¾ full. **8–9** Bake in 300° oven 1½ hours for 6×3×2-inch pan and 2 hours for other two pans, or till cakes test done. (Cover all pans with foil after 1 hour of baking.) Cool on wire rack; remove from pans. **10** Wrap in wine-, brandy-, or fruit juice-moistened cheesecloth. **11** Overwrap with foil. **12** Store in refrigerator. Re-moisten cheesecloth as needed if cakes are stored longer than one week.

238

1 In large mixing bowl stir together the flour, baking powder, cinnamon, salt, nutmeg, allspice, and cloves. Thoroughly combine the dry ingredients so that the baking powder and salt will be evenly distributed.

Add candied fruits and peels, raisins, candied cherries, dates, almonds, pecans, and candied pineapple. Mix with dry ingredients till fruits and nuts are coated.

2 Place the eggs in large mixer bowl. Beat the eggs at high speed of electric mixer till eggs appear foamy, as shown.

7 Using a measuring cup spoon batter into prepared loaf pans, filling each pan about ¾ full, as shown. Use a rubber spatula to distribute the batter evenly around the pans.

8 Adjust the rack in the center of the oven, and place pans on rack. Never let the pans touch each other or the oven wall. To assure even browning, allow some space around the sides of each pan for heat and air circulation.

Bake in 300° oven 1½ hours for the 6×3×2-inch pan and 2 hours for the other two pans, or till the cakes test done. (Cover all pans with foil after 1 hour to prevent overbrowning.)

3 Gradually add the brown sugar to the eggs, a tablespoonful at a time; continue beating the mixture till well blended.

4 Add the orange juice, cooled butter or margarine, and light molasses to egg-sugar mixture; beat with electric mixer to blend ingredients thoroughly.

5 Pour egg mixture over the candied fruit and nut mixture; stir with a spoon till ingredients are thoroughly combined.

6 Grease one 6×3×2-inch loaf pan, one 8×4×2-inch loaf pan, and one 10×3½×2½-inch loaf pan. Use folded paper toweling or a pastry brush to apply shortening, referring to step 1 on page 226.

Line pan bottoms and sides with strips of brown paper, as shown; grease the paper.

If desired, use two 8×4×2-inch pans *and* two 6×3×2-inch pans instead of the three sizes suggested.

239

9 To test fruitcake for doneness, insert a wooden pick in center of the loaf. If pick comes out clean and dry, cake is done. Set cakes in pans on wire rack to cool thoroughly; remove from pans.

10 Dip layers of cheesecloth in wine, brandy, or fruit juice; squeeze to remove excess liquid. Wrap each loaf in several layers of the moistened cheesecloth, as shown.

11 Place each cloth-wrapped loaf on a piece of foil. Bring foil up and around the sides of the loaf, sealing foil over the top.

12 Store the fruitcakes in the refrigerator. Re-moisten the cheesecloth with wine, brandy, or fruit juice once a week.

For a blended and mellow flavor, make the fruitcake 3 to 4 weeks before your intended serving date.

Cakes and Frostings

Pound Cake

Technique: Making pound cake

  1   **cup butter *or* margarine**
  4   **eggs**
  1   **cup sugar**
1½   **teaspoons vanilla**
  2   **cups all-purpose flour**
  ¼   **teaspoon salt**
  ¼   **teaspoon ground nutmeg**

1 Bring butter or margarine and eggs to room temperature. Grease the bottom and about 1 inch up the sides of a 9×5×3-inch loaf pan. **2** In small mixer bowl beat the butter or margarine at medium speed of electric mixer till creamed and fluffy. **3** Gradually add the sugar, beating at medium speed 6 minutes or till light and fluffy. Add vanilla. **4–5** Add the eggs, one at a time, beating about 1 minute after each; scrape the bowl frequently.

6 Stir together flour, salt, and nutmeg. Gradually add the dry ingredients to the egg mixture and beat just till thoroughly blended. **7** Turn the batter into prepared loaf pan. **8** Bake in 325° oven for 60 to 65 minutes or till cake tests done. Cool cake in pan on wire rack 10 minutes; remove from pan. Makes 1 loaf.

1 Remove butter or margarine and eggs from refrigerator; bring to room temperature before using.

Grease the bottom and about 1 inch up the sides of a 9×5×3-inch loaf pan. Use folded paper toweling or a pastry brush to apply shortening, referring to step 1 on page 226. Set pan aside.

5 After adding and beating in the eggs, the cake batter will have a fluffy but somewhat curdled appearance, as shown.

2 In small mixer bowl cream the softened butter or margarine at medium speed of electric mixer till creamed and fluffy. Using a rubber spatula, guide butter toward the beaters for thorough creaming.

3 Gradually add the sugar while beating the mixture at medium speed. Beat about 6 minutes or till light and fluffy. Scrape bowl frequently. Add vanilla.

4 Add the eggs, one at a time, beating about 1 minute after each; scrape the bowl frequently. To avoid mixing eggshell in the batter, break each egg into a small bowl before adding to the creamed mixture.

Again, guide mixture toward the beaters for thorough mixing.

6 In a bowl stir together the flour, salt, and ground nutmeg. Thoroughly combine the dry ingredients before adding them to the egg mixture.

Gradually add dry ingredients to creamed mixture and beat just till thoroughly blended.

7 Turn the batter into the prepared loaf pan, as shown. Use a rubber spatula to distribute the batter evenly around the pan.

Adjust the rack in the center of the oven; place pan on rack as near to the center of the oven as possible.

8 Bake in 325° oven for 60 to 65 minutes or till cake tests done. To test pound cake for doneness, insert a wooden pick in center of baked cake. If pick comes out clean and dry, cake is done. Set cake in pan on wire rack to cool for 10 minutes; remove cake from pan. Cool completely.

Cakes and Frostings

Angel Cake

Technique: Making angel cake

1 **cup sifted cake flour**
¾ **cup sugar**
12 **egg whites (1½ cups)**
1½ **teaspoons cream of tartar**
1½ **teaspoons vanilla**
¼ **teaspoon salt**
¾ **cup sugar**

1 Sift together flour with ¾ cup sugar; repeat sifting. Set aside. **2** In a large mixer bowl beat egg whites with cream of tartar, vanilla, and salt at medium speed of electric mixer till soft peaks form (tips curl over). **3** Gradually add remaining ¾ cup sugar, 2 tablespoons at a time. Continue beating till stiff peaks form (tips stand straight).

4 Sift about ¼ of the flour mixture over whites; fold in. **5** Repeat, folding in remaining flour by fourths. **6** Turn into *ungreased* 10-inch tube pan. **7** Bake in 375° oven 35 to 40 minutes or till cake tests done. **8** Invert cake in pan; cool. **9–10** Using a spatula, loosen cake from pan; remove.

1 On a piece of waxed paper combine flour and ¾ cup sugar. On another piece of waxed paper, place a metal flour sifter; pour flour-sugar mixture into sifter, as shown. Sift mixture onto waxed paper. Repeat sifting; set aside.

If you do not have a sifter, place a metal sieve over a bowl. Add flour mixture, stirring to press mixture through sieve; repeat.

2 In large mixer bowl place egg whites, cream of tartar, vanilla, and salt. (Use a deep, straight-sided glass or metal bowl; do not use a plastic bowl, since the oils retained in the plastic prevent the egg whites from forming peaks.) Beat at medium speed of electric mixer till soft peaks form (tips curl over).

6 Turn the batter into an *ungreased* 10-inch tube pan, as shown. Using a rubber spatula, distribute the batter evenly around the pan.

7 Place pan on the rack as near to the center of the oven as possible.

Bake in 375° oven for 35 to 40 minutes or till cake springs back and leaves no imprint when lightly touched on top, as shown.

3 Gradually add the remaining ¾ cup sugar to egg whites, 2 tablespoons at a time. Continue beating till whites form stiff peaks that stand straight when beaters are removed, as shown.

4 Remove mixer bowl from mixer stand. Sift about ¼ of the flour-sugar mixture over beaten whites. Using a rubber spatula, gently fold in the flour just till blended.

To fold, cut down through the mixture with a rubber spatula; scrape across bottom of bowl and bring spatula up and over mixture, close to the surface. Repeat this circular down-up-and-over motion, turning bowl as you work.

5 Repeat sifting and folding in the remaining flour-sugar mixture by fourths. Press or shake flour mixture through a sieve if you do not have a sifter.

243

TIP Hollow out an angel cake *by first cutting a 1-inch crosswise slice from the top of inverted cake; set aside. With a sharp narrow knife held parallel to cake sides, cut around cake 1 inch from center hole and 1 inch from outer edge, leaving cake walls 1 inch thick, as shown in top photo.*

Remove center with a spoon leaving a 1-inch-thick base, as shown in bottom photo. Place base on serving plate. Fill cavity with a favorite fruit or pudding filling. Replace top slice of cake. Frost the cake with whipped cream. Chill 2 to 3 hours. Slice with serrated or electric knife.

8 Remove cake from oven. Invert cake in pan and place on the counter to thoroughly cool. Inverting the pan prevents the cake from losing volume while cooling.

If cake pan doesn't have long enough legs, invert pan and set tube over a bottle; cool.

9 For a brown crust, remove cake from pan as soon as the cake is cooled. The longer the cooled cake remains in the pan, the more the crust will adhere to the pan sides.

To remove cake, set pan right side up. With a narrow spatula, loosen the cake from the edges of the pan and the center tube.

10 Hold onto the center tube and lift out the removable bottom, being careful not to tear the cake. To loosen the cake, slide a narrow spatula between the cake and the removable bottom. Invert cake onto a plate, letting it slip off of tube. Use your hands to guide cake so that it doesn't tear. This puts the smooth side up for frosting. If cake "rocks," invert again. (If using pan without removable bottom, see step 12 on page 235.)

Cakes and Frostings

Golden Chiffon Cake

Technique: Making chiffon cake

2¼	cups sifted cake flour
1½	cups sugar
1	tablespoon baking powder
1	teaspoon salt
½	cup cooking oil
5	egg yolks
¾	cup water
2	teaspoons finely shredded lemon peel
1	teaspoon vanilla
8	egg whites (1 cup)
½	teaspoon cream of tartar

1 In a small mixer bowl sift together cake flour, sugar, baking powder, and salt; make a well in the center. Add cooking oil, egg yolks, water, lemon peel, and vanilla. **2** Beat mixture at high speed of electric mixer about 5 minutes or till satin smooth. **3** Wash beaters thoroughly. In large mixer bowl combine egg whites and cream of tartar; beat at medium speed till *very stiff* peaks form (tips stand straight). **4–5** Pour batter in a thin stream over entire surface of egg whites; fold in gently. **6** Pour into *ungreased* 10-inch tube pan. **7** Bake in 325° oven 70 minutes or till cake tests done. **8** Invert cake in pan; cool. **9–10** Using a spatula, loosen cake from pan; remove.

1 In a small mixer bowl sift together the cake flour, sugar, baking powder, and salt; make a well in the center. Add cooking oil, egg yolks, water, lemon peel, and vanilla, in that order.

2 Beat at high speed of electric mixer about 5 minutes or till satin smooth. When the mixture is sufficiently beaten, it will flow in a thick stream from the lifted beaters, as shown.

6 Turn the batter into an *ungreased* 10-inch tube pan, as shown. Using a rubber spatula, distribute the batter evenly around the pan.

7 Place pan on the rack as near to the center of the oven as possible.
Bake in 325° oven for 70 minutes or till cake springs back and leaves no imprint when lightly touched on top, as shown.

3 Wash the beaters thoroughly. If any egg yolk or oil is mixed into the egg whites, they will not expand to their proper volume.

In large mixer bowl place egg whites and cream of tartar. (Use a deep, straight-sided glass or metal bowl; do not use a plastic bowl.) Beat at medium speed of electric mixer till *very stiff* peaks form and stand straight when beaters are removed, as shown.

4 Pour the egg yolk mixture in a thin, steady stream over the entire surface of the stiffly beaten egg whites.

5 Gently fold the egg yolk mixture into the egg whites. To fold, cut down through the mixture with a rubber spatula; scrape across bottom of bowl and bring spatula up and over mixture, close to the surface. Repeat this circular down-up-and-over motion, turning bowl as you work. Do not stir; this breaks down the air-retaining structure and fluffy consistency of the carefully beaten whites.

TIP What can you do with egg yolks left over from making chiffon cake? *Stir them into additional beaten eggs for a custard (see recipe, page 86) or scrambled eggs (see recipe, page 72). Or, use the 3 leftover egg yolks in this recipe for tasty cupcakes.*

245

Golden Cupcakes: *Cream 1 cup sugar, ½ cup shortening, and 1 teaspoon vanilla till light. Add 3 beaten egg yolks; beat well. Stir together 2 cups all-purpose flour, 2 teaspoons baking powder, and ½ teaspoon salt.*

Add dry ingredients to creamed mixture alternately with ¾ cup milk, beating well after each addition.

Fill paper bake cups in muffin pans half full. Bake in 350° oven for 30 minutes. Makes 18 cupcakes.

8 Remove cake from oven. Invert cake in pan and place on the counter to cool. Inverting the pan prevents the cake from losing volume while cooling.

If cake pan doesn't have long enough legs, invert pan and set tube over a bottle; cool.

9 For a brown crust, remove cake from pan when completely cooled. The longer the cooled cake remains in the pan, the more the crust will adhere to the pan sides.

To remove cake, set pan right side up. With a narrow spatula, loosen the cake from the edges of the pan and the center tube.

10 Hold onto the center tube and lift out the removable bottom, being careful not to tear the cake. To loosen the cake, slide a narrow spatula between the cake and the removable bottom. Invert cake onto a plate, letting it slip off of tube. Use your hands to guide cake so that it doesn't tear. This puts the smooth side up for frosting. If cake "rocks," invert again. (If using pan without removable bottom, see step 12 on page 235.)

Cakes and Frostings

Hot Milk Sponge Cake

(pictured on page 274)

2 eggs
1 cup sugar
1 cup all-purpose flour
1 teaspoon baking powder
¼ teaspoon salt
½ cup milk
2 tablespoons butter *or* margarine
Broiled Coconut Topping (see recipe, page 259)

Grease a 9×9×2-inch baking pan; set aside. In small mixer bowl beat eggs at high speed of electric mixer about 4 minutes or till thick and lemon-colored. Gradually add sugar; beat at medium speed 4 to 5 minutes or till sugar dissolves. Stir together flour, baking powder, and salt. Add to egg mixture; stir just till blended. In small saucepan heat milk with butter or margarine till butter melts; stir into batter and mix well. Turn into the baking pan. Bake in 350° oven for 20 to 25 minutes or till cake tests done. Frost, while warm, with Broiled Coconut Topping. Serve warm.

TIP Achieve a marbled appearance *by using a narrow spatula to gently swirl through the light and dark batters. Don't swirl too vigorously or you'll lose the marble effect.*

Marble Pound Cake

¾ cup butter *or* margarine
3 eggs
½ cup milk
1¼ cups sugar
1 teaspoon finely shredded lemon peel
1 tablespoon lemon juice
2 cups all-purpose flour
1 teaspoon baking powder
¼ teaspoon salt
2 tablespoons boiling water
1 tablespoon sugar
1 square (1 ounce) unsweetened chocolate, melted and cooled
¼ teaspoon ground cinnamon

Refer to: Making pound cake, page 240. Bring butter, eggs, and milk to room temperature. Grease bottom and about 1 inch up sides of a 9×5×3-inch loaf pan; set aside.

In large mixer bowl beat butter or margarine at medium speed of electric mixer till creamed and fluffy. Gradually add 1¼ cups sugar, beating 6 minutes or till fluffy. Add eggs, one at a time; beat 1 minute after each. Beat 2 to 3 minutes more. Add milk, lemon peel, and juice; beat at low speed till blended. Stir together flour, baking powder, and salt. Gradually add to creamed mixture and beat at low speed just till smooth.

Divide batter in half. Combine the boiling water, 1 tablespoon sugar, chocolate, and cinnamon; stir into one half of the batter. In prepared pan alternate spoonfuls of light and dark batters. Using a narrow spatula stir gently through batter to marble, referring to tip at left.

Bake in 325° oven about 70 minutes or till cake tests done. Cool cake in pan on wire rack 10 minutes; remove from pan. Cool. Sift powdered sugar atop, if desired.

Sour Cream Pound Cake

1 cup butter *or* margarine
6 eggs
2¾ cups sugar
3 cups all-purpose flour
½ teaspoon salt
¼ teaspoon baking soda
1 cup dairy sour cream
½ teaspoon lemon extract
½ teaspoon orange extract
½ teaspoon vanilla
Powdered sugar

Refer to: Making pound cake, page 240. Bring the butter or margarine and the eggs to room temperature. Grease and flour the bottom and sides of a 10-inch tube pan; set aside.

In large mixer bowl beat the butter or margarine at medium speed of electric mixer till creamed. Gradually add the sugar, beating at medium speed till light and fluffy. Add eggs, one at a time, beating about 1 minute after each; scrape the bowl frequently with a rubber spatula, guiding mixture toward the beaters. Beat 2 minutes more.

Stir together the flour, salt, and soda. Add to creamed mixture alternately with sour cream, beginning and ending with the flour mixture. Beat well after each addition. Add lemon extract, orange extract, and vanilla; beat just till thoroughly blended. Turn batter into prepared 10-inch tube pan.

Bake in 350° oven for 1½ hours or till a wooden pick inserted in center of cake comes out clean and dry. Cool cake in pan on wire rack for 15 minutes; remove from pan. Cool completely. Sprinkle with powdered sugar, if desired.

246

Apricot-Cheese Fruitcake

- 2 cups water
- ½ cup snipped dried apricots
- ½ cup light raisins
- ¼ cup sugar
- 1½ cups sugar
- 1 8-ounce package cream cheese, softened
- 1 cup butter *or* margarine
- 1½ teaspoons vanilla
- 4 eggs
- 2¼ cups sifted cake flour
- 1½ teaspoons baking powder
- ½ cup chopped pecans

Grease and flour a 10-inch fluted tube pan; set aside. In saucepan combine water, apricots, raisins, and the ¼ cup sugar; bring to boiling. Reduce heat; cover and simmer 15 to 20 minutes. Drain well; set aside.

continued next column

In mixer bowl combine the 1½ cups sugar, softened cream cheese, butter or margarine, and vanilla; beat at medium speed of electric mixer till creamed. Add eggs, one at a time, beating at medium speed about 1 minute after each; scrape bowl frequently with rubber spatula, guiding mixture toward beaters.

Sift together cake flour and baking powder. Gradually add dry ingredients to creamed mixture and beat till thoroughly blended. Gently fold in apricot mixture and pecans. Turn batter into the fluted tube pan.

Bake in 325° oven for 65 to 70 minutes or till a wooden pick inserted in center of cake comes out clean and dry. Cool completely on rack. Remove cake from pan. Wrap in foil; store overnight before serving.

Sour Cream Pound Cake

Chocolate Chiffon Cake
(pictured on page 258)

- ½ cup water
- 4 squares (4 ounces) unsweetened chocolate, broken up
- ¼ cup sugar
- 2¼ cups sifted cake flour
- 1½ cups sugar
- 1 tablespoon baking powder
- 1 teaspoon salt
- ½ cup cooking oil
- 7 egg yolks
- ¾ cup cold water
- 1 teaspoon vanilla
- 7 egg whites
- ½ teaspoon cream of tartar
  Chocolate Icing (see recipe, page 259)
  Confectioners' Icing (see recipe, page 249)

Refer to: Making chiffon cake, page 244. In saucepan combine ½ cup water, chocolate, and ¼ cup sugar. Cook, stirring constantly, till chocolate is melted and mixture is smooth; cool. In bowl sift together flour, 1½ cups sugar, baking powder, and salt; make a well in center. Add cooking oil, egg yolks, ¾ cup water, and vanilla. Beat egg yolk mixture at high speed of electric mixer for 5 minutes or till satin smooth. Stir in chocolate mixture.

Wash beaters thoroughly. In large mixer bowl combine egg whites and cream of tartar. Beat at medium speed of electric mixer till *very stiff* peaks form (tips stand straight). Pour chocolate mixture in thin stream over entire surface of egg whites; fold in gently. Turn into *ungreased* 10-inch tube pan. Bake in 325° oven for 65 minutes or till cake tests done. Invert cake in pan to cool; remove from pan. If desired, spread Chocolate Icing over top, letting drizzle down the sides. Immediately pipe Confectioners' Icing around top; before icing has set, draw knife through icing at regular intervals to give web effect.

247

Cakes and Frostings

1 In mixer bowl cream butter till light and fluffy. Butter, rather than margarine, is recommended for this recipe to give an authentic "buttery" flavor.

Use an electric mixer to ensure a smooth texture, and guide the butter toward the beaters with a rubber spatula for thorough creaming.

Butter Frosting

Technique: Making butter frosting

6	**tablespoons butter**
1	**16-ounce package powdered sugar, sifted (about 4¾ cups)**
	Milk
1½	**teaspoons vanilla**

1 In mixer bowl cream butter till light and fluffy. **2** Gradually add about *half* the sifted powdered sugar, beating well. **3** Beat in *2 tablespoons* milk and the vanilla. **4** Gradually add remaining powdered sugar, beating constantly. **5–6** Beat in enough additional milk to make frosting of spreading consistency. Frosts tops and sides of two 8- or 9-inch layers.

Chocolate Butter Frosting: Prepare Butter Frosting as above *except* add 2 squares (2 ounces) unsweetened chocolate, melted and cooled, with the vanilla.

Mocha Butter Frosting: Prepare Butter Frosting as above *except* add ¼ cup unsweetened cocoa powder and ½ teaspoon instant coffee crystals to the butter; cream as directed.

248

4 Gradually add the remaining powdered sugar, beating constantly. The frosting will be quite stiff when all the sugar has been added.

2 Gradually add about *half* the sifted powdered sugar, beating well. Keep the electric mixer running constantly at low speed while adding the powdered sugar by spoonfuls. If the mixture splatters onto the sides of the bowl, stop and scrape the sides with a rubber spatula.

3 Beat in *2 tablespoons* milk and the vanilla. Again, keep mixer running on low speed and beat till mixture is thoroughly combined, guiding mixture toward beaters with rubber spatula.

249

TIP Use Confectioners' Icing *to glaze yeast and quick breads, sweet rolls, and cakes. To make the icing, stir together 1 cup sifted powdered sugar, ¼ teaspoon vanilla, and enough milk to make of drizzling consistency (about 1½ tablespoons).*

Using a spoon, drizzle the icing over the bread or cake, as shown, or spread it with a spatula. To glaze rolls or cupcakes, dip the tops in the icing. For easier clean-up, place the bread or cake on a wire rack set on a sheet of waxed paper.

If desired, sprinkle chopped nuts or fruits over the icing before it sets.

5 Beat in enough additional milk to make a frosting of spreading consistency. At this stage, beat in the milk a small amount at a time. Frequently check the consistency of the frosting to avoid adding too much milk. If the frosting becomes too thin, gradually beat in additional powdered sugar.

6 The finished frosting should be smooth and creamy, as shown. To test for proper spreading consistency, spread a small amount of frosting on the cake. If the frosting is too thick or too thin, beat in a little more milk or sugar as directed in step 5.

Cakes and Frostings

1 In top of double boiler combine sugar, unbeaten egg whites, corn syrup or cream of tartar, and salt. Add cold water.

Either light corn syrup or cream of tartar will prevent crystals from forming in the frosting, keeping the frosting smooth. Use whichever you have on hand.

Seven-Minute Frosting

Technique: Making fluffy frosting with a double boiler

1½ **cups sugar**
2 **egg whites**
2 **teaspoons light corn syrup** *or* ¼ **teaspoon cream of tartar**
  Dash salt
⅓ **cup cold water**
1 **teaspoon vanilla**

1 In top of double boiler combine sugar, egg whites, corn syrup or cream of tartar, and salt. Add cold water. **2** Beat ½ minute at low speed of electric mixer to blend. **3** Place over boiling water (water in bottom of double boiler should not touch top pan). **4–5** Beating constantly with electric mixer, cook about 7 minutes or till frosting forms stiff peaks. **6** Remove from heat; add vanilla. **7–8** Beat about 2 minutes more or till of spreading consistency. Frosts tops and sides of two 8- or 9-inch layers, or one 10-inch tube cake.

250

5 Beating the frosting while it cooks produces stiff peaks, as shown. This frosting usually takes about 7 minutes to reach this stage, but remember that this timing is only approximate. Be sure to beat until stiff peaks form.

2 Beat ½ minute at low speed of electric mixer to blend. The mixture should appear well-combined but not fluffy at the completion of this mixing.

3 Place over boiling water (water in bottom of double boiler should not touch top pan). The steam produced by the boiling water surrounds the top of the double boiler and thus heats the mixture evenly.

4 Beating constantly with electric mixer, cook about 7 minutes or till frosting forms stiff peaks (don't cook beyond this stage).

Use a portable electric mixer for easier handling at the range, and beat at the highest speed available. If mixture splatters, reduce mixer speed slightly.

6 Remove from heat; add vanilla. On a gas range, simply turn off the heat. On an electric range, remove the double boiler from the heating unit and set it on the range top, as shown.

7 Beat frosting at high speed of electric mixer about 2 minutes more or till of spreading consistency. Check the consistency by spreading a little of the frosting on the cake. If frosting is too thin, continue beating.

8 The finished frosting should be smooth and fluffy, as shown. Immediately spread the frosting on the cake, and serve the cake as soon as possible since this type of frosting tends to break down if kept very long.

To prevent frosting from sticking to the knife when cutting cake, dip the knife in hot water.

Cakes and Frostings

1 In a heavy 2-quart saucepan combine sugar, water, cream of tartar, and salt. In this type of frosting, the hot sugar syrup cooks the egg whites so a double boiler isn't needed.

Fluffy White Frosting

Technique: Making fluffy frosting without a double boiler

1 **cup sugar**
⅓ **cup water**
¼ **teaspoon cream of tartar**
 Dash salt
2 **egg whites**
1 **teaspoon vanilla**

1 In 2-quart saucepan combine sugar, water, cream of tartar, and salt. **2** Bring to boiling, stirring till sugar dissolves. **3–4** *Very slowly* pour sugar syrup into unbeaten egg whites in mixer bowl, beating constantly with electric mixer about 7 minutes or till stiff peaks form. **5–6** Add vanilla; beat till combined. Frosts tops and sides of two 8- or 9-inch layers, or one 10-inch tube cake.

4 When all the syrup is added, turn mixer to high speed and continue beating and scraping bowl till stiff peaks form, as shown.
  The hot syrup cooks the egg whites, while the continual beating incorporates air into the frosting.

2 Bring to boiling, stirring till sugar dissolves. Since any undissolved sugar will make the frosting "grainy," make sure to scrape down the sides of the saucepan and boil till all the sugar is dissolved. Stir with a figure-8 motion.

3 *Very slowly* pour sugar syrup into unbeaten egg whites in mixer bowl, beating constantly at medium speed of electric mixer. Use a rubber spatula to guide egg whites toward beaters, scraping sides as necessary. This assures that all frosting is evenly mixed.

An electric mixer (preferably a stand mixer) is necessary to provide the continuous hard beating.

253

TIP Shadow icing *(sometimes called allegretti frosting) is an easy dress-up for frosted or unfrosted cakes.*

To make shadow icing, in a small saucepan combine 1 square (1 ounce) unsweetened chocolate and ½ teaspoon shortening. Heat over low heat till melted, stirring constantly. Drizzle melted chocolate mixture from the tip of a teaspoon around the edge of the cake, as shown. Drizzle in a steady stream so the chocolate will run down the sides to form "icicles."

5 Add vanilla; beat till combined. Keep the mixer running at high speed while adding the vanilla, and scrape the sides of the bowl with a rubber scraper to evenly distribute the flavoring.

6 The finished frosting will be smooth and fluffy yet hold stiff peaks, as shown. Spread immediately.

This frosting is somewhat less stable than Seven-Minute Frosting, so frost and serve the cake the same day.

To prevent frosting from sticking to the knife when cutting cake, dip the knife in hot water.

Cakes and Frostings

Fudge Frosting

Technique: Making fudge frosting

> 3 **cups sugar**
> 3 **tablespoons light corn syrup**
> 2 **squares (2 ounces) unsweetened chocolate**
> ¼ **teaspoon salt**
> 1 **cup milk**
> ¼ **cup butter** *or* margarine
> 1 **teaspoon vanilla**

1 Butter sides of heavy 3-quart saucepan. **2** In saucepan combine sugar, corn syrup, chocolate, and salt; stir in milk. **3** Cook and stir over medium heat till sugar dissolves and chocolate melts. **4** Clip candy thermometer to side of pan and continue cooking to 234° (soft-ball stage); stir only as necessary to prevent sticking. **5** Remove from heat; add butter or margarine. **6** Let mixture cool, without stirring, till candy thermometer registers 110°. Add vanilla. **7** Beat till mixture is of spreading consistency. **8** Pour and spread *immediately* atop a 13×9-inch cake.

1 Butter sides of a heavy 3-quart saucepan. Use folded paper toweling or waxed paper to spread butter evenly.

Coating the pan sides in this way helps prevent unwanted sugar crystals from forming along the sides when the mixture bubbles up during cooking.

Using a heavy saucepan helps prevent scorching.

5 Remove saucepan from heat; add butter or margarine. Don't stir in the butter; simply place it on top of the mixture and let the heat of the mixture melt it.

On a gas range, simply turn off the heat. On an electric range, remove the saucepan from the heating unit and set it on the range top.

2 In saucepan combine sugar, corn syrup, chocolate, and salt; stir in milk. Break the chocolate squares in half before adding to speed melting.

3 Cook and stir over medium heat till all the sugar dissolves and the chocolate melts.

Stir gently in a figure-8 motion to avoid splashing the sides of pan.

Remember that any undissolved sugar will cause crystals to form around it, giving the frosting an undesirable grainy texture.

Use medium rather than high heat so the milk and chocolate won't stick or boil over.

4 Clip a candy thermometer to side of pan, referring to the tip on page 317.

Continue cooking over medium heat till thermometer registers 234°; stir only as necessary to prevent sticking. This is the soft-ball stage. (The mixture should boil vigorously, as shown.) Watch closely; the temperature rises quickly above 220°.

If you do not have a candy thermometer, use the cold water test, referring to the tip on page 315.

255

6 Let mixture cool, without stirring, till candy thermometer registers 110°. At this temperature, the bottom of the pan should feel comfortably warm. If necessary, prop the saucepan up slightly so the mixture covers the bulb of the thermometer. Add vanilla.

7 Beat till mixture is of spreading consistency. Using a spoon, beat the mixture vigorously, as shown, with an up-and-over motion.

This is the critical step in making fudge frosting. Be sure to check the consistency frequently so that the frosting doesn't become too stiff. (If the mixture becomes too stiff to spread, pour it into a pan, referring to step 11 on page 313, and use as candy.)

8 Pour and spread *immediately*. The finished frosting will be smooth and satiny, as shown, but will soon become too stiff to spread. Work *quickly*, using a small metal spatula to spread frosting.

To smooth small areas that set up too fast, dip the spatula in warm water and then smooth over these areas.

Cakes and Frostings

Frosting a Cake

Technique: Frosting a cake

Two-layer cake: 1 Completely cool the cake before frosting. Use a pastry brush to brush loose crumbs from the sides of each layer. **2** Arrange strips of waxed paper around edge of serving plate. Position first cake layer, top side down, on the waxed paper-edged plate. **3** Spread about ¼ of the frosting over this first layer. **4** Position second cake layer, top side up, over frosted layer. **5** Spread sides of cake with a thin coat of frosting. **6** Spread a thicker layer of frosting over this thin coat, swirling frosting decoratively. **7** Spread remaining frosting over cake top, swirling decoratively and joining to frosted sides at edge. Carefully remove waxed paper strips. **8** To serve cake, cut into wedges. An 8- or 9-inch two-layer cake makes 12 servings.

One-layer, tube, or loaf cake: Follow instructions given above *except* omit steps 3 and 4.

1 Completely cool the cake before frosting. Use a pastry brush or your hand to brush loose crumbs from the sides of each layer. This helps prevent crumbs from mixing with the frosting as you spread it.

If the cake layer is too rounded, it will not sit securely on the plate. To steady it, use a long-bladed knife to slice a piece from the top, making it level.

5 Spread sides of cake with a thin coat of frosting. This frosting layer seals in any crumbs that weren't brushed off in step 1. For even spreading, hold the spatula vertically, as shown.

2 Arrange strips of waxed paper around edge of serving plate. Position first cake layer, top side down, on the waxed paper-edged plate.

The waxed paper helps prevent the serving plate from becoming smeared with frosting. Make sure that the strips tuck just under the edge of the cake so they can easily be removed when the frosting is finished.

3 Spread about ¼ of the frosting over this first layer. A small metal spatula works well for spreading the frosting.

When using a firm frosting, such as a fudge or butter frosting, spread frosting to edge of cake, as shown.

When using a soft, fluffy frosting, leave about ¼-inch unfrosted around the edge. The weight of the second cake layer will cause the frosting to flow to the edge.

4 Place second cake layer, top side up, over frosted layer. Be sure edges of layers align. This method of assembling the two layers gives the finished cake a slightly rounded top and avoids the space that results when you position the second layer top side down.

If the cake top is too rounded or lopsided, use a sharp, long-bladed knife to level it by slicing off a piece.

TIP Dress up a frosted cake *by sprinkling it with toasted or tinted coconut (see tips on pages 89 and 375). Or, garnish with chocolate curls (see page 375).*

Trim an unfrosted dark-colored cake *with a powdered sugar design. Position a paper doily on the cake top and sift powdered sugar over the doily. Gently press the sugar through the doily with the back of a spoon, then gently lift off the doily.*

257

6 Spread a thicker layer of frosting over this thin coat, swirling frosting decoratively, as shown.

As a guideline, use about ⅔ of the remaining frosting for the cake sides.

7 Spread remaining frosting over cake top, swirling decoratively and joining to frosted sides at edge, as shown. Carefully remove waxed paper strips.

If using butter or fudge frostings, smooth rough areas by dipping a small metal spatula in warm water and then smoothing over the desired areas.

8 To serve cake, cut into wedges. Insert the point of a sharp, thin-bladed knife into center of cake. Slice with an up-and-down motion, pulling knife toward you. Clean frosting and crumbs from knife by occasionally wiping with a damp cloth.

To prevent fluffy frosting from sticking to the knife, dip the knife in hot water before cutting the cake.

Cakes and Frostings

Sea Foam Frosting

1¼ cups packed brown sugar
2 egg whites
2 teaspoons light corn syrup *or*
    ¼ teaspoon cream of tartar
Dash salt
¼ cup cold water
1 teaspoon vanilla

Refer to: Making fluffy frosting with a double boiler, page 250. In top of double boiler combine brown sugar, egg whites, corn syrup or cream of tartar, and salt. Add cold water. Beat ½ minute at low speed of electric mixer to blend. Place over boiling water (water in bottom of double boiler should not touch top pan). Beating constantly with electric mixer, cook about 7 minutes or till frosting forms stiff peaks (don't cook beyond this stage). Remove from heat; add vanilla. Beat about 2 minutes more or till of spreading consistency. Spread on cake. Frosts tops and sides of three 8-inch layers.

Coconut Frosting

1 egg
1 5⅓-ounce can (⅔ cup)
    evaporated milk
⅔ cup sugar
¼ cup butter *or* margarine
Dash salt
1⅓ cups coconut
½ cup chopped pecans

In saucepan beat egg slightly. Stir in milk, sugar, butter or margarine, and salt. Cook and stir over medium heat about 12 minutes or till thickened and bubbly. Add coconut and pecans. Cool. Spread on cake. Frosts top and sides of one 13×9-inch cake or frosts tops of two 8- or 9-inch layers.

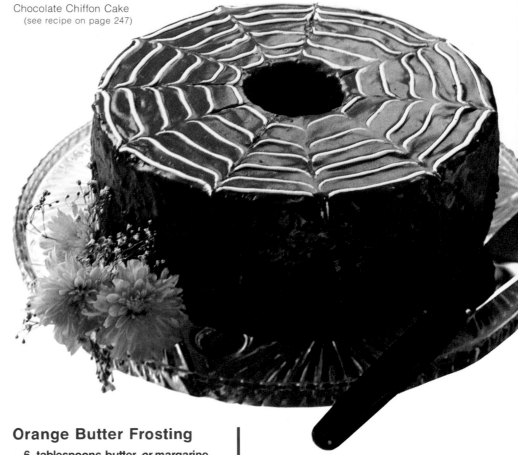

Chocolate Chiffon Cake
(see recipe on page 247)

Orange Butter Frosting

6 tablespoons butter *or* margarine
1 egg yolk
2 teaspoons finely shredded orange
    peel
1 16-ounce package powdered
    sugar, sifted (about 4¾ cups)
3 to 4 tablespoons orange juice

Refer to: Making butter frosting, page 248. In small mixer bowl cream together butter or margarine, egg yolk, and orange peel till light and fluffy. Add about *half* the sifted powdered sugar, beating well. Beat in *2 tablespoons* of the orange juice. Gradually add remaining powdered sugar, beating constantly. Beat in enough additional orange juice to make frosting of spreading consistency. Spread on cake. Frosts tops and sides of two 8- or 9-inch layers.

Banana Frosting

½ cup sugar
¼ cup all-purpose flour
1½ cups milk
2 well-beaten eggs
2 tablespoons butter *or* margarine
1 teaspoon banana flavoring

In saucepan combine sugar and flour; stir in milk. Cook and stir till thickened and bubbly. Gradually stir *half* the hot mixture into eggs, referring to steps 8 and 9 on page 109. Return all to remaining hot mixture in saucepan. Cook 2 minutes more, stirring constantly. Stir in butter or margarine and banana flavoring. Cover surface with plastic wrap or waxed paper. Chill without stirring. Spread chilled mixture on cake. Chill cake. Frosts tops and sides of two 8- or 9-inch layers.

Toasted Pecan Frosting

⅓ cup chopped pecans
1 tablespoon butter *or* margarine
3 cups sifted powdered sugar
¼ cup milk
3 tablespoons butter *or* margarine
¼ teaspoon vanilla

Place chopped pecans in shallow baking pan; dot with 1 tablespoon butter or margarine. Toast in 350° oven 10 to 15 minutes; stir often. Cool.

In mixing bowl combine powdered sugar, milk, the 3 tablespoons butter or margarine, and vanilla. Beat smooth with electric mixer. Stir in toasted pecans. Spread on cake. Frosts 18 cupcakes or top of one 8- or 9-inch layer.

Citrus Frosting

1½ cups sifted powdered sugar
2 tablespoons butter *or* margarine
½ teaspoon finely shredded orange peel
1 tablespoon orange juice
¼ teaspoon finely shredded lemon peel
2 teaspoons lemon juice
Dash salt

In mixing bowl combine powdered sugar, butter or margarine, orange peel, orange juice, lemon peel, lemon juice, and salt. Beat smooth with electric mixer. Spread on cake. Frosts top of one 13×9-inch cake.

Peanut Butter Frosting

¼ cup chunk-style peanut butter
2 tablespoons butter *or* margarine
2½ cups sifted powdered sugar
¼ cup milk
½ teaspoon vanilla

Refer to: Making butter frosting, page 248. Cream peanut butter and butter or margarine, till light and fluffy. Gradually add about *half* the sifted powder sugar, beating well. Beat in milk and vanilla. Gradually blend in remaining powdered sugar. If necessary, blend in a little additional milk by teaspoons to make frosting of spreading consistency. Spread on cake. Frosts top of one 13×9-inch cake.

Maple Frosting

⅓ cup milk
¼ cup packed brown sugar
1 tablespoon butter *or* margarine
3¼ cups sifted powdered sugar
¼ teaspoon maple flavoring

In saucepan combine milk, brown sugar, and butter or margarine; bring to boiling, stirring constantly. Cool; stir in powdered sugar and maple flavoring. Spread on cake. Frosts top of one 9-inch square cake.

Chocolate Icing

1 4-ounce package sweet cooking chocolate
3 tablespoons butter *or* margarine
1½ cups sifted powdered sugar
3 tablespoons hot water

In small saucepan melt together the chocolate and butter or margarine. Remove from heat; stir in powdered sugar and water. Add more hot water if needed to make of pouring consistency. Pour over cake to glaze. Frosts top of 10-inch tube cake.

Broiled Coconut Topping

½ cup packed brown sugar
¼ cup butter, softened
2 tablespoons milk
1 cup coconut

Cream brown sugar and butter till fluffy. Stir in milk. Stir in coconut; spread over warm cake in pan. Broil 4 to 5 inches from heat about 3 minutes or till golden. Serve warm. Frosts top of 9-inch-square cake.

Cream Cheese Frosting

1 3-ounce package cream cheese
¼ cup butter *or* margarine
2 cups sifted powdered sugar
1 teaspoon vanilla
¼ cup chopped nuts

Soften cream cheese and butter or margarine; beat together till fluffy. Gradually add powdered sugar, beating till smooth; stir in vanilla. Spread over cake; sprinkle with nuts. Frosts top of one 13×9-inch cake.

Petits Fours Icing

3 cups granulated sugar
1½ cups hot water
¼ teaspoon cream of tartar
1 teaspoon vanilla
Sifted powdered sugar (about 2½ cups)
Food coloring (optional)

In 2-quart saucepan combine granulated sugar, hot water, and cream of tartar. Cover and cook till boiling. Uncover; clip candy thermometer to saucepan, referring to tip on page 317. Cook till temperature of mixture is 226° on candy thermometer. Remove from heat. Cool at room temperature to 110°. Stir in vanilla. Stir in enough sifted powdered sugar (about 2½ cups) to make of pourable consistency. Tint with food coloring, if desired. Spoon over cake pieces, referring to tip below. Frosts about 36 petits fours.

259

TIP Serve attractive Petits Fours at your next party. *To make these dainty cakes, cut cooled Hot Milk Sponge Cake (see recipe on page 246) into 1½-inch diamonds, squares, or other shapes. Set wire rack over sheet of waxed paper. Place cake pieces on wire rack so pieces don't touch each other. Prepare Petits Fours Icing (see recipe above). Spoon icing over cake pieces, as shown. Lift pieces on rack and spoon icing onto sides of each piece. Let icing dry about 15 minutes. Spoon on second coat of icing. Let dry.*

COOKIES

You'll want to keep your cookie jar filled with favorite treats from this section. Just follow the step-by-step directions for the ever-popular drop cookies, tempting bar cookies, make-ahead refrigerator cookies, and fancier cutout and pressed cookies.

Chocolate Chip Cookies

Technique: Making drop cookies

½	cup butter *or* margarine
½	cup shortening
1	cup packed brown sugar
½	cup granulated sugar
2	eggs
1½	teaspoons vanilla
2½	cups all-purpose flour
1	teaspoon baking soda
½	teaspoon salt
1	12-ounce package (2 cups) semisweet chocolate pieces
1	cup chopped walnuts *or* pecans

1-2 Let butter or margarine stand at room temperature till softened. In mixing bowl cream the softened butter, shortening, brown sugar, and granulated sugar. **3** Add eggs and vanilla; beat well. **4** In a bowl stir together the flour, baking soda, and salt. **5** Add to creamed mixture and stir till well blended. **6** Stir in chocolate pieces and nuts. **7** Drop from a teaspoon 2 inches apart onto an ungreased cookie sheet. Bake in 375° oven for 8 to 10 minutes or till done. **8** Remove from cookie sheet; cool on wire rack. Makes about 6 dozen cookies.

1 Let butter or margarine stand at room temperature till softened. In a bowl cream together the softened butter or margarine, the shortening, brown sugar, and granulated sugar. When creaming by hand, use the back of a wooden spoon to rub mixture against sides of bowl. If desired, use an electric mixer to cream the mixture.

5 Add dry ingredients to creamed mixture and stir with a wooden spoon or beat with an electric mixer till well blended.

2 Continue creaming the mixture until it is thoroughly blended and creamy, as shown. Be sure that there are no uncombined lumps of brown sugar in the mixture.

3 Add the eggs. To avoid getting eggshell in the cookie dough, break eggs one at a time into another bowl and add individually to the creamed mixture. Add the vanilla and beat till well blended using a wooden spoon or an electric mixer.

4 In a bowl stir together the flour, baking soda, and salt. Thoroughly combine the dry ingredients before adding them to the creamed mixture so that the soda and salt will be evenly distributed throughout.

6 Add the semisweet chocolate pieces and the chopped walnuts or pecans and stir into the creamed mixture. Use a wooden spoon for stirring; an electric mixer would break up the chocolate and nuts.

7 Drop dough from a teaspoon onto an ungreased cookie sheet. Use a spatula to push dough off spoon. Drop dough 2 inches apart to allow for spreading.

Bake in 375° oven for 8 to 10 minutes or till done. To test for doneness, gently touch the lightly browned cookie with fingertip; the imprint should be barely visible. Underbaked cookies are doughy; over-baked cookies are dry and hard.

8 When cookies test done, remove from cookie sheet with a pancake turner or wide metal spatula. Cool cookies on wire rack; don't stack them until thoroughly cooled.

If you have a cookie sheet with a non-stick surface, be sure to use an appropriate utensil for removing cookies to prevent scratching the surface of the cookie sheet.

Cookies

Tri-Level Brownies (pictured on page 271)

Technique: Making layered bar cookies

1	**cup quick-cooking rolled oats**
½	**cup all-purpose flour**
½	**cup packed brown sugar**
¼	**teaspoon baking soda**
6	**tablespoons butter, melted**
¾	**cup granulated sugar**
¼	**cup butter, melted**
1	**square (1 ounce) unsweetened chocolate, melted and cooled**
1	**egg**
⅔	**cup all-purpose flour**
¼	**teaspoon baking powder**
¼	**cup milk**
½	**teaspoon vanilla**
½	**cup chopped walnuts**
1	**square (1 ounce) unsweetened chocolate**
2	**tablespoons butter *or* margarine**
1½	**cups sifted powdered sugar**
1	**teaspoon vanilla**
16	**walnut halves**

262

1 Stir together oats, the ½ cup flour, brown sugar, soda, and ¼ teaspoon *salt*. Stir in the 6 tablespoons butter. **2** Pat into 11×7×1½-inch baking pan. Bake in 350° oven for 10 minutes; cool.

3 Mix granulated sugar, the ¼ cup butter, and 1 square melted chocolate. Add egg; beat well. **4-5** Stir together the ⅔ cup flour, baking powder, and ¼ teaspoon *salt*. Add to chocolate mixture alternately with a mixture of milk and the ½ teaspoon vanilla. Stir in chopped nuts. **6-7** Spread over baked layer. Bake in 350° oven for 25 minutes or till done. Cool.

8 To make frosting, melt 1 square chocolate and 2 tablespoons butter or margarine over low heat; stir constantly. **9** Remove from heat; stir in powdered sugar and the 1 teaspoon vanilla. Blend in enough hot *water* (about 2 tablespoons) to make an almost pourable consistency. **10** Frost brownies. **11** Top with walnut halves. **12** Cut into bars. Makes 16 brownies.

1 In mixing bowl stir together the rolled oats, the ½ cup flour, brown sugar, baking soda, and ¼ teaspoon salt. Add the 6 tablespoons melted butter and stir till well blended.

2 Using your hands, pat the oat mixture into an 11×7×1½-inch baking pan. Bake in a 350° oven for 10 minutes. Remove from oven and set aside to cool while preparing second layer.

7 To test brownies for doneness, insert a wooden pick in center of baked brownies. If pick comes out clean, bar cookies are done. Set aside to cool.

8 To make frosting, melt 1 square chocolate and 2 tablespoons butter or margarine in saucepan over low heat. Stir constantly so that mixture heats evenly and chocolate doesn't scorch.

3 For second layer, in a bowl combine the granulated sugar, the ¼ cup melted butter, and the 1 square melted and cooled chocolate. Add the egg and beat well with a wooden spoon.

4 In a bowl stir together the ⅔ cup flour, the baking powder, and ¼ teaspoon salt. Thoroughly combine the dry ingredients so that the baking powder and salt will be evenly distributed throughout. Add *half* of the dry ingredients to chocolate mixture; mix well.

5 Combine the milk and the ½ teaspoon vanilla; add to chocolate mixture. Mix till blended. Stir in remaining dry ingredients till mixed. Stir in the chopped nuts.

6 Spread chocolate mixture over baked layer in pan. Use a metal spatula or knife to spread mixture evenly to the edges.
　Bake in a 350° oven for 25 minutes or till brownies test done.

263

9 Remove saucepan from heat and set on a hot pad. Stir in the sifted powdered sugar and the 1 teaspoon vanilla. Blend in enough hot water (about 2 tablespoons) until frosting is smooth and almost pourable, as shown.

10 Pour frosting over cooled bars and spread evenly with a metal spatula or knife. Be sure to spread frosting to the edges.

11 While frosting is still warm and is not set, decorate top of bars with walnut halves, placing them so that each brownie will be topped with a nut half, as shown.

12 To cut bars into even pieces, first lightly score frosting with a knife. To cut 16 bar shapes, make three lengthwise cuts and three crosswise cuts. To make 20 slightly smaller bars, make four crosswise cuts and three lengthwise cuts.

Cookies

Rolled Sugar Cookies

Technique: Making rolled and cutout cookies

½ **cup butter** *or* **margarine**
1 **cup sugar**
1 **egg**
¼ **cup milk**
½ **teaspoon vanilla**
2¼ **cups all-purpose flour**
2 **teaspoons baking powder**
½ **teaspoon salt**
½ **teaspoon ground mace (optional)**

1 Soften the butter or margarine, referring to step 1 on page 266. In mixer bowl cream together the softened butter or margarine and sugar. **2** Add egg, milk, and vanilla; beat well. **3** Stir together the flour, baking powder, salt, and mace. Add to creamed mixture and beat till blended. **4** Divide dough in half. Cover and chill about 1 hour.

5 On lightly floured surface, roll each half of dough to ⅛-inch thickness for thin crisp cookies, or ¼-inch thickness for thick cookies. **6** Cut into desired shapes with cookie cutters. **7** Place cookies on ungreased cookie sheet. Bake thin cookies in a 375° oven for 7 to 8 minutes; bake thick cookies for 10 to 12 minutes. **8** Remove from cookie sheet; cool on wire rack. Makes about 4½ dozen thin cookies or about 2½ dozen thick cookies.

264

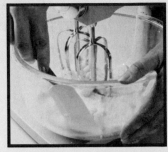

1 Soften the butter or margarine, referring to step 1 on page 266. In mixer bowl cream together the softened butter or margarine and sugar. This step can be done with an electric mixer, as shown. Or, cream mixture by hand, referring to steps 1 and 2 on page 260.

5 After dough has chilled, roll each half on a lightly floured surface to ⅛-inch thickness for thin crisp cookies, or ¼-inch thickness for thick cookies that won't be quite as crisp. Roll out dough from center to edges; use a ruler to measure the thickness.

Keep remaining dough chilled till needed. If dough becomes too soft, chill again or sprinkle a little more flour on the rolling surface.

2 Add the egg. To avoid getting eggshell in the cookie dough, break the egg into another bowl before adding it to the creamed mixture.

Add the milk and vanilla; beat mixture well.

3 In a bowl stir together the flour, baking powder, salt, and mace. (If desired, omit the mace, or substitute ground cinnamon or ground nutmeg.) Thoroughly combine the dry ingredients so that the baking powder, salt, and spice will be evenly distributed.

Add dry ingredients to the creamed mixture and beat till blended.

4 Divide the dough in half and wrap each half in clear plastic wrap or foil. Place in refrigerator for about 1 hour to firm the dough and make it easier to roll.

TIP If you do much rerolling of dough for cutout cookies, *try rolling it on a surface dusted with a mixture of equal parts of all-purpose flour and powdered sugar. The cookies won't be as tough as when rerolled in flour alone. Store any extra flour-sugar mixture for another use.*

265

6 Cut dough into desired shapes using floured cookie cutters, or create your own patterns. Cut shapes out of cardboard, place them on the dough, and trace around edges with the tip of a sharp knife.

Place cutouts as close together as possible so very little dough will need to be rerolled. Too much rolling produces cookies that tend to be dry and tough.

7 Remove the cut cookies from floured surface with a pancake turner or wide metal spatula. Place on ungreased cookie sheet. If desired, sprinkle with colored sugar.

Bake thin cookies in a 375° oven for 7 to 8 minutes; bake thick cookies for 10 to 12 minutes. When done, cookies will be lightly browned around the edges.

Reroll any extra dough to cut and bake as above.

8 Remove cookies with a pancake turner or wide metal spatula. Cool cookies on wire rack; don't stack them until they are thoroughly cooled or they will stick together.

After cookies are thoroughly cooled, decorate them with frosting, if desired.

Cookies

Sugar-Pecan Crisps

Technique: Making refrigerator cookies

¾ **cup butter *or* margarine**
⅔ **cup sugar**
1 **egg**
1 **teaspoon vanilla**
¼ **teaspoon salt**
1¾ **cups all-purpose flour**
½ **cup finely chopped pecans**

1 Soften the butter or margarine. **2** In mixer bowl cream together the butter or margarine and sugar till light and fluffy. **3** Beat in the egg, vanilla, and salt till blended. **4** At low speed of electric mixer gradually blend in the flour; mix well. **5** Cover bowl and chill dough 30 minutes or till it is firm enough to handle.

6 Shape chilled dough into a 12-inch log. **7** Roll the dough in chopped pecans to coat outside of log. **8** Wrap in clear plastic wrap or waxed paper and chill several hours or overnight.

9 Cut dough into ¼-inch-thick slices. Place on ungreased cookie sheet. Bake in 350° oven 10 to 12 minutes or till lightly browned. **10** Remove from cookie sheet; cool on wire rack. Makes 4 dozen cookies.

1 Soften the butter or margarine either by letting it stand at room temperature for a short time or by beating it with an electric mixer until creamy, as shown. Do not let the butter become too soft or melt.

2 In mixer bowl cream together the softened butter or margarine and sugar till light and fluffy, as shown. Use a rubber spatula to scrape sides of bowl often.

6 Shape the chilled dough into a log by working it with your hands and rolling it on the counter until it measures 12 inches long. Use a ruler to check the length.

7 Roll dough in the chopped pecans to coat outside of log. The nuts should be finely chopped for easier slicing of the log. To simplify cleanup, sprinkle nuts on a piece of waxed paper the length of the log, then roll log in nuts, as shown. Gently press the log into the nuts so they will stick.

3 Beat in the egg, vanilla, and salt till blended. The mixture should be very fluffy, as shown, and may have a curdled appearance. Thorough creaming is important to dissolve the sugar crystals for a well-blended mixture.

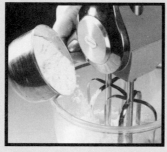

4 At low speed of electric mixer, gradually blend in the flour. Mix thoroughly, using a rubber spatula to scrape sides of bowl often.

5 Cover bowl with clear plastic wrap or foil. Chill the cookie dough 30 minutes or till firm enough to handle and shape.

267

TIP To make round refrigerator cookies the easy way, *fill clean 6-ounce frozen juice containers with dough, packing it into each can till it is level with the open top. Cover open end of each can with foil or clear plastic wrap. Refrigerate dough several hours or till it is thoroughly chilled and you are ready to bake.*

To slice cookies for baking, use a can opener to cut open the sealed end of each container; remove foil or plastic wrap from open end of each can. Pressing in on the loosened can end, push out ¼ inch of the dough at a time. With a sharp, thin-bladed knife, slice dough even with the can rim, as shown, using a back-and-forth sawing motion.

Some cookie doughs may need to stand at room temperature for 5 to 10 minutes before they can be pushed out of the cans for slicing.

8 Wrap log in clear plastic wrap or waxed paper. If desired, cut the 12-inch log in half before wrapping and chilling. Chill dough several hours or overnight. You can store the tightly wrapped dough in the refrigerator for up to one week, or in the freezer for up to 6 months.

9 Cut dough into ¼-inch-thick slices using a sharp, thin-bladed knife. If dough softens during slicing, place it in the freezer till firm enough to slice neatly. Place cookies on ungreased cookie sheet.

Bake in 350° oven for 10 to 12 minutes or till cookies are lightly browned.

10 Remove cookies with a pancake turner or a wide metal spatula; cool on wire rack. After cookies have thoroughly cooled, store in a plastic or metal container with a sealable cover or a canister or cookie jar with a snug-fitting lid.

Cookies

Spritz

Technique: Making pressed cookies

1 cup butter *or* margarine
1 cup sugar
1 egg
1 teaspoon vanilla *or* ½ teaspoon almond extract
2⅓ cups all-purpose flour
½ teaspoon baking powder
¼ teaspoon salt
Colored sugar crystals *or* red and green candied cherries

1 Soften the butter or margarine, referring to step 1 on page 266. In mixer bowl cream together the butter or margarine and sugar. **2** Add the egg and the vanilla or almond extract; beat well. **3** Stir together the flour, baking powder, and salt. Add to creamed mixture and stir till thoroughly mixed. Do *not* chill the dough.

4 Pack dough, half at a time, into cookie press. **5-6** Press into desired shapes on ungreased cookie sheet. **7** Sprinkle with colored sugar crystals. *Or*, trim with pieces of red and green candied cherries, lightly pressing cherries into dough. Bake in a 400° oven for 7 to 8 minutes or till done. **8** Remove from cookie sheet; cool on wire rack. Makes about 6 dozen cookies.

268

1 Soften the butter or margarine, referring to step 1 on page 266. In mixer bowl cream together the softened butter or margarine and the sugar with electric mixer. Use a rubber spatula to scrape sides of bowl during beating.

5 To make ribbon cookies or other shapes requiring a continuous piece of dough, hold cookie press at an angle, as shown. Use an ungreased cookie sheet.
To make filled Spritz, press dough in long ribbons, as shown. Use a star plate to press 2 lengthwise rows of dough atop each strip, making a rim along both edges. Spoon jam or jelly between rims. Bake; cut into 1¼-inch diagonals while cookies are hot.

2 Add the egg. To avoid getting eggshell in the cookie dough, break the egg into another bowl before adding it to the creamed mixture. Add the vanilla or almond extract and beat mixture well.

3 In a bowl stir together the flour, baking powder, and salt. Thoroughly combine the dry ingredients so that the baking powder and salt will be evenly distributed throughout.

Add dry ingredients to the creamed mixture and stir till thoroughly mixed.

Do not chill dough before putting it into the cookie press, since it would become too stiff to handle.

4 Choose a shape for the pressed cookies and insert the proper plate in the cookie press, following manufacturer's directions. Pack the dough into the cookie press, loading about half at a time.

6 For other shapes, hold cookie press upright over ungreased cookie sheet. Press out dough, then give handle a slight turn in reverse to stop dough; lift off the press. Be sure to cool cookie sheet between batches to help cookies retain their shape. Cooling the sheet also makes pressing easier, since dough will cling to the cooled sheet and release better from the press.

7 Sprinkle tops of unbaked cookies with colored sugar crystals or multicolored decorative candies.

Or, trim with pieces of candied cherries, lightly pressing them into dough.

Bake in a 400° oven for 7 to 8 minutes or till the edges of cookies are delicately browned. Bake cookies of like shape on the same cookie sheet so that they will bake the same length of time.

8 Remove cookies from cookie sheet with a pancake turner or wide metal spatula. Cool cookies on wire racks. After cookies have thoroughly cooled, store in a plastic or metal container with a sealable cover or a canister with a snug-fitting lid.

Cookies

Bran Puff Cookies

½ cup butter *or* margarine
½ cup granulated sugar
½ cup packed brown sugar
½ cup dairy sour cream
1 egg
1 teaspoon vanilla
1¾ cups all-purpose flour
½ teaspoon baking soda
1 cup bran flakes
½ cup raisins

Refer to: Making drop cookies, page 260. In bowl cream butter and sugars. Beat in sour cream, egg, and vanilla. Stir together flour, soda, and ½ teaspoon *salt*; stir into creamed mixture. Fold in cereal and raisins. Drop rounded teaspoonfuls onto greased cookie sheet. Bake in 375° oven for 10 to 12 minutes. Cool on rack. Makes 48.

Pumpkin-Face Cookies

¾ cup shortening
½ cup packed brown sugar
1 egg
¼ cup light molasses
1 cup quick-cooking rolled oats
2 cups all-purpose flour
½ teaspoon baking soda
  Pumpkin Filling

Refer to: Making rolled and cutout cookies, page 264. In bowl cream shortening and sugar; beat in egg and molasses. Place oats in blender container; cover. Blend till finely chopped. Stir together oats, flour, soda, and 1 teaspoon *salt*. Stir into creamed mixture. Cover; chill.
  Roll dough on lightly floured surface to ⅛-inch thickness. Cut into 36 three-inch circles. Place a rounded teaspoonful of Pumpkin Filling atop *half* the circles. Place on ungreased cookie sheet. Cut jack-o'-lantern faces in remaining circles; place atop filling. Seal edges. Press on stems cut from dough scraps. Bake in 375° oven 12 minutes. Cool. Makes 18.
  Pumpkin Filling: In saucepan mix ½ cup canned *pumpkin*, ½ cup *granulated sugar*, ½ teaspoon ground *cinnamon*, ½ teaspoon ground *ginger*, and ¼ teaspoon ground *nutmeg*. Cook and stir till mixture boils. Cool.

Molasses-Date Rounds

½ cup butter *or* margarine, softened
¾ cup sugar
1 egg
¼ cup light molasses
2 teaspoons vanilla
2 cups all-purpose flour
½ teaspoon baking powder
½ teaspoon salt
1 cup finely snipped pitted dates
¼ cup sugar
¼ cup water
¼ cup raisins, finely chopped
2 teaspoons lemon juice
½ teaspoon vanilla

Refer to: Making refrigerator cookies, steps 1-3, 5, 8, and 9, page 266. In mixer bowl cream butter or margarine and the ¾ cup sugar; beat in egg, molasses, and the 2 teaspoons vanilla. Stir together flour, baking powder, and salt; stir into creamed mixture. Cover; chill 30 minutes.
  Meanwhile, to prepare date filling, in small saucepan combine dates, the ¼ cup sugar, and water. Bring to boiling; cook and stir over low heat till mixture is thickened and bubbly. Remove from heat. Stir in raisins, lemon juice, and the ½ teaspoon vanilla. Cool slightly.
  On waxed paper, roll dough into a 12×10-inch rectangle. Spread with the date filling to ½ inch from edge. Roll dough jelly roll-fashion, beginning at long side; pinch edges together to seal. Cut roll in half crosswise. Wrap each roll in clear plastic wrap. Chill thoroughly.
  Remove one roll from refrigerator and unwrap. Reshape slightly to round flattened side. Carefully cut into thin (about ⅛-inch-thick) slices. Place on greased cookie sheet. Bake in 375° oven 8 to 10 minutes or till lightly browned. Remove from cookie sheet and cool on wire rack. Repeat with remaining roll. Makes 4½ dozen.

Oatmeal-Molasses Cookies

1½ cups all-purpose flour
1 cup sugar
1 teaspoon baking soda
1 teaspoon ground ginger
½ teaspoon salt
¼ teaspoon ground cloves
½ cup shortening
1 egg
¼ cup molasses
¾ cup quick-cooking rolled oats

In bowl combine flour, sugar, soda, ginger, salt, and cloves. Add shortening, egg, and molasses; beat well. Stir in oatmeal. Drop rounded teaspoonfuls onto ungreased cookie sheet, referring to step 7 on page 261. Bake in 375° oven for 10 to 11 minutes. Wait a few minutes before removing from cookie sheet. Cool on wire rack. Makes 36.

Ribbon Wafers

1 cup sugar
¾ cup butter, melted and cooled
2 eggs
1 teaspoon vanilla
2½ cups all-purpose flour
½ teaspoon baking soda
2 cups crisp rice cereal, slightly crushed
2 squares (2 ounces) semisweet chocolate, melted and cooled

Beat together sugar, butter, eggs, and vanilla at medium speed of electric mixer about 3 minutes or till fluffy. Combine flour and soda; stir into egg mixture. Stir in cereal. Divide dough in half. Stir chocolate into one half.
  Line bottom of 8×4×2-inch loaf pan with waxed paper. Press *half* of the chocolate dough into pan; top with *half* of plain dough, pressing lightly. Repeat layers with remaining dough. Cover and chill about 4 hours or till firm. Remove from pan; discard waxed paper. Cut loaf crosswise into thirds. Starting at narrow end of each portion, cut crosswise into thin slices. Place on ungreased cookie sheet. Bake in 375° oven for 10 to 12 minutes. Cool on rack. Makes about 5½ dozen.

270

Peanut Butter Slices

½ cup butter *or* margarine, softened
½ cup creamy peanut butter
¾ cup sugar
1 egg
3 tablespoons milk
2 teaspoons vanilla
1¾ cups all-purpose flour
½ teaspoon baking powder
½ teaspoon salt
¼ cup wheat germ

Refer to: Making refrigerator cookies, page 266. In mixer bowl cream together the butter or margarine, peanut butter, and sugar; blend in egg, milk, and vanilla. Stir together flour, baking powder, and salt. Stir into creamed mixture. Shape dough into a 12-inch log. Roll in wheat germ. Cut log in half, making two 6-inch logs. Wrap in clear plastic wrap. Chill well. Cut into thin slices; place on greased cookie sheet. Bake in 375° oven for 8 to 10 minutes. Remove from cookie sheet; cool on wire rack. Makes 4 dozen cookies.

Almond Cookies

⅔ cup shortening
1¼ cups sugar
2½ cups all-purpose flour
1 teaspoon baking soda
1 teaspoon salt
2 beaten eggs
2 tablespoons milk
1 teaspoon almond extract
½ teaspoon vanilla

In mixer bowl cream shortening and sugar till light and fluffy. Stir together the flour, baking soda, and salt. Combine eggs, milk, almond extract, and vanilla. Add to creamed mixture alternately with flour mixture, beating well after each addition.

Referring to steps 4-8 on page 264, cover and chill dough 1 to 2 hours or overnight. Roll dough on lightly floured surface to ¼-inch thickness. Cut with floured cookie cutter to desired shapes. Place on ungreased cookie sheet. Bake in 375° oven for 10 to 15 minutes. Remove from cookie sheet; cool on wire rack. Decorate with colored frosting, red cinnamon candies, or small silver decorative candies, if desired. Makes about 3 dozen.

Tri-Level Brownies
(see recipe on page 262)

Three-Way Cookies

1 cup butter *or* margarine
1 8-ounce package cream cheese, softened
1½ cups sugar
1 egg
1 teaspoon vanilla
½ teaspoon almond extract
3½ cups all-purpose flour
1 teaspoon baking powder
  Food coloring
2 squares (2 ounces) semisweet chocolate, melted and cooled
  Powdered Sugar Icing
  Small multicolored decorative candies

Cream together butter, cream cheese, and sugar till fluffy. Add egg, vanilla, and almond extract; beat smooth. Stir together flour and baking powder. Add to creamed mixture; mix well. Divide mixture into thirds; chill one portion 1 to 1½ hours or till firm.

To second portion of dough, add desired food coloring. Press through cookie press onto ungreased cookie sheet, referring to steps 4-8 on page 268. Bake in 375° oven for 8 to 10 minutes. Remove from cookie sheet; cool on rack.

To third portion of dough, blend in chocolate. Pinch off small balls of chocolate dough about the size of a walnut. Roll into logs about 2½ inches long. Place on ungreased cookie sheet and bake in 375° oven for 8 to 10 minutes. Remove from cookie sheet; cool on wire rack. Dip ends in Powdered Sugar Icing, then in multicolored candies.

Referring to steps 5-8 on page 264, roll out the chilled portion of dough on lightly floured surface to ⅛-inch thickness. Cut with cookie cutters. Bake on ungreased cookie sheet in 375° oven for 8 to 10 minutes. Cool on rack. Frost with tinted Powdered Sugar Icing. Makes about 8 dozen cookies.

Powdered Sugar Icing: Beat together 1 cup sifted *powdered sugar*, 1 tablespoon softened *butter or margarine*, and ⅛ teaspoon *almond extract*. Add enough *milk* (1 to 2 tablespoons) to achieve spreading consistency. (To use for dipping, add more milk.) Tint with food coloring, if desired.

271

Cookies

Lemon Rounds

- 1 cup butter *or* margarine, softened
- ½ cup sifted powdered sugar
- 1 teaspoon vanilla
- ½ teaspoon finely shredded lemon peel
- 1 tablespoon lemon juice
- 2½ cups all-purpose flour
- ½ cup finely chopped pecans
  Lemon Glaze

In mixer bowl cream the butter or margarine, sugar, and vanilla. Add lemon peel and lemon juice. Stir in flour, mixing well. Using one rounded teaspoon dough for each, shape dough into balls; dip one side in chopped nuts. Place nut side up on ungreased cookie sheet. Flatten with bottom of glass, referring to tip at right. Bake in 350° oven for 22 to 25 minutes. Cool; drizzle with Lemon Glaze. Makes 3½ dozen cookies.

Lemon Glaze: Combine 1 cup sifted *powdered sugar* and 3 to 4 teaspoons *lemon juice* to make glaze of drizzling consistency.

Chocolate-Oatmeal Cookies

- ½ cup shortening
- 1 cup sugar
- 1 egg
- 2 squares (2 ounces) unsweetened chocolate, melted and cooled
- 2 tablespoons water
- 1 teaspoon vanilla
- ½ teaspoon rum flavoring
- 1 cup all-purpose flour
- ½ teaspoon baking soda
- ½ teaspoon salt
- 1 cup quick-cooking rolled oats
- ½ cup chopped pecans

In bowl cream together shortening and sugar; beat in egg. Blend in melted chocolate, water, vanilla, and rum flavoring. Stir together the flour, soda, and salt; stir into creamed mixture. Stir in oats and nuts. Shape into 1-inch balls; place 2 inches apart on greased cookie sheet. Flatten with sugared bottom of glass, referring to tip at right. Bake in 350° oven for 10 to 12 minutes. Makes 4 dozen cookies.

Chocolate Crinkles

- 1½ cups granulated sugar
- ½ cup cooking oil
- 4 squares (4 ounces) unsweetened chocolate, melted and cooled
- 2 teaspoons vanilla
- 3 eggs
- 2 cups all-purpose flour
- 2 teaspoons baking powder
  Sifted powdered sugar

In mixing bowl combine granulated sugar, oil, melted chocolate, and vanilla. Beat in eggs. Stir together flour and baking powder. Stir into chocolate mixture. Cover and chill. Using 1 tablespoon dough for each, shape into balls; roll in powdered sugar. Bake on a greased cookie sheet in 375° oven for 10 to 12 minutes. While still warm, roll again in powdered sugar. Makes 4 dozen cookies.

Butter Pecan Cookies

- 1 cup butter *or* margarine, softened
- ⅔ cup packed brown sugar
- 1 egg
- 2 cups all-purpose flour
- ½ teaspoon salt
  Pecan halves

Refer to: Making refrigerator cookies, steps 1-5, page 266. In mixing bowl cream together the softened butter and sugar; blend in egg. Stir together flour and salt; stir into creamed mixture. Cover and chill 1 hour. Shape into 1-inch balls; place 2 inches apart on ungreased cookie sheet. Flatten in one direction with fork tines, referring to tip at right. Top each with a pecan half. Bake in 375° oven for 10 to 12 minutes. Makes 4 dozen cookies.

272

Cherry Divinity
(see recipe on page 316)
Gumdrop Bars
Chocolate Crinkles

Gumdrop Bars

- 2 cups all-purpose flour
- 1 cup finely chopped gumdrops of assorted colors, except black (6 ounces)
- ½ cup chopped pecans
- 4 eggs
- 1 tablespoon water
- 2 cups packed brown sugar
- 1 teaspoon ground cinnamon
- ¼ teaspoon salt
  Orange Icing

Thoroughly mix flour, gumdrops, and pecans; set aside. In large mixer bowl beat eggs with water till foamy. Gradually add brown sugar, beating till light. Beat in cinnamon and salt. Stir in gumdrop mixture. Spread evenly in greased 15×10×1-inch baking pan. Bake in 375° oven for 15 to 20 minutes or till done, referring to step 7 on page 262.

While still warm, spread with Orange Icing and cut into bars. Remove from pan. Garnish with sliced gumdrops, if desired. Makes 3 dozen bars.

Orange Icing: In mixing bowl combine 2 cups sifted *powdered sugar*; 3 tablespoons *butter or margarine*, melted; 1 teaspoon finely shredded *orange peel*; and enough *orange juice* to make of spreading consistency (about 2 tablespoons).

Saucepan Fudge Brownies

(pictured on page 274)

- ½ cup butter *or* margarine
- 2 squares (2 ounces) unsweetened chocolate
- 1 cup sugar
- 2 eggs
- 1 teaspoon vanilla
- ¾ cup all-purpose flour
- ½ cup sliced almonds

In saucepan melt butter or margarine and chocolate. Remove from heat; stir in sugar. Blend in eggs, one at a time, beating well after each addition. Add vanilla. Stir in flour; mix well. Spread batter in a greased 8×8×2-inch baking pan. Sprinkle with almonds. Bake in 350° oven for 30 minutes or till done, referring to step 7 on page 262. Cool; cut into bars. Makes 8 to 12.

Cheesecake Cookies

- 1 cup all-purpose flour
- ⅓ cup packed brown sugar
- 6 tablespoons butter *or* margarine, softened
- 1 8-ounce package cream cheese, softened
- ¼ cup granulated sugar
- 1 egg
- 2 tablespoons milk
- ¼ teaspoon finely shredded lemon peel
- 2 tablespoons lemon juice
- ½ teaspoon vanilla
- 2 tablespoons chopped walnuts

Stir together flour and brown sugar. Cut in butter or margarine till mixture forms fine crumbs. Reserve *1 cup* of the crumb mixture for topping. Press remainder over bottom of ungreased 8×8×2-inch baking pan, referring to step 2 on page 262. Bake in 350° oven for 12 to 15 minutes.

In mixer bowl cream the cream cheese and granulated sugar. Add egg, milk, lemon peel, lemon juice, and vanilla; beat well. Spread over partially baked crust. Combine nuts with reserved crumbs; sprinkle over all. Bake in 350° oven for 20 to 25 minutes. Cool; cut into squares. Makes 16 cookies.

Apricot-Oatmeal Bars

- 1 package piecrust mix for 2-crust pie
- 1 cup quick-cooking rolled oats
- ¾ cup packed brown sugar
- 1 12-ounce can apricot cake and pastry filling
- 1 tablespoon lemon juice

In mixing bowl combine piecrust mix, ¾ *cup* of the oats, and the sugar; blend in 2 tablespoons cold *water* till mixture resembles coarse crumbs. Set aside *1 cup* crumb mixture; press remaining into bottom of lightly greased 12×7×2-inch baking dish, referring to step 2 on page 262. Combine apricot filling and lemon juice; spread evenly atop mixture in baking dish. Stir remaining ¼ cup oats into the reserved crumbs; sprinkle atop filling. Bake in 375° oven for 30 to 35 minutes. Cool; cut into bars. Makes 2 dozen.

273

TIP To flatten cookie dough shaped into balls, *there are two easy methods. One way is to dip the bottom of a glass in granulated sugar. Then press the ball of dough on the cookie sheet with the bottom of the glass, referring to top photo above. If desired, use colored sugar crystals for light-colored cookies.*

Another method is to flatten the ball of dough with the tines of a fork. If desired, the fork can be dipped in granulated sugar. Make fork marks in one direction, referring to lower photo above, or crisscross fork markings for a different pattern.

Clockwise from left: Saucepan Fudge Brownies (see recipe, page 273); Baked Custard (see recipe, page 84); Cherry Pie (see recipe, page 282); Cranberry-Orange Bread (see recipe, page 223); and Hot Milk Sponge Cake (see recipe, page 246).

PIES

Home-style or fancy, pie ends a meal deliciously. Serve fruit, custard, cream, or chiffon pies in flaky, tender pastry or flavorful crumb crusts. Whatever your choice, you'll find plenty of help and mouth-watering recipes in this section.

Pastry for a Single-Crust Pie

Techniques: Mixing, rolling, and baking pastry for a single-crust pie

1¼ **cups all-purpose flour**
½ **teaspoon salt**
⅓ **cup shortening *or* lard**
3 **to 4 tablespoons cold water**

1 Stir together flour and salt. Cut in shortening till pieces are the size of small peas. **2** Sprinkle *1 tablespoon* water over part of the mixture; gently toss with a fork. Push to side of bowl; repeat procedure till all is moistened. **3** Form dough into a ball.

4 On lightly floured surface, flatten dough with hands. Roll from center to edge, forming a circle about 12 inches in diameter. **5** Wrap pastry around rolling pin. **6** Unroll onto a 9-inch pie plate. **7** Ease pastry into pie plate, being careful to avoid stretching pastry. **8** Trim edge ½ to 1 inch beyond edge of pie plate; fold excess under. **9** Flute edge.

10 For a baked pie shell, prick bottom and sides. Bake in 450° oven for 10 to 12 minutes. **11** *Or,* for dishes such as quiches, line pastry with foil and fill with dry beans. Bake in 450° oven for 5 minutes. Remove beans and foil. Continue baking 5 to 7 minutes longer or till golden brown. Makes one 9-inch pastry shell.

1 Stir together the flour and the salt. Cut shortening into flour mixture till pieces are the size of small peas, as shown.

Use a pastry blender or blending fork for cutting in shortening. Mixing by hand tends to soften the shortening, making a sticky, hard-to-handle dough.

Avoid blending the fat completely with the flour. This produces pastry that's mealy, rather than flaky.

2 Sprinkle *1 tablespoon* water over part of mixture; gently toss with a fork. Push to side of bowl. Repeat this procedure with the remaining water till all the flour mixture is moistened.

The dough should be stiff, but not crumbly. If too much water is used, the pastry will be tough and may shrink; if too little is used, it will be crumbly.

7 Ease pastry into the pie plate, being careful to avoid stretching the pastry. If pastry is stretched, it will shrink when baked.

8 Use kitchen shears or a sharp knife to trim the edge of the pastry ½ to 1 inch beyond the edge of the pie plate. Fold under the extra pastry to build up the edge, as shown.

3 Once all the flour is moistened, form dough into a ball with a fork.

For a double-crust pie or a lattice-top pie (see recipe on page 278), divide the dough into 2 parts and form into 2 balls.

4 Turn pastry onto lightly floured surface (a pastry cloth is ideal to prevent sticking). Flatten dough and smooth edges with hands.

Roll from center to edge with light, even strokes. forming a circle about 12 inches in diameter (about ⅛ inch thick). Reshape into a circle with your hands as you work. Use a floured rolling pin or one with a floured cover, as shown. Add only as little flour as needed, or pastry may become tough.

5 For easy transfer to the pie plate, wrap pastry around rolling pin. To do this, lift pastry cloth with pastry on it so that pastry slides onto rolling pin and rolls around the pin.

6 Loosely unroll pastry onto a 9-inch pie plate. Do not stretch the dough. To repair tears, moisten edges with a little water and press together.

Use glass, ceramic, or dull metal pans for baking pies and pie shells. These absorb heat to brown the crusts. Shiny metal pans should not be used, since they reflect heat and may cause the crust to become soggy.

277

9 Flute edge of pastry. One good method is to press dough with the forefinger (from outside the pie plate) against the thumb and forefinger of the other hand (placed inside the pie plate), as shown. Continue around the dish till entire edge is fluted.

Hook the fluted edge over the side of the plate all the way around, or press it firmly against rim of pie plate.

10 If pastry is to be baked without a filling, prick bottom and sides of pastry all over with a fork. This helps prevent the crust from puffing up by allowing air and steam to escape.

Do not prick if the filling is to be baked along with the crust.

Bake the pricked pastry in 450° oven for 10 to 12 minutes or till it is golden brown.

11 When preparing dishes such as quiches, line the pastry with foil and fill it with dry beans to assure that the crust does not puff up or shrink. Or, line pastry shell with a double thickness of heavy-duty foil; press down firmly but carefully. The weight of the beans or foil keeps the pastry in shape.

Bake pastry in 450° oven for 5 minutes. Remove beans and/or foil; continue baking 5 to 7 minutes longer or till pastry is golden.

Pies

Pastry for a Double-Crust Pie

Techniques: Rolling and baking pastry for a double-crust pie

2	**cups all-purpose flour**
1	**teaspoon salt**
⅔	**cup shortening** *or* **lard**
6	**to 7 tablespoons cold water**
	Pie filling
	Milk
	Sugar

278

Prepare pastry dough, referring to steps 1-7 on page 276. Combine flour and salt; cut in shortening. Sprinkle *1 tablespoon* water over part of mixture; gently toss with a fork; push to side of bowl. Repeat till all is moistened. Form dough into 2 balls.

1 On floured surface flatten 1 ball of dough. Roll to 12-inch diameter. Transfer to pie plate. Trim pastry even with rim of pie plate. **2** For top crust, roll out second ball of dough; cut slits. **3** *Or,* cut out small pieces of pastry to act as slits. **4** Place desired pie filling in pie shell. Top with pastry for top crust. **5** Trim top crust ½ inch beyond the edge of pie plate. Tuck extra pastry under bottom crust; flute. **6** Brush pastry with milk; sprinkle with sugar. **7** To prevent excessive browning, cover edge with foil. Bake as directed in filling recipe. Remove foil after half the baking time.

Pastry for a Lattice-Top Pie: 8 Prepare bottom crust as described in step 1, except trim bottom crust ½ inch beyond edge of pie plate. Roll out second ball of dough. Cut into strips ½ to ¾ inch wide. **9** Place filling in pie shell. Lay *half* the strips on the filled pie at 1-inch intervals. **10–11** Weave remaining strips to form a lattice. **12** Trim strips even with bottom crust. Fold extra pastry over strips to build up edge. Seal together; flute. If desired, brush with milk; sprinkle with sugar. To prevent excessive browning, cover edge of pie with foil. Bake as directed in filling recipe.

1 To make bottom crust place 1 ball of dough on a floured surface. Flatten with hands; roll out to form circle about 12 inches in diameter. Fit into pie plate, being careful to avoid stretching. Trim the bottom crust even with the rim of the pie plate, using a sharp knife.

If making a lattice-top pie, trim the bottom crust ½ inch beyond the edge of the pie plate; use a kitchen shears or a sharp knife.

2 For top crust, roll out second ball of dough. Cut slits in top crust in a decorative design. The slits allow steam to escape while the pie is baking, keep the underside of the crust from becoming soggy, and prevent steam pressure from tearing the crust.

7 To prevent excessive browning on edge of pie, cover it with foil. Fold a 12-inch square of foil in quarters; cut in circle from center. Unfold, place over pie, molding over edge. *Or,* cut long, narrow strips of foil to mold around edge.

Bake pie according to individual filling recipe; remove foil after about half the baking time to allow edges to brown. Foil is not needed for pies that bake less than 30 minutes.

8 To make a lattice-top pie, roll out dough for bottom crust as described in step 1, trimming bottom crust ½ inch beyond the edge of the pie plate.

Roll out second ball of dough referring to step 4 on page 277. Cut dough into strips ½ to ¾ inch wide with a decorative pastry wheel or a sharp knife. Use a ruler to keep the strips straight and even.

3 *Or,* cut out small pieces of pastry with hors d'oeuvre cutters or small cookie cutters to make a fancy design. These cuts will act as slits to allow steam to escape.

4 Place the desired pie filling in the pie shell. Wrap the pastry around the rolling pin and unroll onto the filled pie, being careful not to stretch the pastry; refer to steps 5 and 6 on page 277.

5 Use kitchen shears or a sharp knife to trim the edge of the pastry ½ inch beyond the edge of the pie plate. Fold the extra pastry under the edge of the bottom crust to build up the edge, as shown.

Flute pie as directed in step 9 on page 277.

6 For a glazed, browner top crust, brush the pastry with a little milk and lightly sprinkle with granulated sugar before baking.

279

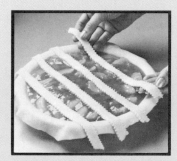

9 Place the desired pie filling in the bottom crust. Lay *half* the strips on the filled pie at 1-inch intervals and all in the same direction, as shown.

10 Fold back alternate strips. Place another pastry strip in center of pie at right angles to the strips that are in place, as shown.

11 Unfold the folded strips and fold back the strips that were straight. Add another pastry strip at right angles to the folded strips and 1 inch away from the last strip, as shown. Repeat this weaving process till lattice top is completed.

12 Trim the pastry strips even with the bottom crust. Fold bottom pastry over the lattice strips to build up the edge. Seal together. Flute edge, referring to step 9 on page 277.

For a glazed, browner top crust, brush pastry with a little milk and lightly sprinkle with granulated sugar before baking.

Put foil in place as described in step 7 at left. Bake as directed in individual filling recipe.

Pies

Graham Cracker Crust

Technique: Making a crumb crust

18	**graham cracker squares**
¼	**cup sugar**
6	**tablespoons butter *or* margarine**

1 Place graham crackers in a plastic bag or between 2 sheets of plastic wrap or waxed paper. Crush into fine crumbs; measure 1¼ cups crumbs. *Or,* crush crackers to fine crumbs in blender. **2** Place crumbs in medium bowl; stir in sugar. **3** Melt the butter or margarine; add to crumb mixture. Mix well.

4 Turn the crumb-butter mixture into a 9-inch pie plate. **5–6** Spread the crumb mixture evenly in the pie plate; pat onto the sides and bottom to form a firm, even crust. Chill at least 45 minutes.

Or, bake in a 375° oven for 6 to 9 minutes or till edges are brown; cool before filling. Makes one 9-inch pie shell.

1 Place the graham crackers in a large plastic bag or between 2 sheets of plastic wrap or waxed paper. Use a rolling pin to crush the crackers into fine crumbs.

Or, break *half* the crackers into blender container; cover and blend till fine crumbs form. Pour into bowl; repeat with remaining crackers.

Measure the crumbs; you should have 1¼ cups.

4 Turn the crumb-butter mixture into a 9-inch pie plate, scraping the crumbs from the bowl with a rubber spatula.

2 Place the graham cracker crumbs in a medium mixing bowl. Add the sugar. Stir with a rubber spatula to combine well.

3 In a small saucepan melt the butter or margarine. Stir the melted butter into the crumb-sugar mixture in the bowl. Mix with a rubber spatula till crumbs are evenly moistened.

TIP Removing a piece of crumb crust pie *from the pie plate is easy if you take a simple precautionary measure. Just before serving, rub the outside of the filled pie plate with a warm, damp towel, as shown. This softens the butter in the crust making it less likely to stick to the pie plate.*

To prepare the towel, rinse it in very hot water, then wring it well.

This procedure is not necessary for crumb crusts that have been baked, since they slide out easily.

5 With your hands, spread the crumb mixture across the pie plate in an even layer. Pat the mixture firmly onto the sides and bottom of the pie plate to form an even crust. Make sure the sides and bottom are the same thickness.

6 To form the top edge of pie shell, press edge firmly between your forefingers, as shown. Make sure the edge is even all the way around.

Before filling, chill the crust for at least 45 minutes to allow it to become firm. *Or,* bake the crust in a 375° oven for 6 to 9 minutes or till the edges are brown. Cool before filling.

Pies

Cherry Pie (pictured on page 274)

Technique: Making a cooked fruit pie filling

  2   **16-ounce cans pitted tart red cherries (water pack)**
1½ **cups sugar**
 ⅓ **cup cornstarch**
  1   **tablespoon butter *or* margarine**
  3   **or 4 drops almond extract**
      Pastry for a Lattice-Top Pie (see recipe, page 278)

1 Drain cherries; reserve 1 cup liquid. **2** Combine ¾ *cup* of the sugar, the cornstarch, and dash *salt;* stir in reserved liquid. **3** Cook and stir till thickened and bubbly. Cook and stir 1 minute more. **4** Remove from heat; stir in remaining ¾ cup sugar, the cherries, butter, and almond extract. If desired, add 10 drops red food coloring. **5** Prepare pastry; fill. **6** Adjust lattice top. Brush with a little milk and sprinkle with sugar, if desired. Cover edges with foil. Bake in 375° oven 25 minutes. Remove foil; bake 25 to 30 minutes more.

282

1 **Cherry Pie**
Drain the cherries by pouring them into a sieve over a large measuring cup or a bowl. Allow the cherry liquid to drain into the cup or bowl.

Reserve 1 cup of the cherry liquid; discard any remaining liquid or reserve it for another use.

2 In a medium saucepan stir together ¾ cup of the sugar, the cornstarch, and dash salt. Blend the cornstarch thoroughly with the sugar so that the starch particles are separated by sugar to prevent lumps from forming. Only half the sugar is added here, because too much sugar can reduce the thickening power of cornstarch.

Slowly stir in the reserved cherry liquid till the mixture is smooth.

Apple Pie (pictured on page 224)

Technique: Making an uncooked fruit pie filling

  2   **pounds apples (6 to 8 apples)**
  1   **tablespoon lemon juice (optional)**
 ¾ **to 1 cup sugar**
  2   **tablespoons all-purpose flour**
 ½ **to 1 teaspoon ground cinnamon**
      Dash ground nutmeg
      Pastry for a Double-Crust Pie (see recipe, page 278)
  2   **tablespoons butter *or* margarine**

1 Peel, core, and thinly slice apples. Sprinkle with lemon juice. **2** Combine sugar, flour, spices, and dash *salt.* **3** Mix with apples. **4** Prepare pastry; fill. **5** Dot with butter. **6** Adjust top crust; brush with milk and sprinkle with sugar, if desired. Cover edges with foil. Bake in 375° oven 25 minutes. Remove foil; bake 20 to 25 minutes more.

1 **Apple Pie**
Peel, core, and thinly slice apples. You should have about 5½ cups. Place the thin apple slices in a large mixing bowl. Use cooking apples such as winesap, jonathan, or McIntosh. If the apples are not very tart, sprinkle with the lemon juice. If the apples are tart, the lemon juice is not needed.

2 In another bowl, stir together the sugar, flour, cinnamon, nutmeg, and dash salt. Blend the flour thoroughly with the sugar so that the starch granules are separated by sugar. This helps prevent lumps from forming when the pie is baked.

If the apples are very tart, use the larger amount of sugar; if they are sweet, you need only the smaller amount.

3 Cook and stir over medium heat till the mixture is thickened and bubbly. Mixture will bubble over entire surface, as shown. Cook and stir 1 minute more so cornstarch will be thoroughly cooked and filling will not taste starchy.

Stir constantly to prevent sticking and scorching; use a figure-8 motion to help filling cook evenly.

4 Remove pan from heat. Stir in the remaining ¾ cup sugar, the cherries, butter or margarine, and almond extract. If desired, stir in about 10 drops of red food coloring. Let cherry mixture stand while preparing pastry.

5 Prepare and roll out the pastry as directed in the recipe. Line a 9-inch pie plate with *half* of the pastry; trim pastry ½ inch beyond the edge of the pie plate.

Pour the cherry mixture into the prepared pastry, as shown.

6 Adjust lattice crust referring to steps 8–12 on page 278. Brush pastry with milk and sprinkle with sugar, if desired. Cover edges of crust with foil to prevent excessive browning.

Bake in 375° oven for 25 minutes. Remove foil; bake 25 to 30 minutes more or till pie is bubbly and crust is golden brown.

If desired, set the pie plate on a shallow baking pan. The pan catches any juice if the pie bubbles over.

283

3 Add the sugar-flour mixture to the apple slices in the large bowl. Use a wooden spoon to toss the apple slices with the dry mixture. When you are finished, the apples should be thoroughly coated with the dry mixture.

4 Prepare and roll out the pastry as directed in the recipe. Line a 9-inch pie plate with *half* of the pastry; trim pastry even with the edge of the pie plate.

Pour the apple slices into the prepared pastry, mounding slightly in the center.

5 Cut the butter or margarine into small pieces; scatter pieces over the apples in the pie shell. The butter adds richness to the pie's flavor.

6 Adjust the top crust as directed in steps 2–7 on page 278. Brush with milk and sprinkle with sugar, if desired. Cover edges of crust with foil to prevent excessive browning.

Bake in 375° oven for 25 minutes. Remove foil; bake 20 to 25 minutes longer or till pie is bubbly and crust is golden brown.

If desired, set the pie plate on a shallow baking pan. The pan catches any juice if the pie bubbles over.

Pies

1 In a large mixing bowl stir together the pumpkin, honey, cinnamon, salt, ginger, nutmeg, and cloves. Mix with a rubber spatula or wooden spoon to thoroughly combine ingredients.

Honey-Pumpkin Pie (pictured on page 224)

Technique: Making a custard-type pie

1	**16-ounce can pumpkin**
¾	**cup honey**
1	**teaspoon ground cinnamon**
½	**teaspoon salt**
½	**teaspoon ground ginger**
¼	**teaspoon ground nutmeg**
¼	**teaspoon ground cloves**
3	**eggs**
1	**5⅓-ounce can (⅔ cup) evaporated milk**
½	**cup milk**
	Pastry for a Single-Crust Pie (see recipe, page 276)

1 In a large mixing bowl stir together pumpkin, honey, cinnamon, salt, ginger, nutmeg, and cloves. **2** Add eggs. **3** Beat eggs into pumpkin mixture with a fork. **4** Stir in the evaporated milk and the milk; mix well.

5 Prepare pastry; fit into a 9-inch pie plate. Flute edges, forming a high rim to hold the filling. Do not prick the shell. Place pie shell on oven rack; pour in filling.

6 Bake in 375° oven for 55 to 60 minutes or till the pie is set. Cool before serving.

4 Add the evaporated milk and the milk; stir in till well combined. The milk is added last so that the mixture will be easier to handle. Once the milk is added, the mixture becomes very thin and is easily splashed.

284

2 Add the eggs. To avoid mixing eggshell in the pumpkin mixture, break each egg into a custard cup or small bowl; skim off any shell fragments before adding the egg to the pumpkin mixture.

3 Lightly beat the eggs into the pumpkin mixture with a fork until blended. It is not necessary to beat air into the mixture, as this recipe makes a very full pie.

TIP Whipped cream *is a favorite garnish for pumpkin pie and other desserts. Make it by beating whipping cream with a rotary or electric mixer till stiff peaks form.*

If you prefer sweetened whipped cream, add 1 tablespoon granulated sugar or 2 tablespoons powdered sugar to each cup of cream before beating it. For best results, chill bowl, beaters, and cream till very cold before whipping.

To freeze dollops of whipped cream for later use, whip cream then drop heaping spoonfuls on a chilled baking sheet, swirling tops with tip of spoon. Place baking sheet in the freezer. When frozen, lift mounds with a spatula; place in a plastic bag. Seal tightly and store till ready to use, up to 3 months. Place atop pie a few minutes before serving to allow cream to thaw.

285

5 Prepare the pastry; fit into a 9-inch pie plate. Flute the edges, forming a high rim to hold the filling. Do not prick the shell or the filling will run underneath and cause pie to stick.

Place pastry shell on oven rack; fill. Pour filling directly from bowl, or transfer mixture to a large measuring cup or pitcher.

If desired, set pie plate on shallow baking pan to catch any filling if it runs over.

6 If desired, cover edges with foil, referring to step 7 on page 278. Bake in 375° oven for 55 to 60 minutes or till the pie is set.

To test for doneness, insert a knife near center of pie. If it comes out clean, the pie is done.

Or, gently shake the pie; if the area that appears to be liquid is less than the size of a quarter, the pie is done. It will continue to set after it is removed from the oven. Cool before serving.

Pies

Oil Pastry

    2   cups all-purpose flour
    1½ teaspoons salt
    ½   cup cooking oil
    5   tablespoons cold water

In medium bowl stir together flour and salt. Pour oil and water into measuring cup; do not stir. Add all at once to flour mixture. Stir lightly with fork till dough holds together. Form into 2 balls; flatten each slightly.

Between 2 pieces of waxed paper, roll out each ball of dough to a 12-inch circle (dampen counter slightly so paper won't slip). Peel off top sheet of waxed paper and fit dough, paper side up, into 9-inch pie plate. Remove paper. Finish pie shell following directions for single- or double-crust pie, referring to pages 276–279. Makes enough pastry for 2 single-crust pies or 1 double-crust pie.

286

TIP Making tart shells *is as simple as making pie crust. To make 10 baked tart shells, prepare Pastry for a Double-Crust Pie, (see recipe on page 278).*

On lightly floured surface, roll half the pastry at a time to ⅛-inch thickness. Cut each half into five 4½-inch circles (reroll scraps, if needed). Fit the dough circles over inverted muffin cups, pinching pleats at intervals to fit around the cups. Prick pastry with a fork. Bake in 450° oven for 7 to 10 minutes or till golden brown. Cool.

Or, cut dough into 5-inch circles and fit into fluted tart pans. Prick pastry with a fork. Bake in 450° oven for 10 to 12 minutes or till golden brown. Cool.

Cookie Crumb Crust

    1½ cups finely crushed vanilla wafers
        (33 cookies) *or* chocolate
        wafers (28 cookies)
    6   tablespoons butter *or* margarine,
        melted

Refer to: Making a crumb crust, page 280. Mix together cookie crumbs and melted butter or margarine. Press firmly into a 9-inch pie plate. Chill till crust is set; do not bake.

Gingersnap Crust

    1½ cups finely crushed gingersnaps
        (23 cookies)
    ¼   cup butter *or* margarine, melted

Refer to: Making a crumb crust, page 280. Mix together gingersnap crumbs and melted butter or margarine. Press firmly into a 9-inch pie plate. Bake in 375° oven for 4 to 5 minutes. Cool before filling.

Deep-Dish Peach Pie

    ¾   cup sugar
    3   tablespoons all-purpose flour
    ¼   teaspoon ground nutmeg
    3   pounds peaches, peeled, pitted,
        and thickly sliced (6 cups)
    3   tablespoons grenadine syrup
    2   tablespoons lemon juice
    2   tablespoons butter *or* margarine
        Pastry for a Single-Crust Pie (see
        recipe, page 276)

Refer to: Making an uncooked fruit pie filling, page 282. In large bowl combine sugar, flour, and nutmeg; toss with peaches till well coated. Let stand 5 minutes. Carefully stir in grenadine and lemon juice. Turn mixture into a 1½-quart casserole or a deep 10-inch round baking dish, spreading evenly; dot with butter or margarine.

Prepare pastry; roll out to a 9-inch or 10-inch circle. Place over peaches. Trim pastry and crimp to edges of dish. Cut slits to allow escape of steam. Cover edges with foil; place dish on baking sheet in oven. Bake in 375° oven for 25 minutes; remove foil and bake 30 to 35 minutes longer or till crust is golden.

Raisin Crisscross Pie

    1   cup packed brown sugar
    3   tablespoons cornstarch
    2   cups raisins
    1⅓ cups water
    1   teaspoon finely shredded orange
        peel
    ½   cup orange juice
    1   teaspoon finely shredded lemon
        peel
    2   tablespoons lemon juice
    ½   cup broken walnuts
        Pastry for a Lattice-Top Pie (see
        recipe, page 278)

Refer to: Making a cooked fruit pie filling, page 282. In medium saucepan combine brown sugar and cornstarch. Stir in raisins, water, orange peel, orange juice, lemon peel, and lemon juice. Cook and stir till thickened and bubbly; cook and stir 1 minute more. Remove from heat; stir in nuts.

Prepare Pastry for a Lattice-Top Pie. Fit half into a 9-inch pie plate. Fill with raisin mixture; adjust lattice top. Seal and flute edges. Bake in 350° oven for about 30 minutes.

Raspberry Tarts

    1   10-ounce package frozen
        raspberries, thawed
    2   tablespoons sugar
    2   tablespoons cornstarch
        Dash salt
    ⅓   cup cream sherry
    6   baked tart shells (refer to tip
        at left)
        Whipped cream (refer to tip,
        page 285)

Refer to: Making a cooked fruit pie filling, page 282. Drain raspberries, reserving syrup. In a small saucepan combine sugar, cornstarch, and salt. Stir in reserved raspberry syrup and the sherry. Cook and stir till thickened and bubbly; cook and stir 1 minute more. Remove from heat; add drained raspberries. Spoon hot mixture into tart shells. Chill. Just before serving, top each tart with a dollop of whipped cream, if desired. Makes 6 tarts.

Cherry-Raspberry Pie

Apple Crumble Pie

- ½ cup sugar
- 2 tablespoons all-purpose flour
- 1 teaspoon finely shredded lemon peel
- 2 pounds apples, peeled, cored, and thinly sliced (5½ cups)
- 3 tablespoons lemon juice
  Pastry for a Single-Crust Pie (see recipe, page 276)
- ½ cup all-purpose flour
- ½ cup sugar
- ½ teaspoon ground ginger
- ½ teaspoon ground cinnamon
- ¼ teaspoon ground mace
- ¼ cup butter *or* margarine

Refer to: Making an uncooked fruit pie filling, page 282. Stir together the ½ cup sugar, the 2 tablespoons flour, and the lemon peel; set aside. Sprinkle apple slices with lemon juice. Toss apples with sugar mixture.

Prepare Pastry for a Single-Crust Pie. Fit into a 9-inch pie plate; do not prick. Fill with apples.

Mix the ½ cup flour, ½ cup sugar, ginger, cinnamon, and mace. Cut in the butter or margarine till crumbly; sprinkle atop the apples.

Cover edges with foil. Bake in 375° oven for 30 minutes. Remove foil; bake 25 to 30 minutes longer. Serve warm with cheese slices, if desired.

287

Cherry-Raspberry Pie

- 1 10-ounce package frozen red raspberries, thawed
- ¾ cup sugar
- 3 tablespoons cornstarch
- ¼ teaspoon salt
- 2 cups pitted fresh tart red cherries, *or* frozen tart red cherries, thawed and drained
  Pastry for a Lattice-Top Pie (see recipe, page 278)

Refer to: Making a cooked fruit pie filling, page 282. Drain raspberries; reserve syrup. Add water to syrup to make 1 cup. In saucepan mix sugar, cornstarch, and salt. Stir in reserved syrup and cherries. Cook and stir over low heat till bubbly; cook and stir 1 minute more. Remove from heat; stir in raspberries.

Prepare Pastry for a Lattice-Top Pie. Fit half into a 9-inch pie plate. Fill with the slightly cooled cherry-raspberry mixture. Adjust lattice top. Seal and flute edges high. Cover edge of pie with foil. Bake in 375° oven for 35 to 40 minutes. Remove foil after half the baking time.

Fruit Melange Pie

- 1½ cups sugar
- ⅓ cup all-purpose flour
- 1½ cups diced fresh pineapple
- 1½ cups diced fresh rhubarb
- 1½ cups sliced fresh strawberries
- 1 banana, sliced
  Pastry for a Double-Crust Pie (see recipe, page 278)
- 1 tablespoon butter *or* margarine

Refer to: Making an uncooked fruit pie filling, page 282. Stir together the sugar and flour. Combine pineapple, rhubarb, strawberries, and banana in a large bowl. Toss with the flour mixture to coat.

Prepare Pastry for a Double-Crust Pie. Fit half into a 9-inch pie plate. Fill with the fruit mixture. Dot with butter or margarine. Cut slits in top crust. Adjust top crust; seal and flute edges. Cover edges with foil. Bake in 400° oven 25 minutes; remove foil and bake about 25 minutes longer.

Rhubarb-Cherry Pie

- 1 21-ounce can cherry pie filling
- 2 cups sliced rhubarb
- ¾ cup sugar
- 2½ tablespoons quick-cooking tapioca
  Pastry for a Lattice-Top Pie (see recipe, page 278)

In bowl combine cherry pie filling, sliced rhubarb, sugar, and tapioca. Let mixture stand 15 minutes.

Meanwhile, prepare Pastry for a Lattice-Top Pie. Fit half the pastry into a 9-inch pie plate. Fill with fruit mixture. Adjust lattice top; seal and flute edges. Cover edges with foil. Bake in 375° oven for 20 minutes. Remove foil and bake 20 to 25 minutes longer.

Pecan Pie

Pecan Pie

1½ cups light corn syrup
½ cup sugar
¼ cup butter *or* margarine
   Pastry for a Single-Crust Pie (see recipe, page 276)
1 cup pecan halves
3 slightly beaten eggs
1 teaspoon vanilla
   Dash salt

In saucepan combine corn syrup, sugar, and butter or margarine; bring to boiling. Boil gently, uncovered, 5 minutes; stir occasionally. Cool slightly.

Prepare Pastry for a Single-Crust Pie. Fit into a 9-inch pie plate; flute edges. Do not prick. Place pecans in pastry shell.

Combine eggs, vanilla, and salt; pour cooled syrup mixture into eggs and beat well. Pour over nuts (pecans will rise to top). Bake in 375° oven for 30 to 35 minutes or till knife inserted near center comes out clean, referring to step 6 on page 285.

Lemon-Pear Pie

2 beaten eggs
1 cup sugar
1 teaspoon finely shredded lemon peel
¼ cup lemon juice
1 tablespoon butter *or* margarine
1 29-ounce can *plus* one 16-ounce can pear halves, drained and diced
   Pastry for a Double-Crust Pie (see recipe, page 278)

In small saucepan combine the beaten eggs, sugar, lemon peel, lemon juice, and butter or margarine. Cook slowly over low heat, stirring constantly, for 3 to 4 minutes or till thickened and bubbly. Remove from heat.

Prepare Pastry for a Double-Crust Pie. Fit half into a 9-inch pie plate. Stir pears into thickened mixture; pour into pie shell. Cut slits in top crust; adjust. Seal and flute edges. Cover edges with foil. Bake in a 375° oven for 20 minutes; remove foil and bake 20 to 25 minutes longer or till top crust is golden brown.

Mock Mince Apple Pie

1⅓ cups sugar
½ teaspoon salt
½ teaspoon ground cinnamon
¼ teaspoon ground cloves
¼ teaspoon ground ginger
3 medium apples, peeled, cored, and finely chopped (3 cups)
½ cup raisins
½ cup jellied cranberry sauce
1 teaspoon finely shredded orange peel
½ teaspoon finely shredded lemon peel
¼ cup lemon juice
   Pastry for a Double-Crust Pie (see recipe, page 278)
1 tablespoon butter *or* margarine

Refer to: Making an uncooked fruit pie filling, page 282. In bowl combine sugar, salt, cinnamon, cloves, and ginger. Add apples, raisins, cranberry sauce, orange peel, lemon peel, and lemon juice; mix well.

Prepare Pastry for a Double-Crust Pie. Fit half into a 9-inch pie plate. Pour in apple mixture. Dot with butter or margarine. Cut slits in top crust; adjust. Seal and flute edges. Cover edges with foil. Bake in 375° oven for 25 minutes. Remove foil and bake 20 to 25 minutes longer.

Cranberry-Raisin Pie

3 cups cranberries
1 cup light raisins
1 cup water
¼ cup lemon juice
¾ cup packed brown sugar
2 tablespoons cornstarch
½ teaspoon salt
½ teaspoon ground cinnamon
½ teaspoon ground nutmeg
¾ cup grape jam
   Pastry for a Double-Crust Pie (see recipe, page 278)

In medium saucepan combine cranberries, raisins, water, and lemon juice; cook and stir about 8 minutes or till cranberries have popped. Combine brown sugar, cornstarch, salt, cinnamon, and nutmeg; add to hot cranberry mixture. Cook quickly, stirring constantly, till thickened and bubbly. Remove from heat; stir in grape jam till melted.

Prepare Pastry for a Double-Crust Pie. Fit half into a 9-inch pie plate. Fill with cranberry mixture. Adjust lattice top. Seal and flute edges. Cover edges with foil. Bake in 375° oven for 20 minutes; remove foil and bake 15 to 20 minutes longer. Cool before serving.

Chocolate-Scotch Pie

1½ cups packed brown sugar
¼ cup butter *or* margarine
3 eggs
1 square (1 ounce) unsweetened chocolate, melted and cooled
½ cup milk
1 teaspoon vanilla
Pastry for a Single-Crust Pie (see recipe, page 276)
Whipped cream (see tip, page 285)

In mixer bowl cream brown sugar and butter. Add eggs, one at a time; beat at low speed of electric mixer just till combined. Blend in chocolate; stir in milk and vanilla. (Mixture may appear slightly curdled.)

Prepare Pastry for a Single-Crust Pie. Fit into a 9-inch pie plate. Flute edges; do not prick. Pour in filling. Bake in 350° oven about 40 minutes or till knife inserted near center comes out clean; refer to step 6 on page 285. Cool; chill, if desired. Top with whipped cream.

Banana-Nut Turnovers

Pastry for a Double-Crust Pie (see recipe, page 278)
4 medium bananas, sliced
2 tablespoons lemon juice
½ cup chopped pecans
⅓ cup packed brown sugar
½ teaspoon ground cinnamon
Milk
Granulated sugar

Prepare Pastry for a Double-Crust Pie; divide in half. On floured surface roll and trim each half to a 12-inch square. Cut each into four 6-inch squares. Place several banana slices on each pastry square; sprinkle with a little lemon juice. Top *each* with 1 tablespoon nuts. Mix brown sugar and cinnamon; sprinkle about 1 tablespoon over each. Fold each square in half to form a triangle; moisten edges and seal. Place on ungreased baking sheet; brush with a little milk and sprinkle with a little granulated sugar. Bake in 375° oven for 25 to 30 minutes or till golden brown. Makes 8.

Apple Turnovers

3 cups all-purpose flour
1 teaspoon salt
1 cup shortening
6 to 8 tablespoons cold water
6 tablespoons butter *or* margarine, softened
4 cups chopped, peeled apples
1 tablespoon lemon juice
⅔ cup sugar
½ teaspoon ground cinnamon
¼ teaspoon ground nutmeg
⅛ teaspoon salt
Milk

Refer to: Mixing and rolling pastry, steps 1–4, page 276. In mixing bowl thoroughly stir together flour and the 1 teaspoon salt. Cut in shortening till mixture resembles small peas. Sprinkle *1 tablespoon* water over part of mixture, gently toss with fork. Push to side of bowl; repeat procedure till all is moistened. Form dough into a ball. Divide dough in half.

On lightly floured surface roll *each half* to an 11-inch square. Spread *each half* with *3 tablespoons* of the softened butter or margarine. Fold each in thirds; cover and chill 30 minutes. Re-roll each portion to an 18×12-inch rectangle. Cut each rectangle into six 6-inch squares.

Refer to: Making an uncooked fruit pie filling, page 282. Sprinkle apples with lemon juice. Combine sugar, cinnamon, nutmeg, and the ⅛ teaspoon salt, toss with apples. Put ⅓ cup apple mixture in center of each pastry square. Moisten edges of pastry with a little milk. Fold in half diagonally, sealing edges well by pressing with tines of fork; place on baking sheet. Prick tops. Brush with more milk; sprinkle with a little sugar and cinnamon, if desired. Bake turnovers in 375° oven for 30 to 35 minutes or till pastry is golden brown. Serve turnovers warm or cool; top with vanilla ice cream or whipped cream, if desired. Makes 12 turnovers.

Fresh Apricot Pie

2 pounds fresh apricots, pitted and sliced (4 cups)
1 tablespoon lemon juice
1 cup sugar
¼ cup all-purpose flour
Dash ground nutmeg
Pastry for a Double-Crust Pie (see recipe, page 278)
1 tablespoon butter *or* margarine

Refer to: Making an uncooked fruit pie filling, page 282. In a large bowl sprinkle the apricots with lemon juice. Combine the sugar, flour, and ground nutmeg; mix with the sliced apricots.

Prepare Pastry for a Double-Crust Pie. Fit half into a 9-inch pie plate. Fill with apricot mixture; dot with butter or margarine. Cut slits in top crust. Adjust top crust; seal and flute edges. Cover edges with foil. Bake in 375° oven for 20 minutes. Remove foil; bake 20 to 25 minutes longer or till golden brown.

Lemon Custard Pie

2 lemons
1¾ cups sugar
Pastry for a Double-Crust Pie (see recipe, page 278)
4 eggs

Finely shred peel from lemons to make 2 teaspoons; set aside. Peel lemons, discarding all white membrane; cut lemons into very thin slices. Remove seeds. In bowl mix lemon slices, shredded peel, and sugar. Let stand 20 minutes, stirring occasionally.

Meanwhile, prepare Pastry for a Double-Crust Pie. Fit half into a 9-inch pie plate.

Beat eggs just till blended. Stir eggs into lemon mixture; pour into pastry-lined plate. Cut slits in top crust. Adjust top crust; seal and flute edges. Cover edges with foil. Bake in 400° oven for 20 minutes. Remove foil and bake 15 to 20 minutes longer.

Pies

Vanilla Cream Pie

Technique: Making a cream pie

Pastry for a Single-Crust Pie (see recipe, page 276)
- **1 cup sugar**
- **½ cup all-purpose flour** *or* **¼ cup cornstarch**
- **¼ teaspoon salt**
- **3 cups milk**
- **4 egg yolks**
- **3 tablespoons butter** *or* **margarine**
- **1½ teaspoons vanilla**
- **4 egg whites**
- **1 teaspoon vanilla**
- **½ teaspoon cream of tartar**
- **½ cup sugar**

1 Prepare pastry; fit into a 9-inch pie plate. Flute edges and prick pastry. Bake in 450° oven for 10 to 12 minutes or till golden. Cool.

2 In saucepan combine the 1 cup sugar, the flour or cornstarch, and salt. **3** Gradually stir in milk. **4** Cook and stir till thickened and bubbly. Reduce heat, cook and stir 2 minutes more. Remove from heat. **5** Beat yolks slightly. Stir in *1 cup* of the hot mixture. **6** Return mixture to pan. Return to gentle boil; cook and stir 2 minutes more. **7** Stir in butter and the 1½ teaspoons vanilla. **8** Pour hot mixture into cooled pastry.

9 To make meringue, beat egg whites with the 1 teaspoon vanilla and the cream of tartar till soft peaks form. **10–11** Gradually add the ½ cup sugar, beating to stiff peaks. **12** Spread over hot filling; seal to edges. Bake in 350° oven for 12 to 15 minutes or till golden. Cool; refrigerate.

Dark Chocolate Pie: Prepare Vanilla Cream Pie as directed above *except* increase sugar to 1¼ cups. Chop 3 squares (3 ounces) *unsweetened chocolate;* add to filling along with milk in step 3.

1 Prepare Pastry for a Single-Crust Pie. On a lightly floured surface roll out to form circle about 12 inches in diameter (about ⅛ inch thick). Fit into a 9-inch pie plate; trim edges ½ to 1 inch larger than pie plate. Turn under and flute edges; prick pastry all over with a fork.

Bake in 450° oven for 10 to 12 minutes or till golden. Set aside to cool.

2 In a medium saucepan combine the 1 cup sugar, the flour or cornstarch, and the salt. Thoroughly blend the flour or cornstarch with the sugar so that the starch particles are separated by sugar. This helps prevent lumps from forming when the liquid is added.

7 Stir in the butter or margarine and the 1½ teaspoons vanilla. The butter will melt from the heat of the filling, and can easily be stirred in.

The vanilla is not added earlier with the other ingredients because some of its flavor evaporates during the cooking process.

8 Pour the hot filling mixture from the saucepan into the cooled baked pastry shell. Use a wooden spoon or rubber spatula to guide the mixture into the pastry shell.

3 Gradually add the milk, stirring till the dry ingredients are thoroughly blended with the milk. A wooden spoon is a good utensil to use for stirring in a saucepan, since the handle remains cool even when the mixture becomes hot.

4 Cook and stir over medium-high heat till thickened and bubbly. Mixture will bubble over surface, as shown. Reduce heat to medium so mixture bubbles gently. Cook and stir 2 minutes more so the starch will thoroughly cook and filling won't taste starchy. Remove from heat.

Use medium-high heat initially because high heat may scorch the mixture, and low heat will cook it too slowly. Stir constantly to prevent sticking.

5 In a medium bowl beat egg yolks slightly. Remove about 1 cup of the hot mixture from the saucepan and gradually stir it into the beaten egg yolks.

This step warms the egg before it is added to the hot mixture. If eggs are added directly to a hot mixture, they often curdle.

6 Immediately return the mixture to saucepan. Bring to gentle boil. Cook and stir 2 minutes more to cook the egg. Stir with a figure-8 motion to keep mixture from sticking. Remove from heat.

Avoid cooking the filling mixture too long. The thickeners tend to lose some of their strength with excessive heat. If cooked too much at this point, the filling may become thin when the meringue is baked.

291

9 To make meringue, in mixer bowl beat egg whites with the 1 teaspoon vanilla and cream of tartar at medium speed of electric mixer about 1¼ minutes or till soft peaks form.

The egg white foam will turn white and the tips of the peaks will bend over in soft curls when beaters are removed, as shown.

Do not beat the egg whites too much at this point or the meringue may leak later.

10 Gradually add the ½ cup sugar, about a tablespoon at a time, beating at high speed of electric mixer for about 4½ minutes or till mixture forms stiff peaks. Using a rubber spatula, guide egg whites toward beaters to thoroughly beat in sugar.

11 When the mixture forms stiff peaks, the foam becomes even whiter and forms glossy peaks that stand up straight when beaters are removed, as shown.

Rub a little meringue between your fingers. When sugar is dissolved, you will not feel any granules.

12 Immediately spread the meringue over the hot filling. Spoon meringue around the edges first, spreading toward the center. Be sure to seal the crust all the way around to prevent shrinkage of the meringue during baking.

Bake pie in 350° oven for 12 to 15 minutes or till meringue is golden brown. Cool; store in the refrigerator. To cut, see tip on page 296.

Pies

Strawberry Chiffon Pie

Technique: Making a chiffon pie

Pastry for a Single-Crust Pie (see recipe, page 276)
- **1 pint fresh strawberries**
- **¼ cup sugar**
- **1 tablespoon lemon juice**
- **¼ cup sugar**
- **1 envelope unflavored gelatin**
- **¾ cup water**
- **2 egg whites**
- **¼ cup sugar**
- **½ cup whipping cream**

1 Prepare Pastry for a Single-Crust Pie; fit into a 9-inch pie plate. Flute edges and prick pastry. Bake in a 450° oven for 10 to 12 minutes or till golden. Cool.

2 Reserve a few strawberries for garnish. In large bowl crush enough of the remaining strawberries to make 1¼ cups crushed berries. Stir in ¼ cup sugar and the lemon juice; let stand 30 minutes.

3 In small saucepan stir together ¼ cup sugar and the gelatin. Stir in the water; heat and stir till sugar and gelatin dissolve. Cool. **4–5** Stir the cooled gelatin mixture into the strawberry mixture; chill till partially set, stirring occasionally.

6 In mixer bowl beat egg whites till soft peaks form. **7–8** Gradually add ¼ cup sugar, beating till stiff peaks form. **9** Fold egg whites into the strawberry mixture.

10 Beat whipping cream till soft peaks form. **11** Fold whipped cream into the strawberry mixture. Chill, if necessary, till mixture mounds. **12** Pour into the cooled baked pastry shell. Chill 8 hours or overnight, till firm. Garnish with the reserved strawberries and more whipped cream, if desired.

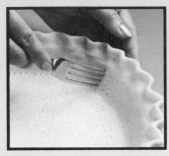

1 Prepare Pastry for a Single-Crust Pie. On lightly floured surface roll out to form a circle about 12 inches in diameter (about ⅛ inch thick). Fit into a 9-inch pie plate; trim edges ½ to 1 inch larger than pie plate. Turn under and flute edges; prick pastry all over with a fork.

Bake in 450° oven for 10 to 12 minutes or till golden. Set aside to cool.

2 Set aside a few of the prettiest strawberries for garnish. In a large bowl crush enough of the remaining berries with a potato masher to make 1¼ cups crushed berries.

Stir in ¼ cup sugar and the lemon juice; let stand for 30 minutes.

7 Gradually add ¼ cup sugar, about a tablespoon at a time, beating at high speed of electric mixer about 3 minutes or till mixture forms stiff peaks. Using a rubber spatula, guide egg whites toward beaters to thoroughly beat in the sugar.

The sugar helps to stabilize the foam, thus preventing it from separating.

8 When the mixture forms stiff peaks, the foam becomes even whiter and forms glossy peaks that stand up straight when the beaters are removed, as shown.

3 In a small saucepan stir together ¼ cup sugar and the gelatin. Stir in the water, combining well. Heat, stirring constantly, till the sugar and gelatin dissolve; cool.

4 Stir the cooled gelatin mixture into the strawberry-sugar mixture. Place the bowl in the refrigerator to chill till partially set, stirring occasionally. Or, set bowl in larger bowl of ice water for faster cooling.

5 Gelatin is partially set when it has the consistency of unbeaten egg whites. Since the strawberries are not smooth, the mixture will appear lumpy, as shown.

Remove bowl from refrigerator or bowl of ice water to prevent the gelatin from further setting while you beat the egg whites.

6 In mixer bowl beat egg whites at medium speed of electric mixer for about 1 minute or till soft peaks form.

At this stage, the egg white foam turns white and the tips of the peaks bend over in soft curls when beaters are removed, as shown.

293

9 Fold egg whites into the partially set gelatin mixture. To fold, cut down through the mixture with a rubber spatula; scrape across the bottom of the bowl; then bring spatula up and over mixture, close to the surface. Repeat this circular down-up-and-over motion till mixture is completely folded together, turning the bowl as you work.

10 Beat well-chilled whipping cream at medium speed of electric mixer till soft peaks form. For best results, thoroughly chill the bowl and beaters before whipping the cream.

Be careful not to beat the cream too much or it will turn to butter. Peaks should mound slightly when beaters are removed, as shown.

11 Fold the whipped cream into the strawberry mixture, using same down-up-and-over motion that is described in step 9.

Chill the mixture, if necessary, till it begins to set and mounds when dropped from a spoon. The mixture will be thick and fluffy, as shown. The mixture may mound without chilling.

12 Pour the strawberry mixture into the cooled baked pastry shell. Use a rubber spatula or a wooden spoon to guide the mixture into the pastry shell.

Chill the pie for 8 hours or overnight, till it is firm. Garnish with the reserved strawberries and additional whipped cream, if desired.

Pies

Lemon Meringue Pie (pictured on page 224)

Technique: Making a lemon meringue pie

Pastry for a Single-Crust Pie (see recipe, page 276)
1½ **cups sugar**
3 **tablespoons cornstarch**
3 **tablespoons all-purpose flour**
 Dash salt
1½ **cups water**
3 **egg yolks**
2 **tablespoons butter** *or* **margarine**
½ **teaspoon finely shredded lemon peel**
⅓ **cup lemon juice**
3 **egg whites**
½ **teaspoon vanilla**
¼ **teaspoon cream of tartar**
6 **tablespoons sugar**

294

1 Prepare Pastry for a Single-Crust Pie; fit into a 9-inch pie plate. Flute edges and prick pastry. Bake in 450° oven for 10 to 12 minutes or till golden. Cool. 2 In saucepan combine the 1½ cups sugar, the cornstarch, flour, and salt. Gradually stir in the water. 3 Cook and stir over medium-high heat till thickened and bubbly. Reduce heat; cook and stir 2 minutes more. Remove from heat. 4 Beat egg yolks slightly. Stir *1 cup* of the hot mixture into the beaten yolks. 5-6 Immediately return mixture to saucepan. Return to gentle boil. Cook and stir 2 minutes more. Remove from heat. 7 Add butter or margarine and lemon peel. Gradually stir in lemon juice, mixing well. 8 Turn filling into pastry shell. 9 For meringue, beat egg whites with vanilla and cream of tartar till soft peaks form. 10-11 Gradually add the 6 tablespoons sugar, beating till stiff peaks form. 12 Immediately spread meringue over hot filling. Bake in 350° oven for 12 to 15 minutes or till meringue is golden brown. Cool; refrigerate.

1 Prepare Pastry for a Single-Crust Pie. On lightly floured surface roll out to form a circle about 12 inches in diameter (about ⅛ inch thick). Fit into a 9-inch pie plate; trim edges ½ to 1 inch larger than pie plate. Turn under and flute edges; prick pastry all over with a fork.

Bake in 450° oven for 10 to 12 minutes or till golden. Set aside to cool.

2 In medium saucepan combine the 1½ cups sugar, the cornstarch, flour, and salt. Blend flour and cornstarch thoroughly with the sugar so that the starch particles are separated by sugar. This helps prevent lumps from forming when the liquid is added.

Gradually stir in the water till liquid and dry ingredients are well mixed.

7 Add the butter or margarine and the lemon peel to the hot mixture in the saucepan. Gradually stir in the lemon juice, mixing well.

The lemon juice must be added last, since the acid in lemon juice can decrease the thickening power of the starch and curdle the egg. Heating the lemon mixture at this point could cause it to curdle.

8 Turn the hot filling mixture from the saucepan into the cooled baked pastry shell. Use a rubber spatula or wooden spoon to guide the mixture into the pastry shell.

3 Cook and stir over medium-high heat till thickened and bubbly. Mixture will bubble over entire surface; as shown. Reduce heat; cook and stir 2 minutes more so the starch will cook thoroughly and filling won't taste starchy. Remove from heat.

Use medium-high heat; higher heat may cause the mixture to scorch, while lower heat will cook it too slowly. Stir constantly so filling doesn't scorch.

4 In a medium bowl beat egg yolks slightly. Gradually pour about 1 cup of the hot mixture (measure for best results) from the saucepan into the beaten yolks, stirring constantly.

This step gradually warms the egg before it is added to the hot mixture. If eggs are added directly to hot mixture, they often curdle.

5 Immediately return all of the egg yolk mixture to the saucepan. Return to gentle boil. Cook and stir 2 minutes more to cook the egg. Stir with a figure-8 motion to keep mixture from sticking. Remove pan from heat.

Avoid cooking the filling mixture too long. Thickeners tend to lose some of their strength with excessive heat. If cooked too much at this point, the filling may become thin when the meringue is baked.

6 After the egg mixture has been cooked, it will be very thick, as shown.

Three thickening agents are used in this recipe—cornstarch, flour, and egg yolks. Because of the high acidity of the lemon juice, all three are needed to keep the filling thick.

Cooking too much at this point will cause the mixture to become thinner, as the thickening agents tend to break down with excess heat.

295

9 To make meringue, in mixer bowl beat egg whites with vanilla and cream of tartar at medium speed of electric mixer about 1 minute or till soft peaks form.

The egg white foam will turn white and the tips of the peaks will bend over in soft curls when beaters are removed, as shown.

Do not beat the egg whites too much at this point or the meringue may leak later.

10 Gradually add the 6 tablespoons sugar, about a tablespoon at a time, beating at high speed of electric mixer about 4 minutes longer or till mixture forms stiff peaks. Using a rubber spatula, guide egg whites toward beaters to thoroughly beat in the sugar.

11 When the mixture forms stiff peaks, the foam becomes even whiter and forms glossy peaks that stand up straight when beaters are removed, as shown.

Rub a little meringue between your fingers. If sugar is sufficiently dissolved, you will not feel any granules.

12 Immediately spread the meringue over the hot lemon filling. Spread meringue from the edges to the center, making sure the meringue seals the crust all the way around. This contact prevents shrinkage of the meringue during baking.

Bake pie in 350° oven for 12 to 15 minutes or till meringue is golden brown. Cool; store in refrigerator. To cut, see tip on page 296.

Pies

Meringue for Pie

3 egg whites
½ teaspoon vanilla
¼ teaspoon cream of tartar
6 tablespoons sugar

Refer to: Making a lemon meringue pie, steps 9–12, page 295. In a mixer bowl beat egg whites with vanilla and cream of tartar at medium speed of electric mixer for about 1 minute or till soft peaks form.

Gradually add the sugar, about 1 tablespoon at a time, beating at high speed of electric mixer about 4 minutes longer or till mixture forms stiff, glossy peaks and sugar is dissolved. Spread over pie, sealing to edges of pastry to prevent shrinkage. Bake as directed in pie filling recipe.

TIP Cutting a meringue pie *is made simple by first dipping the knife into a cup or glass filled with water. The meringue does not stick to the wet knife as it would to a dry one, so the pieces are neater and easier to cut.*

Be sure to cut completely through the crust so the piece of pie does not tear apart as you remove it.

Strawberry Cream Pie

Pastry for a Single-Crust Pie (see recipe, page 276)
⅔ cup sugar
3 tablespoons cornstarch
¼ teaspoon salt
2 cups milk
3 slightly beaten egg yolks
2 tablespoons butter *or* margarine
1 teaspoon vanilla
1 10-ounce package frozen sliced strawberries, thawed
4 teaspoons cornstarch
Meringue for Pie (see recipe at left)

Refer to: Making a cream pie, page 290. Prepare Pastry for a Single-Crust Pie. Fit into a 9-inch pie plate; bake and cool.

In saucepan combine the sugar, the 3 tablespoons cornstarch, and the salt. Stir in milk. Cook, stirring constantly, over medium-high heat till mixture is thickened and bubbly; cook and stir 2 minutes more.

Stir *1 cup* of the hot mixture into beaten yolks; return to pan. Return to a gentle boil. Cook and stir 2 minutes more. Remove from heat; stir in butter or margarine and vanilla. Pour into cooled, baked pastry shell. Cover surface with plastic wrap or waxed paper, referring to the tip on page 339. Set aside to cool.

Meanwhile, in small saucepan combine strawberries and the 4 teaspoons cornstarch. Cook, stirring constantly, till thickened and bubbly. Cook and stir 2 minutes longer. Remove from heat. Cover with plastic wrap or waxed paper, referring to the tip on page 339; cool.

Spread cooled strawberry mixture over vanilla mixture in pastry shell. Prepare Meringue for Pie; spread over pie, sealing to edges. Bake in 350° oven for 12 to 15 minutes or till meringue is golden. Cool; chill.

Milk Chocolate Pie

Pastry for a Single-Crust Pie (see recipe, page 276)
¾ cup sugar
5 tablespoons cornstarch
2½ cups milk
3 squares (3 ounces) semisweet chocolate, melted
3 slightly beaten egg yolks
2 tablespoons butter *or* margarine
2 teaspoons vanilla
Meringue for Pie (see recipe at left)

Refer to: Making a cream pie, page 290. Prepare Pastry for a Single-Crust Pie. Fit into a 9-inch pie plate; bake and cool. In saucepan combine sugar, cornstarch, and dash *salt.* Stir in milk. Cook and stir till bubbly. Reduce heat; cook and stir 2 minutes more. Add chocolate. Stir *1 cup* hot mixture into yolks; return to pan. Return to gentle boil. Cook and stir 2 minutes. Stir in butter and vanilla. Turn into pastry shell. Prepare Meringue for Pie; spread atop pie, sealing to edges. Bake in 350° oven 12 to 15 minutes. Cool; chill.

Marmalade Meringue Pie

Pastry for a Single-Crust Pie (see recipe, page 276)
½ cup sugar
3 tablespoons cornstarch
3 tablespoons all-purpose flour
½ cup orange marmalade
3 slightly beaten egg yolks
2 tablespoons butter *or* margarine
2 tablespoons lemon juice
Meringue for Pie (see recipe at left)

Refer to: Making a lemon meringue pie, page 294. Prepare Pastry for a Single-Crust Pie. Fit into a 9-inch pie plate; bake and cool. In saucepan mix sugar, cornstarch, flour, and dash *salt;* stir in 1½ cups *water.* Add marmalade; cook and stir till bubbly. Reduce heat; cook and stir 2 minutes more. Stir *1 cup* hot mixture into yolks; return to pan. Return to gentle boil. Cook and stir 2 minutes. Remove from heat. Add butter; stir in lemon juice. Pour into pastry shell. Spread Meringue for Pie atop, sealing to edges. Bake in 350° oven 12 to 15 minutes. Cool; chill.

Coconut Cream Pie

Pastry for a Single-Crust Pie (see recipe, page 276)
1 cup sugar
½ cup all-purpose flour *or* ¼ cup cornstarch
¼ teaspoon salt
3 cups milk
4 slightly beaten egg yolks
3 tablespoons butter *or* margarine
1½ teaspoons vanilla
1 3½-ounce can (1⅓ cups) flaked coconut
4 egg whites
1 teaspoon vanilla
½ teaspoon cream of tartar
½ cup sugar

Refer to: Making a cream pie, page 290. Prepare Pastry for a Single-Crust Pie. Fit into a 9-inch pie plate; bake and cool.

In a medium saucepan combine the 1 cup sugar, the flour or cornstarch, and salt; gradually stir in milk. Cook and stir over medium-high heat till thickened and bubbly. Cook and stir 2 minutes longer. Remove saucepan from the heat.

Stir *1 cup* of the hot mixture into the beaten egg yolks; immediately return all mixture to the hot mixture in the saucepan. Return to gentle boil. Cook and stir 2 minutes more. Remove from heat. Stir in butter or margarine and the 1½ teaspoons vanilla. Stir in *1 cup* of the coconut. Pour into cooled baked pastry shell.

To make meringue, beat egg whites with the 1 teaspoon vanilla and the cream of tartar till soft peaks form. Gradually add the ½ cup sugar, beating to stiff peaks. Spread over hot filling, sealing to edges. Sprinkle meringue with the remaining coconut. Bake in 350° oven for 12 to 15 minutes or till meringue is golden brown. Cool; chill.

Banana-Apricot Pie

Pastry for a Single-Crust Pie (see recipe, page 276)
2 cups dried apricots, snipped
1¼ cups sugar
¼ cup all-purpose flour
3 slightly beaten egg yolks
2 tablespoons butter *or* margarine
2 medium bananas, thinly sliced
Meringue for Pie (see recipe at left)

Refer to: Making a cream pie, page 290. Prepare and bake Pastry for a Single-Crust Pie; cool.

In saucepan combine apricots and 1½ cups *water*. Cover and simmer 10 minutes or till tender. Combine sugar, flour, and ¼ teaspoon *salt;* stir into apricot mixture. Cook and stir till thickened and bubbly; cook and stir 2 minutes more. Stir *1 cup* of the hot mixture into yolks; return all to saucepan. Return to gentle boil. Cook and stir 2 minutes. Stir in butter. Arrange bananas in pastry shell; pour apricot mixture atop. Prepare Meringue for Pie; spread over hot filling. Bake in 350° oven for 12 to 15 minutes. Serve warm or cool.

Rhubarb-Raisin Pie

1 cup sugar
2 tablespoons all-purpose flour
½ cup orange juice
3 slightly beaten egg yolks
3 cups chopped fresh rhubarb (1 pound)
¼ cup raisins
Pastry for a Single-Crust Pie (see recipe, page 276)
Meringue for Pie (see recipe at left)

In mixing bowl combine the 1 cup sugar and the flour; stir in orange juice and egg yolks. Stir in rhubarb and raisins.

Prepare Pastry for a Single-Crust Pie; fit into 9-inch pie plate. Flute edges; do not prick. Fill with rhubarb mixture. Cover edges with foil. Bake in 375° oven 30 minutes. Remove foil; bake 25 minutes more or till nearly set.

Prepare Meringue for Pie; spread over hot filling, sealing to edges, referring to step 12 on page 291. Bake in 375° oven for 12 minutes or till meringue is golden. Cool.

297

Coconut Cream Pie

Pies

Peppermint Chiffon Pie

Pastry for a Single-Crust Pie (see recipe, page 276)
½ cup crushed peppermint candy
¼ cup sugar
1 envelope unflavored gelatin
1¼ cups milk
3 slightly beaten egg yolks
3 egg whites
¼ cup sugar
½ cup whipping cream

Refer to: Making a chiffon pie, steps 5–12, page 293. Prepare and bake Pastry for a Single-Crust Pie; cool.

In saucepan combine candy, ¼ cup sugar, gelatin, and ¼ teaspoon *salt*. Stir in milk and yolks. Cook and stir till candy melts and mixture thickens slightly. If desired, tint pink with a few drops of red food coloring. Pour into large bowl; chill till partially set, stirring occasionally. Beat egg whites to soft peaks; gradually add ¼ cup sugar, beating to stiff peaks. Fold into gelatin mixture. Whip cream; fold in. Chill till mixture mounds slightly; turn into baked pastry shell. Chill till firm. Top with additional whipped cream and crushed candy, if desired.

Cranberry Chiffon Pie

Pastry for a Single-Crust Pie (see recipe, page 276)
1 envelope unflavored gelatin
½ cup cold water
1 16-ounce can whole cranberry sauce
1 teaspoon finely shredded lemon peel
1 tablespoon lemon juice
2 egg whites
¼ cup sugar

Refer to: Making a chiffon pie, steps 5–9, page 292. Prepare and bake Pastry for a Single-Crust Pie; cool.

Soften gelatin in water; stir over low heat till gelatin dissolves. Mix with cranberry sauce, lemon peel and juice, and dash *salt*. Chill till partially set, stirring occasionally. Beat egg whites to soft peaks; gradually add sugar, beating to stiff peaks. Fold into cranberry mixture; chill till mixture mounds. Turn into pastry shell. Chill.

Upside-Down Berry Pie

Pastry for a Single-Crust Pie (see recipe, page 276)
2 egg whites
½ teaspoon vanilla
¼ teaspoon vinegar
⅛ teaspoon salt
⅓ cup sugar
2 pints fresh strawberries
½ cup sugar
3 tablespoons cornstarch
¾ cup water
1 cup whipping cream

Prepare and bake Pastry for a Single-Crust Pie; cool.

Referring to steps 9–11 on page 295, beat egg whites, vanilla, vinegar, and salt to soft peaks. Gradually add the ⅓ cup sugar, beating to stiff peaks. Spread on bottom and sides of baked pastry shell. Bake in 350° oven for 12 minutes or till meringue is golden; cool.

Mash and sieve *3 cups* of the berries to make 1 cup puree. In saucepan combine the ½ cup sugar and cornstarch. Add water and the puree. Cook and stir till thickened and bubbly. Cook and stir 2 minutes more. Spread over meringue; chill till set. Whip cream; spread atop. Slice remaining berries over top for garnish.

Sugar Tartlets

Pastry for a Double-Crust Pie (see recipe, page 278)
¾ cup packed brown sugar
⅓ cup whipping cream
¼ cup chopped walnuts

Prepare Pastry for a Double-Crust Pie; roll to ⅛-inch thickness. Cut sixteen 4-inch circles. Fit circles into 2-inch muffin pans.

In saucepan mix brown sugar and cream. Bring to boiling; stir in nuts. Spoon *1 tablespoon* filling into each pastry-lined muffin cup (*do not fill any fuller*). Bake in 375° oven 15 to 18 minutes. Cool 10 minutes. Remove from pans. Makes 16 tartlets.

Pumpkin Chiffon Tarts

¾ cup packed brown sugar
1 envelope unflavored gelatin
1 teaspoon ground cinnamon
½ teaspoon salt
¼ teaspoon ground nutmeg
¼ teaspoon ground ginger
¾ cup milk
3 slightly beaten egg yolks
1¼ cups canned pumpkin
3 egg whites
¼ cup granulated sugar
10 baked tart shells (refer to tip, page 286)

Refer to: Making a chiffon pie, page 292. In saucepan combine brown sugar, gelatin, cinnamon, salt, nutmeg, and ginger. Stir in milk and egg yolks. Cook and stir till slightly thickened. Remove from heat; stir in pumpkin. Chill till partially set, stirring occasionally.

Beat egg whites to soft peaks; gradually add granulated sugar, beating to stiff peaks. Fold into pumpkin mixture; chill till mixture mounds. Turn into tart shells. Chill till firm. Makes 10.

Coffee-and-Cream Pie

⅓ cup sugar
3 tablespoons instant coffee granules
1 envelope unflavored gelatin
¼ teaspoon salt
1½ cups milk
2 slightly beaten egg yolks
1 teaspoon vanilla
2 egg whites
¼ cup sugar
½ cup whipping cream
Cookie Crumb Crust (see recipe, page 286)

Refer to: Making a chiffon pie, page 292. In saucepan combine the ⅓ cup sugar, coffee, gelatin, and salt. Stir in milk and yolks. Cook and stir till slightly thickened. Remove from heat. Add vanilla. Pour into large bowl; chill till partially set, stirring occasionally.

Beat egg whites to soft peaks; gradually add the ¼ cup sugar, beating to stiff peaks. Fold into gelatin mixture. Whip cream; fold in. Chill till mixture mounds. Turn into 9-inch Cookie Crumb Crust; chill till firm.

Apple Swirl Pie

> **Pastry for a Single-Crust Pie (see recipe, page 276)**
> ¼ cup sugar
> 1 envelope unflavored gelatin
> ¼ teaspoon salt
> 1⅓ cups milk
> 1 cup tiny marshmallows
> 2 slightly beaten egg yolks
> ½ teaspoon finely shredded lemon peel
> 2 teaspoons lemon juice
> 2 egg whites
> 2 tablespoons sugar
> ½ cup whipping cream
> 1 cup apple butter

Refer to: Making a chiffon pie, steps 5–12, page 293. Prepare and bake Pastry for a Single-Crust Pie; cool.

In saucepan mix the ¼ cup sugar, gelatin, and salt. Stir in milk; add marshmallows. Cook and stir till gelatin dissolves and marshmallows melt. Stir *half* the hot mixture into yolks; return to pan. Return to gentle boil. Cook and stir 2 minutes. Cool slightly; stir in lemon peel and juice. Turn into large bowl; chill till partially set, stirring occasionally. Beat egg whites to soft peaks; gradually add 2 tablespoons sugar, beating to stiff peaks. Fold into gelatin mixture. Whip cream; fold in. Chill till mixture mounds. Spoon apple butter over; fold in just till marbled. Turn into pastry shell. Chill.

Lime Chiffon Pie

(pictured on page 224)

> ½ cup sugar
> 1 envelope unflavored gelatin
> ¼ teaspoon salt
> 4 egg yolks
> 1 teaspoon finely shredded lime peel
> ½ cup lime juice
> ¼ cup water
> Green food coloring
> 4 egg whites
> ½ cup sugar
> 1 cup whipping cream
> Cookie Crumb Crust (see recipe, page 286)

Refer to: Making a chiffon pie, page 292. In saucepan combine ½ cup sugar, gelatin, and salt. Beat yolks, lime peel, lime juice, and water till blended; stir into gelatin. Cook and stir till mixture thickens slightly. Remove from heat; stir in food coloring to tint dark green. Chill till partially set, stirring mixture occasionally.

Beat egg whites to soft peaks. Gradually add ½ cup sugar, beating to stiff peaks. Fold lime mixture into whites. Whip cream to soft peaks; fold in. Chill till mixture mounds. Pile filling into 9-inch Cookie Crumb Crust. Garnish with shaved chocolate, if desired.

Eggnog Tarts

> 2 tablespoons sugar
> 1 envelope unflavored gelatin
> ¼ teaspoon salt
> ⅛ teaspoon ground nutmeg
> 1 cup milk
> 3 slightly beaten egg yolks
> ¼ cup rum *or* brandy
> 3 egg whites
> ¼ cup sugar
> ½ cup whipping cream
> 10 baked tart shells (refer to tip, page 286)
> 10 candied cherries

Refer to: Making a chiffon pie; steps 5–12, page 293. In saucepan combine the 2 tablespoons sugar, gelatin, salt, and nutmeg; stir in milk and yolks. Cook and stir till slightly thickened. Cool; stir in rum or brandy. Pour into large bowl; chill till partially set, stirring occasionally. Beat egg whites to soft peaks; gradually add ¼ cup sugar, beating to stiff peaks. Fold into gelatin mixture. Whip cream; fold in. Chill till mixture mounds. Spoon into tart shells; top each with a cherry. Chill till firm. Makes 10.

Blueberry-Yogurt Pie

> ¼ cup sugar
> 1 envelope unflavored gelatin
> ½ teaspoon salt
> ¼ cup water
> 2 slightly beaten egg yolks
> 1 cup cream-style cottage cheese
> 1 8-ounce carton blueberry yogurt
> 2 egg whites
> ¼ cup sugar
> Graham Cracker Crust (see recipe, page 280)

Refer to: Making a chiffon pie, steps 3–9, page 293. In saucepan combine ¼ cup sugar, the gelatin, and salt; add water and yolks. Cook and stir till mixture thickens slightly; cool.

Sieve cottage cheese; stir in gelatin mixture. Add yogurt; beat till blended. Beat egg whites to soft peaks. Gradually add ¼ cup sugar, beating to stiff peaks. Fold into yogurt mixture. Chill till mixture mounds. Turn into 9-inch Graham Cracker Crust; chill till firm. Top with whipped cream, if desired.

299

Eggnog Tarts

BAKED SPECIALTIES

Nothing whets the appetite like the aroma of home-baked specialties. In this section, you'll learn how to bake popovers, cream puffs, Danish pastries, and cheesecakes. Try your hand at baking these delicacies, or choose one of the additional recipes at the end of the section.

Popovers

Technique: Making popovers

3	**teaspoons shortening**
2	**eggs**
1	**cup milk**
1	**cup all-purpose flour**
½	**teaspoon salt**
1	**tablespoon cooking oil**

1 Grease six 6-ounce custard cups with *½ teaspoon* of the shortening per cup. **2** Place eggs and milk in 4-cup liquid measure or mixing bowl; add flour and salt. **3** Using an electric mixer or rotary beater, beat 1½ minutes or till smooth. **4** Add oil; beat only 30 seconds more. **5** Fill the well-greased custard cups half full. Arrange cups on baking sheet; place on lower rack in the preheated oven. **6** Bake in 475° oven for 15 minutes. Reduce oven to 350° and bake 25 to 30 minutes more or till browned and firm. (If popovers brown too quickly, turn off the oven and finish baking in oven till very firm.) A few minutes before removing from oven, prick each popover with a fork to let steam escape. Serve popovers hot. Makes 6.

If you like popovers dry and crisp, *turn off the oven and leave popovers in oven 30 minutes more with door ajar.*

1 Grease the bottoms and sides of custard cups with about ½ teaspoon of shortening for each cup. Use a piece of folded paper toweling or waxed paper to spread shortening evenly. Cups should be greased so that popovers will be easy to remove after baking. Cups that are too heavily greased will hinder popovers from rising properly.

4 Add the cooking oil to the well-beaten batter. Oil greatly contributes to the tenderness of the final popover product.

Beat only 30 seconds more. Avoid excessive beating, which will result in popovers that have a tough, heavy texture.

2 Place eggs and milk in 4-cup liquid measure or mixing bowl. Add flour and salt (sifting is not necessary). Flour forms gluten when mixed with a liquid. As the batter is beaten, the gluten develops an elastic quality that later allows it to stretch, forming a shell around the expanding steam.

3 Using an electric mixer or rotary beater, beat eggs, milk, flour, and salt about 1½ minutes or till smooth. The popover batter will be thin.

TIP Prepare Yorkshire Pudding *to accompany roast beef by following the mixing technique for making popovers.*

In a 15½×10½×2-inch roasting pan, retain ¼ cup roast beef pan drippings. Place 4 eggs and 2 cups milk in mixing bowl. Add 2 cups all-purpose flour and 1 teaspoon salt; beat mixture about 2 minutes or till batter is smooth. Pour batter into pan atop drippings. Bake in 400° oven about 40 minutes. Cut into squares; serve immediately with roast beef or other meat.

301

5 Arrange greased custard cups on baking sheet. Carefully pour batter from liquid measure or mixing bowl, filling each cup about ½ full. Slide baking sheet into preheated oven to bake. Do not peek in at popovers during baking. Opening the oven door lets in cool air, which will condense the steam inside the popovers and cause them to collapse.

6 Bake popovers in 475° oven for 15 minutes. Reduce oven to 350° and continue baking 25 minutes more or till browned and firm. A few minutes before removing from oven, prick each popover with a fork to allow steam to escape. This prevents popovers from being soggy. Serve hot.

Baked Specialties

Cream Puffs

Technique: Making cream puffs

½ **cup butter** *or* **margarine**
1 **cup boiling water**
1 **cup all-purpose flour**
¼ **teaspoon salt**
4 **eggs**

1 Grease baking sheet. **2** In saucepan melt butter in boiling water. **3** Add flour and salt all at once; stir vigorously. **4** Cook and stir till mixture forms a ball that doesn't separate. Remove from heat; cool 10 minutes. **5-6** Add eggs, one at a time, beating about 30 seconds after each addition or till smooth.

7 Drop batter by heaping tablespoonfuls 3 inches apart onto greased baking sheet. Bake in 400° oven about 30 minutes or till golden brown and puffy. **8** Remove from oven; split, removing any soft dough. Cool on wire rack. Fill with sweetened whipped cream or a favorite pudding or fruit mixture. Makes 10.

1 Grease baking sheet using a piece of folded paper toweling or waxed paper to spread shortening evenly. Greasing the baking sheet will allow cream puffs to lift easily off sheet when done.

5 Add eggs, one at a time, to the slightly cooled mixture. Beat after each addition about 1 to 2 minutes or till smooth.

(This slight cooling prevents the eggs from cooking before they can be blended into flour-butter mixture.)

2 In large heavy saucepan add butter or margarine to boiling water. Cook over low heat, stirring with wooden spoon, till butter has melted.

3 Immediately after butter has melted, add flour and salt all at once. Stir vigorously over medium heat till thoroughly blended.

4 Once the flour is mixed into the liquid, cook mixture over medium heat, stirring constantly, till it forms a smooth ball that doesn't separate, as shown. Remove from heat and cool 10 minutes.

303

TIP Make eclairs with the same dough you use for cream puffs. *Refer to steps 1–6 of the cream puff technique. Spoon some of the dough into a pastry tube fitted with a number 10 or larger tip. Pipe the batter through the tube onto a greased baking sheet, as shown. Make eclairs about 4 inches long and ¾ inch wide. Bake, split, and cool as for Cream Puffs. Fill with your favorite pudding or fruit filling and frost with a chocolate icing. Makes 14.*

6 After the second egg has been added, the mixture will appear to be separated into clumps, as shown. Continue by adding one egg at a time, beating till mixture is thick, smooth, and slightly sticky to the touch.

7 Drop batter by heaping tablespoonfuls 3 inches apart onto greased baking sheet. Use a spatula to push the sticky batter off spoon. Shape batter into fairly even mounds for baking. Bake in preheated 400° oven about 30 minutes or till golden brown and puffy.

8 Cream puffs are leavened by steam and, being a delicate pastry, may collapse when removed from the oven. This can be prevented by immediately splitting each puff. The puff may have a slightly soggy center. This soft membrane of dough may be removed to leave a crisp, hollow puff. Gently lift out the soft dough with a fork, as shown. Cool.

Baked Specialties

Danish Pastry

Technique: Making Danish pastry

- 1 **cup butter**
- ⅓ **cup all-purpose flour**
- 3¾ **to 4 cups all-purpose flour**
- 2 **packages active dry yeast**
- 1¼ **cups milk**
- ¼ **cup sugar**
- 1 **egg**
  Almond Filling
  Prune Filling
  Confectioners' Icing (see recipe, page 249)

1 Cream butter with the ⅓ cup flour. **2** Roll into a 12×6-inch rectangle; chill. **3** Combine *1½ cups* of the flour and yeast. Heat milk, sugar, and 1 teaspoon *salt* till warm (115 to 120°). Add to flour mixture; add egg. Beat at low speed ½ minute; beat 3 minutes at high speed. Stir in enough of the remaining flour to make soft dough. Turn out onto floured surface; knead about 5 minutes. Let rest 10 minutes. Roll into a 14-inch square. Place *chilled* butter mixture on *half* of dough. **4** Fold over other half of dough; seal. **5** Roll into a 20×12-inch rectangle. **6–7** Fold into thirds. Roll again to 20×12-inch rectangle. Repeat folding and rolling 2 more times. Chill 30 minutes. Divide dough into thirds. Return ⅔ to refrigerator.

8 To make *Almond Fans*, roll ⅓ of dough into a 12×8-inch rectangle. Cut into 4×2-inch rectangles; spoon 1 teaspoon Almond Filling down *center* of each. **9** Fold each lengthwise; seal edges. **10** Place on ungreased baking sheet. Curve rolls; snip side opposite sealed edge. **11** To make *Bunting Rolls*, form remaining ⅔ dough into a ball. Roll into an 18×12-inch rectangle. Cut into 3-inch squares. Place on ungreased baking sheet. Spoon 1 teaspoon Prune Filling in *center* of each square. **12** Fold corners to center; seal.

Let rolls rise till almost double (45 to 60 minutes). Bake in 450° oven about 8 minutes. Drizzle with Confectioners' Icing. Serve warm. Makes 36.

Almond Filling: Cream ¼ cup *butter* and ¼ cup *sugar.* Stir in ¼ cup chopped, blanched *almonds.*

Prune Filling: Combine ½ cup cooked, pitted dried *prunes,* ¼ cup *sugar,* 1 tablespoon all-purpose *flour,* 1 tablespoon *lemon juice,* and dash *salt.*

304

1 In mixing bowl cream together butter and ⅓ cup flour using a wooden or metal spoon. (For easier creaming, bring butter to room temperature.)

2 On baking sheet roll out the butter-flour mixture between 2 sheets of waxed paper. Using a ruler as a guide, roll into a 12×6-inch rectangle. Chill well.

7 Stretch dough gently to even the layers. On the lightly floured surface, roll out the 3-layer piece of dough into a 20×12-inch rectangle. Repeat folding and rolling the dough 2 more times. If necessary, chill dough in between rollings. Chill dough 30 minutes after last rolling. Divide dough into thirds. Return ⅔ to refrigerator.

8 Working on a floured surface, make *Almond Fans* by rolling ⅓ of dough into a 12×8-inch rectangle. Cut dough into 4×2-inch rectangles. Carefully spoon 1 level teaspoon Almond Filling down *center* of each dough rectangle.

3 Refer to steps 1–9 on page 186. Combine 1½ cups of flour and yeast. Heat milk, sugar, and 1 teaspoon *salt* till warm (115 to 120°). Add to flour mixture; add egg. Beat at low speed ½ minute, then 3 minutes at high speed. Stir in enough remaining flour to make soft dough. Knead on floured surface till elastic (about 5 minutes); let rest 10 minutes. Roll into a 14-inch square. Place chilled butter mixture on *half* of dough, as shown.

4 Carefully lift the other half of dough and lay over butter mixture to cover. With heel of hand, seal all 3 edges of dough. Sealing the butter mixture between layers of dough contributes to the rich, flaky layers of the baked pastry.

5 On lightly floured surface, roll out dough into a 20×12-inch rectangle. If dough sticks to rolling pin, lightly rub rolling pin with flour. Apply even pressure when rolling to ensure uniform dough thickness.

6 Gently lift dough, without stretching, and fold into thirds. If butter mixture has softened, refrigerate dough 30 minutes before continuing with next step.

305

9 Using fingertips, gently fold dough lengthwise over filling, as shown. Moisten edges with a little water and seal well.

10 Transfer each sealed pastry to ungreased baking sheet. Curve filled pastries slightly to form crescent shapes. With kitchen shears, snip side opposite sealed edge at 1-inch intervals, as shown.

11 To prepare *Bunting Rolls*, roll remaining dough into an 18×12-inch rectangle. Cut dough into 3-inch squares. Place on ungreased baking sheet. Carefully spoon 1 teaspoon Prune Filling in *center* of each square.

12 Fold 2 opposite corners of pastry to center and overlap edges. Moisten with a little water and seal edges well so they will not unfold. Repeat with 2 remaining corners.

Let Almond Fans and Bunting Rolls rise in warm place till almost double (45 to 60 minutes). Bake in 450° oven about 8 minutes. Drizzle with Confectioners' Icing; serve warm. Makes 12 Almond Fans and 24 Bunting Rolls.

Baked Specialties

Cheesecake Supreme

Technique: Making cheesecake

- ¾ **cup all-purpose flour**
- 3 **tablespoons sugar**
- ¾ **teaspoon grated lemon peel**
- 6 **tablespoons butter** *or* **margarine**
- 1 **slightly beaten egg yolk**
- ½ **teaspoon vanilla**
- 3 **8-ounce packages cream cheese**
- 1 **cup sugar**
- 2 **tablespoons all-purpose flour**
- 2 **eggs**
- 1 **egg yolk**
- ¼ **cup milk**
- 1 **cup halved fresh strawberries**
  Strawberry Glaze

1 To prepare crust, combine ¾ cup flour, 3 tablespoons sugar, and *½ teaspoon* lemon peel. Cut in butter till crumbly. **2** Stir in 1 slightly beaten egg yolk and *¼ teaspoon* vanilla. **3** Pat ⅓ of dough onto bottom of 8-inch springform pan (sides removed). Bake in 400° oven 7 minutes or till golden; cool. **4** Butter sides of pan; attach to bottom. **5** Pat remaining dough onto sides of pan to a height of 1¾ inches. **6** To prepare filling, let cream cheese soften to room temperature. Beat till creamy; add remaining lemon peel and remaining vanilla. **7** Mix 1 cup sugar, 2 tablespoons flour, and ¼ teaspoon *salt;* gradually blend into cheese. **8** Add 2 eggs and 1 egg yolk all at once; beat just till blended. **9** Stir in milk. **10** Turn into crust-lined pan. Bake in 450° oven 10 minutes. **11** Reduce heat to 300°; bake 55 minutes more or till center appears set. **12** Remove from oven; cool 15 minutes. Loosen sides of cheesecake from pan with spatula. Cool ½ hour more; remove sides of pan. Cool 2 hours longer. Place halved fresh strawberries on cooled cheesecake. Pour Strawberry Glaze over strawberries. Chill at least 2 hours. Makes 12 servings.

Strawberry Glaze: Crush ¾ cup fresh *strawberries;* add ½ cup *water.* Cook 2 minutes; sieve. In saucepan combine ⅓ cup *sugar* and 4 teaspoons *cornstarch;* gradually stir in sieved berry mixture. Bring to boil; stir constantly. Cook and stir till thickened and clear. Cool to room temperature.

1 To prepare crust, combine ¾ cup flour, 3 tablespoons sugar, and ½ teaspoon lemon peel. Using a pastry blender, cut in butter till flour mixture is crumbly (butter should be cut up to size of peas).

2 In a custard cup or small bowl slightly beat 1 egg yolk; stir in ¼ teaspoon vanilla. Using a rubber spatula, combine egg yolk mixture and crumbly flour-butter mixture. Mix well to form a soft, pliable dough.

7 Mix 1 cup sugar, 2 tablespoons flour, and ¼ teaspoon salt. Beating on low speed of electric mixer, gradually add sugar mixture to cheese mixture. Use a rubber spatula to scrape sides of bowl. Beat on higher speed to mix all ingredients thoroughly till cream cheese-sugar mixture is light and fluffy.

8 Add 2 eggs and 1 egg yolk all at once to beaten cream cheese-sugar mixture. Beat on low speed till mixture is just blended.

3 Using fingertips, pat ⅓ of dough onto bottom of 8-inch springform pan. Be sure to equally distribute dough on pan bottom so dough will bake evenly. Before adding sides of springform pan, bake bottom in 400° oven about 7 minutes or till golden; cool to room temperature. The specially designed springform pan allows the whole cheesecake to be removed from the pan.

4 Butter sides of springform pan. Use a piece of folded paper toweling or waxed paper to spread butter evenly. Attach buttered sides to cooled bottom portion of pan.

5 With fingertips, gently pat remaining dough onto sides of pan to a height of 1¾ inches. Make sure dough is of equal thickness throughout.

6 To prepare filling, let cream cheese stand at room temperature 1 to 1½ hours or till softened. In mixer bowl beat cream cheese till creamy; add remaining lemon peel and remaining vanilla.

9 Pour in milk, stirring gently with a rubber spatula or spoon till batter is smooth and creamy. Do not beat vigorously, or the excess air incorporated will cause the cheesecake to puff up, then fall and crack.

10 Carefully turn filling into the prepared crust-lined pan. Distribute filling evenly by smoothing with a rubber spatula. Bake in 450° oven for 10 minutes.

11 Reduce heat to 300°; bake about 55 minutes more or till center appears set. Test for doneness by inserting a knife near center. If batter doesn't cling to knife, filling is done.

12 Cool baked cheesecake on wire cooling rack about 15 minutes. Carefully loosen sides of cheesecake from pan with metal spatula. Cool ½ hour more; remove sides of pan. Cool 2 hours longer. Place halved fresh strawberries atop *cooled* cheesecake; pour Strawberry Glaze over strawberries. Chill at least 2 hours.

Baked Specialties

Rhubarb Cheesecake

1½ cups finely crushed zweiback *or* rusks
⅓ cup sugar
¾ teaspoon ground cinnamon
6 tablespoons butter, melted
3 eggs
2 8-ounce packages cream cheese, softened
1 cup sugar
2 teaspoons vanilla
½ teaspoon ground nutmeg
3 cups dairy sour cream
½ cup sugar
2 cups fresh rhubarb, cut into 1-inch pieces (½ pound)
1 pint fresh strawberries
2 teaspoons cornstarch
7 *or* 8 drops red food coloring (optional)

Refer to: Making cheesecake, page 306. Combine crushed zweiback or rusks, the ⅓ cup sugar, and cinnamon; add butter and mix till blended. Press crumb mixture on bottom and 2 inches up sides of a buttered 8- or 9-inch springform pan. Chill.

In bowl beat eggs till foamy. Add cream cheese, the 1 cup sugar, vanilla, nutmeg, and ¼ teaspoon *salt;* beat till smooth. Blend in sour cream. Pour into crust. Bake in 375° oven for 45 to 50 minutes or just till set (filling will be soft). Cool.

In saucepan combine the ½ cup sugar and ½ cup *water.* Heat and stir to dissolve sugar; add rhubarb. Bring to boiling; reduce heat. Simmer, uncovered, about 1 minute or till almost tender, being careful not to break up rhubarb. Remove from heat. Lift rhubarb out with slotted spoon; reserve ½ cup of the cooking liquid. In blender container combine ¾ *cup* of the strawberries and reserved cooking liquid. Cover and blend till smooth. In small saucepan blend cornstarch and dash *salt* with 1 tablespoon *water;* add blended mixture. Cook and stir till thickened and bubbly; cook 1 minute longer. Remove from heat; stir in food coloring, if desired. Cool to room temperature. Halve remaining strawberries; arrange on cooled cheesecake along with rhubarb. Spoon cooked strawberry mixture atop. Cover and chill. Makes 12 servings.

Coffee Cheesecakes

1 tablespoon butter *or* margarine
½ cup crushed vanilla wafers
1 tablespoon sugar
4 egg whites
½ cup sugar
2 8-ounce packages cream cheese, softened
¼ cup coffee liqueur

Melt butter or margarine. Combine with wafer crumbs and the 1 tablespoon sugar. Press into bottom of six 6-ounce custard cups. In large mixer bowl beat egg whites to soft peaks (tips curl); gradually add the ½ cup sugar, beating to stiff peaks (tips stand straight). Beat together cream cheese and liqueur. Fold half of the egg whites into cheese mixture. Fold into remaining egg whites. Fill each prepared custard cup with about ⅔ cup filling. Bake in 350° oven for 20 minutes. (Cheesecakes will puff, then fall when removed from oven.) Cool in cups. Dip bottom of each cup in warm water. Loosen sides of cake with knife; invert onto serving plate. Cover; chill. Drizzle with additional liqueur, if desired. Makes 6 servings.

Banana-Ginger Cheesecake

1½ cups finely crushed gingersnaps
¼ cup butter, melted
1 8-ounce package cream cheese, softened
2 tablespoons sugar
2 egg yolks
½ of a 14-ounce can (⅔ cup) *sweetened condensed* milk
½ cup mashed ripe banana
1 teaspoon vanilla
1 tablespoon all-purpose flour
⅛ teaspoon *each* salt, ground ginger, and ground cinnamon
2 stiff-beaten egg whites
Sour Cream Topper

Refer to: Making cheesecake, page 306. Combine gingersnaps and butter. Press firmly into buttered 9-inch pie plate. Cream together cheese and sugar. Add egg yolks; beat well. Blend in milk, banana, and vanilla. Combine flour, salt, and spices; stir into cream cheese mixture. Fold in beaten egg whites. Turn into crust. Bake in 350° oven 25 minutes or till knife inserted near center comes out clean. Spread Sour Cream Topper over hot cheesecake. Cool; chill. Serves 6 to 8.

Sour Cream Topper: Combine ½ cup dairy *sour cream,* 1 tablespoon *sugar,* and ½ teaspoon *vanilla;* blend well.

Rhubarb Cheesecake

308

Choco-Almond Cheesecake

- 1 8½-ounce package chocolate wafers, finely crushed (2½ cups)
- ½ cup butter *or* margarine, melted
- 2 8-ounce packages cream cheese, softened
- ½ cup sugar
- 2 eggs
- 1 6-ounce package (1 cup) milk chocolate pieces, melted and cooled
- ½ cup dairy sour cream
- ⅓ cup Amaretto liqueur
- 1 teaspoon vanilla
- ½ cup dairy sour cream
- 1 tablespoon Amaretto liqueur
  Toasted sliced almonds

Refer to: Making cheesecake, page 306. In medium mixing bowl combine crushed cookies and the melted butter or margarine. Press firmly in bottom and 2 inches up sides of 8-inch springform pan. Chill.

In mixer bowl beat cream cheese and sugar till fluffy. Add eggs; beat just till combined. Blend in chocolate, ½ cup sour cream, the ⅓ cup liqueur, and the vanilla. Pour into prepared crust. Bake in 350° oven 55 to 60 minutes or just till set. Stir together ½ cup sour cream and 1 tablespoon liqueur; spread over cheesecake. Return to oven for 3 minutes. Cool to room temperature. Loosen sides. Cover and chill. Remove from pan. Garnish with toasted sliced almonds. Makes 12 to 16 servings.

Double Chocolate Eclairs

- ½ cup butter *or* margarine
- 1 cup boiling water
- 1 cup all-purpose flour
- ¼ teaspoon salt
- 4 eggs
  Chocolate Custard Filling
  Chocolate Glaze

Refer to tip on page 303. In saucepan melt the butter or margarine in boiling water. Add flour and salt all at once; stir vigorously. Cook and stir till mixture forms a ball that doesn't separate. Remove from heat; cool slightly. Add eggs, one at a time, beating well after each addition. Pipe dough through a pastry tube fitted with a number 10 or larger tip onto a greased baking sheet, making 4 × ¾-inch strips. Bake in 400° oven about 30 minutes or till golden brown and puffy. Remove from oven. Cut off tops of eclairs; remove soft centers. Cool completely on rack. Just before serving, fill each with Chocolate Custard Filling. Drizzle tops with Chocolate Glaze. Makes 14 eclairs.

Chocolate Custard Filling: Combine 1 cup granulated *sugar*, 2 tablespoons all-purpose *flour*, 2 tablespoons *cornstarch*, and ½ teaspoon *salt*. Gradually stir in 3 cups *milk* and 2 squares (2 ounces) *unsweetened chocolate*, cut up. Cook and stir till bubbly; cook and stir 2 to 3 minutes longer. Stir about 1 cup hot mixture into 2 slightly beaten *egg yolks;* return to hot mixture. Cook and stir just till mixture boils. Add 2 teaspoons *vanilla;* cool. Beat till smooth. Whip ½ cup *whipping cream* to soft peaks (tips curl). Fold into chocolate mixture.

Chocolate Glaze: Melt 1 square (1-ounce) *unsweetened chocolate* and 1 tablespoon *butter* over low heat. Stir in 1 cup sifted *powdered sugar* and 2 to 3 tablespoons *milk*, blending till smooth and of drizzling consistency.

Cinnamon Popovers

- 3 eggs
- 1 cup milk
- 1 cup all-purpose flour
- 3 tablespoons butter *or* margarine, melted
- 1 teaspoon ground cinnamon
- ¼ teaspoon salt
  Butter *or* margarine (optional)

Refer to: Making popovers, page 300. In blender container combine eggs, milk, flour, butter or margarine, cinnamon, and salt. Cover and blend 30 seconds or till combined. Fill 6 to 8 well-greased 6-ounce custard cups half full. Bake in 400° oven for 40 minutes. Remove from custard cups. Serve hot with butter or margarine, if desired. Makes 6 to 8.

Strawberry Dream Puffs

- 2 cups tiny marshmallows
- 1 cup dairy sour cream
- ¼ cup sugar
  Cream Puffs (see recipe, page 302)
- 1 quart fresh strawberries

In mixing bowl combine marshmallows, sour cream, and sugar. Cover and chill several hours.

Meanwhile, prepare Cream Puffs. Wash and hull strawberries. Crush *2 cups* of the berries; slice remaining. Fold all berries into chilled marshmallow mixture. Spoon ¼ cup berry mixture into each cream puff. Spoon 1 tablespoon berry mixture atop each cream puff. Makes 10 servings.

From left: Chocolate-Mint Bombe (see recipe, page 337).
Apricot Chiffon Ice Cream (see recipe, page 334);
Cherry-Almond Ice Cream (see recipe, page 335); Brown
Sugar Peanut Brittle (see recipe, page 318); Fudge (see
recipe, page 312); Divinity (see recipe, page 316); Penuche
(see recipe, page 320); and Caramels (see recipe, page 314).

CANDY

Candies are crystalline and creamy in texture, such as fudge and divinity; non-crystalline and hard, such as brittle; or chewy, such as caramels. All candies are best when made in cool, dry weather.

Fudge (pictured on page 310)

Technique: Cooking candy to the soft-ball stage

2	**cups sugar**
¾	**cup milk**
2	**squares (2 ounces) unsweetened chocolate**
1	**teaspoon light corn syrup**
	Dash salt
2	**tablespoons butter *or* margarine**
1	**teaspoon vanilla**
½	**cup coarsely chopped nuts (optional)**

1 Butter an 8×8×2-inch pan; set aside. **2** Butter the sides of a heavy 2-quart saucepan. **3** In saucepan combine the sugar, milk, chocolate, corn syrup, and salt. **4** Cook and stir over medium heat till sugar dissolves and mixture comes to boiling. **5** Clip candy thermometer to side of pan and continue cooking to 234° (soft-ball stage); stir only as necessary to prevent sticking. **6** Immediately remove pan from heat; add butter but do not stir. **7** Cool, without stirring, till thermometer registers 110°; add vanilla. **8** Beat with wooden spoon. **9** Continue beating till fudge becomes very thick and starts to lose its gloss. **10** Quickly stir in nuts, if desired. **11** Immediately spread fudge in the buttered pan. **12** While fudge is still warm, mark into squares; cut into pieces when fudge is cooled. Makes about 1¼ pounds.

If you live in a high altitude area, *see page 374 for information on adapting recipes for high-altitude cooking.*

1 Butter the bottom and sides of an 8×8×2-inch pan; set aside. Use a folded piece of paper toweling to spread butter evenly.

For thicker fudge use a 9×5×3-inch loaf pan.

Be careful not to butter too heavily or the fudge will feel greasy when eaten.

2 Butter the sides of a heavy, high-sided, 2-quart saucepan from top to bottom. Use a folded piece of paper toweling to spread butter evenly.

Coating the pan sides in this way helps prevent unwanted sugar crystals from forming along the sides when the mixture bubbles up during cooking.

Using a heavy saucepan helps prevent scorching.

7 Let candy mixture cool, without stirring, till the candy thermometer registers 110°. At this temperature the bottom of the pan should feel comfortably warm.

Add the vanilla and remove the thermometer.

8 Beat, lifting candy up and over. Since this fudge mixture is quite heavy, many candy makers prefer to use a wooden spoon for beating. Metal spoons tend to make the hand sore after long use. Do not use an electric mixer, as the heavy fudge could easily burn out the mixer motor.

3 In the buttered saucepan combine the sugar, milk, chocolate, corn syrup, and salt. Besides adding flavor, the corn syrup and the fat in the chocolate help slow down the crystallization of the fudge so that the texture will be creamy and smooth instead of grainy. The corn syrup also helps keep the fudge moist and improves its keeping quality.

4 Cook and stir over medium heat till all the sugar is dissolved and the mixture starts to boil.

Stir gently to avoid splashing over sides of pan.

Remember that any undissolved sugar will cause crystals to form around it and give the fudge an undesirable grainy texture.

Use medium rather than high heat so the milk and chocolate won't tend to stick or boil over.

5 Clip candy thermometer to side of pan, referring to the tip on page 317.

Continue cooking till thermometer registers 234°, stirring only as necessary to prevent sticking; this is the soft-ball stage. Watch closely; the temperature rises quickly above 220°.

If you do not have a candy thermometer, use the cold water test, referring to the tip on page 315.

6 Immediately remove the pan from the heat; set on a protected countertop. Add the butter or margarine, but do not stir.

313

9 Continue beating till the fudge becomes very thick and starts to lose its gloss, as shown. At this point the fudge will seem to stiffen slightly.

10 If you want to add chopped nuts to the fudge now is the time to stir them in. Work quickly (have the nuts chopped beforehand); once the fudge begins to stiffen, it is important to quickly pour it into the pan before it sets.

11 Pour fudge into the buttered pan, spreading evenly. Do not scrape the saucepan; these scrapings have a stiffer, less creamy texture.

If the fudge becomes too stiff before it's put into the pan, try kneading it with your hands till softened; press into pan, or shape into a roll and slice.

If fudge doesn't set, stir in an additional ¼ cup milk; repeat steps 4–9. Do not add more butter or vanilla.

12 While the fudge is still warm, mark it into squares using the tip of a sharp knife; dip knife in water when necessary.

If desired, press a nut half on each square. Cut into pieces when fudge is cool and firm.

To keep fudge at its freshest, cover tightly with waxed paper, foil, or clear plastic wrap and store in an airtight container in a cool, dry place.

Candy

Caramels (pictured on page 310)

Technique: Cooking candy to the firm-ball stage

1 cup butter *or* margarine
1 16-ounce package (2¼ cups packed) brown
sugar
Dash salt
1 cup light corn syrup
1 14-ounce can *sweetened condensed* milk
314   **1 teaspoon vanilla**

1 Butter a 9×9×2-inch pan; set aside. **2** Melt the 1 cup butter or margarine in a heavy 3-quart saucepan. Add sugar and salt; stir thoroughly. Stir in corn syrup. **3** Gradually add the sweetened condensed milk, stirring constantly. **4** Clip candy thermometer to side of pan. Cook and stir over medium heat to 245° (firm-ball stage). This will take 12 to 15 minutes. **5** Remove from heat; stir in vanilla. Pour into buttered pan. **6** When cooled, cut into squares. **7** Wrap pieces individually in clear plastic wrap. Makes about 2½ pounds.

Chocolate Caramels: Prepare as above, except add two squares (2 ounces) *unsweetened chocolate,* cut up, with the milk in step 3.

1 Butter the bottom and sides of a 9×9×2-inch pan; set aside. Use a folded piece of paper toweling to spread butter evenly.

    Be careful not to butter too heavily or caramels will feel greasy when eaten.

5 Remove pan from heat. Stir in the vanilla. Immediately pour the hot mixture into the buttered pan.

    It's a good idea to set the pan on a wire rack so that the candy will cool more evenly.

    If desired, stir some chopped nuts into the candy before pouring it into the pan.

2 Melt the 1 cup butter or margarine in a heavy 3-quart saucepan. Add sugar and salt; stir thoroughly. Stir in the corn syrup.

The chewy texture of caramels is due to the large proportion of corn syrup that is used; this also slows the formation of crystals.

3 Gradually pour in the *sweetened condensed* milk, stirring constantly but gently till blended. The reaction between the milk and sugar during cooking helps give caramels their characteristic color and flavor. Be sure to use sweetened condensed milk rather than evaporated milk, which does not have the needed sugar.

To make chocolate caramels, cut up the squares of unsweetened chocolate and add just after the milk.

4 Clip a candy thermometer to the side of the pan, referring to the tip on page 317. Cook over medium heat, stirring occasionally, to 245°; this is the firm-ball stage. For this recipe, this should take 12 to 15 minutes.

If you do not have a candy thermometer, use the cold water test, referring to the tip below.

315

6 When candy has cooled, cut into squares. For even pieces, use a ruler to mark lines before cutting, as shown. Dip knife in water between cuts, if necessary.

7 Remove caramels from pan. Wrap each piece in a square of clear plastic wrap, overlapping the two long sides and folding under the ends, as shown.

If caramels are difficult to remove from pan, warm over low heat for a few seconds to loosen bottom; turn out onto board.

Wrapping caramels keeps them from sticking to each other. Store in an airtight container in a cool, dry place.

TIP Use the cold water test *if a candy thermometer is not available. Remove pan of candy from heat. Immediately drop a few drops of the boiling syrup into a cup of very cold (but not icy) water, as shown in top photo at right. Use fresh water and a clean spoon for each test. Form drops into a ball with fingers, as shown in bottom photo. The firm-*

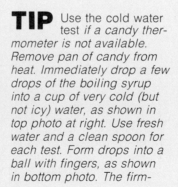

ness of the ball indicates the temperature of the syrup. If the right stage has not been reached, quickly return pan to heat. Remove pan and re-test candy every 2 to 3 minutes till desired stage is reached.

Stage	Cold Water Test
Thread (230°–234°)	Syrup dropped from spoon spins 2-inch thread.
Soft-ball (234°–240°)	Syrup can be shaped into a ball that flattens when removed from water.
Firm-ball (244°–248°)	Syrup can be shaped into a firm ball that does not flatten when removed from water.
Hard-ball (250°–266°)	Syrup forms a hard ball that is pliable.
Soft-crack (270°–290°)	Syrup separates into threads that are not brittle.
Hard-crack (300°–310°)	Syrup separates into hard, brittle threads.

Candy

Divinity (pictured on page 310)

Technique: Cooking candy to the hard-ball stage

2½   cups sugar
½   cup light corn syrup
½   cup water
¼   teaspoon salt
2   egg whites
1   teaspoon vanilla

316

1 In a heavy 2-quart saucepan stir together the sugar, corn syrup, water, and salt. **2** Clip candy thermometer to side of pan. Cook and stir till sugar dissolves. Continue cooking to 260° (hard-ball stage); remove from heat. **3** Immediately beat the egg whites to stiff peaks. **4** Remove candy thermometer from pan. Gradually pour syrup over egg whites, beating at high speed of electric mixer. **5** Add the vanilla and continue beating for 4 to 5 minutes or till candy holds its shape. **6** Quickly drop candy from a teaspoon onto waxed paper. **7** *Or* spread candy into a 10×6×2-inch baking dish and cut into squares. Makes about 40 pieces.

Cherry Divinity (pictured on page 272): Prepare as above, except fold in ½ cup chopped red *candied cherries* after beating candy in step 5.

1 In a heavy 2-quart saucepan stir together the sugar, corn syrup, water, and salt. Using a heavy saucepan helps to prevent scorching.

5 Add the vanilla and continue beating for 4 to 5 minutes or till candy holds its shape. Test as soon as candy starts to lose its gloss. Turn off mixer and lift beaters. When candy falls in a ribbon but mounds, as shown, try dropping a few spoonfuls onto waxed paper. It should stay mounded and not flatten out.

If desired, fold in chopped candied fruits or nuts just before spooning out.

2 Clip a candy thermometer to the side of the pan, referring to the tip at right. Cook and stir mixture till sugar dissolves. Stir gently to avoid splashing syrup on sides of pan.

Continue cooking, without stirring, to 260°. This is the hard-ball stage. Remove pan from heat.

If you don't have a candy thermometer, use the cold water test, referring to the tip on page 315.

3 Immediately beat egg whites at medium speed of electric mixer for 1¼ to 1½ minutes or till stiff peaks form. Tips of peaks will stand straight when beaters are lifted, as shown. Use a large bowl since syrup will be added. Do not use a plastic bowl; oils retained in the plastic may prevent egg whites from forming peaks. For best results, let egg whites stand at room temperature an hour before beating.

4 Remove candy thermometer from pan. Gradually pour the hot syrup over egg whites while beating at high speed of electric mixer.

Be careful not to add syrup too rapidly or egg whites will cook too fast and will not blend smoothly.

The beaten egg whites give divinity its light, airy texture.

TIP Using a candy thermometer *is the best way to ensure a successful candy-making session. Be sure to check the accuracy of the thermometer each time it is used. To test, place in boiling water. If the thermometer registers either above or below 212°, add or subtract the same number of degrees from the recipe temperature and cook to that temperature.*

For accuracy, be sure to read the thermometer at eye level.

Humidity affects the cooking of candy. *If you have to make candy on a rainy or very humid day, cook the candy to a degree or two higher than the temperature given in the recipe.*

If you live in a high altitude area, *see page 374 for information on recipe changes you'll need to make.*

When clipping thermometer to side of pan, *make sure the bulb is completely covered with boiling liquid, not just foam, and that it doesn't touch the pan bottom. This ensures a more accurate reading.*

317

6 Drop candy by spoonfuls onto waxed paper. Work quickly or ask someone to help you so candy doesn't set up in pan. Use a second spoon to push candy off the first one. Swirl the top of each piece, or add a piece of candied fruit or a nut half, if desired. Sticky candy cannot be remedied. To avoid it next time, don't let syrup become too cool before adding to egg whites. Also be sure to beat syrup long enough.

7 If desired, instead of dropping candy into mounds, pour beaten candy into a 10×6×2-inch baking dish; spread evenly. Decorate with candied fruits or nuts, if desired. When candy is firm, cut into squares.

Divinity dries out quickly and is best when fresh. To keep moist, wrap or cover with waxed paper or clear plastic wrap and store in a covered container.

Candy

Brown Sugar Peanut Brittle (pictured on page 310)

Technique: Cooking candy to the hard-crack stage

1	**cup granulated sugar**
1	**cup packed brown sugar**
1	**cup light corn syrup**
½	**cup water**
½	**teaspoon salt**
¼	**cup butter *or* margarine**
2 to 3	**cups raw peanuts**
1½	**teaspoons baking soda**

1 Butter two 15×10×1-inch pans or two baking sheets; set aside. **2** In a heavy 3-quart saucepan combine the sugars, corn syrup, water, and salt. **3** Cook and stir till the sugars dissolve. **4** Continue cooking till the mixture boils; stir in the butter or margarine. **5** Clip candy thermometer to side of pan. Continue cooking, without stirring, to 230° (thread stage). Cook and stir to 280° (soft-crack stage) **6** Stir in the peanuts. **7** Cook, stirring constantly, to 300° (hard-crack stage). Remove pan from heat. **8** Quickly stir in the soda, mixing well. **9** Pour onto the buttered pans, spreading evenly. **10** As candy cools, stretch it by lifting and pulling with two forks. **11** Break candy into pieces when cool. Makes about 2 pounds.

318

1 Butter two 15×10×1-inch pans or two baking sheets. Use a folded piece of paper toweling to evenly spread a small amount of butter or margarine over the bottom of the pans; set aside.

Be careful not to butter too heavily or the candy will feel greasy when eaten.

2 In a heavy 3-quart saucepan combine the sugars, corn syrup, water, and salt. The corn syrup helps to prevent crystallization and so helps to keep the candy from becoming sugary. Using a heavy saucepan helps prevent scorching.

7 Continue cooking; stir constantly but gently, till thermometer registers 300°. Immediately remove pan from heat; further cooking will give candy a burned taste. This is the hard-crack stage. At this point the sugar starts to caramelize, giving candy a darker color. This caramelization plus the use of corn syrup helps prevent crystallization. If you don't have a candy thermometer, use the cold water test, referring to tip on page 315.

8 Quickly stir in the soda, mixing well. The candy will foam as the baking soda reacts chemically to neutralize the acid of the caramelized sugar. This makes the brittle porous and tender.

3 Cook and stir mixture over medium heat till all the sugar is dissolved. Stir gently to avoid splashing syrup on the sides of the pan where it may form undesirable crystals. Undissolved sugar also may cause crystals to form, giving the candy a grainy texture.

Use a wooden spoon since it won't become uncomfortably hot.

4 Continue cooking, stirring only occasionally, until the syrup begins to boil. Stir in the butter or margarine; it adds richness to the flavor of the brittle.

5 Clip a candy thermometer to the side of the pan, referring to the tip on page 317. Continue cooking, without stirring, to 230°. This is the thread stage.

Continue cooking, stirring frequently but gently, till thermometer registers 280°. This is the soft-crack stage.

If you don't have a candy thermometer, use the cold water test, referring to the tip on page 315.

6 Stir in the peanuts; there's no need to skin them. Make sure you use raw (unroasted) peanuts because roasted nuts would taste overcooked and scorched.

If desired, other unroasted nuts may be substituted for the peanuts.

319

9 Immediately pour the candy onto the buttered pans, spreading as evenly as possible. Do not scrape the sides of the pan.

10 As the candy cools, stretch it by lifting and pulling with two forks, as shown. Stretch gently to avoid tearing the candy.

11 When candy is completely cooled, break it into pieces. An easy way to do this is to crack it with the handle of a wooden spoon or with the back of a heavy knife, as shown.

Candy

Coconut Bonbons

⅓ cup light corn syrup
¼ cup sugar
2 tablespoons water
1 3½-ounce can (1⅓ cups) flaked coconut
¼ teaspoon vanilla
1½ pounds white almond bark *or* confectioners' coating, finely chopped or grated
Food coloring (optional)

Lightly butter the bottom of a shallow baking pan; set aside. In 1-quart saucepan mix corn syrup, sugar, and water. Cook and stir over low heat till sugar dissolves. Cook, without stirring, to 238° (soft-ball stage); refer to step 5 on page 313. Stir in coconut and vanilla. Spread in buttered pan. Cool 1 hour. Shape into 36 balls. Cover; chill 1 hour.

In small saucepan melt almond bark or confectioners' coating over low heat; stir constantly. Tint with food coloring, if desired. Spoon 1 teaspoon coating mixture into each of thirty-six 1¼-inch paper bonbon cups. Place one coconut ball in each. Add enough coating mixture to cover coconut and fill cups. Makes 36.

TIP Controlling the formation of sugar crystals *is the candymaker's goal. Do this by stirring until all the sugar dissolves. Stirring throws some of the syrup onto the sides of the pan where sugar crystals can form. To dissolve them by steaming, cover the pan for 3 minutes; watch carefully so the candy doesn't boil over. Once the sugar is dissolved, avoid stirring unless directed.*

During later cooking, any sugar crystals may be wiped from the sides of the pan with a pastry brush or cloth-wrapped fork. Keep a glass of water handy for rinsing. Also rinse and dry the spoon every time it is removed.

Eggnog Fudge

2 cups sugar
1 cup eggnog
1 tablespoon light corn syrup
2 tablespoons butter *or* margarine
1 teaspoon vanilla
½ cup chopped walnuts
2 tablespoons semisweet chocolate pieces
2 teaspoons butter *or* margarine

Refer to: Cooking candy to the soft-ball stage, page 312. Butter bottom and sides of an 8×4×2-inch loaf pan; set aside. Butter sides of a heavy 3-quart saucepan. In saucepan combine the sugar, eggnog, and corn syrup. Cook over medium heat, stirring constantly, till sugar dissolves and mixture comes to a boil. Cook to 238° (soft-ball stage), stirring only as necessary. Immediately remove from heat. Add the 2 tablespoons butter or margarine and the vanilla. Cool to 110°; do not stir.

Beat till fudge becomes very thick and starts to lose its gloss. Quickly stir in nuts. Spread in prepared pan. In glass 1-cup measure, combine chocolate pieces and 2 teasooons butter or margarine; set in saucepan filled with 1 inch of water; heat till chocolate melts. Drizzle over top of fudge; score in squares while warm. Cut when cool and firm. Makes about 1 pound candy.

Maple Sponge Candy

1 cup maple-flavored syrup
½ cup sugar
2 teaspoons white vinegar
2 teaspoons baking soda

Refer to: Cooking candy to the hard-crack stage, page 318. Butter a 9×9×2-inch pan; set aside. In heavy 2-quart saucepan combine syrup, sugar, and vinegar. Bring to boiling over medium heat, stirring till sugar dissolves. Continue cooking without stirring to 300° (hard-crack stage).

Remove from heat; quickly stir in soda and mix well. Immediately pour into buttered pan; do not spread. Cool; break into pieces. Makes about ½ pound candy.

Penuche

(pictured on page 310)

1½ cups granulated sugar
1 cup packed brown sugar
⅓ cup light cream
⅓ cup milk
2 tablespoons butter *or* margarine
1 teaspoon vanilla
½ cup chopped walnuts *or* pecans

Refer to: Cooking candy to the soft-ball stage, page 312. Butter an 8×8×2-inch pan; set aside. Butter sides of a heavy 2-quart saucepan. In saucepan combine sugars, cream, and milk. Cook over medium heat, stirring constantly, till sugars dissolve and mixture boils. Cook to 238° (soft-ball stage), stirring only as necessary. Immediately remove from heat. Cool to 110°; do not stir. Add butter or margarine and vanilla. Beat till candy becomes very thick and loses its gloss. Quickly stir in nuts and spread in prepared pan. Score while warm. Cover and refrigerate. Cut when firm. Makes about 1¼ pounds.

Mocha Fudge

3 cups sugar
½ cup unsweetened cocoa powder
1 cup strong coffee
3 tablespoons butter *or* margarine
1½ teaspoons vanilla
Pecan halves

Refer to: Cooking candy to the soft-ball stage, page 312. Butter bottom and sides of a 9×5×3-inch loaf pan; set aside. Butter sides of heavy 3-quart saucepan. In saucepan combine sugar and cocoa powder. Stir in coffee. Cook over medium heat, stirring constantly, till sugar dissolves and mixture boils. Cook to 238° (soft-ball stage), stirring only as necessary. Immediately remove from heat; add butter or margarine and vanilla. Cool to 110°; do not stir. Beat till mixture thickens and loses its gloss. Turn into prepared pan. Score in squares while warm. Press a pecan half into each square. Cover and refrigerate. Cut when firm. Makes about 1 pound.

Sesame Seed Brittle

2 1⅞-ounce cans (¾ cup) sesame
  seed
1 cup sugar
½ teaspoon vanilla

Butter a baking sheet; set aside. Spread sesame seed in large baking pan. Toast in 350° oven for 15 to 20 minutes or till lightly browned; stir occasionally. In heavy saucepan cook and stir sugar over low heat till melted and golden brown, referring to caramelizing sugar, page 371. Remove from heat; quickly stir in sesame seed and vanilla. Pour onto buttered baking sheet; spread thinly, referring to steps 9 and 10 on page 319. Cool; break up. Makes about ½ pound.

Brown Sugar Pralines

2 cups packed dark brown sugar
1 cup light cream
2 tablespoons butter *or* margarine
2 cups pecan halves *or* pieces

In heavy 2-quart saucepan combine sugar and cream; mix well. Bring to boiling over medium heat, stirring constantly. Cook and stir to 238° (soft-ball stage), referring to step 5 on page 313. Remove from heat; add butter. Stir in pecans. Beat about 1 minute or till candy just begins to lose its gloss. Drop by tablespoonfuls onto waxed paper, shaping into patties with back of spoon. If the candy becomes too stiff to drop, add a little hot water to make the right consistency. Makes 24.

Jewel Candies

1 cup sugar
½ cup light corn syrup
⅓ cup water
¼ teaspoon anise oil
3 or 4 drops food coloring (any
  color)

Refer to: Cooking candy to the hard-crack stage, steps 2, 3, and 7, page 318. Line an 8×8×2-inch pan with foil, extending foil up sides; butter foil. Butter sides of heavy 1-quart saucepan; add sugar, corn syrup, and water, mixing well. Bring to boiling, stirring constantly till sugar is dissolved. Cook over medium heat to 300° (hard-crack stage). Remove from heat; add anise oil and food coloring. Pour into prepared pan at once.

After about 5 minutes, when candy is just beginning to set around the edges, carefully lift foil out of pan; candy will still be hot and pliable. Cut candy into 1-inch strips by pressing straight down with a knife. *Working quickly,* use scissors to cut strips into very small pieces of irregular shape. *This requires 2 or 3 people cutting at once;* make only one batch at a time. Makes about ¾ pound.

321

Jewel Candies
Brown Sugar Pralines

Peanut Butter Divinity

2½ cups sugar
½ cup light corn syrup
½ cup water
2 egg whites
½ cup chunky peanut butter

Refer to: Cooking candy to the hard-ball stage, page 316. In heavy 2-quart saucepan combine sugar, corn syrup, and water. Bring to boiling. Cook to 260° (hard-ball stage), stirring only till sugar dissolves; remove from heat. In large mixer bowl immediately beat egg whites to stiff peaks. Gradually pour syrup over egg whites, beating at high speed of electric mixer. Add peanut butter and beat for 3 to 4 minutes more or till candy holds its shape. Quickly drop from a teaspoon onto waxed paper. Makes about 40 pieces.

Chocolate Caramel Apples

Chocolate Caramel Apples

12 small, crisp, tart apples
12 wooden skewers
 1 cup butter *or* margarine
 1 16-ounce package (2¼ cups packed) brown sugar
   Dash salt
 1 cup light corn syrup
 1 14-ounce can (1⅓ cups) *sweetened condensed* milk
 2 squares (2 ounces) unsweetened chocolate
 1 teaspoon vanilla
 1 cup chopped peanuts

Refer to: Cooking candy to the firm-ball stage, page 314. Butter a baking sheet; set aside. Wash and dry apples; remove stems. Insert a skewer into stem end of each; set aside. In heavy 3-quart saucepan melt butter or margarine. Stir in brown sugar and salt. Add corn syrup; mix well. Gradually stir in milk; add chocolate. Cook over medium heat, stirring constantly, 12 to 15 minutes or till candy thermometer registers 245° (firm-ball stage). Remove from heat; stir in vanilla. Dip each apple into chocolate mixture, turning to coat. With narrow spatula, scrape excess caramel from bottom of apple and let drip back into pan. Immediately dip bottom half of apples in chopped peanuts. Set on buttered baking sheet to cool. Makes 12 caramel apples.

Liqueur-Flavored Wafers

 ¼ cup butter *or* margarine
 ⅓ cup green crème de menthe *or* coffee liqueur *or* crème de cacao *or* Galliano liqueur
 1 package creamy white frosting mix

Melt butter with liqueur over (but not touching) boiling water in top of double boiler. Add frosting mix; mix well. Cook and stir about 5 minutes or till smooth and glossy. Drop from teaspoon onto waxed paper, swirling tops of candies. If candy hardens, add a few drops warmed milk. Cool. Makes 72 pieces (about 1 pound).

Chewy Maple Caramels

1½ cups light cream
 1 cup granulated sugar
 ½ cup packed brown sugar
 ½ cup light corn syrup
 ¼ cup butter *or* margarine
 1 teaspoon maple flavoring

Refer to: Cooking candy to the firm-ball stage, page 314. Line 9×5×3-inch loaf pan with foil; lightly butter bottom and sides. In 2-quart saucepan combine cream, sugars, corn syrup, and butter. Cook and stir over low heat till sugars dissolve. Cook over medium heat to 248° (firm-ball stage); stir occasionally. Remove from heat; stir in flavoring. Turn into prepared pan; cool. Turn out onto cutting board; cut into 48 pieces. Wrap individually in waxed paper or clear plastic wrap. Makes 48 caramels.

Marshmallow Fudge

 4 cups sugar
 1 13-ounce can evaporated milk
 1 cup butter *or* margarine
 1 12-ounce package semisweet chocolate pieces
 1 7-, 9-, *or* 10-ounce jar marshmallow creme
 1 cup chopped walnuts
 1 teaspoon vanilla

Refer to: Cooking candy to the soft-ball stage, page 312. Lightly butter bottom and sides of a 13×9×2-inch baking pan; set aside. In 3-quart saucepan cook sugar, evaporated milk, and butter to 236° (soft-ball stage); stir frequently. Remove from heat. Stir in chocolate, marshmallow creme, walnuts, and vanilla till blended. Pour into buttered pan. Score while warm; cut when cool. Makes 54 pieces.

Brazil Nut Fudge Slices

- 2 cups sugar
- 1 cup maple-flavored syrup
- ½ cup milk
- 2 squares (2 ounces) unsweetened chocolate, cut up
  Dash salt
- 2 tablespoons butter or margarine
- 1 teaspoon vanilla
- 1 cup coarsely chopped Brazil nuts

Refer to: Cooking candy to the soft-ball stage, page 312. Butter a baking sheet; set aside. Butter sides of a heavy 3-quart saucepan. In saucepan combine sugar, maple-flavored syrup, milk, chocolate, and salt. Cook and stir over medium heat till sugar dissolves and mixture comes to boiling. Cook to 236° (soft-ball stage), stirring occasionally. Immediately remove pan from heat. Add butter or margarine; cool, without stirring, to 110°. Add vanilla. Beat about 10 minutes or till mixture begins to lose its gloss. Beat in nuts. Divide into two equal portions, spooning each onto buttered baking sheet. Shape with buttered hands into two 8-inch logs; cool. Slice when firm, or wrap unsliced logs in waxed paper and store at room temperature. Makes about 1½ pounds candy.

Molasses Popcorn

- 1 cup sugar
- ½ cup water
- ¼ cup molasses
- 1 tablespoon vinegar
  Dash salt
- 1 tablespoon butter or margarine
- 1 teaspoon vanilla
- 2 quarts popped corn (½ cup unpopped)
- 1 cup Spanish peanuts

In heavy 1½-quart saucepan combine sugar, water, molasses, vinegar, and salt. Place over medium heat; cover and heat to boiling. Uncover; clip on candy thermometer. Cook to 272° (soft-crack stage) referring to step 5 on page 319. Stir in butter or margarine and vanilla. In large bowl combine popped corn and peanuts; slowly pour on syrup, tossing till well-coated. Makes 2 quarts.

Pecan Roll

- 1 7-, 9-, or 10-ounce jar marshmallow creme
- 2 tablespoons butter or margarine, softened
- 1 tablespoon vanilla
- 1 16-ounce package (4½ cups) powdered sugar, sifted
- 1 14-ounce package vanilla caramels
- ¼ cup milk
- 1½ cups chopped pecans

In a small mixer bowl combine marshmallow creme, butter or margarine, and vanilla. Using low speed of electric mixer, gradually beat in about half of the powdered sugar. By hand, stir in enough of the remaining sugar to make a stiff mixture. Turn out onto a clean surface and knead in the remaining sugar. Wrap and chill about 2 hours or till firm.

In saucepan combine caramels and milk. Heat over low heat till melted, stirring occassionally. Cool slightly. Form chilled marshmallow creme mixture into four 6-inch logs. Sprinkle nuts on a sheet of waxed paper. With knife or narrow spatula, spread melted caramel over the top and sides of one log; invert onto nuts. Spread uncoated side with caramel; coat with nuts. Repeat with remaining logs. Wrap. Store in refrigerator; slice ½-inch-thick. Makes 48 slices.

Pecan Candy

- 1 cup granulated sugar
- 1 cup finely chopped pecans
- 1 teaspoon vanilla
- ⅛ teaspoon salt

Butter a baking sheet or board and a rolling pin; set aside. In 10-inch skillet over low heat, cook and stir sugar till melted and golden brown. Stir in pecans, vanilla, and salt. Pour immediately onto buttered baking sheet or board. Roll quickly with buttered rolling pin to 8×8-inch square; cut into diamonds or squares or break into small pieces. Makes about ½ pound.

Cranberry Fudge

- 2 cups sugar
- ½ cup milk
- ½ cup light cream
- 1 tablespoon light corn syrup
- ½ teaspoon salt
- 1 tablespoon butter or margarine
- 1 teaspoon vanilla
- ½ cup fresh cranberries, chopped

Refer to: Cooking candy to the soft-ball stage, page 312. Butter a 9×5×3-inch loaf pan; set aside. Butter sides of heavy 2-quart saucepan. In saucepan combine sugar, milk, cream, corn syrup, and salt. Cook and stir over medium heat till mixture boils. Cook to 238° (soft-ball stage). Immediately remove from heat. Add butter or margarine. Cool to 110°; do not stir. Add vanilla. Beat about 5 minutes or till mixture becomes very thick and starts to lose its gloss. Quickly stir in cranberries; spread in buttered pan. Score while warm; cut when cool. Use candy within a few days; since cranberries tend to water out. Makes 30 pieces.

Buttery Molasses Taffy

- 2 cups sugar
- 1½ cups water
- 1 cup molasses
- ½ cup butter or margarine
- ¼ cup light corn syrup

Butter a platter or shallow baking pan; set aside. Butter a heavy 3-quart saucepan. In saucepan combine sugar, water, molasses, butter or margarine, and corn syrup. Cook over low heat, stirring till sugar is dissolved. Bring to boiling; boil gently till candy thermometer registers 266° (hard-ball stage), referring to step 2 on page 317. Pour onto buttered platter or pan.

Cool 10 to 15 minutes or till easily handled. Butter hands lightly and pull candy till light in color and difficult to pull; you'll need 3 or 4 helpers. On countertop, rub and twist candy into ropes, ½ inch in diameter; cut into 1-inch pieces. Wrap each piece individually in clear plastic wrap. Makes about 1½ pounds.

ICE CREAM AND FROZEN DESSERTS

In this section, learn to make ice cream in a crank-type freezer, as well as in your refrigerator freezer. Then discover elegant ways to serve ice cream in bombes, baked alaskas, and other frozen desserts.

Vanilla Custard Ice Cream

Technique: Freezing cooked ice cream in an ice cream freezer

1½	cups sugar
¼	cup all-purpose flour
4	cups milk (1 quart)
4	beaten eggs
4	cups whipping cream (2 pints)
3	tablespoons vanilla
	Rock salt

1 Combine sugar, flour, and ½ teaspoon *salt*. Stir in milk. **2** Cook and stir over medium-high heat till slightly thickened and bubbly. **3** Stir about 1 cup hot mixture into eggs. **4** Return to hot mixture. Cook and stir 1 minute. Chill.

5 Stir in cream and vanilla. **6** Pour into ice cream freezer can till ⅔ full. **7** Fit can into freezer. Adjust dasher; cover. Pack *crushed ice* and rock salt around can. Turn handle till crank turns hard. **8** Remove ice to below lid. Remove lid and dasher, scraping off ice cream.

9 Cover can with several thicknesses of waxed paper or foil. Plug opening in lid; replace lid. Pack more ice and salt around can. Cover with heavy cloth or newspaper. Let ripen 4 hours. **10** Uncover freezer. Remove ice to below lid; remove lid. Makes 2½ quarts.

1 In a 3-quart saucepan thoroughly stir together the sugar, flour, and ½ teaspoon salt. Gradually stir in milk till ingredients are thoroughly combined and mixture is smooth.

The sugar contributes a smooth texture as well as added flavor. The level of sugar in ice cream also affects the freezing point.

2 Cook the mixture over medium-high heat, stirring constantly, till slightly thickened and bubbly. Remove saucepan from heat. Use a wooden spoon for more comfortable stirring.

6 Pour the chilled mixture into an ice cream freezer can to ⅔ capacity. A measuring cup is a handy pouring utensil.

An ice cream freezer is a container equipped with a dasher turned by hand or by an electric motor. If using an electric ice cream freezer, follow the manufacturer's directions.

Filling the can not more than ⅔ full allows room for expansion produced by beating in air.

7 Fit can securely into ice cream freezer. Adjust dasher; cover with lid. Alternately pack layers of crushed ice and rock salt into the outer container; use 6 parts ice to 1 part salt, by weight. Fit handle or motor into place; secure.

Turn handle slowly till there's a slight pull, then faster to beat air into the ice cream. Continue until turning is difficult.

Use rock salt because table salt dissolves too fast.

3 Stir about 1 cup of the hot thickened mixture into the beaten eggs in a mixing bowl.

Gradually adding the hot mixture to the eggs prevents them from curdling.

4 Return the egg-milk mixture to the remaining hot mixture in the saucepan. Cook over medium heat, stirring constantly, for 1 minute. Then chill the mixture in the refrigerator. Chilling the mixture speeds freezing.

The eggs also give the ice cream a smooth texture. Additional cooking permits the eggs to further thicken the mixture.

5 Stir in the whipping cream and vanilla; mix well.

The fat in the cream contributes richness and smoothness, while the vanilla flavoring imparts a mild, pleasant flavor.

The proportion of flavoring in frozen desserts is rather high because flavors are less pronounced in cold mixtures.

TIP Keeping ice crystals small *is the key to making smooth homemade ice cream.*

Solids such as sugar, eggs, milk fat, and gelatin break up and separate the ice crystals, preventing large, coarse crystals from forming.

Air cells also keep the crystals small. Agitating the ice cream in an ice cream freezer incorporates air, thus refining and smoothing the texture. The same goal is achieved in refrigerator-frozen ice cream by beating the partially frozen mixture and by folding in beaten egg whites.

325

8 Remove ice to below level of the can lid so that no melted ice seeps into the can. Wipe can and lid with a damp cloth to remove salt and ice. Remove lid and dasher, scraping ice cream from the dasher back into the can.

9 Cover can with several thicknesses of waxed paper or foil. Plug the opening in lid with a cork; replace lid. To ripen ice cream, pack additional layers of ice and salt into the outer container; use 4 parts ice to 1 part salt, by weight. Cover freezer with heavy cloth or newspaper. Let ripen about 4 hours.

During ripening, the ice cream hardens slightly and becomes smoother.

10 Uncover ice cream freezer and remove ice to below level of the can lid. Wipe can and lid with a damp cloth to remove salt and ice. Remove lid.

To dip ice cream with an ice cream scoop, press scoop into the ice cream, twist scoop to keep the ice cream rounded, then lift scoop out of container.

Ice Cream and Frozen Desserts

Strawberry Ice Cream

Technique: Freezing uncooked ice cream in a refrigerator-freezer

- **1 envelope unflavored gelatin**
- **¼ cup cold water**
- **2 well-beaten egg yolks**
- **2 cups whipping cream (1 pint)**
- **1 pint fresh strawberries, crushed (1½ cups)**
- **¾ cup sugar**
- **1½ teaspoons vanilla**
- **¼ teaspoon salt**
- **10 to 12 drops red food coloring (optional)**
- **2 egg whites**
- **¼ cup sugar**

1 In a glass measure or bowl soften gelatin in cold water. **2** Place glass measure in a saucepan of hot water. Warm over low heat, stirring occasionally, till dissolved. **3** In a bowl combine egg yolks, whipping cream, strawberries, ¾ cup sugar, vanilla, and salt. Add food coloring, if desired. **4** Add gelatin; mix well. **5** Turn into a 13×9×2-inch pan. Cover and freeze till partially frozen.

6 Beat egg whites to soft peaks. **7–8** Gradually add ¼ cup sugar, beating till stiff peaks form. **9** Break frozen mixture into chunks. **10** Beat with electric mixer till fluffy. **11** Fold in beaten egg whites. **12** Return to pan. Cover and freeze till firm. Serves 8 to 10.

1 In a 1-cup liquid measuring cup or bowl sprinkle an envelope of unflavored gelatin over the cold water. Let stand for a few minutes to soften.

Softening the gelatin in cold water enables the gelatin granules to disperse throughout the liquid.

2 Place measuring cup with the softened gelatin in a saucepan of hot water, as shown. Warm over low heat, stirring occasionally, till gelatin mixture is clear and no granules remain.

7 Gradually add the ¼ cup sugar, about a tablespoon at a time. Beat at high speed of electric mixer.

The sugar helps the beaten egg whites hold their shape. It is added gradually so that the sugar granules will dissolve completely.

8 Beating to very stiff peaks will take about 7 minutes.

At this stage the foam becomes even whiter and forms stiff peaks that stand straight when beaters are removed, as shown. The whites now contain all of the air they can hold.

3 In mixing bowl combine beaten egg yolks, whipping cream, crushed berries, the ¾ cup sugar, vanilla, and salt. Add food coloring, if desired.

Blend with a rubber spatula till ingredients are well mixed.

The fat in the whipping cream contributes richness and smoothness to the ice cream.

4 Stir the gelatin into the strawberry mixture until well combined.

Gelatin helps stabilize the ice cream mixture during freezing, resulting in a smooth texture.

5 Using a rubber spatula, turn the strawberry mixture into a 13×9×2-inch pan or other shallow container (for example, you can use one 6-cup or two 3-cup metal refrigerator trays with removable dividers).

Cover mixture with clear plastic wrap or foil. Freeze till partially frozen.

6 In mixer bowl beat egg whites to soft peaks. Use an electric mixer at medium speed; this will take about 1 minute.

At this stage, the egg white foam turns white and stiffens so that soft peaks form when beaters are lifted from the bowl. The tips of peaks will bend over in soft curls, as shown.

327

9 Break the partially frozen strawberry mixture into chunks with a wooden spoon. Transfer the broken-up mixture to a large chilled mixer bowl. The frozen chunks should be small enough for easy mixing with an electric mixer.

10 Beat the partially frozen mixture with an electric mixer till smooth and fluffy. Do not let the ice cream melt. Scrape down sides of bowl with a rubber spatula.

Beating the mixture before it is completely frozen incorporates air, which improves the consistency of the ice cream.

11 Fold the beaten egg whites into the strawberry mixture just till distributed. To fold, cut down through the mixture with a rubber spatula; scrape across bottom of bowl; then bring spatula up and over mixture, close to the surface. Repeat this circular down-up-and-over motion, turning bowl as you work. Don't fold too vigorously or the ice cream will lose air.

12 Return the strawberry mixture to the pan. Cover with clear plastic wrap or foil. Freeze in a freezer or the freezer compartment of a refrigerator till firm.

Rapid freezing improves the texture of the ice cream.

Refrigerator-frozen ice creams are best eaten soon after freezing.

Ice Cream and Frozen Desserts

Double Dip Sundaes

Technique: Making ice cream sundaes

- **1   quart strawberry ice cream**
- **1   cup crumbled soft coconut macaroons (6 cookies)**
- **1   tablespoon sugar**
- **1   teaspoon cornstarch**
- **1   8¼-ounce can crushed pineapple**
- **1   5⅓-ounce can evaporated milk (⅔ cup)**
- **½   cup milk chocolate pieces**
- **½   cup peanut butter**
- **1   quart vanilla ice cream**
- **1   small banana, sliced**
- **Whipped cream (optional)**
- **Coarsely chopped peanuts (optional)**

1 Stir strawberry ice cream just enough to soften. **2** Fold in macaroons. Cover and return to freezer.

3 For pineapple sauce, in small saucepan stir together sugar and cornstarch. **4** Stir in *undrained* pineapple. **5** Cook and stir till thickened and bubbly. Cool.

6 For chocolate sauce, in small heavy saucepan combine evaporated milk, chocolate pieces, and peanut butter. **7** Cook and stir over low heat till chocolate and peanut butter are blended and mixture is slightly thickened. Cover and keep warm.

8 Place 1 scoop strawberry-macaroon ice cream and 1 scoop vanilla ice cream into each of 8 sundae dishes. **9** Stir sliced banana into pineapple sauce. **10** Spoon pineapple sauce over strawberry-macaroon ice cream. Stir warm chocolate sauce and spoon over vanilla ice cream. **11** If desired, garnish sundaes with whipped cream and coarsely chopped peanuts. Serve immediately. Makes 8 servings.

1 In a medium mixing bowl stir the strawberry ice cream just enough to soften. Use a wooden spoon for more comfortable stirring.

2 Fold the crumbled macaroons into the softened strawberry ice cream. Cover mixing bowl with clear plastic wrap or foil and return ice cream mixture to the freezer.

7 Cook over low heat, stirring constantly, till the chocolate pieces and peanut butter are blended and the mixture is slightly thickened. Cover saucepan and keep warm over very low heat.

8 Place 1 scoop strawberry-macaroon ice cream and 1 scoop vanilla ice cream into each of 8 sundae dishes.

Scoop ice cream by pressing an ice cream scoop into the ice cream. Twist the scoop to keep the ice cream rounded, then lift the scoop from container.

3 For pineapple sauce, in a small saucepan stir together the sugar and cornstarch till dry ingredients are thoroughly blended.

Mixing with sugar disperses the cornstarch and reduces the possibility of a lumpy sauce.

4 Stir undrained crushed pineapple into the sugar-cornstarch mixture till the ingredients are well combined.

For help in removing the pineapple from the bottom and sides of the can, use a wooden spoon or rubber spatula.

5 Cook over medium heat, stirring constantly, till mixture is thickened and bubbly. The mixture should reach this stage in about 5 minutes.

Remove saucepan from heat and let the mixture cool.

6 For chocolate sauce, in a small heavy saucepan combine evaporated milk, chocolate pieces, and peanut butter.

Creamy peanut butter will give the sauce a smoother texture, but you may use chunk-style peanut butter if you prefer.

329

9 Stir the sliced banana into the pineapple sauce till the banana is coated with sauce. Stir gently with a wooden spoon, being careful not to break up the banana slices.

10 Spoon some of the pineapple sauce over the scoop of strawberry-macaroon ice cream in each sundae dish.

Remove chocolate sauce from heat. Uncover and stir till smooth. Spoon some of the chocolate sauce over the scoop of vanilla ice cream in each dish.

11 If desired, garnish with whipped cream and coarsely chopped peanuts. Serve ice cream sundaes immediately, before the warm chocolate sauce melts the ice cream.

Raspberry Cream Bombe

Technique: Making a bombe

1 **cup finely crushed graham crackers (14 crackers)**
½ **cup finely chopped toasted almonds**
¼ **cup sugar**
6 **tablespoons butter *or* margarine, melted**
2 **pints raspberry sherbet *or* strawberry ice cream**
½ **cup sugar**
2 **tablespoons all-purpose flour**
   Dash salt
1 **cup milk**
2 **slightly beaten egg yolks**
½ **cup diced mixed candied fruits and peels**
1 **teaspoon vanilla**
1 **cup whipping cream**

330

1 Combine crackers, almonds, and the ¼ cup sugar. Stir in butter or margarine. 2 Press firmly onto sides and bottom of an 8-cup tower or bombe mold; freeze. 3 Soften sherbet or ice cream. 4 Quickly spread over crumb mixture. (If sherbet or ice cream slips, freeze in mold till workable.) Freeze till firm.

5 Meanwhile, in small saucepan combine the ½ cup sugar, flour, and salt. Stir in milk. 6 Cook and stir till thickened and bubbly. 7 Stir *half* of the hot mixture into egg yolks. Return to hot mixture. Cook and stir 2 minutes more. 8 Remove from heat. Stir in candied fruits and vanilla. Cool to room temperature; chill. 9 Beat whipping cream to soft peaks. Fold into fruit mixture. 10 Pile into mold atop sherbet or ice cream. Cover with foil; freeze till firm. 11 Invert mold onto chilled plate. Rub mold with a hot damp towel. 12 Lift off mold. Let stand 10 to 15 minutes. Makes 8 to 10 servings.

1 In a medium mixing bowl combine crushed graham crackers, chopped almonds, and the ¼ cup sugar. Stir in melted butter or margarine till well combined.

2 Turn crumb mixture into an 8-cup tower or bombe mold. Using your hand, firmly press the mixture onto the sides and bottom of the mold, distributing evenly. Freeze till firm.

7 Remove saucepan from heat. Gradually stir *half* of the hot mixture into beaten egg yolks.

This step warms the egg yolks before they're added to the hot mixture. If eggs are added directly to a hot mixture, they often curdle.

Return the egg mixture to remaining mixture in saucepan. Cook and stir 2 minutes more.

8 Remove saucepan from heat and stir in the candied fruits and peels and the vanilla. Cool the mixture to room temperature, then chill in refrigerator.

3 In a medium mixing bowl soften the raspberry sherbet or strawberry ice cream by using a wooden spoon to stir and press it against sides of bowl, as shown. Soften just till pliable. Use a wooden spoon for more comfortable stirring.

4 Using the back of a wooden spoon, quickly spread the softened sherbet or ice cream over the frozen crumb mixture, making an even layer on sides and bottom of mold. (If sherbet or ice cream slips, freeze in mold till workable.) Freeze till firm.

5 In small saucepan combine the ½ cup sugar, flour, and salt. Stir in milk till ingredients are well blended and mixture is smooth. A wooden spoon is a good utensil to use for stirring in a saucepan.

6 Cook over medium heat, stirring constantly, till thickened and bubbly. Mixture will bubble over the entire surface.

Stir constantly so the milk mixture doesn't stick to bottom of pan and scorch, giving an unpleasant flavor. Stirring with a figure-8 motion helps cook the mixture evenly.

9 In a small mixing bowl beat whipping cream to soft peaks (see step 3 on page 161). Using a rubber spatula, gently fold whipped cream into the chilled fruit mixture.

10 Pile the whipped cream-fruit mixture into center of mold atop sherbet or ice cream, as shown.

If the mold is not reasonably full, add additional softened sherbet or ice cream, forming a smooth layer.

Cover with foil and freeze till firm.

11 Invert the mold onto a chilled serving plate. Rub all outside surfaces with a hot damp towel to loosen the frozen dessert.

12 Carefully lift off the mold so that the pattern formed in the dessert remains intact. For easier slicing, let stand for 10 to 15 minutes before serving.

Using a sharp, thin-bladed knife, cut dessert into wedges. Transfer wedges to serving plates with a pie server or spatula.

Ice Cream and Frozen Desserts

1 Lay ice cream bricks side by side, as shown in step 2. Measure length and width of ice cream bricks.

Place sponge cake or layer cake on a cutting board. With a serrated knife, trim the cake to measure 1 inch larger on all sides than the ice cream.

Use your favorite flavors of cake and ice cream. You'll need a 9×9-inch or 13×9-inch layer cake.

Baked Alaska

Technique: Making a baked alaska

2 pints *or* 1 quart brick-style ice cream
1 1-inch-thick piece sponge cake *or* layer cake
5 egg whites
1 teaspoon vanilla
½ teaspoon cream of tartar
⅔ cup sugar

1 Lay ice cream bricks side by side, as shown in step 2. Measure length and width of ice cream bricks. Trim cake 1 inch larger on all sides than ice cream measurements. **2** Place cake on a piece of foil. Center ice cream on cake. Cover; freeze till firm.

3 At serving time, beat together egg whites, vanilla, and cream of tartar to soft peaks. **4–5** Gradually add sugar, beating till stiff peaks form. **6** Transfer cake with ice cream to baking sheet. **7** Spread with egg white mixture, sealing to edges of cake and baking sheet all around. Swirl to make peaks. **8** Bake in 500° oven about 3 minutes or till golden. Slice and serve immediately. Makes 8 servings.

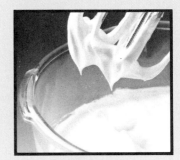

5 Beating to stiff peaks will take about 7 minutes at high speed.

At this stage, the foam becomes even whiter and forms stiff peaks that stand straight when beaters are removed, as shown. The whites now contain all of the air they are capable of holding.

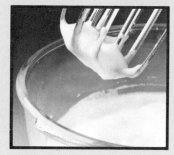

2 Place the trimmed cake on a piece of foil. Center ice cream on cake.

If using 2 pints ice cream, place them side by side. If using *half* of a ½ gallon container, set the ice cream on its wide side and cut in half lengthwise. Then turn over onto the cut side and center on cake. Use metal spatulas to help transfer the ice cream.

Cover lightly with an additional piece of foil and freeze till firm.

3 At serving time, beat together egg whites, vanilla, and cream of tartar to soft peaks. Use an electric mixer at medium speed; this will take about 1 minute.

At this stage, the egg white foam turns white and stiffens so that soft peaks form when the beaters are lifted from the bowl. The tips of the peaks will bend over in soft curls.

The cream of tartar acts as a stabilizer to help the egg whites hold their shape.

4 Gradually add the sugar, about a tablespoon at a time, as shown. Beat at high speed of an electric mixer.

The sugar also helps the beaten egg whites hold their shape. Sugar should be added gradually so that it will dissolve completely.

TIP If you can't locate brick-style ice cream, *re-shape the ice cream you have to fit atop a round cake base.*

First, select a mixing bowl with a diameter 2 inches smaller than the diameter of a 1-inch-thick round layer cake. Then stir the ice cream in the bowl with a wooden spoon just enough to soften, referring to step 3 on page 331. Cover and return the ice cream to the freezer. When firm again, center the ice cream on the cake and continue preparing the baked alaska.

333

6 Transfer the frozen cake with ice cream to a baking sheet. Use 2 large metal spatulas, 1 under each end, to avoid breaking the cake.

(If you have an unfinished wooden cutting board, you can use it instead of the baking sheet. Check the board carefully, since any varnish or other finish can burn when the board is heated in the oven.)

7 Using a narrow metal spatula, spread beaten egg white mixture over ice cream and cake. Make sure ice cream and cake are completely covered with egg white mixture. Carefully spread egg whites to edges of cake and the baking sheet, sealing all around. Swirl the egg white mixture in a circular motion to make decorative peaks.

The egg white mixture helps insulate the ice cream during baking.

8 Bake in a 500° oven about 3 minutes or till the egg white mixture is golden brown. Slice with a serrated knife and serve immediately, using a wide metal spatula to transfer slices to serving plates.

Baking for only a short time at a high temperature browns the egg white mixture without melting the ice cream.

Ice Cream and Frozen Desserts

Taffy Apple Ice Cream

- 1 cup granulated sugar
- ½ cup packed brown sugar
- ¼ cup all-purpose flour
- ¼ teaspoon salt
- 2 13-ounce cans (3⅓ cups) evaporated milk
- 2 tablespoons molasses
- 4 beaten eggs
- 2 cups finely chopped peeled apples
- 2 cups whipping cream
- 1 teaspoon vanilla
- Apple slices (optional)

Refer to: Freezing cooked ice cream in an ice cream freezer, page 324. In saucepan combine sugars, flour, and salt; gradually stir in evaporated milk and molasses. Cook and stir over low heat till slightly thickened. Stir about 1 cup of the hot mixture into beaten eggs; return to hot mixture in saucepan. Cook and stir for 1 minute. Stir in chopped apples, whipping cream, and vanilla.

Freeze in 4- or 5-quart ice cream freezer. Garnish servings with apple slices, if desired. Makes 2½ quarts.

Deluxe Fruit Ice Cream

- 2 ripe medium bananas, cut up
- 2 cups chopped pitted fresh apricots
- 1 pint fresh strawberries
- 1 cup orange juice
- ½ cup lemon juice
- 3 cups milk
- 2 cups sugar
- 2 cups whipping cream
- ¼ teaspoon salt

In blender container place bananas, apricots, strawberries, orange juice, and lemon juice; cover and blend at medium speed till smooth. Turn mixture into a large bowl.

In same blender container combine milk, sugar, whipping cream, and salt; cover and blend till smooth. Stir milk mixture into fruit mixture.

Freeze in 4- or 5-quart ice cream freezer, referring to steps 6–10 on page 324. Makes 3½ quarts.

Cookies and Ice Cream

- 4 beaten eggs
- 2 cups milk
- 1¼ cups sugar
- 3 cups whipping cream
- 1 tablespoon vanilla
- 10 oatmeal cookies, coarsely crushed (2 cups)
- ½ cup toasted chopped almonds
- ½ cup light raisins, chopped

In medium saucepan combine eggs, milk, and sugar. Cook and stir over medium heat just till mixture coats a metal spoon, referring to step 4 on page 86. Chill. Stir in whipping cream and vanilla.

Freeze in 4- or 5-quart ice cream freezer till *almost* firm, referring to steps 6–7 on page 324. Remove lid and add crushed oatmeal cookies, almonds, and raisins. Resume freezing 1 to 2 minutes more or till ingredients are mixed throughout. Remove dasher and replace lid, referring to steps 8–10 on page 325. Let ice cream ripen. Makes about 3 quarts.

Apricot Chiffon Ice Cream
(pictured on page 310)

- 1 cup dried apricots
- 3 beaten egg yolks
- ¼ cup water
- 3 egg whites
- ½ cup sugar
- 1 cup whipping cream

Rinse apricots and place in saucepan. Cover with water 1 inch above fruit. Cover pan and simmer gently for 20 to 25 minutes; drain. Place drained apricots in blender container; cover and blend till smooth (makes about ¾ cup puree). In saucepan combine apricot puree, egg yolks, and water. Cook and stir till thickened. Cool.

Beat egg whites to soft peaks, referring to step 6 on page 327. Gradually add sugar and beat till stiff peaks form, referring to steps 7–8 on page 326. Fold into cooled apricot mixture. Whip cream to soft peaks. Fold whipped cream into apricot mixture. Turn into 13×9×2-inch pan. Cover and freeze till firm. Makes about 5½ cups ice cream.

English Toffee Ice Cream

334

English Toffee Ice Cream

    4 1⅛-ounce chocolate-coated
       English toffee bars, chilled
    2 cups whipping cream
    1 14-ounce can *sweetened
       condensed* milk
    ½ cup strong coffee, cooled
  1½ teaspoons vanilla

Crush toffee bars by placing them between 2 pieces of waxed paper and crushing with a rolling pin; set aside. Combine cream, milk, coffee, and vanilla. Cover and chill.

Beat cream mixture till it is custard-like in consistency. Fold in crushed toffee bars. Turn into 13×9×2-inch pan. Cover and freeze till firm. If desired, sprinkle servings with additional crushed chocolate-coated English toffee bars. Makes 2 quarts.

Cherry-Almond Ice Cream

(pictured on page 310)

    1 6-ounce jar (½ cup) maraschino
       cherries
    1 cup sugar
    3 tablespoons all-purpose flour
  2¼ cups milk
    3 beaten eggs
    2 cups whipping cream
    2 teaspoons vanilla
    ½ teaspoon almond extract
    ½ cup finely chopped toasted
       almonds

Drain cherries, reserving ¼ cup syrup (if necessary, add water to syrup to make ¼ cup). Set aside. Finely chop cherries; set aside.

In large saucepan combine sugar, flour, and ¼ teaspoon *salt,* referring to steps 1–4 on page 324. Gradually stir in milk and reserved cherry syrup. Cook and stir over low heat till slightly thickened. Stir about 1 cup hot mixture into eggs; return to hot mixture. Cook and stir for 1 minute. Chill well.

Beat whipping cream, vanilla, and almond extract to soft peaks. Fold whipped cream mixture, almonds, and cherries into chilled milk-egg mixture. Turn into 13×9×2-inch pan. Place in freezer. Stir every 30 minutes for the first 1½ hours. Freeze till firm. Makes 1¾ quarts.

Pear Sherbet

    1 3-ounce package lemon-flavored
       gelatin
    1 cup boiling water
  1¼ cups sugar
    1 16-ounce can pear halves
    4 cups milk
       Dash salt

In large mixing bowl dissolve lemon gelatin in boiling water. Stir in sugar; cool. Mash *undrained* pears; stir gelatin mixture, milk, and salt into mashed pears. Turn into a 9×9×2-inch pan. Cover and freeze.

Break frozen mixture into chunks, referring to steps 9–10 on page 327. Beat till fluffy. Return to pan. Cover; freeze firm. Makes 8 servings.

Almond-Strawberry Slices

    1 envelope unflavored gelatin
    ¼ cup cold water
    1 quart fresh strawberries *or* 1
       20-ounce package frozen whole
       strawberries, thawed
    ⅓ cup strawberry preserves, cut up
    1 cup whipping cream
    2 tablespoons sugar
    ½ teaspoon vanilla
    ¼ teaspoon almond extract
    ½ cup chopped almonds

Soften gelatin in cold water, referring to steps 1–2 on page 326. Dissolve gelatin over hot water. Sieve fresh or frozen berries. Blend in strawberry preserves and *2 tablespoons* of the dissolved gelatin. Turn into an 8×8×2-inch pan; freeze about 45 minutes or till slushy.

Turn into chilled bowl; beat well. Divide mixture between two 16-ounce fruit or vegetable cans; freeze about 1½ hours or till almost firm. With long-handled spoon, push mixture evenly up sides of cans, leaving centers hollow. Beat cream with sugar, vanilla, and almond extract till mixture begins to thicken. Add the remaining gelatin (remelt, if necessary). Beat to soft peaks. Fold in almonds. Spoon into hollows in cans. Cover; freeze till firm. Remove from cans; cut into slices. Serves 8 to 10.

Frozen Pineapple Custard

  1½ cups crushed vanilla wafers
       (33 wafers)
    ¼ cup butter *or* margarine, melted
    3 slightly beaten egg yolks
    1 8-ounce can crushed pineapple
       (juice pack)
    ½ cup sugar
    2 tablespoons lemon juice
    ⅛ teaspoon salt
    3 egg whites
    2 tablespoons sugar
    1 cup whipping cream
       Strawberry Sauce

Combine wafer crumbs and melted butter or margarine. Reserve ½ cup crumb mixture; press remaining mixture in bottom of 10×6×2-inch dish. In saucepan combine egg yolks, *undrained* pineapple, the ½ cup sugar, lemon juice, and salt. Cook and stir over low heat till slightly thickened and bubbly. Cover surface with clear plastic wrap or waxed paper; cool.

Beat egg whites to soft peaks, referring to steps 6–8 on page 326. Gradually add the 2 tablespoons sugar, beating till stiff peaks form. Beat cream to soft peaks. Fold egg whites and whipped cream into egg yolk mixture. Pour into crumb crust. Sprinkle with the reserved ½ cup crumb mixture. Cover and freeze till firm. Cut into squares and serve with Strawberry Sauce. Makes 8 servings.

Strawberry Sauce: In small saucepan crush one 10-ounce package frozen *strawberries,* thawed. Blend in 1 tablespoon *cornstarch.* Add ½ cup *water.* Cook and stir till thickened and bubbly. Cook 1 minute longer. Strain and chill.

335

Ice Cream and Frozen Desserts

Individual Baked Alaskas

1 package fluffy white frosting mix
  (for 2-layer cake)
4 cake dessert cups
  Preserves, ice cream toppings, *or* liqueurs
1 pint ice cream *or* sherbet

Prepare frosting mix according to package directions. Place cake dessert cups on a baking sheet. Fill center of each with preserves or ice cream topping *or* sprinkle with 1 teaspoon liqueur. Scoop out 4 balls of ice cream. Top each cake with scoop of ice cream. If desired, make an indentation in the top of each ice cream ball with a spoon handle; spoon in about 1 teaspoon liqueur.

Cover completely with frosting, referring to step 7 on page 333. Spread to edges of cake and baking sheet, sealing all around. Swirl to make peaks. Freeze up to 24 hours or till firm. Bake in 500° oven for 2 to 3 minutes or till golden brown. Sprinkle with crushed peppermint candies, if desired. Serve immediately. Makes 4 servings.

Suggested preserves: *Apricot, blackberry, red or black raspberry, cherry, peach, pineapple, plum, or strawberry preserves.*

Suggested ice cream toppings: *Butterscotch, caramel, fudge, cherry, pineapple, strawberry or pecan ice cream topping.*

Suggested liqueurs: *Coffee, cherry, or orange liqueur; crème de menthe; crème de cacao; or apricot or peach brandy.*

Suggested ice creams or sherbets: *Chocolate, chocolate-mint, coffee, vanilla, French vanilla, cherry-nut, or strawberry ice cream; or raspberry, pineapple, or orange sherbet.*

Peanut Butter and Jelly Sundaes

6 eggs
2 cups sugar
2 cups whipping cream
2 cups light cream
1 cup peanut butter
4 teaspoons vanilla
  Strawberry preserves

In mixing bowl thoroughly beat eggs, sugar, whipping cream, light cream, peanut butter, and vanilla. Turn into 13×9×2-inch pan. Cover and freeze till partially frozen. Break partially frozen mixture into chunks, referring to steps 9–10 on page 327. Beat till fluffy. Return to pan. Cover; freeze firm.

To serve, scoop frozen mixture into sherbet dishes. Drizzle strawberry preserves over each serving. Makes about 2 quarts ice cream.

Hot Butterscotch Sundaes

2 tablespoons cornstarch
¼ teaspoon salt
1¼ cups milk
¼ cup light corn syrup
1 cup packed dark brown sugar
2 tablespoons butter *or* margarine
  Vanilla ice cream

For butterscotch sauce, in heavy saucepan stir together cornstarch and salt. Stir in milk and corn syrup. Cook over medium heat, stirring constantly, till mixture is thickened and bubbly. Cook for 2 minutes more, stirring occasionally. Remove from heat. Stir in brown sugar and butter or margarine.

Serve sauce warm over scoops of ice cream. Store remaining butterscotch sauce in screw-top jar in the refrigerator. Serve chilled or reheat to use. Makes about 1¾ cups sauce.

Individual Baked Alaskas

Peppermint Sundaes

2 7-, 9-, *or* 10-ounce jars
    marshmallow creme
1/3 cup milk
1/2 cup finely crushed peppermint
    candy
    Red food coloring (optional)
    Vanilla ice cream

In saucepan heat and stir marshmallow creme over low heat till softened. Blend in milk; stir in crushed peppermint candy. Tint pink with a little red food coloring, if desired.

Stir marshmallow creme mixture before serving; if necessary, add additional milk to achieve pouring consistency. Serve warm or chilled over ice cream. Makes about 2½ cups sauce.

Chocolate-Mint Bombe

(pictured on page 310)

1 cup whipping cream
1/3 cup *sweetened condensed* milk,
    chilled
2 tablespoons green crème de
    menthe
1/4 teaspoon vanilla
1 pint chocolate *or*
    chocolate-almond ice cream
1 quart vanilla *or* French vanilla
    cream

Refer to: Making a bombe, page 330. Place a 6-cup tower or bombe mold in the freezer to chill. Combine whipping cream, sweetened condensed milk, crème de menthe, and vanilla; beat to soft peaks. Freeze till partially firm. Spread evenly over bottom and up sides of chilled mold, leaving center open (if mixture slips, freeze in mold till workable). Freeze firm.

Stir chocolate ice cream just enough to soften. Quickly spread over the crème de menthe layer to cover completely, leaving center open. Freeze till firm. Stir the vanilla ice cream just enough to soften. Pile into center of mold atop chocolate ice cream, smoothing the top. Cover with foil; freeze till firm.

To serve, invert mold onto a chilled plate. Rub mold with hot damp towel to loosen. Lift off mold. Let stand about 10 minutes before slicing. Makes 6 to 8 servings.

Hot Fudge Sundaes

1/3 cup water
2 squares (2 ounces) unsweetened
    chocolate
1/2 cup sugar
    Dash salt
3 tablespoons butter *or* margarine
1/4 teaspoon vanilla
    Vanilla ice cream

For fudge sauce, in small heavy saucepan combine water and chocolate. Cook over low heat, stirring constantly, till chocolate is melted. Stir in sugar and salt. Cook over medium heat, stirring constantly, about 8 minutes or till sugar is dissolved and mixture is slightly thickened. Remove from heat.

Add butter or margarine and vanilla, stirring till fudge sauce is smooth. Serve sauce warm over scoops of ice cream. Makes about 1 cup sauce.

Caramel-Pear Sundaes

1 cup packed brown sugar
2 tablespoons cornstarch
1/4 teaspoon salt
1/2 cup water
3/4 cup light cream
1/4 cup light corn syrup
1/2 cup coarsely chopped pecans
2 tablespoons butter *or* margarine
1 tablespoon rum *or* brandy
    Canned pear halves
    Vanilla ice cream

For pecan sauce, in heavy saucepan combine brown sugar, cornstarch, and salt; stir in water. Blend in light cream and corn syrup. Cook, stirring constantly, till thickened and bubbly (mixture may appear curdled during cooking). Stir in pecans, butter or margarine, and rum or brandy.

Serve pecan sauce warm or chilled atop pear halves filled with vanilla ice cream. Makes 2⅓ cups sauce.

Sweet Cherry Bombe

1 14-ounce can *sweetened*
    condensed milk
2 cups fresh dark sweet cherries,
    pitted and finely chopped (12
    ounces)
1 teaspoon vanilla
    Few drops almond extract
1 cup whipping cream
1 pint chocolate-almond ice cream

Refer to: Making a bombe, page 330. Combine milk, cherries, vanilla, and almond extract. Turn into a 9×9×2-inch pan, freeze firm. Place a 5-cup tower or bombe mold in freezer to chill.

Break frozen cherry mixture into chunks, referring to steps 9–10 on page 327. Beat till fluffy. Beat whipping cream to soft peaks; fold into cherry mixture. Remove 1 cup of the cherry mixture and freeze till almost firm.

Freeze remaining cherry mixture till partially firm. Spread evenly over bottom and up sides of chilled mold, leaving center open (if mixture slips, freeze till workable). Freeze firm. Stir chocolate ice cream just enough to soften. Pile into center of mold atop cherry mixture, smoothing the top. Spread the reserved 1 cup cherry mixture over top. Cover with foil; freeze firm.

To serve, invert mold onto a chilled plate. Rub mold with hot damp towel to loosen. Lift off mold. Let stand about 10 minutes before slicing. Makes 6 to 8 servings.

Orange-Chocolate Pops

1 pint chocolate ice cream
1 cup chocolate milk
1/2 of a 6-ounce can (1/3 cup) frozen
    orange juice concentrate
1/4 cup powdered sugar
10 wooden sticks

In blender container combine ice cream, milk, orange concentrate, and powdered sugar. Cover; blend till smooth. Pour into ten 3-ounce waxed paper drink cups. Freeze till partially frozen. Insert wooden sticks; freeze firm. To serve, peel off paper cup wrapping. Makes 10 servings.

337

PUDDINGS

Puddings come in various textures and colors, as well as flavors. Here you'll learn to make puddings that are creamy and fluffy, soft and firm—and even puddings that are half cake, half pudding.

Chocolate Pudding

Technique: Making cream pudding

1 cup sugar
2 tablespoons cornstarch
¼ teaspoon salt
2 cups milk
2 squares (2 ounces) unsweetened chocolate
2 slightly beaten egg yolks *or* 1 well-beaten egg
2 tablespoons butter *or* margarine
1 teaspoon vanilla

1 In saucepan combine the sugar, cornstarch, and salt. **2** Stir in the milk. **3** Chop the chocolate; stir in. **4** Cook and stir over medium heat till mixture is thickened and bubbly. Cook and stir 2 minutes more. **5** Remove from heat. Gradually stir about 1 cup of the hot mixture into egg yolks or egg. **6** Return to mixture in saucepan. Cook and stir 2 minutes more. **7** Remove pan from heat; stir in the butter or margarine and the vanilla. Cool. **8** Pour mixture into sherbet or dessert dishes and chill. Makes 4 or 5 servings.

Vanilla Pudding: Follow recipe for Chocolate Pudding *except* reduce sugar to ¾ cup and omit chocolate.

1 In a medium saucepan combine the sugar, cornstarch, and salt.

Blend the cornstarch thoroughly with the sugar so that the starch particles are separated by sugar. This helps prevent lumps from forming when the liquid is added.

5 Remove saucepan from heat. Remove about 1 cup of the hot pudding from the saucepan and gradually stir it into the beaten egg yolks or the beaten whole egg.

This step warms the egg before it is added to the hot mixture. If eggs are added directly to a hot mixture, they often curdle.

2 Add the milk and stir until the dry ingredients are thoroughly blended with the milk. A wooden spoon is a good utensil to use for stirring in a saucepan.

3 Chop the chocolate on a cutting board with a French knife.

Or, blender-chop the chocolate. First cut each square into quarters, then add pieces to the blender through the opening in the center of cover while blender is running. Cover and continue blending till chocolate is chopped.

Add the chopped chocolate to the saucepan; stir in.

4 Cook and stir over medium heat till thickened and bubbly. Mixture will bubble over entire surface, as shown. Cook and stir 2 minutes longer so cornstarch will be thoroughly cooked and pudding will not taste starchy.

Stir constantly so the chocolate mixture doesn't stick to bottom of pan and scorch, giving pudding an unpleasant flavor. Stirring with a figure–8 motion helps cook pudding evenly.

339

TIP To keep a "skin" from forming *on the top of a pudding mixture while cooling, carefully place a piece of clear plastic wrap or waxed paper directly on the surface of the hot pudding, as shown. After pudding has cooled, remove paper and spoon pudding into dessert dishes.*

6 Return the egg-chocolate mixture to remaining mixture in saucepan. Cook and stir 2 minutes more.

Use a figure–8 motion for stirring to keep the pudding from sticking to pan.

7 Remove saucepan from heat and stir in the butter or margarine and the vanilla. The butter will melt from the heat of the pudding and can easily be stirred in.

Cover, referring to tip at right; set aside to cool. Do not stir during cooling, as the stirring may cause the pudding to soften.

8 Spoon the chocolate pudding mixture from saucepan into four or five sherbet or dessert dishes. Cover and chill thoroughly.

Puddings

Fluffy Tapioca Pudding

Technique: Making fluffy tapioca pudding

½	**cup sugar**
¼	**cup quick-cooking tapioca**
¼	**teaspoon salt**
4	**cups milk**
3	**slightly beaten egg yolks**
1½	**teaspoons vanilla**
3	**egg whites**

340

1 In 2-quart saucepan combine sugar, tapioca, and salt. Stir in the milk, mixing well; let stand 5 minutes. **2** Stir in the egg yolks. **3** Bring mixture to boiling, stirring constantly. **4** Remove saucepan from heat (tapioca mixture will be thin). Stir in vanilla.

　5 Beat egg whites till stiff peaks form. **6** Put one-third of the beaten egg whites into a large bowl. Slowly stir in the tapioca mixture. **7** Fold in remaining egg whites, leaving little fluffs of egg white. Chill. **8** Spoon tapioca mixture into sherbet or dessert dishes. Garnish as desired. Makes 8 to 10 servings.

1 In a 2-quart saucepan combine the sugar, tapioca, and salt. Stir in the milk, mixing well. Let the mixture stand 5 minutes to soften tapioca.

5 Beat the egg whites about 1½ minutes or till stiff peaks form, using a rotary beater or electric mixer. Peaks will stand up straight when the beaters are removed. Egg whites should still appear glossy.

　Do not use a plastic bowl when beating egg whites, since oils retained in the plastic prevent the egg whites from forming peaks. For the same reason, be sure the beaters are clean.

2 Stir in the slightly beaten egg yolks. A slightly beaten yolk is one that has been mixed with a fork only till the yolk is broken.

3 Bring mixture to boiling, stirring constantly to prevent sticking. Use a wooden spoon or rubber spatula to stir mixture in the saucepan.

4 Remove saucepan from heat and stir in the vanilla. The mixture will appear thin at this point, and will pour readily off a spoon, as shown.

6 Put one-third of the stiff-beaten egg whites into a large bowl. Slowly add the cooked tapioca mixture, stirring while mixture is being added.

7 Fold in the remaining egg whites. To fold, cut down through the mixture with a rubber spatula; scrape across bottom of bowl, and bring spatula up and over mixture, close to the surface. Repeat this circular down-up-and-over motion, turning bowl as you work.

Do not completely fold the egg whites into the pudding, but leave little fluffs of egg white throughout the mixture. Cover and chill.

8 Spoon the chilled tapioca mixture into eight to ten sherbet or dessert dishes. If desired, garnish the top of the pudding with tart jelly, canned fruit, toasted coconut, or maraschino cherries.

Puddings

Fluffy Rice Pudding (pictured on page 349)

Technique: Making saucepan rice pudding

¾   **cup long grain rice**
¼   **cup sugar**
4   **cups milk**
¼   **cup dry sherry** *or* **milk**
1½ **teaspoons vanilla**
¼   **teaspoon almond extract**
½   **cup whipping cream**
1   **10-ounce package frozen red raspberries, thawed**
1   **tablespoon cornstarch**
½   **cup currant jelly**

342

1 In heavy 2-quart saucepan combine uncooked rice and sugar. Stir in the 4 cups milk. **2–3** Bring mixture to boiling. Reduce heat; cover and cook 25 to 30 minutes or till rice is tender, stirring occasionally. **4** Stir in the ¼ cup sherry or milk, the vanilla, and almond extract. Cool to room temperature. **5** Whip cream to soft peaks. **6** Fold whipped cream into rice mixture. Cover and chill thoroughly.

   7 To make sauce, in saucepan crush raspberries. **8** Stir in the cornstarch; add currant jelly. **9** Cook and stir till mixture is thickened and bubbly; cook 1 minute more. **10** Sieve sauce; discard seeds. Cover surface of sauce with waxed paper or plastic wrap. Cool sauce to room temperature.

   11 To serve, spoon rice pudding into sherbet dishes. **12** Drizzle some of the raspberry sauce over each serving. Makes 6 to 8 servings.

1 In a heavy 2-quart saucepan combine the uncooked long grain rice and sugar. Add the 4 cups milk and stir till mixture is blended.

2 Place saucepan on range over medium heat and bring mixture to boiling. When mixture reaches boiling, reduce heat so that mixture simmers. Cover saucepan and simmer for 25 to 30 minutes or till rice is tender, stirring occasionally.

7 To make the sauce, in a small saucepan crush the thawed raspberries in syrup. Use a potato masher to quickly mash the berries, or use the back of a fork for mashing.

8 Sprinkle cornstarch over crushed raspberries. Stir in, making sure cornstarch is thoroughly blended to prevent lumps from forming in the sauce. Stir in the currant jelly.

3 To test rice for done-ness, squeeze grains of cooked rice between thumb and forefinger. If there is no hard core, rice is properly cooked.

4 Remove saucepan from heat and stir in the ¼ cup sherry or milk, the vanil-la, and almond extract. Set saucepan aside to cool rice mixture to room temperature.

5 Whip the cream till soft peaks form when beat-ers are removed, as shown. Avoid beating the cream too much or it will break down when folded in.

6 Fold the whipped cream into the cooled rice mix-ture. To fold, cut down through the mixture with a rubber spatula; scrape across bottom of bowl, and bring spatula up and over mixture, close to the surface. Repeat this circular down-up-and-over motion, turning bowl as you work.

Cover mixture and chill thoroughly before serving.

343

9 Cook and stir with a wooden spoon till mix-ture is thickened and bub-bly. Cook 1 minute longer to be sure starch granules are thoroughly cooked. Mixture will bubble over entire sur-face and should be clear in appearance when cooked.

10 To sieve sauce, place sieve over bowl and pour mixture through. You will need to work the sauce through the sieve with the back of a wooden spoon. Discard seeds.

Cover surface of sieved mixture with waxed paper or plastic wrap, referring to the tip on page 339. Cool sauce to room temperature before serving.

11 To serve, spoon the chilled rice pudding into six to eight sherbet dishes, mounding the mix-ture attractively in each dish.

12 Drizzle some of the cooled raspberry sauce over each serving of pudding with a spoon. Serve pudding at once.

If desired, garnish pud-ding and sauce with a few whole raspberries, as pic-tured on page 349.

Puddings

Lemon Pudding-Cake

Technique: Making pudding-cake

¾   **cup sugar**
¼   **cup all-purpose flour**
     Dash salt
3   **tablespoons butter *or* margarine, melted**
1   **teaspoon finely shredded lemon peel**
¼   **cup lemon juice**
3   **egg yolks**
1½   **cups milk**
3   **egg whites**

344

1 In a mixing bowl combine sugar, flour, and salt. Stir in the melted butter or margarine, lemon peel, and lemon juice. **2** In another bowl beat egg yolks till well beaten. **3** Add milk to beaten yolks and stir together. **4** Pour yolk-milk mixture into lemon mixture, mixing well. **5** Beat egg whites till stiff peaks form. **6** Fold egg whites into the lemon mixture.

7 Pour batter into an ungreased 8×8×2-inch baking pan. **8** Place a 13×9×2-inch baking pan on oven rack; place the batter-filled pan in the 13×9×2-inch pan. Carefully pour hot water into the larger pan to a depth of 1 inch. **9** Bake in 350° oven for 40 minutes or till done. Serve warm or chilled in dessert dishes. Makes 9 servings.

1 In a mixing bowl combine the sugar, flour, and salt. Add the melted butter or margarine, lemon peel, and lemon juice; stir till blended.

Shred the lemon peel before cutting lemon in half and squeezing for juice.

6 Fold stiff-beaten egg whites into the lemon mixture. To fold, cut down through the mixture with a rubber spatula; scrape across bottom of bowl, and bring spatula up and over mixture, close to the surface. Repeat this circular down-up-and-over motion, turning the bowl as you work.

2 In a smaller bowl beat the egg yolks till they are well-beaten, as shown.

When separating eggs, use cold, fresh eggs so the yolks and whites will be easier to separate. Be sure none of the yolk gets into the whites; if this happens, remove yolk with a spoon. Otherwise, the egg whites will not beat to the proper stiffness.

3 Pour the milk into the well-beaten egg yolks. Stir till the mixture is blended, using a wooden spoon or rubber spatula for mixing.

4 Pour the egg yolk-milk mixture into the lemon mixture, scraping out the bowl with rubber spatula. Stir together till thoroughly combined.

5 Using a rotary beater or electric mixer, beat the egg whites about 1½ minutes or till stiff peaks form. Peaks will stand up straight when beaters are removed, as shown.

Do not use a plastic bowl when beating egg whites, since oils retained in the plastic prevent the egg whites from forming peaks.

If you reuse the beaters that were used to beat egg yolks, be sure to wash them thoroughly.

345

7 Pour batter into an ungreased 8×8×2-inch baking pan. Use a rubber spatula to push the batter into pan and to clean out the bowl. Batter will be very thin.

8 Place a 13×9×2-inch baking pan on oven rack; place the batter-filled pan in the 13×9×2-inch pan. Carefully pour hot water into the larger pan to about a 1-inch depth, being careful not to spill any into batter.

The water in larger pan helps keep temperature more even, and prevents curdling of the pudding.

9 Bake in a 350° oven for 40 minutes or till done. To test for doneness, insert a wooden pick into the cake layer without going into the pudding mixture below. If pick comes out clean from cake portion, the pudding-cake is done. To serve, spoon warm or chilled pudding-cake into nine dessert dishes.

Puddings

Steamed Carrot Pudding

Technique: Making steamed pudding

2 medium carrots, cut up
2 medium apples, peeled, cored, and cut up
1 medium potato, peeled and cut up
4 ounces suet, cut up
1 cup sugar
⅓ cup orange juice
1 beaten egg
1 teaspoon vanilla
1½ cups all-purpose flour
1½ teaspoons baking soda
1 teaspoon ground cinnamon
1 teaspoon ground nutmeg
½ teaspoon ground cloves
½ teaspoon salt
1 cup snipped pitted dates
1 cup raisins
  Brown Sugar Sauce

346

1 Grease a 2-quart mold. 2 Grind together carrots, apples, potato, and suet. 3 Combine sugar, orange juice, egg, and vanilla. Stir into carrot mixture. 4 Stir together flour, soda, spices, and salt. 5 Stir into carrot mixture; fold in dates and raisins. 6 Pour batter into mold. 7 Cover with foil. 8 Add water to a deep kettle to a depth of 1 inch. 9 Place mold on rack in kettle. Bring water to boiling. Cover kettle; steam 3½ hours, adding more water if needed. 10 Remove mold from kettle. Cool 10 minutes. Unmold; serve warm with Brown Sugar Sauce. Makes 8 to 10 servings.

Brown Sugar Sauce: In a saucepan mix ½ cup packed *brown sugar* and 2 teaspoons *cornstarch;* stir in ⅓ cup *water* and 2 tablespoons *butter.* Cook and stir till thickened and bubbly. Gradually stir hot mixture into 1 beaten *egg;* return to saucepan. Cook and stir 1 minute more. Stir in 1 teaspoon *vanilla.*

1 Using folded paper toweling or a pastry brush, thoroughly grease a 2-quart mold with shortening. Do not use a ring mold, as the pudding would cook too quickly.

2 Using the coarse blade of a food grinder, grind together the carrots, apples, potato, and suet. Place a pie plate or other shallow dish under the grinder blades to catch the ground mixture.

6 Pour batter into the well-greased mold. Use a wooden spoon or rubber spatula to push batter from the bowl into the mold. Spread evenly and scrape the bowl clean.

7 Cover mold with foil and tie securely with string so that the cover is tight. Make a bowknot or other closing that is easily untied.
   The foil is used to keep water that condenses on the lid of the kettle from dropping onto the pudding.

3 In a bowl combine the sugar, orange juice, egg, and vanilla; stir into the ground carrot mixture, blending well with a wooden spoon.

Be sure to add the egg to the sugar only after the orange juice has been added. When large amounts of sugar are mixed with such a small amount of egg, hard lumps of egg-sugar mixture often form.

4 In a bowl combine the flour, baking soda, cinnamon, nutmeg, cloves, and salt. Stir together till ingredients are thoroughly mixed.

The soda, spices, and salt must be evenly distributed in the flour to avoid any unblended ingredients in the pudding.

5 Stir the dry ingredients into the carrot mixture. Mix till dry ingredients are thoroughly moistened, as shown. Fold in the snipped dates and raisins, mixing with a wooden spoon.

347

TIP To cook Steamed Carrot Pudding in an electric slow crockery cooker, *turn the batter into a greased container, choosing any heatproof pan, can, or dish that fits inside your particular crockery cooker. A 3-pound shortening can and a 2-pound coffee can are examples of containers that fit into most cookers. Each holds about 8 cups. Be sure to remove any paper labels from the can before using it for steaming.*

Cover can with foil and tie tightly with a string, referring to step 7 at left. Place in the crockery cooker (add no water to cooker). Cover and cook on high-heat setting about 4 hours. Remove from cooker with pot holders and cool 10 minutes before unmolding onto a plate.

8 Place rack in bottom of a deep kettle large enough to accommodate the mold. Place kettle on range and add hot water to a depth of 1 inch.

9 Place covered mold on rack in kettle. Bring water to boiling. Cover kettle and steam pudding for 3½ hours. Add more boiling water during the steaming process, if needed to maintain the 1-inch depth.

10 Remove mold from kettle and cool 10 minutes to let the pudding firm. Remove foil cover and invert a plate on top of mold. Using pot holders to handle the mold, invert mold and plate together and lift off the mold. Steamed puddings have a firm texture and will conform to the shape and design of the mold in which they are cooked.

Serve the steamed pudding warm with sauce spooned atop.

Puddings

Lemon Snow Pudding

¾ cup sugar
5 tablespoons cornstarch
¼ teaspoon salt
2¼ cups water
⅓ cup lemon juice
2 egg whites
Custard Sauce

Refer to: Making cream pudding, steps 1, 2, and 4, page 338. In saucepan combine sugar, cornstarch, and salt; blend in water. Heat to boiling; cook 2 minutes, stirring constantly. Cool. Stir in lemon juice.

Referring to steps 5 and 6 on page 344, beat egg whites till stiff peaks form; fold into lemon mixture. Pour into 4-cup mold; chill till firm. Unmold. Serve pudding with Custard Sauce. Makes 6 servings.

Custard Sauce: Refer to: Making stirred custard, page 86. In saucepan combine 2 slightly beaten *egg yolks,* ¼ cup *sugar,* and ⅛ teaspoon *salt.* Stir in 1½ cups *milk.* Cook and stir over low heat till mixture thickens. Stir in ½ teaspoon *vanilla.* Cover and chill sauce till ready to serve.

Baked Pineapple Tapioca

1 20-ounce can pineapple chunks (juice pack)
¾ cup hot water
½ cup sugar
3 tablespoons quick-cooking tapioca
1 tablespoon lemon juice
½ teaspoon salt
Dash ground nutmeg
Frozen whipped dessert topping, thawed
½ cup chopped walnuts

In a bowl combine undrained pineapple, hot water, sugar, tapioca, lemon juice, salt, and nutmeg. Let stand 10 minutes. Pour into a 1-quart casserole. Bake, uncovered, in 325° oven 40 to 50 minutes or till tapioca granules are clear and pudding is thick; stir occasionally. Cool slightly. Serve topped with whipped dessert topping and sprinkled with chopped walnuts. Makes 6 servings.

Holiday Bread Pudding

2 slightly beaten eggs
2¼ cups milk
½ cup packed brown sugar
1 teaspoon vanilla
¼ teaspoon salt
5 slices day-old firm-textured white bread, cut into 1-inch pieces
⅓ cup raisins
Wine Sauce

In mixing bowl combine eggs, milk, brown sugar, vanilla, and salt; stir in bread pieces and raisins. Let stand 5 minutes. Turn mixture into an ungreased 8×1½-inch round baking dish. Place dish in a 13×9×2-inch baking pan on oven rack. Carefully pour hot water into larger pan to depth of 1 inch, referring to step 8 on page 345. Bake, uncovered, in 350° oven about 50 minutes or till knife comes out clean. Serve warm with Wine Sauce. Makes 6 servings.

Wine Sauce: Referring to steps 7–10 on page 342, in a saucepan crush one 10-ounce package frozen sliced *strawberries,* thawed. Stir in 2 tablespoons cold water, 1 tablespoon *cornstarch,* and ¼ teaspoon ground *cinnamon.* Cook and stir till mixture is thickened and bubbly; cook 1 minute more. Sieve sauce; discard seeds. Return sauce to saucepan. Stir in ½ cup *dry white wine.* Add several drops *red food coloring,* if desired; heat through.

Honey Rice Pudding

4 cups milk
½ cup long grain rice
½ cup raisins (optional)
¼ to ⅓ cup honey *or* sugar
½ teaspoon salt
½ teaspoon vanilla
½ teaspoon ground cinnamon

In a 1½-quart casserole combine milk, rice, raisins, honey or sugar, salt, and vanilla. Bake, uncovered, in 300° oven about 2 hours, stirring gently every 20 minutes. Sprinkle with cinnamon. Serve warm. Makes 6 to 8 servings.

Chocolate Bread Pudding

4 beaten eggs
2⅔ cups milk
½ cup sugar
1½ teaspoons vanilla
1 teaspoon ground cinnamon
½ teaspoon salt
4 cups dry bread cubes (6 slices)
¾ cup tiny semisweet chocolate pieces
⅓ cup chopped walnuts

In mixing bowl combine eggs, milk, sugar, vanilla, cinnamon, and salt. Stir in bread cubes, chocolate, and nuts. Turn mixture into an ungreased 10×6×2-inch baking dish. Place dish in a 13×9×2-inch baking pan on oven rack. Carefully pour hot water into larger pan to depth of 1 inch, referring to step 8 on page 345. Bake in 350° oven for 65 to 70 minutes or till a knife inserted just off-center comes out clean. Serve warm. Makes 8 servings.

Chocolate Rice Pudding

1½ cups milk
½ cup long grain rice
½ cup raisins
2 squares (2 ounces) semisweet chocolate
2 tablespoons butter *or* margarine
2 tablespoons sugar
1 tablespoon cornstarch
½ cup milk
2 beaten egg yolks
2 egg whites
¼ cup sugar

In saucepan combine the 1½ cups milk, the rice, and raisins. Simmer, covered, 25 to 30 minutes or till rice is tender, referring to steps 2 and 3 on page 342. In medium saucepan over low heat, melt chocolate and butter or margarine. Combine the 2 tablespoons sugar and the cornstarch. Stir into chocolate; add remaining milk and the egg yolks. Cook and stir till bubbly. Stir in rice mixture. In mixing bowl beat egg whites to soft peaks. Gradually add the ¼ cup sugar and beat to stiff peaks, referring to steps 6–8 on page 292. Fold into rice mixture. Cover and chill. Makes 8 servings.

Indian Pudding

- 3 cups milk
- ½ cup molasses
- ⅓ cup yellow cornmeal
- ½ teaspoon ground ginger
- ½ teaspoon ground cinnamon
- ¼ teaspoon salt
- 1 tablespoon butter *or* margarine

In saucepan mix milk and molasses; stir in cornmeal, ginger, cinnamon, and salt. Cook and stir about 10 minutes or till thick. Stir in butter or margarine. Turn into an ungreased 1-quart casserole. Bake, uncovered, in 300° oven about 1 hour. Makes 6 servings.

Lemonade Fluff Parfaits
Fluffy Rice Pudding
(see recipe on page 342)

Lemonade Fluff Parfaits

- ½ cup sugar
- 3 tablespoons cornstarch
- ¼ teaspoon salt
- 1½ cups milk
- 2 beaten egg yolks
- 1 3-ounce package cream cheese, softened
- 2 tablespoons butter *or* margarine
- 1 teaspoon vanilla
- ½ cup frozen lemonade concentrate, thawed
- 2 egg whites
- ¼ cup sugar
- ½ cup crushed vanilla wafers (about 12 cookies)
- 2 tablespoons chopped walnuts
- 2 tablespoons butter *or* margarine, melted

Refer to: Making cream pudding, steps 1, 2, 4, 5, and 6, page 338. In saucepan combine the ½ cup sugar, the cornstarch, and salt; stir in milk. Cook and stir over medium heat till thickened and bubbly. Remove from heat. Gradually add *1 cup* of the hot mixture to beaten egg yolks, mixing well. Return to saucepan; cook and stir 2 minutes more. Remove from heat.

Add cream cheese, 2 tablespoons butter or margarine, and vanilla; beat until smooth with rotary beater. Stir in lemonade concentrate. Cover surface with waxed paper, referring to tip on page 339; cool 10 minutes.

With clean beaters, beat egg whites to soft peaks; gradually add the ¼ cup sugar and beat to stiff peaks, referring to steps 6–8 on page 292. Fold into pudding mixture.

Combine vanilla wafer crumbs, chopped nuts, and 2 tablespoons butter or margarine. Layer pudding and crumbs in parfait glasses, beginning with pudding and ending with crumbs. Cover and chill. Makes 6 servings.

Victorian Plum Pudding

- 4 slices bread, torn into pieces
- 1 cup prepared mincemeat
- ½ cup milk
- 2 slightly beaten eggs
- 1 cup packed brown sugar
- 4 ounces suet, very finely chopped (about 1 cup)
- ¼ cup brandy
- 1 teaspoon vanilla
- 1 cup all-purpose flour
- 2 teaspoons ground cinnamon
- 1 teaspoon baking soda
- 1 teaspoon ground cloves
- 1 teaspoon ground mace
- ½ teaspoon salt
- 1½ cups chopped mixed candied fruits and peels (12 ounces)
- 1 cup raisins
- ½ cup slivered almonds
  Brandy Hard Sauce

349

Refer to: Making steamed pudding, steps 1 and 6–10, page 346. Generously grease a 2-quart mold; set aside.

In a bowl combine bread, mincemeat, and milk; beat together. Stir in eggs, brown sugar, finely chopped suet, brandy, and vanilla. Thoroughly stir together the flour, cinnamon, soda, cloves, mace, and salt. Add mixed candied fruits and peels, raisins, and almonds. Stir in bread mixture. Pour batter into the prepared mold. Cover mold with foil and secure with string.

Place a rack in a large, deep kettle; add 1 inch hot water to kettle. Place covered mold on rack. Bring water to boiling. Cover kettle and steam pudding for 3½ hours. Add more boiling water to kettle, if needed.

When pudding is done, remove from kettle and cool 10 minutes; unmold. Serve with Brandy Hard Sauce. Makes 8 to 10 servings.

Brandy Hard Sauce: In a bowl cream together 2 cups sifted *powdered sugar* and ½ cup *butter or margarine.* Beat in 1 *egg yolk,* 2 tablespoons *brandy,* and 1 teaspoon *vanilla.* Beat 1 *egg white* till stiff peaks form, referring to step 5 on page 345. Fold egg white into butter mixture; chill. Garnish sauce with an orange peel twist, if desired. Makes about 1¾ cups sauce.

BEVERAGES

Beverages are an important part of every meal. Whether you prefer coffee, tea, hot chocolate, or a cold drink such as lemonade, this section will give you pointers on making the beverage as well as serving it.

Coffee

Technique: Brewing coffee using a percolator or a drip coffee maker

¾ **cup water (for each 6-ounce cup)**
1 **to 2 tablespoons ground coffee (for each 6-ounce cup)**

Percolator Coffee: 1 Pour water into percolator; stand the stem and basket firmly in the pot. **2** Measure coffee into the basket. Replace basket lid and cover pot. **3** Bring water to boiling; reduce heat and perk gently for 5 to 8 minutes. **4** Let stand for a minute or two; remove basket. Keep coffee warm over low heat.

Drip Coffee: 1 Measure coffee into the basket of the pot. **2** Measure water. For electric drip coffee makers, pour cold water into upper compartment. For non-electric drip coffee makers, pour boiling water over the coffee in basket. **3** For electric drip coffee makers, place pot on heating element and allow water to drip through coffee basket. For non-electric drip coffee makers, simply allow water to drip into bottom section.

When coffee is finished dripping, remove basket and discard grounds. Stir the brewed coffee and serve. Keep warm over low heat.

When a recipe calls for hot strong coffee, *simply make coffee by any method you prefer, using a little more coffee than you usually would. You can also use instant coffee crystals, following the directions on the label.*

1 Percolator Coffee: Pour water into percolator. Use at least ¾ of the capacity of the pot, but do not allow the water level to come above the bottom of the basket. Stand the stem and basket firmly in the pot.

To make the best coffee, use fresh, cold water. And, start with a clean coffeepot so that any sediment and oils from the previous pot do not disturb the flavor.

1 Drip Coffee: Measure coffee into the basket of the pot, being careful to distribute it evenly. Use a filter if the manufacturer recommends one for your pot.

Use "regular grind" or the finer "drip grind" according to the pot manufacturer's directions.

2 Measure coffee into the basket of the pot; distribute coffee evenly. Replace basket lid and cover pot.

To prevent excessive sediment, use "regular grind" coffee in a percolator. Keep coffee in an airtight container in a cool place. The refrigerator or freezer is often recommended. If you store it there, avoid letting it stand out because condensed moisture can speed staling.

3 Bring water to boiling; reduce heat and perk gently for 5 to 8 minutes. Perking longer than 8 minutes adds bitterness to the coffee rather than flavor. If you use an automatic percolator, you will not need to time it since it will shut off automatically.

The best way to tell when coffee is done to the preferred strength is to pour a little into a cup and taste it.

4 Remove percolator from heat a minute or two before serving to allow all the coffee to finish dripping through the basket. Then remove basket using a pot holder to protect fingers. The basket must be removed to prevent steaming the grounds and releasing bitterness and burned flavors.

Serve coffee immediately. Keep remaining coffee warm over low heat for a short time. Or, to keep it longer, let it cool; reheat later.

351

2 Use the pot to measure the water, if manufacturer directs. *Or* use standard measuring cups. For electric drip coffee makers, pour fresh, cold water into the coffee maker. For non-electric drip coffee makers, pour boiling water over the coffee in basket.

3 For electric drip coffee makers, place the pot on the heating element with the coffee basket in its proper position. Allow pot to drip till all the water has dripped through. For non-electric pots, allow water to drip into bottom section.

When coffee is finished dripping, remove basket and discard grounds. Stir coffee and serve immediately. Keep remaining coffee warm over low heat.

Beverages

Tea

Technique: Brewing tea

Boiling water
3 to 6 teaspoons loose tea *or* **3 to 6 tea bags**
4 cups boiling water
Sugar
Lemon wedges
Milk

352

1 Warm a teapot by rinsing it with boiling water. **2** Measure tea into tea ball. **3** Empty teapot; add tea ball or tea bags to pot. **4** Measure boiling water. **5** Immediately add the 4 cups boiling water to teapot. Cover pot and let steep 3 to 5 minutes. **6** Remove tea ball or bags; stir tea and serve at once. Pass sugar, lemon, and milk. Makes 5 (6-ounce) servings.

Iced Tea: Prepare tea as directed above *except* use 4 to 8 teaspoons loose tea or 4 to 8 tea bags. Pour over ice in glasses; pass sugar and lemon.

Keep tea at room temperature to avoid clouding. If tea does become cloudy, restore the clear amber color by adding a little boiling water to the tea.

1 Warm the teapot by filling it with boiling water. Let the water stand in the pot for a few moments till the pot is hot. This prevents the pot from cooling the water below the best temperature for brewing and drinking tea.

4 Measure the boiling water. Be sure to use fresh, cold water just brought to a boil to avoid tea with a flat or leftover taste.

2 Fill the tea ball with the loose tea. Experiment to find the amount and variety of tea you prefer.

The three basic types are the light, unfermented green teas; the semi-fermented oo-long teas; and the hearty, fermented black teas. Black tea is the most popular type in the United States. Other variations are derived by adding herbs, spices, or flowers to the leaves. Store tea in an airtight container up to 6 months.

3 Pour the hot water out of the teapot. Add the tea ball or tea bags to the warm teapot, securing tea ball chain to the rim of the pot for easy removal later.

TIP You don't have to boil water to make iced tea. *Place 6 tea bags in a pitcher with 4 cups fresh, cold water. Cover and refrigerate several hours or overnight. Pour tea over ice in glasses; pass sugar and lemon. Makes 4 servings.*

353

5 Immediately pour the measured water into teapot. Cover pot and let tea steep for 3 to 5 minutes. The tea leaves need this amount of time to release all their flavor.

Don't depend on the color of the tea to tell you when it has finished brewing, since teas vary greatly in color. If tea is too strong, add a little hot water to each cup of tea. If it's too weak, next time increase the amount of tea.

6 Remove tea ball or tea bags from the pot when tea is finished brewing. Do not leave the tea leaves or bags in the pot, as the tea may become bitter. Stir tea and serve in cups; pass sugar, lemon wedges, and milk.

Beverages

Breakfast Cocoa

Technique: Making hot chocolate

⅓ **cup sugar**
⅓ **cup unsweetened cocoa powder**
    Dash salt
½ **cup water**
3½ **cups milk**
½ **teaspoon vanilla**

354

1 In a saucepan stir together sugar, cocoa, and salt. **2** Stir in the water. **3** Bring to boiling, stirring constantly. Cook 1 minute longer. **4** Stir in milk. **5** Heat just to the boiling point; *do not boil.* **6** Remove from heat; stir in vanilla. **7** Beat with a rotary beater till frothy. Serve in cups or mugs; top with marshmallows or whipped cream, if desired. Makes 4 (8-ounce) servings.

1 In a saucepan stir together the sugar, cocoa, and salt. Blend the ingredients thoroughly so that the starch particles in the cocoa are separated by sugar. This helps prevent lumps from forming when the liquid is added.

Dry cocoa powder is used to make this hot beverage rather than solid chocolate because the fat in solid chocolate tends to separate when heated.

5 Heat the cocoa-milk mixture just to the boiling point, stirring often. At this point, tiny bubbles will form around the edges of the saucepan. *Do not boil* the mixture.

2 Add the water and stir till the dry ingredients are thoroughly blended with the water. A wooden spoon is a good utensil to use for stirring in a saucepan.

3 Bring mixture to boiling, stirring constantly with a wooden spoon. Allow mixture to bubble over entire surface, as shown. Boil 1 minute longer. This step helps prevent cocoa from settling out and ensures that the starchy components of the cocoa will be thoroughly cooked.

4 Add the milk to the hot cocoa mixture in the saucepan, stirring constantly with a wooden spoon to assure complete blending.

6 Remove pan from heat. Stir the vanilla into the chocolate mixture in the saucepan. The vanilla is not added with the other ingredients because some of its flavor would evaporate during cooking.

7 Just before serving, beat the mixture with a rotary beater till the cocoa is very frothy. The froth prevents the formation of a skin on the surface of the cocoa.

Serve cocoa in cups or mugs. Garnish with marshmallows or whipped cream, if desired.

Beverages

Orange Lemonade

Technique: Using syrup method to make lemonade

2	**cups sugar**
2½	**cups water**
3	**oranges**
6	**lemons**
¼	**cup lightly packed fresh mint leaves (optional)**
	Ice
	Water

1 Place sugar in saucepan; stir in the 2½ cups water. Heat over medium heat till sugar dissolves, stirring occasionally. **2** Remove from heat; cool.

3 Finely shred enough orange peel to make 2 tablespoons; set aside. **4** Squeeze juice from oranges and lemons; you should have about 1½ cups orange juice and 1½ cups lemon juice. **5** Add juices and peel to cooled syrup. Pour over mint leaves, if desired. Cover and steep for 1 hour. **6** Strain mixture. **7** Pour into jars. Cover and refrigerate. **8** Fill glasses with ice. Pour equal parts of water and fruit syrup over ice; stir to combine. Makes 6 cups fruit syrup or 12 (8-ounce) servings of lemonade.

356

1 Place the sugar in a saucepan. Stir in the 2½ cups water. Heat the sugar-water mixture till the sugar dissolves, stirring mixture occasionally.

5 Add the orange juice, lemon juice, and orange peel to the cooled syrup. Pour over the mint leaves, if they are to be used. Cover and steep for 1 hour.

2 When sugar dissolves completely, no grains of sugar will be visible and the mixture will be a clear syrup, as shown. Remove pan from heat and allow mixture to cool to room temperature.

3 Meanwhile, rub an orange across a very fine shredding surface to make 2 tablespoons of shredded peel. Shred only the outer orange layer of skin, since the inner white layer is very bitter. Set aside.

4 Cut the oranges and lemons in half crosswise. Squeeze the juice from the fruit, rotating the fruit on a citrus juicer with a firm motion. You should have about 1½ cups orange juice and 1½ cups lemon juice.

357

6 Set a sieve over a large bowl or pitcher. Pour fruit syrup through the sieve to strain out seeds, peel, pulp, and mint leaves.

7 Pour the strained syrup into jars, if desired; or place in a pitcher. Cover and chill the fruit syrup. Store in refrigerator till ready to serve.

8 To serve lemonade, fill glasses with ice. Half-fill each glass with water; finish filling with the fruit syrup. Stir to combine.

Or, mix equal parts of fruit syrup and water in a pitcher. Pour into ice-filled glasses.

Garnish glasses with additional fruit slices and mint leaves, if desired.

Beverages

Amber Tea Punch

- 4 cups hot tea (see recipe on page 352)
- ½ cup sugar
- 2 12-ounce cans apricot nectar
- 2 cups orange juice
- ½ cup lemon juice
- 1 28-ounce bottle ginger ale, chilled
  Ice cubes

Combine hot tea and sugar; stir to dissolve sugar. Stir in nectar and juices. Chill. Pour mixture into punch bowl; carefully pour ginger ale into bowl. Serve over ice cubes. Makes 24 (4-ounce) servings.

Strawberry-Eggnog Shake

- 1 quart strawberry ice cream
- 1 cup fresh strawberries, mashed
- 2 cups canned eggnog, chilled
  Ground nutmeg

Referring to step 3 on page 331, soften ice cream in a large chilled mixer bowl. Add mashed berries; beat with electric mixer just to blend. Stir in eggnog. Serve in tall chilled glasses; sprinkle with nutmeg. Makes 4 (12-ounce) servings.

Firetong Punch

- 1 fifth dry red wine (750 ml)
- ½ cup sugar
- 6 whole cloves
- 1 3×1½-inch strip orange peel
- 1 2×1½-inch strip lemon peel
- ½ cup orange juice
- ¼ cup lemon juice
- ¼ cup rum
- 8 sugar cubes

Heat together the wine, the ½ cup sugar, cloves, peels, and juices. *Do not boil.* Pour the hot mixture into a heat-proof punch bowl.

Warm the rum; soak the sugar cubes in the rum. Place cubes in a strainer over punch bowl. Referring to the tip on page 151, ignite cubes; as they flame, gradually spoon more warm rum over the cubes. When all sugar has melted, garnish punch with orange slices, if desired. Serve hot. Makes 10 (4-ounce) servings.

Sangria

- 2 oranges
- 2 lemons
- 2 fifths rosé, burgundy, *or* other red wine (1.5 liters)
- ¼ cup sugar
- ¼ cup brandy
- 1 apple
- 1 28-ounce bottle carbonated water, chilled

Chill *one* orange and *one* lemon for garnish. Squeeze juice from the second orange and lemon, referring to step 4 on page 357. Place juices, wine, sugar, and brandy in a large pitcher or bowl. Stir to dissolve sugar; chill. Just before serving, divide mixture into 2 pitchers or pour into punch bowl. Cut chilled orange into wedges. Slice chilled lemon into cartwheels. Cut apple into wedges; remove core. Thread fruit on wooden picks to stand in glasses, or float fruit in punch bowl. Slowly add carbonated water. Makes about 24 (4-ounce) servings.

Spiced Percolator Punch

- 2 32-ounce bottles cranberry juice cocktail
- 1 46-ounce can unsweetened pineapple juice
- 1 cup packed brown sugar
- 4 teaspoons whole cloves
- 12 inches stick cinnamon, broken
  Peel of ¼ orange, cut in strips
- 1 fifth light rum (750 ml)

Refer to: Brewing coffee using a percolator, page 350. In 24-cup electric percolator combine cranberry juice, pineapple juice, and brown sugar. Place cloves, cinnamon, and orange peel in coffee maker basket. Assemble coffee maker; plug in and percolate. Just before serving, remove basket and stir in rum. Keep hot. Float a quartered lemon slice on each serving, if desired. Makes about 34 (4-ounce) servings.

Citrus-Rhubarb Cooler

- 1 pound rhubarb, cut up (4 cups)
- 3 cups water
- ¾ cup sugar
- ⅔ cup orange juice
- 3 tablespoons lemon juice
  Ice cubes
- 1 28-ounce bottle ginger ale, chilled

In saucepan cook rhubarb with water and sugar about 15 minutes or till fruit is very soft; press through sieve. Add to the fruit juices. Cover; chill. To serve, pour ½ cup of rhubarb liquid over ice cubes in a tall glass, referring to step 8 on page 357. Fill glass with ginger ale; stir. Makes about 12 (6-ounce) servings.

Cinnamon Iced Coffee

- 3½ cups hot strong coffee (see recipe on page 350)
- 6 inches stick cinnamon
- ½ cup whipping cream
  Cracked ice
  Sugar

Pour hot coffee over cinnamon; let stand 1 hour. Discard cinnamon; stir in cream. Chill. To serve, pour over ice in glasses. Stir in sugar to taste. Makes about 5 (6-ounce) servings.

Brandied Chocolate

- 1 cup cold water
- 1 tablespoon cornstarch
- 2 inches stick cinnamon
- 2⅓ cups milk
- ½ cup packed brown sugar
- 1 square (1 ounce) unsweetened chocolate, cut up
- 1 beaten egg yolk
- ¼ cup brandy

In saucepan stir water into cornstarch; add cinnamon. Cook and stir till bubbly. Add milk, sugar, and chocolate; stir till chocolate melts. Discard cinnamon. Beat with rotary beater. Combine yolk and brandy; stir *1 cup* of the hot mixture into yolk mixture, referring to steps 5–6 on page 338. Return all to pan; cook and stir over low heat 1 to 2 minutes. *Do not boil.* Makes 6 (5-ounce) servings.

Frosty Spiced Tea

- ¾ cup water
- 3 tablespoons sugar
- 6 inches stick cinnamon, broken
- ½ teaspoon whole cloves
- ¼ teaspoon ground nutmeg
- 4 teaspoons loose tea *or* 4 tea bags
- 4 cups boiling water
  Ice cubes

Refer to: Brewing tea, page 352. In small saucepan combine the ¾ cup water with sugar, cinnamon, cloves, and nutmeg. Bring to boil; reduce heat. Cover and simmer for 20 minutes. Strain to remove spices.

Place loose tea in tea ball; add tea ball or tea bags to teapot. Pour the 4 cups boiling water over loose tea or tea bags; steep for 3 to 5 minutes. Remove tea ball or tea bags. Combine sugar mixture with brewed tea; pour over ice in glasses. Makes 6 (6-ounce) servings.

Brandy-Eggnog Deluxe

- 6 egg yolks
- ¾ cup sugar
- ½ teaspoon vanilla
- ¼ teaspoon ground nutmeg
- 1½ cups brandy
- ⅓ cup bourbon
- 3 cups whipping cream, chilled
- 2 cups cold milk
- 6 egg whites
- 6 tablespoons sugar

Beat egg yolks at high speed of electric mixer about 6 minutes or till they are thick and lemon-colored. Gradually add the ¾ cup sugar, vanilla, and nutmeg, beating constantly. Stir in brandy and bourbon; chill. Stir in cream and milk. Beat egg whites till soft peaks form; gradually add the 6 tablespoons sugar and beat to stiff peaks, referring to steps 3–5 on page 92. Fold into yolk mixture just till combined, leaving a few small fluffs of egg white. Serve at once. Sprinkle with additional nutmeg, if desired. Makes 24 (4-ounce) servings.

Minted Lime Soda

- 6 tablespoons crème de menthe syrup
- 6 tablespoons lime juice
- 1 quart vanilla ice cream
- 1 28-ounce bottle lemon-lime carbonated beverage, chilled

To each of 6 chilled 12-ounce glasses, add *1 tablespoon* of the crème de menthe syrup and *1 tablespoon* of the lime juice. To each glass add a *small amount* of the ice cream and ½ *cup* of the carbonated beverage. Stir to muddle. Place additional scoops of ice cream in glasses; fill with remaining carbonated beverage. Garnish with mint sprigs, if desired. Makes 6 (12-ounce) servings.

Sangria
Minted Lime Soda
Brandy-Eggnog Deluxe
Frosty Spiced Tea

Honeyed Chocolate

- 1 4-ounce package sweet cooking chocolate
- ¼ cup honey
- ½ teaspoon salt
- 7 cups milk
- 1 teaspoon vanilla

Chop the chocolate, referring to step 3 on page 339. In saucepan combine chocolate, honey, salt, and 1 cup *water.* Cook and stir over low heat till smooth. Referring to steps 4–6 on page 354, add milk; heat. Stir in vanilla. Makes 8 (8-ounce) servings.

SPECIAL HELPS

Have you ever started a recipe and realized at the last minute that you're out of an ingredient? Or, gotten halfway through something you're preparing for tonight's meal only to find it has to chill overnight? To avoid such problems, follow these three steps whenever you cook.

1 Read the recipe and make sure you understand it. If any terms in the directions are unfamiliar, look them up. And if it's your first time making the dish, allow plenty of extra time—you may run into steps that take longer than you might think.

2 Gather all the ingredients you'll need to make the recipe. It's a good idea to put everything together on a tray so you can find it easily, then put it all away at the same time. Check to see that you have enough of each ingredient before you begin. If something should be chilled, make sure it's in the refrigerator; if an ingredient should be cut up, chopped, drained, toasted, peeled, or sliced, now is the time to do it.

3 Assemble all the equipment you're going to need. Get out mixing bowls and spoons, spatulas, baking pans, and measuring utensils (for instance, make sure that your only pie plate isn't in the dishwasher). This step also saves floury hand prints on cabinets.

COOKING TERMS

Bake: Cook in an oven or oven-like appliance. Always bake a dish uncovered unless recipe specifies otherwise.

Baste: Brush or spoon a glaze, a sauce, or drippings over a food as it cooks to add flavor and to help keep the surface moist.

Beat: Use a brisk up-and-over motion to add air to a mixture and make it smooth. Or, use an electric mixer or rotary beater to achieve similar results.

Blanch: Briefly boil or steam a food to prevent spoilage during freezing, or to loosen skins for peeling.

Blend: Process a food in an electric blender to mix, chop, or puree. Or, combine by hand with a stirring motion to make a uniform mixture.

Boil: Cook in liquid that is heated until bubbles rise to the surface and break (refer to photo on page 363). In a full rolling boil, bubbles form rapidly throughout the mixture.

Braise: Cook slowly with a small amount of liquid in a covered pan on the range top or in the oven.

Broil: Cook by direct heat under a broiler in an electric or gas range.

Caramelize: Cook sugar over low heat till it melts and turns brown (refer to photo on page 371).

Chill: Refrigerate to reduce temperature of a food.

Chop: Cut into small irregular-shaped pieces (refer to photo on page 363).

Cool: Let stand at room temperature to reduce the temperature of a food. When a recipe says, "cool quickly," the food should be refrigerated or set in a bowl of ice water to quickly reduce its temperature.

Cream: Beat with a spoon or electric mixer to make mixture light and fluffy.

Cube: Cut into pieces that are the same size on each side—at least ½ inch (refer to photo on page 363).

Dice: Cut into cubes that are ⅛ to ¼ inch on each side (refer to photo on page 363).

Dissolve: Stir a dry ingredient into a liquid until the dry ingredient is no longer visible.

Fillet: Cut lean meat or fish into pieces without a bone.

Flake: Gently break into small pieces.

Fold: Gently combine two or more ingredients (refer to step 4 on page 81).

Fry: Cook in hot fat. When a large amount of fat is used, the process is called deep-fat frying.

Garnish: Decorate a food, usually with another food.

Glaze: Brush mixture on a food to give a glossy appearance or a hard finish. Usually the glaze adds flavor.

Grate: Rub across a grater to break a food into fine particles (refer to photo on page 363).

Grill: Cook over hot coals.

Grind: Use a food grinder to cut a food into very fine pieces.

Knead: Work dough with the hands in a pressing, folding, and turning motion (refer to steps 6–8 on page 182).

Marinate: Allow a food to stand in a liquid that adds flavor to the food (refer to tip on page 19).

Mince: Cut into very tiny, irregular-shaped pieces (refer to photo on page 363).

Mix: Combine ingredients by stirring.

Partially set: A term used to describe gelatin mixtures at the point in setting when the consistency resembles raw egg whites.

Pit: Remove the seed from a piece of fruit.

Poach: Cook in hot liquid, being careful that the food holds its shape.

Puree: Use a blender, food processor, or food mill to convert a food into a liquid or heavy paste.

Reduce: Boil rapidly to evaporate liquid so mixture becomes thicker.

Roast: Cook a meat, uncovered, in the oven. "Pot roasting" refers to braising a meat roast.

Sauté: Cook in a small amount of butter, margarine, oil, or shortening.

Scald: Bring to a temperature just below boiling so that tiny bubbles form at the edges of the pan.

Score: Cut shallow grooves or slits through the outer layer of a food.

Sear: Brown surface of meat quickly with intense heat.

Shred: Rub on a shredder to form long, narrow pieces (refer to photo on page 363).

Sift: Pass flour or a dry mixture through a sieve or sifter to incorporate air and break up lumps.

Simmer: Cook in liquid that is just below the boiling point. Bubbles burst before reaching surface (refer to photo on page 363).

Steam: Cook using steam, sometimes under pressure.

Steep: Extract the flavor or color from a substance by letting it stand in hot liquid.

Stew: Cook slowly in simmering liquid.

Stir: Use a spoon to combine ingredients with a circular or figure-8 motion.

Stir-fry: Cook quickly in a small amount of hot fat, stirring constantly (refer to page 134).

Toss: Mix ingredients lightly by lifting and dropping with a spoon, or a spoon and fork.

Whip: Beat lightly and rapidly, incorporating air into a mixture to make it light and to increase its volume.

What's the difference?

Understanding the difference between similar cooking terms can be essential to a recipe's success. Here's an explanation of some often-confused terms.

Cube: Cut a food into uniform-size pieces ½ inch or larger on each side. Use a chef's knife to make lengthwise cuts of the desired width, then cut crosswise to make cubes. Cube meat and vegetables when you want larger pieces that you can identify.

Dice: Cut a food into uniform pieces ⅛ to ¼ inch on each side. Use a chef's knife to cut the food into strips of the desired width. Then pile strips together and cut crosswise into even cubes. Dice when you need small, even pieces that cook quickly.

Chop: Cut a food into irregular-shaped pieces about the size of a pea. Use a chopper, blender, food processor, or a chef's knife. Chop foods when their shape is not important, as in salads, breads, and casseroles.
To finely chop, cut into slightly smaller pieces.

363

Mince: Cut a food into very tiny, irregular-shaped pieces. A utility knife is the right utensil to use for mincing. Mincing is primarily used for garlic, so that its strong flavor is evenly distributed through a dish.

Finely shred: Rub a food across a fine shredding surface to form very narrow strips. This is usually done for lemon and orange peel, and when very small pieces of other potent seasonings are needed.

Shred: Cut a food into long, narrow strips, usually by rubbing it across a shredding surface. Some vegetables, such as lettuce or cabbage, can be shredded by thinly slicing with a knife. Use a shredder for other vegetables and for cheeses.

Grate: Rub a food across a rough grating surface to make very fine particles. Grate potent seasonings such as gingerroot, and hard cheeses such as parmesan.

Simmer: Cook in liquid that is kept just below boiling. A few bubbles form slowly and burst before they reach the surface. Simmering usually takes place between 185°F. (85°C) and 210°F. (99°C).

Boil: Cook in liquid kept at the temperature at which bubbles rise to the surface of the liquid and break. Water boils at 212°F. (100°C).

INGREDIENTS AND HOW TO USE THEM

Flour

All-purpose flour is a blend of hard- and soft-wheat flours. The combination allows it to be used in all types of baked goods, as well as for thickening.

Self-rising flour is an all-purpose flour that contains added leavening and salt. It may be substituted for all-purpose flour in quick bread recipes, but the salt, baking powder, and baking soda must be omitted.

Cake flour is a flour made from a softer wheat. It is used for making tender, delicate cakes.

Other types of flour include whole wheat, rye, and buckwheat flours, which are used mainly for specialty breads.

Thickeners

Flour (all-purpose) may be used to thicken gravies, sauces, and puddings. It gives sauces an opaque appearance.

Cornstarch is used to thicken sauces and puddings when a translucent product is desired. Its thickening power is about twice that of flour.

Tapioca may be used to thicken pie fillings and puddings. It forms a lumpy, but clear, mixture. Pearl tapioca is a slow-cooking variety, while quick-cooking tapioca cooks quickly and requires less soaking.

Eggs also may be used to thicken mixtures, as well as add richness.

Fats and Oils

Fats and oils differ in consistency and function. Fats are solid at room temperature, while oils are liquid. Both make baked products tender, add flavor, and can be used for frying. But no single fat does all three tasks equally well.

Hydrogenated shortenings may be composed of vegetable or animal fat or a combination of the two. They are processed to give the desired flavor, consistency, storage quality, and functional characteristics. This process makes them solid at room temperature and ideal for baking, but less suitable for frying (although they may be used).

Lard is a rendered pork fat and has a distinctive flavor. It is excellent for making pastry and biscuits, but is less suitable for making cakes and other products that require creaming. Although it can be used for frying, lard varies too much from batch to batch to make it reliable for deep-fat frying.

Butter is made from milk fat. Since it is 80% fat and 20% moisture and solids, it has different characteristics from other fats. Butter lends flavor to baked goods as well as some shallow-fried foods. However, butter is not suitable for deep-fat frying since it smokes before reaching the required temperatures.

Margarine, like butter, is only 80% fat. It is made from vegetable oil to simulate the characteristics of butter, and it performs like butter. Soft margarine also is available; it can be used like butter, but is made softer for easy spreading. Diet margarine has less fat, and cannot be substituted for butter in baking.

Drippings are fats rendered from cooking meat fats. Although most often used for shallow frying, drippings—particularly bacon drippings—are sometimes used as a seasoning.

Oils are fats that are liquid at room temperature. They are a good choice for frying, but should not be interchanged with solid fats for baking purposes, since they cannot be creamed to hold air. However, certain recipes for baked goods are designed specifically for oil. Oils also are used for salad dressings.

Unlike other oils, olive oil is not suited for deep-fat frying, and its flavor is too strong for use in baked goods. Use it only when you want its special flavor in salad dressings and for shallow frying.

Sweeteners

Besides their primary function of adding flavor, sweeteners affect the tenderness of baked goods and the consistency of puddings and sauces.

Granulated sugar is a basic sweetener made from sugar cane or sugar beets (both kinds are the same).

Powdered sugar or **confectioners' sugar** is granulated sugar crushed and screened till grains are tiny. Starch is then added to keep lumping to a minimum. It's designed for use in uncooked frostings and to dust over baked products.

Brown sugar is a less refined form of granulated sugar. It derives a special flavor and moistness from the molasses that clings to the granules. Dark brown sugar has a stronger flavor than light. A granulated form is available, but it can't be substituted for regular brown sugar in baking because its moisture content is lower.

Honey is made by bees from the nectar of flowers. It is sweeter than sugar, and adds a characteristic flavor to foods.

Syrups include corn, cane, sorghum, maple, maple-flavored syrups, and molasses. Each adds its distinctive flavor to foods. They are used as toppings as well as recipe ingredients.

Artificial sweeteners sweeten foods without the use of natural sugars. They cannot be substituted for sugar in baked foods because they do not have the other properties of sugar. However, artificial sweeteners are widely used to sweeten beverages and cereals.

364

Leavenings

Leavenings are the ingredients that cause a baked food to rise in the oven or on the griddle. In some products, such as cream puffs and angel cakes, the water turning to steam and air expanding are sufficient to leaven the food. But most baked goods require additional leavening agents.

Baking soda reacts with the acid in food to form carbon dioxide gas. The soda and acid begin to react as soon as liquid is added, so a product containing soda should be baked immediately after it is mixed. Some acidic foods that help complete the reaction are vinegar, lemon juice, cream of tartar, buttermilk, sour milk, brown sugar, and molasses.

Baking powder is a combination of baking soda and an acidic ingredient. It does not produce its full amount of leavening till heated, so the unbaked product is more stable than with soda.

Yeast is a microscopic plant that produces carbon dioxide from starch or sugar when placed in suitable conditions for growth. It can be purchased in the active dry or compressed form.

Eggs

Eggs have many functions in cooking. They can thicken mixtures, bind ingredients, or form a structure in baked goods. All recipes in this book were tested using large eggs.

Slightly beaten eggs are whole eggs beaten with a fork just long enough to break up yolks and form streaks of white and yellow.

Beaten eggs are whole eggs beaten with a fork till the whites and yolks are blended and no streaks remain.

Well-beaten eggs are whole eggs beaten with an electric mixer or rotary beater till they are very light in color and texture.

Thick and lemon-colored yolks are yolks beaten with an electric mixer till very thick and lemon-colored. They flow in a thick stream when beaters are lifted.

Egg whites beaten to soft peaks are whites beaten with an electric or rotary beater till they form peaks with tips that curl over when beaters are lifted.

Egg whites beaten to stiff peaks are whites beaten with an electric or rotary beater till they form peaks that stand straight when beaters are lifted. Further beating makes them dry, flaky, and unsuitable for most purposes.

Dairy Products

Homogenized whole milk is milk that has been processed so that the fat does not rise to the top. The fat content is at least 3.25%. **Skim milk** has most of its fat removed, so its fat content is less than 0.5%. **Low-fat milk** has a fat content of 0.5% to 2%.

Nonfat dry milk is milk with both fat and water removed. It is processed to mix easily with water. **Evaporated milk** has 60% of the water removed, and is processed in cans. **Sweetened condensed milk** is milk with about half the water removed and a large amount of sugar added, and is also processed in cans.

Buttermilk is the liquid left after the butter-making process. More widely sold is cultured buttermilk, a product made by adding a bacteria to skim milk. The two are interchangeable. **Yogurt** is a creamy product made by fermenting milk.

Whipping cream also may be called heavy cream or light whipping cream. It contains 30% to 40% fat, and is suitable for whipping. **Light cream** contains 10% to 30% fat and includes half-and-half. it adds richness to recipes. **Dairy sour cream** is a commercially cultured light cream used to add a tangy flavor and richness to food.

Natural cheese is a product made from milk that is cured to add flavor, and often ripened by bacteria or mold. Natural cheese in cooked foods can become grainy or stringy. **Process cheese** is made by combining several natural cheeses with an emulsifying agent. It is not cured. When cooked it is smoother than natural cheese.

INGREDIENT EQUIVALENTS

Food	Amount Before Preparation	Approximate Measure After Preparation
CEREALS		
Macaroni	1 cup (3½ oz.)	2½ cups cooked
Noodles	3 cups (4 oz.)	3 cups cooked
Spaghetti	8 oz.	4 cups cooked
Long grain rice	1 cup (7 oz.)	3 cups cooked
Quick-cooking rice	1 cup (3 oz.)	2 cups cooked
Popcorn	¼ cup	5 cups popped
CRUMBS		
Bread	1 slice	¾ cup soft or ¼ cup fine dry crumbs
Saltine crackers	28 squares	1 cup finely crushed
Rich round crackers	24 crackers	1 cup finely crushed
Graham crackers	14 squares	1 cup finely crushed
Chocolate wafers	19 cookies	1 cup finely crushed
Gingersnaps	15 cookies	1 cup finely crushed
Vanilla wafers	22 cookies	1 cup finely crushed
FRUITS		
Apples	1 medium	1 cup sliced
Apricots	1 medium	¼ cup sliced
Avocados	1 medium	1¼ cups sliced
Bananas	1 medium	⅓ cup mashed
Cherries, red	1 lb.	2 cups pitted
Grapes	1 lb.	2½ cups seeded
Lemons	1 medium	3 tablespoons juice 2 teaspoons peel
Limes	1 medium	2 tablespoons juice 1½ teaspoons peel
Oranges	1 medium	¼ to ⅓ cup juice 4 teaspoons peel
Peaches, Pears	1 medium	½ cup sliced
Rhubarb	1 lb. (4 cups)	2 cups cooked
Strawberries	4 cups whole	4 cups sliced

Food	Amount Before Preparation	Approximate Measure After Preparation
VEGETABLES		
Beans and peas, dried	1 lb. (2½ cups)	6 cups cooked
Cabbage	1 lb. (1 small)	5 cups shredded
Carrots, without tops	1 lb. (6 medium)	3 cups shredded or 2½ cups diced
Celery	1 medium bunch	4½ cups chopped
Corn	1 medium ear	½ cup cut from cob
Green beans	1 lb. (3 cups)	2½ cups cooked
Green onions	1 bunch (7)	½ cup sliced
Green peppers	1 large	1 cup diced
Mushrooms	1 lb. (6 cups)	6 cups sliced or 2 cups cooked
Onions	1 medium	½ cup chopped
Potatoes	1 medium	⅔ cup cubed or ½ cup mashed
Radishes	1 bunch	1 cup sliced
Spinach	1 lb. (12 cups)	1½ cups cooked
Tomatoes	1 medium	½ cup cooked
Zucchini	1 medium	1 cup sliced
NUTS		
Almonds	1 lb. in shell	1¼ cups shelled
Pecans	1 lb. in shell	2 cups shelled
Walnuts	1 lb. in shell	1½ cups shelled
MISCELLANEOUS		
Cheese, blue	4 oz.	1 cup crumbled
Cheese, Swiss or American	4 oz.	1 cup shredded or cubed
Eggs	1 large	3 tablespoons egg
Egg whites	1 large	2 tablespoons white
Egg yolks	1 large	1 tablespoon yolk
Whipping cream	1 cup	2 cups whipped
Ground beef	1 lb. raw	2¾ cups cooked
Boneless meat	1 lb. raw	2 cups cooked, cubed
Cooked meat	1 lb.	3 cups diced

HOW TO MEASURE

Measurements are important for consistent results, but all ingredients are not measured in the same way!

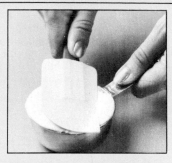

To measure liquids, use a standard glass or clear plastic measuring cup. Place it on a level surface and bend down so your eye is level with the marking you wish to read, as shown. Fill the cup to the marking.

Don't lift the cup off the counter to your eye, since your hand is not as steady or as level as a countertop.

To measure dry ingredients, use a dry measure with exactly the capacity you wish to measure. Pile the ingredient lightly into the cup with a spoon, then level with a metal spatula, as shown.

Never pack dry ingredients except brown sugar, which must be packed into the cup so that it holds the shape of the measure when turned out.

See below for information about measuring flour.

To measure solid shortening, pack it into a dry measure using a spatula, as shown. Run the spatula through the shortening in the cup to make sure there are no air pockets remaining.

The easiest way to measure butter or margarine is to use a quarter-pound stick for ½ cup, half of a stick for ¼ cup, or an eighth of a stick for 1 tablespoon.

To measure dried herbs, lightly fill a measuring spoon to the top—it's not necessary to level with a spatula—keeping the level as close to the top as possible. Then empty the spoon into your hand and crush the herb with your other hand. This breaks the leaves to better release their flavor.

Is sifting necessary?

Until recently, it was essential to sift all-purpose flour to lighten it for accurate measurement and to remove any lumps. But today's flour is no longer lumpy and compact, and now stirring it with a spoon is sufficient.

To measure flour, stir it in the canister to lighten it. Then gently spoon it into a dry measure, as shown, and level off the top with a metal spatula. This method applies to most flours.

The notable exception is *cake flour* which is very soft and tends to pack down. It should still be sifted to remove lumps and to lighten it. *Powdered sugar* also requires sifting to remove lumps.

What's a dash?

Recipes often call for a dash of pepper or a dash of bottled hot pepper sauce. What does "dash" really mean? It's a measure of less than ⅛ teaspoon (the smallest amount you can accurately measure using standard measuring spoons).

Most times a dash is used, it is for seasoning, and the actual amount is up to you. However, as a guide, consider a dash to be about ¹/₁₆ teaspoon.

MIXING TOOLS

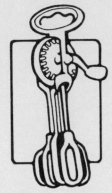

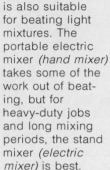

For stirring and beating, there are several types of tools. The *wire whip (whisk)* is the simplest, but can only be used on light mixtures such as egg whites. The *rotary beater,* operated by a hand crank, is also suitable for beating light mixtures. The portable electric mixer *(hand mixer)* takes some of the work out of beating, but for heavy-duty jobs and long mixing periods, the stand mixer *(electric mixer)* is best.

Essential for mixing are the *mixing bowl* and *mixer bowl*. These differ in that the mixer bowl is fitted to the stand of an electric mixer so it turns while the mixer is operating. The mixing bowl is simply an all-purpose bowl used with any mixing utensil.

A variety of spoons is needed for different jobs. *Wooden spoons* are recommended for beating since they're silent against a glass or metal bowl. When stirring hot mixtures, wooden spoons prevent burned fingers.

368

Metal spoons are essential for testing custard and jelly and for skimming fat. Use a *slotted spoon* to lift large pieces from liquid.

Spatulas also differ in design for different purposes. A *rubber spatula* scrapes the bowl clean of batter. A *flexible metal spatula* works to frost a

cake or to loosen bread from a pan. The *large metal spatula* is used primarily as a pancake or egg turner.

For measuring, you'll need *liquid measures, dry measures,* and *measuring spoons.* See page 367 to learn how to use these and why you need all three.

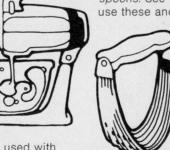

A *pastry blender* is needed for making pie crusts and biscuits. Use this tool to cut in shortening for flaky baked products.

You'll also need a *rolling pin* to roll out pastry, breads, and cookies.

Knives are used for all types of cutting jobs, although each is specialized to do one job better than another. Use a *paring knife* or *utility knife* for peeling fruits and other small cutting jobs.

Use a *chef's knife* for chopping and for large cutting jobs, and a *serrated knife* for slicing tomatoes and bread. Other knives include boning, grapefruit, butcher, and carving knives.

A *vegetable peeler* makes peeling easy and helps reduce waste. *Kitchen shears* make short work of snipping parsley and fruits, and heavy-duty shears will even cut up chicken.

Choose a *meat mallet* with both fine and coarse sides. Use the fine side for flattening chicken or veal, and the coarse side for tenderizing meat.

Strainers (sieves) and *colanders* differ in size and function. A strainer is made of fine wire mesh, while a colander has larger holes and stands freely on legs.

Be careful to use *thermometers* only for jobs for which they were intended, since some cannot perform in certain temperature ranges.

Saucepans are basic for top-of-the-range cooking. It's best to use about ⅔ of their capacity, so select a small (1- to 1½-quart), a medium (2- to 2½-quart), and a large (3- to 4-quart) covered saucepan when choosing your cookware.

Skillets are wider and shallower than saucepans. Small (6-inch), medium (8-inch), and large (12-inch) skillets with covers will suit most needs.

You'll need a kettle or Dutch oven for larger quantities. Saucepans and kettles differ in that the latter have two handles for easy carrying.

Baking pans (metal) and baking dishes (nonmetal) are most commonly used in the oven. These come in a variety of sizes and shapes—round, square, and rectangular are the most often used.

A baking sheet or cookie sheet is a flat metal pan that may have a raised edge on one or two sides. It differs from a jelly roll pan (also called a shallow baking pan) in that the jelly roll pan has 1-inch sides and can be used to make a jelly roll or bar cookies as well as other types of cookies.

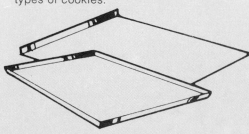

Muffin pans are used for baking cupcakes and muffins. The standard muffin cup measures 2½ inches across the top; smaller sizes are available to use for making tarts and tiny pastries. Usually 6 or 12 cups are included in a single muffin pan for ease in carrying the muffins to and from the oven.

Custard cups are 6-ounce glass or ceramic dishes for oven use. These may be used in place of muffin pans, or for making custards and individual desserts or casseroles.

Loaf pans (metal) and loaf dishes (nonmetal) are deeper than baking pans

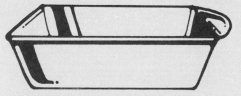

and dishes. They are used for making breads, cakes, and meat loaves.

A pie plate or pie pan is used for making pies. Choose one of glass or dull metal, since shiny metal keeps the crust from browning properly.

A casserole dish differs from a baking dish in that it is deeper and may be of any shape, but is usually round or oval. It is made of glass or ceramic materials. To find its volume, fill to the top with water, measuring as you fill.

A roasting pan is a shallow pan with a rack designed to keep the meat out of the drippings while roasting (see step 3 on page 9). A covered roasting pan is deeper, has a deep cover, and is used for pot roasting.

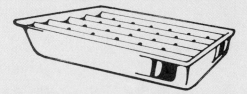

A broiler pan is a shallow pan with a fitted rack designed to keep meat out of the drippings while broiling.

A tube pan has a cylinder in its middle and is used to make angel and chiffon cakes (see step 6 on page 242). It may or may not have a removable bottom. Fluted tube pans also are available for making fancier cakes.

Springform pans have removable sides for making desserts with delicate crusts that could be disturbed by removing the food from the pan (see step 3 on page 307).

Use a wire rack for cooling finished baked products (see step 11 on page 229). It allows the food to cool without becoming soggy from the steam remaining in it.

STORAGE & PREPARATION HELPS

Storing Food

Considering today's prices, food is an investment well worth protecting. Because food is always subject to some sort of spoilage, keep these precautions in mind.

Store perishable foods in the refrigerator or freezer immediately after purchase. Two hours at room temperature is time enough to allow microorganisms to start growing on some foods.

Thaw frozen foods with care. If there's time, thaw all foods in the refrigerator. Otherwise, place in a sealed bag under cold running water.

Once food is cooked, refrigerate or freeze leftovers immediately after serving. Again, a 2-hour period of time can give germs a foothold.

Keep clean everything that will contact the food—hands, utensils, and counters. Be especially careful that cooked meat or poultry doesn't touch plates or knives used with raw meat.

The freezer is a good place to keep most foods that you'll store for a long time. The low temperature slows the growth of microorganisms and keeps fat from becoming rancid so quickly. But it rarely kills microorganisms, so use foods before they lose quality and safeness. Keep freezer at 0°F. (−18°C) or lower for maximum protection.

The refrigerator is the best place for perishable foods that you'll use within a few days. But it allows microorganisms to grow. To preserve maximum freshness, make sure the refrigerator is between 34°F. (1°C) and 40°F. (4°C). If it's any lower, food may alternately freeze and thaw—a process that reduces its quality.

The shelf is for storing foods that are fairly sturdy—such staples as flour and sugar, as well as stable vegetables like potatoes and onions. The best temperature here is 50°F. (10°C) to 70°F. (21°C) with ventilation and no sunlight. Foods stored here keep well because they are low in moisture, so keep the area as dry as possible.

Crumbs & Croutons

Make soft bread crumbs by tearing slices of fresh bread into crumbs. Or, tear bread into quarters. Place a few at a time in blender container; cover and blend till coarsely chopped. Each slice makes about ¾ cup crumbs.

Make fine dry bread crumbs by oven-toasting bread in a 300° oven till crisp and dry. Crush with a rolling pin. Or, place in blender container; cover and blend till finely crushed. Each slice makes about ¼ cup crumbs.

Make buttered crumbs by adding 1 tablespoon melted butter or margarine to each ¼ cup dry crumbs or ¾ cup soft bread crumbs. Toss to coat crumbs.

To make croutons, brush bread slices lightly with cooking oil or melted butter, if desired. Cut into ½-inch cubes. For seasoned croutons, sprinkle with garlic powder or crushed dried herbs.

Spread bread cubes in a shallow baking pan. Bake in a 300° oven for 20 to 25 minutes or till cubes are dry; stir at least once.

Using a Pastry Cloth

One valuable tool in the kitchen is a pastry cloth. Not only is it useful when you roll out cookies or pastry, it comes in very handy for kneading bread, and can minimize sticking problems with any dough.

To use a pastry cloth, sprinkle it with some flour, then rub it in. As you work, you may need to add a little more, but don't use extra flour unless the dough is sticking.

After using, the pastry cloth may be washed with your laundry. Or if it doesn't appear fat-soaked, store it in a tightly closed plastic bag in a cool place or in the refrigerator. This will prevent any fat that did adhere from becoming rancid.

Should You Preheat?

At one time, all recipes recommended preheating your oven, no matter what you were baking. But with rising energy costs and low fuel supply, avoiding this step is often a good idea.

When you bake a delicate cake, preheat the oven because the rapid increase in oven temperature may cause the cake to rise too quickly, then fall later.

But, for casseroles and roasts, the preheating time is not necessary. Simply turn the oven on when you begin to bake the food.

However, remember that the timings in many recipes are based on a preheated oven, so you may need to add an extra minute or two to the baking time.

Cooking Bacon

To fry: Place bacon strips in an unheated skillet. Cook over medium-low heat for 6 to 8 minutes, turning often. Drain well on paper toweling to remove excess fat.

To broil: Place bacon strips side by side on the unheated rack of a broiler pan. Broil 3 to 5 inches from heat till done, turning once. Watch closely to prevent burning.

To bake: Place bacon strips side by side on unheated rack of broiler pan. Bake in 400° oven for 10 minutes or till bacon is done.

To clarify butter, melt it over low heat in a heavy pan without stirring. When butter is completely melted, you'll see a clear oily layer atop a milky layer. Slowly pour clear liquid into a dish, leaving milky layer in pan. Discard the pan liquid; the clear liquid is the clarified butter.

Melt chocolate over low heat in a small heavy saucepan. Stir often to avoid scorching. If recipe calls for cooled chocolate, simply remove pan from the heat and let stand till lukewarm. Scrape chocolate from pan with a rubber spatula.

Snipping parsley or another fresh herb is easy to do right in the measuring cup. Place the uncut parsley in the cup and snip it with kitchen shears, then check to make sure you have the proper quantity for the particular recipe.

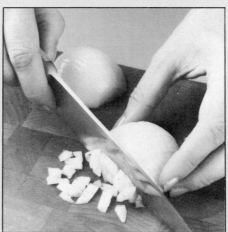

Separate eggs by gently cracking shell in center with a knife. Over a bowl, slip yolk back and forth from one shell half to the other, allowing white to fall into bowl. Drop yolk into another bowl. If yolk breaks into whites, remove *all* yolk traces since they can prevent whites from whipping.

It's easier to separate cold eggs, but bring them to room temperature before beating for best results.

Chop onions the easy way—cut them in half, then use the cut side as a stable base. Slice onion half in one direction. Then, holding onion slices together with one hand, as shown, slice in the other direction. Use a very sharp chef's knife to make the job even easier.

This technique works well for chopping other vegetables such as carrots and potatoes, too.

Carmelizing sugar is actually melting it; the sugar becomes a golden liquid. Place sugar in a heavy skillet or saucepan; heat and stir over low heat till sugar melts and turns golden brown.

To make a syrup from this melted sugar (it will harden when cooled), add hot water to the liquid very slowly, stirring constantly and using proportions specified in the recipe.

EMERGENCY SUBSTITUTIONS

*For best results, use ingredients specified in the recipe,.
since substitutions often change flavor and texture.
But when you're in a bind, use this chart to find an
acceptable substitute.*

If you don't have:	Substitute:
1 cup cake flour	1 cup minus 2 tablespoons all-purpose flour
1 tablespoon cornstarch (for thickening)	2 tablespoons all-purpose flour
1 teaspoon baking powder	¼ teaspoon baking soda plus ½ cup buttermilk or sour milk (to replace ½ cup of liquid called for)
1 package active dry yeast	1 cake compressed yeast
1 cup granulated sugar	1 cup packed brown sugar *or* 2 cups sifted powdered sugar
1 cup honey	1¼ cups granulated sugar plus ¼ cup liquid
1 cup corn syrup	1 cup granulated sugar plus ¼ cup liquid
1 square (1 ounce) unsweetened chocolate	3 tablespoons unsweetened cocoa powder plus 1 tablespoon butter or margarine
1 cup whipping cream, whipped	2 cups whipped dessert topping
1 cup sour milk or buttermilk	1 tablespoon lemon juice or vinegar plus enough whole milk to make 1 cup (let stand 5 minutes before using)*or* 1 cup whole milk plus 1¾ teaspoons cream of tartar
1 cup buttermilk	1 cup plain yogurt
1 cup whole milk	½ cup evaporated milk plus ½ cup water *or* 1 cup reconstituted nonfat dry milk (plus 2 teaspoons butter or margarine, if desired)
1 cup light cream	2 tablespoons butter plus 1 cup minus 2 tablespoons milk
1 whole egg	2 egg yolks (for most uses)
2 cups tomato sauce	¾ cup tomato paste plus 1 cup water
1 cup tomato juice	½ cup tomato sauce plus ½ cup water
1 clove garlic	⅛ teaspoon garlic powder or minced dried garlic
1 small onion	1 teaspoon onion powder *or* 1 tablespoon minced dried onion, rehydrated
1 teaspoon dry mustard	1 tablespoon prepared mustard
1 teaspoon finely shredded lemon peel	½ teaspoon lemon extract

THE METRIC SYSTEM

You've probably noticed in your supermarket shopping the metric measurements on cans and packages of food. But what does it mean to you?

The metric system or System Internationale (SI) is far from new. It was conceived in 1790 as a standard to simplify measurement throughout the world. And as of now, the United States is the only major country in the world that has not converted to this system.

But the change is coming, however slowly. Because SI is easier to learn and use and will simplify world trade, the United States is moving toward the metric system. Presently, however, the changeover is voluntary and many questions are yet to be decided. Until food manufacturers can tell us how large packages will be, we cannot predict the future of metrics in the grocery store.

However, based on the experience of Canada and other countries already using SI, there is some information that can help you become acquainted with the system.

Because it is based on multiples of 10, the metric system is easy to learn. Once you know the basic units (meter for length, liter for volume, etc.), you can convert to convenient units simply by moving the decimal point.

The smaller and larger units are named by adding a prefix to the basic unit. Thus, a meter becomes a kilometer (1000 meters), a centimeter (0.01 meter), or a millimeter (0.001 meter).

Volume: The metric system is really quite simple since there are fewer units of measure to remember. You will be trading teaspoons, tablespoons, fluid ounces, cups, pints, quarts, and gallons for milliliters and liters. And no more will you have to wonder about the difference between fluid ounces and *avoirdupois* ounces.

Measuring cups will change slightly, but measuring techniques should remain the same. Liquid measures will probably be sized 250 ml, 500 ml, and 1000 ml (1 liter)—only slightly larger than the present 1-cup, 2-cup, and 4-cup measures, respectively.

Dry measures will probably be sized 50 ml (just under ¼ cup), 125 ml (just over ½ cup), and 250 ml (just over 1 cup).

Measuring spoons will probably include spoons with 1 ml, 2 ml, 5 ml, 15 ml, and 25 ml capacities. These range from just under ¼ teaspoon to the size of a coffee measure.

Weight: No more will the decimals on a package of meat be difficult to convert to ounces. Since the metric system is based on decimals, they'll make more sense in relation to the kilogram (a measure of slightly more than 2 pounds).

Length: Pan sizes will also change to correspond with the new system. The centimeter is what you'll see most. Based on the meter (about 3 inches longer than a yard), the centimeter is 1/100 of a meter or between ⅓ and ½ of an inch.

Temperature: You're probably already familiar with the SI method of measuring heat. Measured in degrees Celsius, water freezes at 0°C and boils at 100°C (at sea level). Although the conversion from degrees Fahrenheit is oversimplified here, for the range of cooking temperatures, the reading in degrees Fahrenheit is nearly double that in degrees Celsius.

Putting Metric Units Into Perspective

Measures	Unit	Example
Volume	milliliter (ml)	Dash of salt is about 1 ml.
	liter (l)	Quart of milk is just less than 1 liter.
Weight (mass)	gram (g)	Paper clip weighs 1 g. Soda cracker weighs 3 g.
	kilogram (kg)	Small chicken weighs 1 kg. Large turkey weighs 10 kg.
Length	millimeter (mm)	Thickness of a dime is 1 mm.
	centimeter (cm)	Width of your little finger is 1 cm.
	meter (m)	With face turned to side and arm stretched in opposite direction, distance from nose to fingertips is 1 m.
	kilometer (km)	10 to 15 minutes' walk is 1 km. National speed limit is 90 km/hour.
Temperature	degrees Celsius (°C)	Water freezes at 0°C. Water boils at 100°C. Room temperature is 20°C to 25°C.

COOKING AT HIGH ALTITUDES

Many cooks have searched for the magic conversion that will adjust favorite recipes for high altitude cooking. Unfortunately, there is no formula, since ingredients and proportions vary with each recipe. Your best bet is to become familiar with how altitude affects food, then experiment with recipes to find a balance suitable to your location. Since recipes are more sensitive to high altitudes, be sure to measure accurately instead of guessing. And keep a record of the amounts you use and the results each time you cook.

Baking

Almost every ingredient in baked goods is affected by the lower air pressure at high altitudes, especially leavenings, liquids, and sugar.

Leavenings: With less air pressure to control expansion, baked products rise too quickly and textures are coarse and crumbly.

Liquids: Evaporation is accelerated at high elevations causing foods to dry.

Sugar: As liquid evaporates, sugar becomes more concentrated. This weakens the cell structure of cakes and breads causing them to fall.

Cakes leavened by air, such as angel cake, expand too much if egg whites are beaten according to sea-level directions. Beat whites only till *soft* peaks form. Cakes leavened with baking powder or soda have a delicate structure and need more adjustment than others. Use the chart at right to compensate for altitude.

Cookies, biscuits, and muffins are more stable than cakes and need little adjustment. Experiment, reducing sugar and baking powder and increasing liquid.

For cakes and cookies, increase oven temperature about 20°F. and decrease time. This allows cakes to set before leavening expands too much, and keeps cookies from drying out.

Yeast bread doughs rise more quickly at high altitudes, resulting in a weaker structure. To compensate, shorten the rising time. You may need to add extra liquid to compensate for rapid evaporation during rising.

Pie crusts are not greatly affected. A slight increase in liquid may help keep them from being dry. But use as little flour as possible when rolling out dough.

Range Top Cooking

Liquids boil at lower temperatures at high altitudes, which means foods take longer to cook. Three-minute eggs may take 4 minutes, vegetables need more time to become tender, and boiling soup isn't as hot. Increase cooking time rather than heat, since doing the latter can scorch food on the bottom of the pan. Also increase liquid, as it will evaporate more quickly.

Deep-fat fry foods at a lower temperature for a longer time. Since moisture in the food has a lower boiling point, food fried at recommended sea-level temperature will be crusty outside and underdone inside. Lower the temperature of the fat 3°F. for each 1000 feet above sea level.

Candies, frostings, syrups, and jellies become more concentrated at high altitudes because of rapid evaporation. The cold water test and sheet test are still reliable to determine doneness, but if you use a candy thermometer, decrease temperature about 2°F. for each 1000 feet above sea level.

Processing time for canning must be adjusted for high altitudes to allow ample time for safe processing. A general suggestion is to increase processing time 1 to 2 minutes for each 1000 feet above sea level when processing for 20 minutes or less. Increase time 2 minutes per 1000 feet when processing for more than 20 minutes. In pressure canners, the steam pressure must be increased 1 pound for every 2000 feet above sea level to raise the temperature at which water boils.

Packaged foods such as cake mixes have special high altitude instructions on their side panels. For other foods, follow the general principles of increasing the liquids and cooking longer and at lower temperatures.

For more information on cooking at high altitudes, contact your County Extension Office or write to: Colorado State University Experiment Station Bulletin Room, Fort Collins, Colorado 80523.

High Altitude Adjustments for Cakes

When making cakes, use this chart as a guide. Adjust all ingredients listed. You may need to experiment with each recipe to discover the best formula; where two amounts appear, try the smaller first, and adjust next time, if necessary.

Ingredients	3000 feet	5000 feet	7000 feet
Liquid: Add for each cup	1 to 2 tablespoons	2 to 4 tablespoons	3 to 4 tablespoons
Baking powder: Decrease for each teaspoon	⅛ teaspoon	⅛ to ¼ teaspoon	¼ teaspoon
Sugar: Decrease for each cup	0 to 1 tablespoon	0 to 2 tablespoons	1 to 3 tablespoons

MAKING FOOD ATTRACTIVE

A colorful garnish can make the difference between an everyday meal and a festive occasion. For main dishes and vegetables, add interest with snipped parsley, sliced green onions or olives, wedges of tomatoes or hard-cooked eggs, or whole or sliced mushrooms or cherry tomatoes.

For desserts, garnish with whipped cream, sifted powdered sugar, chopped nuts, or crushed candies.

The following tips make fancy garnishes from ordinary foods. A small amount of time spent preparing them will be well worth it.

Radish Roses: Cut root tip off radish. Make 4 or 5 petals around the radish by cutting thin slices from top to—*but not through*—bottom of radish. Leave a little red between the petals. Chill in ice water till petals spread open. Drain before serving.

Scored Cucumbers: Run tines of fork lengthwise down cucumber, pressing to break through peel. Repeat at regular intervals around cucumber. Slice crosswise or on the bias.

Pickle Fans: Make 3 or 4 lengthwise slices from one end *almost* to the other. Spread slices apart to resemble a fan; press uncut end to hold in place.

Carrot Curls and Zigzags: With a vegetable peeler, shave thin, wide strips from a carrot. Roll up each strip; secure with a wooden pick. Or, make zigzags by threading carrot strips on picks accordion-style. Place curls or zigzags in ice water to crisp. Remove picks before serving.

Celery or Green Onion Brushes: Trim ends from celery stalks or green onions. At one or both ends, cut several lengthwise gashes about 2 inches long. Place stalks in ice water to crisp. Drain well before serving.

Chocolate Curls: For the most luscious curls, use a milk chocolate bar (you may also use sweet baking chocolate, semisweet chocolate, or unsweetened chocolate). Chocolate should be at room temperature; cold chocolate breaks instead of curling, while warm chocolate melts in the hand. Shave chocolate with a vegetable peeler or sharp knife into long thin strips that curl as you cut them. Use a wooden pick to place the curls exactly where you want them.

Tinted Coconut: Place shredded or flaked coconut in a screw-top jar; add a few drops of desired food coloring. Secure lid and shake till all is colored.

375

INDEXES

To aid you in your use of the Complete Step-By-Step Cook Book, *we include an index of cooking techniques as well as an index of recipes.*

Look in the **technique index,** *which appears first, when you want to learn a specific cooking technique or process. For example, look up "Creaming" to learn how to cream butter or margarine. (You'll find the reference listed as the step number(s) followed by the page number.) Where no specific action is involved, simply look up the food product. The entry "Baked alaska," for instance, refers you to the technique for making a baked alaska.*

The **recipe index** *begins on page 379 and lists recipes in the book by title and food category.*

Technique Index

A–C

Technique Index

Recipe Index

A–B

Recipe Index

Recipe Index

383

HUNDREDS OF OTHER RECIPES

All from
Better Homes and Gardens®

Now that you've learned the techniques of successful cooking, try your expertise on the many recipes from America's favorite cook books . . .

New Cook Book

The best-selling cook book of all time has been updated and is now better than ever—with over 1,500 recipes, plus extra features on microwave and crockery cooking, canning, and wines.

Meat Cook Book

This "main dish" cook book features over 275 recipes, as well as tips on how to buy, store, and serve meat.

Homemade Cookies

Here are 219 recipes for everything from brownies to refrigerator cookies, plus tips on storing and mailing cookies.

All-Time Favorite Barbecue Recipes

This comprehensive barbecue book has all you need to know about grilling meat, poultry, fish, and vegetables, as well as breads and desserts.

Meals For One Or Two

This "small-scale" cook book includes 195 recipes for elegant dishes as well as quick-and-easy meals, plus planning and preparation tips.

Microwave Cook Book

Choose from 200 kitchen-tested recipes for main dishes, vegetables, soups, and desserts, plus menu ideas that make the most of microwave convenience.

All-Time Favorite Beef Recipes

You'll enjoy these classic recipes for steaks, roasts, and less-expensive cuts, and the tips on how to use leftovers will save you money.

All-Time Favorite Vegetable Recipes

From artichokes to zucchini, here's everything you need to know about storing, preparing, and cooking vegetables—with 184 tasty recipes.

All-Time Favorite Salad Recipes

Sample this selection of America's favorite vegetable salads, fruit salads, traditional salads, full-meal salads, molded salads, and salad dressings—161 recipes in all.

All-Time Favorite Casserole Recipes

Try these delicious all-occasion oven recipes, from dishes that use leftovers to elegant entrées for entertaining.

Homemade Bread Cook Book

Enjoy over 185 recipes for oven-fresh loaves, rolls, coffee cakes, and sourdough and natural breads, most of which use the easy-mix yeast method.

OTHER BETTER HOMES AND GARDENS® TITLES

Oriental Cook Book

Casual Entertaining Cook Book

Crepes Cook Book

More From Your Microwave

Crockery Cooker Cook Book

After Work Cook Book

Calorie-Trimmed Recipes

New Junior Cook Book

Blender Cook Book

Low-Cost Cooking